European Integration and Supranational Governance

European Integration and Supranational Governance

EDITED BY

Wayne Sandholtz and **Alec Stone Sweet**

Oxford University Press

1998

Oxford University Press, Great Clarendon Street, Oxford OX2 6DP

Oxford New York

Athens Auckland Bangkok Bogotá Buenos Aires Calcutta
Cape Town Chennai Dar es Salaam Delhi Florence Hong Kong Istanbul
Karachi Kuala Lumpur Madrid Melbourne Mexico City Mumbai
Nairobi Paris São Paulo Singapore Taipei Tokyo Toronto Warsaw
and associated companies in
Berlin Ibadan

Oxford is a registered trade mark of Oxford University Press

Published in the United States
by Oxford University Press Inc., New York

British Library Cataloguing in Publication Data
Data available

Library of Congress Cataloging in Publication Data
Data available

ISBN 0–19–829457–3
ISBN 0–19–829464–6 (pbk.)

1 3 5 7 9 10 8 6 4 2

Typeset by BookMan Services, Ilfracombe
Printed in Great Britain
on acid-free paper by
Biddles Ltd, Guildford and King's Lynn

PREFACE

This book is the product of four years of intensive collaboration among a small group of people, some of whom had not met each other before the project began. We are friends now, which we count as the project's most important achievement. If the group has achieved more scholarly ambitions, it is largely due to the generous financial and logistic support of two research centers. We thank the University of California Center for German and European Studies, its directors, Richard Buxbaum and Gerald Feldman, and its administrator, Beverly Crawford. We also thank the University of California, Irvine, Institute for Global Peace and Conflict Studies, and its director, Patrick Morgan. This support provided us with a great luxury, enough time—to get to know one another, to reflect on common purposes, and to revise (and revise again) each of our respective contributions. Earlier versions of these chapters were presented at the conference, *Supranational Governance: The Institutionalization of the European Union*, hosted by the Center for German and European Studies at Berkeley, November 1996, and at panels organized for the European Community Studies Association meetings at Seattle, May 1997. We are grateful to the discussants at these conferences, who both encouraged and provided us with many helpful criticisms.

Wayne Sandholtz
Alec Stone Sweet

Irvine, California
February 1998

CONTENTS

CONTRIBUTORS

David R. Cameron
Department of Political Science, Yale University

James A. Caporaso
Department of Political Science, University of Washington

Russell J. Dalton
Department of Politics and Society, University of California, Irvine

Richard C. Eichenberg
Political Science Department, Tufts University

Neil Fligstein
Department of Sociology, University of California at Berkeley

Jason McNichol
Department of Sociology, University of California at Berkeley

Dolores O'Reilly
School of Public Policy, Economics, and Law, University of Ulster

Paul Pierson
Department of Government, Harvard University

Mark A. Pollack
Department of Political Science, University of Wisconsin, Madison

Wayne Sandholtz
Department of Politics and Society, University of California, Irvine

Alberta M. Sbragia
Department of Political Science, University of Pittsburgh

Michael E. Smith
Department of Politics and Society, University of California, Irvine

Alec Stone Sweet
Department of Politics and Society, University of California, Irvine

1

Integration, Supranational Governance, and the Institutionalization of the European Polity

ALEC STONE SWEET AND WAYNE SANDHOLTZ

SIX governments, moved by a hope for enduring peace in a prosperous Europe, in 1957 signed the Treaty of Rome establishing the European Community. The EC thus began its life as an agreement among independent nation-states. Forty years later, the European Community[1] has developed into something more than a pact among governments. In fact, it is now commonplace to compare the Treaty of Rome to a constitution, and to refer to the European Community in terms[2] that imply an analogy with nation-states. In this book we theorize, and assess empirically, the institutionalization of the European Community, that is, its remarkable transformation from an interstate bargain into a multidimensional, quasi-federal polity. We propose a theory of European integration, focusing on the process through which supranational governance—the competence of the European Community to make binding rules in any given policy domain—has developed.

We therefore confront some of the most puzzling questions posed by the evolution of the Community. Why does policymaking sometimes migrate from the nation-state level to the European Community? Why has integration proceeded more rapidly in some policy domains than it has in others? To what extent is the Community governed by "intergovernmental" or "supranational" modes of decision-making? What accounts for the relative dominance of the neoliberal project, and for the relative failure of social democratic visions of

---

[1] We recognize the important formal distinctions between 'European Community' and 'European Union.' However, since most of the activities we refer to in this chapter occur under the aegis of the European Community, in this chapter we consistently use 'EC' and 'European Community.'

[2] e.g. "system of multilevel governance," "quasi-federal polity," or "complex of policy networks."

Europe to gain influence? We do not claim to have definitively settled all controversies. But our theory yields responses to these questions in the form of testable propositions. The chapters of the book demonstrate the resilience of these propositions in a wide range of contexts.

We do not explain the founding of the EC, but rather its institutional development. Our starting point, therefore, is the Treaty of Rome. The Treaty established a cluster of organizations (Council, Commission, Court, and Parliament) and a set of rules whose central purpose was to promote exchange across national borders. The founders of the European Community reasoned that a "common market," linking their diverse national economies, would both accelerate the generation of wealth and make war among the member-states unthinkable. The Treaty of Rome thus created a social and political space that intentionally privileged transnational economic interests. That is, the point of the EC was to facilitate exchange among its member countries. Because the Community was designed to promote intra-EC exchange, its rules and organizations have favored economic actors with a stake in cross-border transactions (trade, investment, production, distribution). Rising levels of transnational exchange trigger processes that generate movement toward increased supranational governance. We do not claim to explain policy processes, or their substantive outcomes, in terms of increasing cross-border exchange; specific policies are the product of complex political interactions. Rather, increasing exchange provokes behaviors and processes that are decisively shaped by the institutional context of the EC, and these processes tend to produce or reinforce supranational rule-making.

In other words, we emphasize the role of transnational exchange (e.g. trade, investment, the development of Euro-groups, networks, and associations) in pushing the EC's organizations to construct new policy and new arenas for policy-relevant behavior. Once constituted, these arenas sustain integration in predictable ways, not least, by promoting additional transnational exchange. Some chapters of the book demonstrate how rising levels of cross-border exchange produced demands for EC-level rules and policies, to which EC organizations and national governments responded (Chapters 4, 5, 6, and 7). A number of chapters focus on the emergence and institutionalization of supranational policy domains (Chapters 3, 4, 5, 7, 10, and 11). Chapters 2 and 8 assess the consequences of institutionalization for policymaking; still others examine the reciprocal impact of supranational governance and national politics (Chapter 4) and national public opinion (Chapter 9).

Our analytical goals, and thus our theory, differentiate us from existing approaches. "Intergovernmentalism" denies the significance of supranational governance, arguing instead that the member-states control policy processes and outcomes. Institutionalization is not an issue because the EC remains as it began, a set of bargains among independent nation-states. Scholars who analyze the EC in terms of "multilevel governance" or "policy networks" focus on the processes by which the contemporary EC produces policy outcomes. That is, they take a certain amount of supranational governance for granted. But the policy-centered approaches do not take as part of their task the explanation of how the EC developed from an interstate treaty to a system of governance, or why some policy domains have become more integrated than others. The latter questions define the analytical terrain that this volume occupies.

This chapter proceeds as follows. In Section 1, we briefly contrast our theory with the main features of neofunctionalism and intergovernmentalism. Some urge that the neofunctionalist–intergovernmentalist debate be abandoned. We would respond that there has been no genuine debate; since the mid-1970s, very few have claimed the neofunctionalist banner, much less offered a systematic, full-fledged neofunctionalist argument on European integration. Instead, theoretical discussions tend to involve a ritual dismissal of neofunctionalism followed by either a critique or an endorsement of intergovernmentalism. That hardly constitutes a debate. Sometimes the impatience with the neofunctionalist–intergovernmentalist debate simply amounts to claim that no general theory of European integration is possible (often tied to a preference for analyses of individual policies or sectors). In reply, we are placing on the table a general theory along with supportive empirical evidence that includes both aggregate data and process-tracing case studies. The onus is on those who reject the possibility of broad theories to show why our results should not be taken seriously.

In Sections 2 and 3 of this chapter, we elaborate a theory that offers a positive alternative to intergovernmentalism. We define key concepts, discuss causal relationships between variables, and derive hypotheses about how European integration proceeds. The fourth section describes the structure of the book and how the remaining contributions fit together. In the concluding section we clarify our differences with intergovernmentalist theories of integration.

1. Theoretical Context

The primary theoretical divide in EC studies has been between intergovernmentalism and neofunctionalism. Endless nuance and distinction exist within each approach, but in the end most theorizing on integration endorses either the following statement or its opposite: the distribution of preferences and the conduct of bargaining among the governments of the member-states broadly explain the nature, pace, and scope of integration, and neither supranational organization nor transnational actors generate political processes or outcomes of seminal importance. In recent decades, intergovernmentalists have worked to refine their framework, and some have aggressively proclaimed its superiority (e.g. Moravcsik 1993, 1995). At the same time, neofunctionalism has gradually been abandoned. Its original adherents have moved away from integration studies, and critics of intergovernmentalism have not developed their own general theory, least of all by refining neofunctionalism (e.g. Sandholtz 1993*a*, 1996; Sbragia 1993*b*; Marks *et al.* 1996; Pierson 1996).

We set ourselves the task of developing and testing a theory of how supranational governance evolves over time. What we are seeking to explain, the nature and extent of supranational governance, varies along a number of dimensions. In some sectors, the competence to govern is held exclusively by the Community; in others, national institutions are the primary sites of policymaking; and in many domains, the transfer of power from the national to the supranational level has been only partial. Within the same policy sector, the answer to the question, "who governs?" has changed over time. And in those areas in which EC institutions have become sites of policy innovation and change, one finds variation in the relative capacity of the member-state governments, acting in summits and in the Council of Ministers, to control that policy. In specifying the research problem in this way, we commit ourselves to theorizing integration as a dynamic process that yields divergent outcomes. We therefore problematize the notion, strongly implied by neo-functionalist theories, that integration is the process by which the EC gradually but comprehensively replaces the nation-state in all of its functions. And we reject the comparative statics of intergovernmentalists as a mode of analysis incapable of capturing crucial temporal elements of European integration.

Our theory, set out in Sections 2 and 3 below, privileges the expansion of transnational exchange, the capacities of supranational organizations to respond to the needs of those who exchange, and the role of supranational rules in shaping subsequent integration. We argue that supranational governance serves the interests of (i) those individuals, groups, and firms who transact across borders, and (ii) those who are advantaged by European rules, and disadvantaged by national rules, in specific policy domains. The expansion of transnational exchange, and the associated push to substitute supranational for national rules, generates pressure on the EC's organizations to act. Generally, EC organizations, such as the Commission and the Court, respond to this pressure by working to extend the domain of supranational rules, in order to achieve collective (transnational) gains and to accomplish the purposes of the Treaties, broadly interpreted. A first hypothesis, then, is that the relative intensity of transnational activity, measured across time and policy sectors, broadly determines variation on the dependent variable (supranational governance).

We claim that transnational activity has been the catalyst of European integration; but transnational exchange can not, in and of itself, determine the specific details, or the precise timing, of Community rule-making. Instead it provokes, or activates, the Community's decision-making bodies, including the Council of Ministers. Member-state governments often possess (but not always) the means to facilitate or to obstruct rule-making, and they use these powers frequently. Nevertheless, we argue, among other things, that as transnational exchange rises in any specific domain (or cluster of related domains), so do the costs, for governments, of maintaining disparate national rules. As these costs rise, so do incentives for governments to adjust their policy positions in ways that favor the expansion of supranational governance. Once fixed in a given domain, European rules—such as relevant treaty provisions, secondary legislation, and the ECJ's case law—generate a self-sustaining dynamic, that leads to the gradual deepening of integration in that sector and, not uncommonly, to spillovers into other sectors. Thus, we view intergovernmental bargaining and decision-making as embedded in processes that are provoked and sustained by the expansion of transnational society, the pro-integrative activities of supranational organizations, and the growing density of supranational rules. And, we will argue, these processes gradually, but inevitably, reduce the capacity of the member-states to control outcomes.

Our theory has important affinities with neofunctionalism. We acknowledge the insights of two of the founders of integration theory, Karl Deutsch and Ernst Haas. On crucial questions, we believe, they got it right. What we find complementary are Deutsch's emphasis on social exchange, communication, and transactions, and Haas's attention to the relationship between global interdependence, political choice, and the development of supranational institutions.

Deutsch and his collaborators held that increasing density of social exchange among individuals over prolonged periods of time would lead to the development of new communities (shared identity) and, ultimately, to the creation of a super-state with centralized institutions (e.g. Deutsch 1953; Deutsch *et al.* 1957). We agree that social exchange across borders drives integration processes, generating social demands for supranational rules, and for higher levels of organizational capacity to respond to further demands. If this demand is not supplied, the development of higher levels of exchange will be stunted. We set aside Deutsch's concern with the formation of communities and identities per se, and the issue of whether or not identity formation precedes state-building. Our dependent variable remains mode of governance, not the construction of a pan-European identity or of a super-state.

Haas (e.g. 1958, 1961) conceived of integration as the product of growing international interdependence and pluralist, interest-driven politics. Mitrany had theorized what would happen in a world increasingly beset by policy problems that transcended national borders: governmental functions would steadily migrate from national governments, who would act on the basis of "politics," to global technocrats, who would act on the basis of expertise. Haas recognized that the transfer of functions to supranational bodies would always be intensely contested, as some groups foresaw gains while others feared losses. He consequently saw the initial construction of supranational authority as the crucial political hurdle. Stripped down, Haas's neofunctionalist argument runs something like this. Some elite groups (leadership of political parties, industry associations, and labor federations) begin to recognize that problems of substantial interest cannot be solved at the national level. These groups push for the transfer of policy competence to a supranational body, finding each other and establishing cross-national coalitions along the way. If the problem is important enough and pro-integration elites are able to mount sufficient political leverage, governments establish supranational institutions.

Once supranational institutions are born, a new dynamic emerges. Haas pioneered in theorizing the logic of institutionalization at the supranational level (1961). He suggested a dynamic process. The creation of supranational authority leads to changes in social expectations and behavior, which feedback onto supranational policymaking, and so on. As supranational bodies begin to deliver the coordinative solutions that pro-integrationists hoped for, they become the locus of a new kind of politics. Groups increasingly seek influence over supranational policies, opening up new political channels, but also helping supranational organizations acquire expertise, information, and legitimacy, thus bolstering their authority. The dynamic is reinforced by the potential, inherent in integration processes, for functional "spillover." Spillover is achieved when supranational authority is extended to new, but related functional domains, as it becomes evident that initial policy objectives can not be adequately attained without such an extension. Neofunctionalists—especially Philippe Schmitter (1969, 1970)—also attended to the role of bargaining among member governments. But they at least implicitly argued (and we argue explicitly) that, as integration proceeds, member-state governments become less and less proactive, and more and more reactive to changes in the supranational environment to which they belong.

The three constituent elements of our theory are prefigured in neofunctionalism: the development of transnational society, the role of supranational organizations with meaningful autonomous capacity to pursue integrative agendas, and the focus on European rule-making to resolve international policy externalities. Further, we appreciate Haas's insight that supranational policymaking (governance) generates a dynamic process of institutionalization. We do not, however, embrace all of Haas's neofunctionalism. Haas defined integration as "the process whereby political actors . . . are persuaded to shift their national loyalties, expectations, and political activities to a new and larger center" (Haas 1961: 367). Again, we leave as an open question the extent to which the loyalties and identities of actors will shift from the national to the European level. There is substantial room for supranational governance without an ultimate shift in identification. And we will specify somewhat differently the causal mechanisms by which integration is provoked and sustained, tying both to the development of transnational society and to contemporary theories of institutions and institutionalization.

Intergovernmentalists (especially Moravcsik 1991, 1993; but see also Garrett 1992), conceptualize EC politics as a subset of international relations, namely as an example of interstate cooperation sustained by an international regime. Successful regimes facilitate the ongoing coordination of policy among member-states, by reducing the costs of information, policy innovation, and negotiation (e.g. Keohane 1984). In Andrew Moravcsik's "liberal intergovernmentalism" (1993, 1994), regime theory has been supplemented to take account of domestic politics. At times, Moravcsik conceives European politics as a two-level game (Evans *et al.* 1994). The crucial actors are national executives, who continuously mediate between domestic interests and the activities of the international regime. At other times, Moravcsik sequences, for analytical purposes, national preference formation (domestic politics) and intergovernmental bargaining (regime politics). National executives are constrained by, but also aggregate, domestic interests as national preferences; once fixed, the distribution of preferences among, and the "relative bargaining power" of, member-state governments determines outcomes.

European integration is a product of these outcomes. As Moravcsik puts it: "the EC has developed through a series of celebrated intergovernmental bargains, each of which set the agenda for an intervening period of consolidation" (1993: 473). In order to consolidate these bargains efficiently, member-state governments establish and delegate powers to the EC's organizations, like the Commission and the Court of Justice (ECJ). Although intergovernmentalists rarely focus empirical attention on the process of consolidation, they claim that the EC's organizations broadly pursue goals previously determined by the member-state governments, or are called to order if they pursue divergent agendas (Garrett 1992; Moravcsik 1995).

National executives construct the EC's capacity to govern, Moravcsik argues, for two main reasons. First, for electoral reasons executives may find it in their interest to respond to international policy externalities by pooling their sovereignty at the supranational level. Such externalities are generated by international interdependence. Second, in order to enhance their own autonomy vis-à-vis domestic actors, national executives may shift competence to govern to an arena (such as the Council of Ministers) that operates with fewer constraints on executive authority than national arenas. Why executives do so in some policy domains, but not in others, appears to be indeterminate.

For Moravcsik, the following sequence encompasses virtually all that is important: rising interdependence > domestic politics and national preference formation > intergovernmental bargaining > delegation to supranational authorities > consolidation. Integration proceeds, but the sequence never varies in any meaningful way. In this imagery, transnational actors and society do not exist; instead, he notices domestic groups impacted by increasing interdependence. And supranational organizations do not impact integration processes in autonomous and decisive ways; instead, in accordance with their place in the sequence, they behave as rather faithful agents of intergovernmental bargains. By our reading, rising interdependence constitutes the only important causal factor that both provokes integration and is not decisively determined by intergovernmental bargaining. On this point, intergovernmentalism hardly displaces neofunctionalism, but rather relies on a causal argument developed by the neofunctionalists.

We will return to our differences with intergovernmentalists in the concluding section.

2. A Transaction-Based Theory of Integration

As most students of EC policymaking have observed, simple characterizations of the Community, as either "intergovernmental" or "supranational," will not do. The brute fact is that integration has proceeded unevenly, and theories of integration have failed to explain this unevenness. Most recent research on EC politics has focused either on the grand bargains (the Single European Act or the Maastricht Treaty, for instance), or on how day-to-day policy is made in specific sectors. Neither emphasis has provided an adequate basis for theorizing the dynamic nature of integration over time across policy domains. When we began our joint efforts we perceived the need for a unifying heuristic capable of capturing this dynamic.

2.1. From intergovernmental to supranational politics

We thus propose a continuum that stretches between two ideal-typical modes of governance: the intergovernmental (the left-hand pole), and the supra-national (the right-hand pole). One pole is constituted by intergovernmental politics. The central players in intergovernmental politics are the national exec-utives of the member-states, who bargain with each other to produce common policies. Bargaining is shaped by the relative powers of the member-states, but also by state preferences, which emerge from the pulling and hauling among domestic groups. These preferences are then given agency, as negotiating positions, by national executives in EC organizations such as the Council of Ministers. The EC level of governance operates as an international regime in the functional, transaction-costs mode: it is a "passive structure" that enhances the efficiency of interstate bargaining (Moravcsik 1993; Keohane 1984).

The other pole is constituted by supranational politics. A "supranational" mode of governance is one in which centralized governmental structures (those organizations constituted at the supranational level possess jurisdiction over specific policy domains within the territory comprised by the member-states. In exercising that jurisdiction, supranational organizations are capable of con-straining the behavior of all actors, including the member-states, within those domains. Many would argue that "federal politics" would be the appropriate label (Lenaerts 1990; Sbragia 1992, 1993b). We use the term "supranational" to emphasize that the EC is an international organization, and that EC politics is a form of international politics. And we have avoided using the term "federal" here in order to avoid an argument about the precise nature of the EC polity

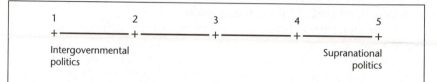

Fig. 1.1. Governance in the European Union

Note: From left to right, the continuum measures the increasing influence of three factors on policymaking processes and outcomes within any given policy sector. These factors are: (1) supranational organizations, (2) supranational rules, and (3) transnational society.

and how it compares with other federal polities. Movement from left to right along the continuum indicates that a shift away from intergovernmentalism, and toward supranationalism, has taken place.

In principle, the continuum is capable of situating—and therefore of characterizing—all international regime forms as sites (more or less) of intergovernmental or sites (more or less) of supranational politics. Unlike most regimes, which tend to organize interstate cooperation in one or a few closely related sectors, the EC possesses differing degrees of competence across a diverse range of policy areas. In principle, one could use the continuum to characterize the development of the EC as a whole, in terms of the composite picture of all policy areas. One could also use the continuum to chart the comparative development or lack of development of different policy sectors comparatively. Thus, policy sector A may be located at point 2, shading toward intergovernmental politics, while policy sector B may be located at point 4, exhibiting strong features of supranationalism. Used in this way, the continuum asserts that there are potentially many ECs. As discussed in the next section, we hope that by disaggregating EC governing processes by policy sector, we will be able to learn more about the nature of European integration than we can by working to characterize, in a blanket fashion, the EC as an "intergovernmental" or "supranational" regime.

2.2. Dimensions of institutionalization

The continuum measures the movement from intergovernmental to supranational governance in three interrelated dimensions:

- *EC rules*: the legal, and less informal, constraints on behavior produced by interactions among political actors operating at the European level;
- *EC organizations*: those governmental structures, operating at the European level, that produce, execute, and interpret EC rules; and
- *transnational society*: those non-governmental actors who engage in intra-EC exchanges—social, economic, political—and thereby influence, directly or indirectly, policymaking processes and outcomes at the European level.

For any given policy area or process, movement from left to right along the continuum therefore measures the growing presence and intensity of each of these factors.

We understand these dimensions to be crucial indicators of levels of integration in the EC. By "integration," we mean the process by which the horizontal and vertical linkages between social, economic, and political actors emerge and evolve. Vertical linkages are the stable relationships, or patterned interactions, between actors organized at the EC level and actors organized at or below the member-state level. Horizontal linkages are the stable relationships, or patterned interaction, between actors organized in one member-state with actors organized in another. We understand these linkages to be "institutionalized" to the extent that they are constructed and sustained by EC rules.

The three dimensions are analytically distinct, although we expect them to covary, as integration proceeds, in predictable ways. As we move from left to right along the continuum the influence of EC (or supranational) organizations on policymaking processes and outcomes increases. Supranational EC organizations include the Commission, the Court of Justice, the Parliament, and even at times the Council of Ministers. At the left-hand pole, the regime's organizations exhibit little if any meaningful autonomy from the most powerful member-states. By autonomy, we mean an organization's capacity to define and pursue, on an ongoing basis, a politically relevant agenda. In intergovernmental politics, organizations facilitate intergovernmental bargaining and logistical coordination (they lower the transaction costs for governments). At point 3 on the continuum, supranational organizations may often be the source of successful policy innovation, a form of "relative"—but meaningful—autonomy. At the supranational pole, institutions may exercise substantial autonomy, as when they are able to innovate, in policy-relevant ways, at times even in the face of member-state indifference or hostility.

The second dimension built into the continuum is legal-normative. As we move from left to right along the continuum, EC rules achieve higher degrees of clarity and formalization. Consider those rules that govern the production, application, and interpretation of all other rules, such as secondary legislation, within the Community. At the far left of the continuum, rules are few and weak; they do not trump individual governmental interests that conflict with them. As we move along the continuum, rules stabilize state bargaining, delegitimize exit, and—at the level of law—lay down binding standards of conduct enforceable by courts. Many of the rules governing EC policymaking are behavioral, that is, they have resulted from many years of constant interaction between state and supranational officials in a myriad of settings. But many of these rules are also highly formal, codified in treaty law, secondary legislation, and the ECJ's jurisprudence. Within any given policy domain, as we move leftward the rules governing the interactions of all actors, public and private, grow more dense and elaborate.

The third dimension captured by the continuum is the presence and influence of transnational actors—interest groups, business, knowledge-based elites—on policy processes and outcomes. In intergovernmental politics, national executives mediate between domestic actors and supranational organizations and rules. In supranational politics, transnational actors have a choice of fora in which to exert their influence. They may target national governmental structures—executive, legislative, or judicial—as well as supranational bodies, and they may play one level off against the other.

Taken together, these dimensions are constitutive of supranational politics. If this is so, the group believes, these three factors must move together, and that disjunctures that do occur in movement are short-lived. Organizations, rules, and social exchange are closely linked in the development of society and systems of governance (March and Olsen 1989; North 1990; Stone Sweet forthcoming); they are similarly connected in supranational politics. Organizations produce and transmit the rules that guide social interaction. They structure access to policy processes, defining political power and privileging some parts of society more than others. As supranational organizations acquire and wield autonomy, they are able to shape not only specific policy outcomes but also the rules that channel policymaking behaviors. As supranational organizations and rules emerge and solidify, they constitute transnational society by establishing bases for interaction and access points for influencing policy. As transnational society endures and expands, the organizations and rules that structure behaviors become more deeply rooted as "givens," taken for granted as defining political life. Growth in one element of the supranational trio (organizations, rules, transnational society) creates conditions that favor growth in the other two. An expansion of the tasks or autonomy of supranational organizations creates opportunities for political action, which actors and groups will seek to exploit, thus expanding transnational society. As societal actors adjust their behaviors in response to new supranational rules, these rules can gradually be locked in. If broader, global trends promote the growth of transnational society, there will be a corresponding demand for increased organizational capacity and rules to coordinate and to guide interactions.

2.3. Why movement occurs

The continuum gives us tools with which to describe EC governance. We have also offered a proposition that would account for some of the dynamics of integration, namely that movement in any one of the dimensions will tend to produce movement in the other two. In other words, there is an internal dynamic of institutionalization. But important questions remain to be theorized. Why does movement on any of the dimensions occur in the first place? Why do some policy domains move farther and faster toward the supranational pole than others? In this section we offer a theoretical account that can generate answers to such questions.

Our starting point is society, in particular, non-state actors who engage in transactions and communications across national borders, within Europe. These are the people who need European standards, rules, and dispute resolution mechanisms—who need supranational governance. In the beginning, the causal mechanism is quite simple: increasing levels of cross-border transactions and communications by societal actors will increase the perceived need for European-level rules, coordination, and regulation. In fact, the absence of European rules will come to be seen as an obstacle to the generation of wealth and the achievement of other collective gains. Separate national legal regimes constitute the crucial source of transaction costs for those who wish to engage in exchanges across borders: customs and other border controls, differing technical standards, divergent health and environmental regulations, distinct systems of commercial law, diverse national currencies, and so on. Further, the costs of transacting across borders are higher than those involved in contracting within a single member-state, to the extent that there exists no secure common legal framework at the supranational level, comparable in its efficacy to that of national legal systems. As transnational exchanges rise, so does the societal demand for supranational rules and organizational capacity to regulate. Trans-actors can exert pro-integration pressure on their own governments, but when these are reticent, transactors can access supranational arenas dominated by the Commission and the European Court of Justice.

Governmental actors clearly have their own interests, which may include maximizing their autonomy and control over resources. They may resist the shift toward supranational policymaking. But as they do so, they inhibit the generation of wealth within their territories by those actors that depend on European transactions. Such resistance is therefore sustainable only at a cost in prosperity (Mattli 1996). They can also attempt to slow integration or push it in directions favorable to their perceived interests, but they do not drive the process nor fully control it. In a fundamental sense, governments are reactive, constantly adjusting to the integration that is going on all around them.

On this point, the contrast between our theory and intergovernmental approaches to the EC could hardly be greater, but we have not written national governments out of the story. In fact, intergovernmental decision-making is ubiquitous in the EC, present even at the far right-hand pole of our continuum (as it is in Canada and other federal systems). EC summits, intergovernmental conferences, and meetings of the Council of Ministers are practically defined by tough, interest-driven negotiation. But that is part of the problem with intergovernmental approaches to integration. Adherents of these approaches always begin by announcing that the "grand bargains" are the defining moments of European integration, and then these historic agreements become the object of empirical research. But the grand bargains are, by definition, inter-governmental. The research results are quite predictable when one looks to intergovernmental bargains for evidence of intergovernmental bargaining. Thus the observation that bargaining among governments is ubiquitous in the EC does not settle theoretical controversy. Put differently, the term "inter-governmental" is useful as a description of a specific mode of decision-making within the EC policy process. But to attend to what is intergovernmental about the construction of supranational governance does not require us to adopt, or to accept the validity of, "intergovernmentalism-as-theory."

Indeed, we argue that intergovernmental bargaining in the EC more often than not is responsive to the interests of a nascent, always developing, trans-national society. Indeed, the demand for EC rules and regulation provides the subject matter for the bargaining. With very few exceptions, EC legislation concerns, directly or indirectly, the creation of rules that facilitate or regulate intra-EC exchange and communications. The configuration of social interests that will be affected by European policy innovation may vary from state to state, which creates the differences over which governments must negotiate. But rather than being the generator of integration, intergovernmental bargain-ing is more often its product.

The exclusive focus on grand intergovernmental bargains can also lead to serious distortions of the historical record. The 1970s have generally been regarded as disconfirmation of neofunctionalism; intergovernmentalists typically note that member-state preferences diverged during those years and that few of the EC's ambitious plans at the beginning of the decade bore fruit (e.g. Taylor 1983). We do not read the story of European integration as one of stop-and-go, at least not in any general or comprehensive sense. At the height of de Gaulle's power in the 1960s, the ECJ moved aggressively to "constitutionalize" the treaties (Stein 1981; Weiler 1981, 1991). In the worst days of "Eurosclerosis" in the 1970s, levels of intra-EC trade and other forms of exchange soared. And, as we would expect, both the amount of legislation and the number of organized EC pressure groups grew steadily through the 1970s (Chapter 3). Integration always proceeded, in some sectors and from some vantage points, despite the Luxembourg compromise and despite the divergence of state preferences.

Empirical research supports the transaction-driven theory of European integration. Stone Sweet and Caporaso (Chapter 4) focus on the political impact of the "constitutionalization" of the treaty system. They find that cross-national exchange, transnational judicial activity, and supranational rule-making rose steadily after the move to constitutionalization by the ECJ (1960s). In analyses of aggregate data, and in case studies of the sources and consequences of the judicial rule-making, they demonstrate the causal link we have proposed: transactors seek to reduce obstacles, which triggers a process leading to the production of EC rules (Chapter 4).

The telecommunications case is equally clear. By the 1980s, Europe's fragmentation into national telecommunications monopolies was increasingly costly to a variety of actors who depended on reliable, advanced telecommunications facilities spanning national borders. Telecommunications provide the infrastructure for the modern economy, and businesses from a multitude of sectors needed pan-European telecommunications for their transnational activities (trade, strategic partnering, investment, finance, design, production, distribution, sales). These businesses, plus telecommunications equipment makers and suppliers of new services and infrastructures, became ready allies of the Commission when it undertook to create a liberalized EC telecommunications market. Governments resisted, but found that ECJ rulings and the Commission's use of Art. 90 directives (that do not require Council approval) severely curtailed their ability to prevent liberalization and rule-making at the EC-level. In fact, intergovernmental bargaining continued in the Council of Ministers, but always under the shadow of the Commission's capacity to bypass the Council with Art. 90 (Chapter 5). A remarkably similar story is that of the liberalization of the European airline industry (Chapter 6). At a time of sustained increase in levels of passenger and freight transported by airlines, supranational organizations, in complicity with business and consumer groups, were gradually able to overcome the resistance of governments that had been hostile to deregulation. Once removed from national control, reregulation—at the European level—proceeded.

Finally, Fligstein and McNichol report that through the 1970s, both the quantity of EC legislation and the number of EC pressure groups expanded. Most significantly, pressure groups and legislation grew during the 1970s in domains where EC competences would later be enhanced by Treaty revisions. In other words, the interstate bargains that amended the Treaty in the 1980s were a response to the prior growth in transnational activity. "The Treaty revisions of the 1980s took place in the context of a demand for more cooperation at the European level. One can infer that the crisis of the 1980s was partially precipitated by the limits of the institutions and organizations of the EC to deal with these activities" (Chapter 3).

The transactions-based theory implies a coherent answer to the question, why does integration proceed faster or farther in some policy areas than in others? We would look to variation in the levels of cross-border interactions and in the consequent need for supranational coordination and rules. In sectors where the intensity and value of cross-national transactions are relatively low, the demand for EC-level coordination of rules and dispute resolution will be correspondingly low. Conversely, in domains where the number and value of cross-border transactions are rising, there will be increasing demand on the part of the transactors for EC-level rules and dispute-resolution mechanisms. It makes sense, then, that the EC has moved farthest toward the supranational pole with respect to managing the internal market. Intra-EC trade and investment have grown steadily since the founding of the EEC, creating the need for greater degrees of supranational governance in issue areas closely linked to expanding the common market. Naturally, the EC rules for the single market have in turn encouraged increases in the cross-border transactions they were meant to facilitate. In contrast, there are few societal transactions that are impeded by the absence of a common foreign and security policy. Or, put differently, though some argue for the political benefits that CFSP would bring, few societal transactors find its absence costly. There is therefore minimal social demand for integration in that policy domain.

Furthermore, the capacity of supranational organizations to make rules in a given policy domain appears to vary as a function of the level of transnational activity. As Stone Sweet and Caporaso document (Chapter 4), litigation of free movement of goods disputes dominates the work of the European Court of Justice, and legal principles developed by the ECJ in that domain have animated the Court's decision-making in other areas. Mark Pollack (Chapter 8) finds that the Commission exercises greater autonomy in some policy sectors than in others. The Commission's authority is greatest when it is supported by EC rules, pro-integrative Court decisions, and transnational interests. We would argue that variation in these factors is not random: higher levels of transactions push the EC to legislate, the Court to clarify the rules, and interests to organize. It is therefore not surprising that in Pollack's comparative case studies, the Commission's powers are greater in competition policy than in structural funds or external trade. Even within competition policy, the Commission acts with greater authority where transaction levels are high (telecommunications) relative to where they are low (electricity).

The theory also allows us to explain the general direction of integration in the common market. Business is likely to be the segment for which the material stake in cross-border transactions is greatest and most obvious. Indeed, the Treaty of Rome created rules whose purpose was to promote cross-national economic activities. Companies with an interest in cross-national sales or investment will press for the reduction of national barriers, and for the establishment of regional rules and standards. By the same token, the consequences of integration for people in their roles as workers and consumers are less transparent. This would explain why European companies have had a greater impact on integration than have labor or consumers (Sandholtz and Zysman 1989; Sandholtz 1992*a*; Green-Cowles 1993). We can thus account for the decisively neoliberal (pro-market) character of recent events like the 1992 program and the Maastricht provisions on EMU. If integration is driven fundamentally by private transactors, and if capital is the group with the clearest immediate stake in intra-EC transactions (not to mention the resources required for political influence), it is not surprising that the major steps in integration should be congenial to those segments of business.

We can now also respecify the spillover mechanism. As the most obvious hindrances to cross-national exchange are removed, or their effects reduced by the transaction-cost-reducing behavior of supranational organizations and rules, new obstacles to such transactions are revealed and become salient. With the removal of tariffs and quotas, for example, differences in national regulatory standards—for the environment, health and safety, technical compatibility, and so on—become more apparent as obstacles to exchange. Economic actors seeking to benefit from intra-Community exchange will then target these obstacles, both by attacking regulatory barriers through litigation and by pressuring EC legislative institutions to widen the jurisdiction of the EC into new domains. Transactors will always prefer, other things being equal, to live under (or adapt to) one set of rules rather than six, or twelve, or fifteen. As governments and EC institutions respond, spillover occurs.

Globalization, which is integration of a broader geographic scope, can also stimulate movement toward increased supranational governance within Europe. The integration of national markets (for goods, services, and capital) and multilateral approaches to global problems (ozone, climate change, weapons proliferation) can create pressures for integration from above the nation-state. Transnational actors are sometimes the conduit through which globalization stimulates advances in European integration. For instance, with the goal of increasing their competitiveness in world markets, European multinationals pressed for active EC high-technology programs (ESPRIT, RACE) as well as the creation of a genuine internal market (Sandholtz and Zysman 1989; Sandholtz 1992*b*). But globalization can also exert pressure directly on EC organizations. For example, the involvement of the EC in global environmental negotiations has strengthened Commission competencies and roles (Chapter 10).

3. Institutionalization

Once movement toward the supranational pole begins, European rules generate a dynamic of its own, which we call institutionalization. In laying out the continuum, the objective was to establish analytic categories for conceptualizing and identifying movement toward supranational politics. In a subsequent section, we offered a theory as to why policy domains move toward the supranational pole. Our transaction-based theory of movement leads us, when we observe rising levels of transnational exchange, to expect more EC rules. We can thus explain why some policy domains move more quickly toward supranational governance than others. The theory does not tell us what specific rules and policies will emerge, nor what organizational form supranational governance will acquire.

In this section, we propose a theoretical account for why shifts toward supranational governance tend to generate additional movement in the same direction, or at least make it difficult to reverse the shifts that have already occurred. In other words, the EC is not at any given moment simply the organizational instantiation of state interests, combined through negotiation into a lowest-common-denominator agreement. The supranational content of the EC does not fluctuate up and down to reflect the interstate bargain *du jour*. Rather, because of institutionalization, EC policy domains can become more supranational without some, or at times a majority of, governments wanting it or being able to reverse it.

Like Haas, we argue that there is a logic of institutionalization. Rules and rule-making are at the heart of this logic. Rules define roles (who is an actor) and establish the social context in which actors' interests and strategies take shape. Rules define the game, establishing for players both the objectives and the range of appropriate tactics or moves. Actors behave in self-interested ways, but both the interests and the behaviors take form in a social setting defined by rules. Actors will try to exploit the rules for selfish advantage, or to change the rules to favor achievement of their objectives. But at any given moment, they take the rules as given. Institutions are systems of rules (Jepperson 1991: 149, 157; North 1990: 3, 6), and institutionalization is the process by which rules are created, applied, and interpreted by those who live under them.

Institutions, contrary to the image of fixity frequently associated with them, are in constant evolution. People acting within a rule context inevitably encounter the limits of the rules, that is, situations in which their content is unclear or disputed. Rules may not provide clear guidance for new kinds of transactions or behaviors. Or two actors may disagree as to what the rules require in a specific instance. In either case, actors will then make demands on the dispute resolution processes. They may push for the creation of new rules (legislation). Or they may seek reinterpretation of the existing rules (adjudication). As they interpret and apply the rules, courts, legislators, and administrators necessarily modify the rules by establishing their effective meaning. The new or changed rules then guide subsequent interactions, as people adapt their behaviors to the rules. The disputes that arise thereafter take shape in an altered rule structure and initiate the processes that will again reinterpret and modify the rules. The new rules guide actor behaviors, and so on (Stone Sweet forthcoming; Sandholtz 1997).

The logic of institutionalization is at work in the European Community and is crucial to understanding integration as a process. As European rules emerge and are clarified and as European organizations become arenas for politics, what is specifically supranational shapes the context for subsequent interactions: how actors define their interests, what avenues are available to pursue them, how disputes are to be resolved. This creates the "loop" of institutionalization. Developments in EC rules delineate the contours of future policy debates as well as the normative and organizational terms in which they will be decided. Since rules are central to institutionalization, the Treaty of Rome is the crucial starting point for subsequent integration. The Treaty established EC rules and rule-making procedures, and constituted EC organizations like the Commission and the ECJ.

We would expect that, in general, integration would occur most readily in policy domains included in the Treaty. Policy domains mentioned in the Treaty have the advantage of a legal basis in the Union's fundamental rules. Treaty-based policy domains should move more quickly toward supranational governance, other things being equal, than policy areas for which a competence or legal basis would have to be constructed from scratch. Fligstein and McNichol show that "most of the arenas in which the EC built competencies were laid down in the Treaty of Rome and the original language and definitions gave rise to organizational structures oriented towards producing legislation in those domains" (Chapter 3).

Integration, however, is not limited to those domains specifically called out in the Treaty. Where cross-border activities are of increasing importance, we expect to find the creation and growth of supranational governance. When there is no Treaty-based competence for such a development, the relevant actors will create one. (Conversely, policy domains mentioned in the Treaty but lacking cross-border transactions are not likely to move toward supranational governance.) Rising levels of cross-border transactions generate demand for EC rules and dispute resolution. Member governments can respond by amending the Treaty, or stretching Treaty clauses to cover new legislation. Art. 236, for instance, permits the EC to establish supranational governance to achieve the general objectives of the Community. This provision has served as the legal basis for EC action in policy domains not specifically mentioned in the Treaty. Perhaps more important in practice, the ECJ has interpreted the Treaty so as to permit the expansion of supranational policy domains (Weiler 1981). Again: the Court does not choose its questions; it responds to the cases brought, frequently, by transactors seeking clearer EC rules or enforcement of existing rules. The landmark Dassonville line of case law, which underpinned immensely consequential Commission initiatives and intergovernmental bargaining in the move to complete the common market, was sustained by private actors desiring the elimination of national practices that limited intra-EC trade (Alter and Meunier-Aitsahalia 1994).

A clear example of a policy domain becoming supranational despite the absence of a treaty basis is the telecommunications sector. The Treaty of Rome makes no mention of telecommunications. In fact, various Treaty provisions (Art. 90 (2) and Art. 222) had traditionally been interpreted as exempting national telecommunications monopolies from EC competition rules. A series of ECJ rulings undermined that supposed exemption. The Commission took advantage of the Court's decisions to attack the national telecommunications monopolies with Art. 90 directives. In short, the ECJ's reinterpretation of the Treaty enabled the Commission, supported by transnational coalitions, to effect a liberalization of telecommunications that was faster, more far-reaching, and more coordinated at the EC level than almost any of the member governments wanted at any stage along the way (Chapter 5). Or, as Michael Smith shows, interactions within the framework of European Political Cooperation, which were completely outside the Treaty structure, generated a body of informal rules and practices that significantly shaped government behaviors and interactions (Chapter 11).

Thus, though the Treaty is the indispensable starting point, over time supranational rules and rule-making processes evolve in ways that are not predictable from the ex ante perspective of those who establish them. The new rules create legal rights and open new arenas for politics; in this fashion they structure political processes thereafter. Actors—including governments, private entities, and EC bodies—adapt to the new rules and arenas. This dynamic is wholly absent in the intergovernmentalist account. Intergovernmentalists see governments as the sole mediators between non-state actors and EC policymaking. In contrast, our theory leads us to expect (and we do observe) private actors successfully employing the EC judicial process against member governments and pursuing political strategies directly at the Commission. Intergovernmentalists depict governments as directing the process of integration and establishing its limits. Our approach, in contrast, views governments as powerful actors that cannot always impose their preferred outcomes on other players in the EC political system (transnational actors, the Commission and the ECJ), who also possess substantial legal and political powers.

Finally, governments are ultimately constrained by rules whose production they do not control. National courts, guided by ECJ decisions, can compel their governments to comply with EC rules they have opposed. For example, though the UK has taken the most anti-integration position in the Council with respect to social provisions, British courts responding to private litigants and ECJ rulings have forced the government to change domestic policies so that they align with EC laws that Britain opposed (Chapter 4). Similarly, though member governments bargained with each other with respect to telecommunications liberalization, that bargaining took place during the crucial phase under the shadow of the Commission's newfound capacity, affirmed by the Court, to enact its preferred policies via Art. 90 directives (Chapter 5).

The rule-centered logic of institutionalization also suggests why it is difficult, and sometimes impossible, for governments to reverse the shifts toward supranational governance that have occurred. The Treaty—the constitution of the European polity—fixes the rule-making processes of the EC and the ECJ is authoritative interpreter of this constitution. As substantive rules, such as secondary legislation, evolve, actors (including governments, as well as EC bodies and non-state entities) adjust their behaviors. The rules, since the impetus behind them is to facilitate cross-border transactions and communications, lead to new kinds and higher levels of transactions. The new transactions entrench interests. The result is a high degree of "stickiness" in movement along the continuum.

Two logics, or languages, capture the essence of that stickiness. The first has to do with path-dependence, the second with principal–agent relations. Paul Pierson (Chapter 2) makes two interrelated points: first, that significant gaps emerge between member-state preferences and the functioning of EC policies and institutions; and second, that once such gaps develop states cannot simply close them. The latter point is the crucial one with respect to the difficulty of reversing shifts toward supranational governance. Pierson argues that institutional change is a "path-dependent" process; once institutional and policy changes are in place, social actors adapt to those changes, frequently making substantial investments in the process. A policy turnabout would entail the loss of these sunk costs, thus raising the costs for governments seeking to unwind supranational governance. Furthermore, decision rules often constitute major obstacles to reversing course. The process of adaptation to change in complex social settings also produces unintended consequences that are difficult to unwind. Thus institutional and policy outcomes become "locked in," channeling politics down specific paths and closing previously plausible alternatives.

Mark Pollack assesses the conditions under which the EC Commission can act autonomously, recognizing that the Commission is the most constrained of the EC's supranational bodies (as compared to the Parliament and the ECJ). He employs principal–agent imagery to argue that the administrative and oversight mechanisms that principals (member governments) use to rein in agents (the Commission) can be costly and of limited effectiveness. Furthermore, agents can exploit divergent preferences among multiple principals, especially under more demanding decision rules, like unanimity (Chapter 8).

The path-dependence and principal–agent logics reinforce our argument that institutionalization in the EC is not reducible to the preferences of, or bargaining among, member governments. The expansion of transnational society pushes for supranational governance, which is exercised to facilitate and regulate that society. Once in place, supranational rules alter the context for subsequent transactions and policymaking. Actors—governments, supranational organizations, and non-state entities alike—adapt their preferences, strategies, and behaviors to the new rules. These adaptations, plus the importance of rules in shaping preferences and behaviors, are what make shifts toward supranational governance sticky and difficult to undo. Finally, because specific policies and organizational forms emerge through a path-dependent process, in which numerous social systems interact in quite contingent ways, those outcomes can only be analyzed through historical, process-tracing case studies. Thus, whereas broad aggregate data reflect the causal link between cross-border transactions and EC rule-making (Chapter 4), case studies are essential for explaining the specific content and form of EC rules and policies (Chapters 2, 4, 5, 8, and 11).

4. Overview of the Book

Each contribution to this volume addresses several themes relating to the institutional development of the European Community. Some authors speak directly to the proposition that rising levels of cross-border transactions (other things being equal) trigger the policy-relevant behaviors that produce supranational rules, showing how prior institutionalization shapes EC policy processes and outcomes (Chapters 4, 5, and 7). Others focus on the dynamics of institutionalization (Chapters 2, 8, 10, and 11). Still others provide broad views of the development of EC institutions, in terms of the organizational construction of policy domains (Chapter 3) or in terms of public conceptions of the EC as a policymaking space (Chapter 9).

The empirical contributions range from the specific to the panoramic. Some chapters assess issue areas in considerable detail, including free movement, competition policy, external trade, monetary and exchange rate policies, social provisions, structural policy, telecommunications, environment, and foreign and security policies. Others analyze the overarching configuration of EC policy domains. Some of the chapters include a focus on a specific EC organization, such as the Commission (Chapter 8), or on the interactions between EC bodies (Chapters 4, 5, and 10). Chapters 7 and 11 trace the emergence of new EC organizational structures in the monetary and foreign policy realms. A striking feature of the EC's development has been the expansion of its competences into issue areas not enunciated in the Treaty; several chapters detail the construction of EC policy domains in such areas (environment, foreign and security policies, monetary policy, social provisions, telecommunications). Though the primary focus of the book is on the dynamic of institutionalization within the EC, some of the chapters analyze the impact on EC institutions and policymaking of external actors and events (Chapters 10 and 11). Uniting all of these studies is a shared concern with institutional processes, with explaining how and why policy domains move along the continuum between intergovernmental and supranational modes of governance.

In the following paragraphs, we briefly introduce the various chapters. For the purposes of this overview, we cluster the chapters into three groups. In the first group we place those contributions that directly engage the transactions-driven theory of integration. The second group includes essays whose primary concern is institutionalization, including both the evolution of rules and organizations and the changing pattern of member-state control. Chapters in the third group take a broad perspective of the development of the EC in its organizational structures and in public opinion.

4.1. Transnational activity and the demand for integration

Alec Stone Sweet and James Caporaso in Chapter 4 elaborate and test a theory of legal integration that is broadly congruent with the theory presented here. In analyses of the evolution of relationships that have developed between three variables—transnational exchange, transnational judicial activity, and supranational rules—the chapter provides strong support for our claim that, in Europe, transnational society, organizational capacity, and rule-making bind together as integration proceeds.

Sandholtz (Chapter 5) applies the transactions-based theory of integration to the telecommunications sector. Until recently, European telecommunications were a patchwork of national monopolies. By the 1980s, this fragmentation was increasingly dysfunctional for the rising number of actors who needed advanced pan-European telecommunications. These actors became natural allies for the Commission, which had set the objective of a liberalized EC telecommunications market as early as 1979. Key decisions by the ECJ held that the Community's competition rules applied to state monopolies. The Commission exploited this opening, issuing a series of Art. 90 directives (that did not need Council assent) that opened up the Community markets in telecommunications equipment, services, and, ultimately, networks. The chapter shows that the Commission, bolstered by alliances with transnational coalitions, was able to deploy EC rules to liberalize telecommunications in a more rapid, far-reaching, and coordinated fashion than the member governments would collectively have preferred.

Chapter 6 on the Europeanization of air transport traces the process by which the competence to regulate the market for aviation services was transferred from national governments, who had operated completely outside of EC auspices, to supranational organs. Much of their focus is on the role of EC governments, who ultimately made the decisions to dismantle the system of national monopoly and control, and to replace it with a more liberal system to be governed by EC rules. The authors show that in the 1980s transnational activity, Commission initiatives, and a crucial ECJ ruling conspired to fatally undermine national control. The Council could have blocked the move to supranational governance, but only at increasingly exorbitant costs.

Chapter 7 analyzes the emergence of supranational authority in monetary and exchange-rate policy. Rising levels of cross-border transactions play a crucial, though indirect, role in this policy domain as well. The elimination of internal tariffs, and the steadily increasing dependence on intra-EC trade, raised the salience of exchange-rate relations within the Community. After the removal of capital controls pursuant to the single market program in the 1980s, policymakers became increasingly conscious of the incompatibility among national monetary autonomy, free capital movements, and fixed exchange rates. Cameron explains why monetary union came to be seen as the preferred response to that dilemma. Central to his account is the transformation of the Committee of Central Bank Governors of the EC from an informal body only loosely connected to the organizational structure of the EC, into the Community's supranational monetary policymaking authority in the future European Central Bank.

4.2. On institutionalization

We begin with Paul Pierson's elaboration of an historical institutionalist account of the development of supranational governance. Focusing on the cumulative impact of the EC's organizations and EC rule-making, Pierson argues that, over time, institutional effects like path-dependence and lock-in overwhelm the capacities of governments to control the course of integration. This is due in part to the fact that governments tend to act on short-term interests, while being unable to anticipate the long-range consequences of delegating authority to EC organizations. It is also due to the forging of multidimensional relationships between societal actors and the Court and the Commission; to the fact that complex policy feedback loops, potentially encompassing even governments, become commonplace; and to the extent to which EC organizations develop and exploit information asymmetries within specific policy arenas, thereby enhancing their own authority vis-à-vis governments. Given the decision-making rules in place, governments are often incapable of reversing, blocking, or rerouting specific paths being carved out. Indeed, how governments define, express, and pursue their own preferences may itself be best understood in path-dependent ways, that is, as endogenous to processes of integration. Pierson applies these arguments to EC social policy, demonstrating the extent to which the Commission and the Court, in conjunction with private actors affected, have succeeded in extending the scope of social policy beyond the "minimalist" parameters envisaged by governments.

The collaborators of this volume agree for the need to evaluate empirically the extent of member-state government control, or of the autonomy exercised by supranational organizations and transnational processes within EC policy processes over time. Two chapters in this volume explicitly employ the principal–agent framework to do so. In Chapter 8, Mark Pollack argues that the role of the Community's supranational organizations is "best understood in terms of principal–agent analysis." As Pollack employs it, the principal–agent framework focuses attention on how and under what conditions member-state governments delegate authority to Community organs, on the means available to the former to "control" the latter, and on the iterated and interstitial nature of the relationship between principals and agents. In his detailed examination of the role of the Commission in developing policies on regional development, antitrust, and external trade, Pollack shows that the Commission has been a central actor in policy deliberations, and indeed exercises "considerable autonomy and influence." Nevertheless, the extent of this influence varies widely across issue area as a function of the interplay between five basic factors. In any given sector, the more that member-state government preferences diverge, the rules authorizing Commission policy discretion are explicit, information asymmetries benefit the Commission, alliances with transnational actors have been forged, and the ECJ backs an increase in the EC's competence to govern, the greater autonomy we are likely to find.

Although more skeptical about the utility of the principal–agent construct, Stone Sweet and James Caporaso use it as a tool in their effort to assess the impact of the European Court in the development of two domains of EC law: the free movement of goods and social provisions (Chapter 4). They find that governments have been largely incapable of controlling how the legal system operates. Indeed, the ECJ, in complicity with national judges, consistently generates policy outcomes that many powerful governments would have rejected had they been proposed in legislative processes. As important, judicial policymaking has altered the conduct of policymaking at both the national and supranational levels (see also Chapters 5 and 6).

Two chapters examine the extent to which processes of institutionalization have served to construct the external personality of the EC. Michael Smith (Chapter 11) examines the evolution of European Political Cooperation (EPC) and its impact on the European polity. At first, EPC—the process through which common foreign and security policies are elaborated among EC member-states—operated as a stable forum for government-to-government diplomacy. Diplomats eschewed fixed rules, procedures, and bureaucratic support, taking care to exclude the domain from EC affairs, and to insulate it from the influence and scrutiny of the Community's organizations. With experience, intergovernmental trust grew and, in consequence, rules and procedures, reflecting the development of shared understandings and expectations, appeared. Smith shows that as incentives to coordinate foreign policies increased, so did the density of transgovernmental networks and communications to manage this coordination, and these communications pushed the system to institutionalize further. Finally, as EPC matured and became more participatory, and as European integration proceeded, the distinction between EPC and the EC, and therefore between "high" and "low" politics, broke down. Community organizations, like the Commission and the Council of Ministers were gradually included in EPC deliberations. At the same time, informal rules and "soft" law were codified as "hard" law. The Single European Act and the Maastricht Treaty hardwired EPC rules, procedures, and the new organizational capacities of EC organizations into the institutional structure of the European Union.

Alberta Sbragia (Chapter 10) examines the impact of the institutionalization of the EC on the Commission's competence to act as an actor in the international system. Although the body's authority to participate in international organizations and to represent the Community in multilateral treaty negotiations is now both extensive and secure, such an outcome was not preordained. There is neither a rich tradition in international relations nor a strong precedent in international law for a body like the Commission to participate alongside sovereign states in international fora. Further, EC member-states themselves assumed that, with the single exception of commercial policy, they retained, individually, sovereignty over their external relations. As Sbragia shows, the Commission acquired its international personality through an internal and an external dynamic. First, the drive to achieve a European common market coupled with the ECJ's constitutionalization of the treaty system constructed the context for the Commission's own bid to expand its authority internationally. In 1971, as the Commission was busily working to reduce national barriers to trade, the ECJ ruled that the EC, and not member-states, was responsible for the external relations of the Community in those areas preempted by EC law. In effect, the ECJ's doctrine of supremacy (1964) implied preemption, and preemption deprived the member-states of control at the international levels. Second, in order for the Commission to be successful, the international community had to, in effect, accept it as a member of the club. The chapter documents the Commission's struggle for acceptance, focusing on the body's participation in international environmental treaty negotiations. Sbragia characterizes the system by which the member-states and the Community represent themselves externally today as a complex combination of the intergovernmental and the federal.

4.3. The EC polity

Two chapters take as their empirical focus the overarching configuration of the EC's policy domains and how it has developed over time. Fligstein and McNichol trace the evolution of policy domains in the EC (Chapter 3). They present and analyze rich data on the evolution of EC organizations (structures, budgets, and employees), legislation, and transnational interest groups. They demonstrate that the Commission and the Council are both organized into units that mirror the policy domains articulated in the Treaty and its revisions. They also document a close relationship between the production of EC legislation and transnational pressure group activities. Relevant to the transactions-based theory of integration offered by Stone Sweet and Sandholtz, they find that growth in the number of transnational pressure groups in a number of domains preceded the Treaty revisions that established EC competences. Interest group activity and EC legislation grew during the 1970s in policy areas that would later be given a treaty basis in the 1980s and 1990s.

Dalton and Eichenberg (Chapter 9) argue that as the European Community has moved from intergovernmental toward supranational modes of governance, public opinion has assumed an increasingly important role. Furthermore, they suggest that public opinion influences which areas are most susceptible to further integration efforts. Their chapter analyzes public opinion data on the extent to which Europeans believe that policy responsibility in specific areas should be transferred from national governments to the European Community. They find that policy areas involving technical complexity, interdependence, and management of the common market attract high levels of public support. The original six EC members (arguably the most integrated economically) display the greatest net support for EC-level action; newer members are less enthusiastic. Chapter 9 also provides more detailed analyses of public opinion in three policy areas addressed in other chapters: environment, monetary, and foreign and security policies.

In a concluding chapter, Caporaso places the themes of this volume in a broader perspective of past and present theorizing on European integration.

5. Conclusion

We have proposed a theory of integration that relies on three causal factors: exchange, organization, and rules. Transnational exchange provokes supranational organizations to make rules designed to facilitate and to regulate the development of transnational society. To the extent that supranational organizations are successful at doing so, specific causal connections between our three factors will be constructed. These connections sustain an inherently expansionary process, not least, by means of policy feedback. As the structure of European rules becomes more dense and articulated, this structure itself will encourage private and public actors at all levels of the Community to forge new, or intensify existing, linkages (vertical and horizontal). Member-state governments are important actors in this process. Nevertheless, we argue that the integration-relevant behavior of governments, whether acting individually or collectively, is best explained in terms of the embeddedness of governments in integration processes, that is, in terms of the development of transnational society and its system of governance.

We do not want to be misunderstood on this last point. No one denies that certain elements, or stages, of the European policymaking process are intergovernmental. Governments are repositories of immense resources, both material (e.g. financial) and non-material (e.g. legitimacy). In the EC, national executives pursue what they take to be their own interests, which they express as constituting the national interest. And in the bargaining process, executives from the larger states command greater resources and tend to wield greater influence on EC policy outcomes than those from the smaller states. But noticing governments and power does not entail accepting intergovernmentalism as a body of causal propositions about how integration has proceeded. Although we dismiss as untenable Moravcsik's proclamation that his version of intergovernmentalism is the "indispensable and fundamental point of departure for any general explanation of regional integration" (1995: 625) we have no trouble recognizing that intergovernmental bargaining is an ubiquitous feature of supranational governance (as it is in many federal polities). Indeed, in our research we constantly attend to the question of whether and how integration shapes the preferences of governments over time, and the extent to which it casts (and recasts) the nature and content of intergovernmental bargaining. In our opinion, Moravcsik has developed a theory of intergovernmental bargaining within a specific institutional context, that of the EC, but not a satisfying general theory of integration.

Our theory accounts for causal relationships between variables that are systematically downplayed or de-emphasized by intergovernmentalism and, we argue, these relationships will regularly produce outcomes that significantly impact the trajectory of integration. Intergovernmentalism is rigid: integration proceeds, but nothing essential in European politics ever changes. In contrast, we expect that integration produces new political arenas; that the politics in these arenas will qualitatively differ from purely intergovernmental politics; and that this difference will have an impact downstream, on subsequent policy processes and outcomes. In Moravcsik's view, supranational organizations, like the Commission, are virtually always "perfectly reactive agents," responding only to the "delegation" of tasks pursuant to the "pooling" of state sovereignty (1995: 616, 621). In contrast, we expect supranational bodies to work to enhance their own autonomy and influence within the European polity, so as to promote the interests of transnational society and the construction of supranational governance. In Moravcsik's view, "Only where the action of supranational leaders *systematically* bias outcomes away from the long term self-interest of member-states can we speak of a serious challenge to an intergovernmentalist view" (1993: 514, emphasis in original). In response, we expect what intergovernmentalism is not capable of explaining, namely that, as integration proceeds, the Court and the Commission will routinely produce rules (policy outcomes) that would not have been adopted by governments in the Council of Ministers, or in summitry. And we argue that the long-term interests of member-state governments will be increasingly biased toward the long-term interests of transnational society, those who have the most to gain from supranational governance.

2

The Path to European Integration: A Historical-Institutionalist Analysis

PAUL PIERSON

T HE evolution of the European Community has long fascinated political scientists. For four decades, some of the world's most enduring nation-states have conducted an extraordinary political experiment. Progressing sporadically but in a consistent direction, the member-states of the European Community have "pooled" increasing areas of policy authority, introducing prominent collective institutions. The creation of these institutions initiated a process which has transformed the nature of European politics.

How the evolution of these arrangements of collective governance can be explained and the nature of the current system understood remain matters of considerable controversy. Within American political science, it has been students of international relations who have maintained the most theoretically driven discussions of the EC. Despite significant internal disputes, the dominant paradigm in international-relations scholarship regards European integration as the practice of ordinary diplomacy under conditions creating unusual opportunities for providing collective goods through highly institutionalized exchange (Garrett 1992; Moravcsik 1993). From this "intergovernmentalist" perspective the EC is essentially a forum for interstate bargaining. Member-state governments remain the only important actors at the European level. Societal actors exert influence only through the domestic political structures of member-states. Policymaking is made through negotiation among member-state governments or through carefully circumscribed delegations of authority. Whether relying on negotiation or delegation, Chiefs of Government ("COGs") are at the heart of the EC, and each seeks to maximize its own advantage. Debate within this perspective has concerned such questions as why member-state governments desired certain observed outcomes, which governments

An earlier version of this chapter appeared in *Comparative Political Studies* (see Pierson 1996).

have the most influence on collective decision-making, and which alignment of COG interests can best explain policy or institutional development in the EC (Moravcsik 1991; Lange 1993; Martin 1993).

This perspective has not been without its challengers. European scholars have generally depicted the EC as a more complex and pluralistic political structure, less firmly under the control of member-state governments. Much of this scholarship is not particularly concerned with advancing broad theories of integration, concentrating instead on the detailed investigation of day-to-day policy development in areas where the EC's role is prominent. From this perspective, the Community looks more like a single (if highly fragmented) polity than the site of diplomatic maneuvering among autonomous member-state governments. Within Europe, analyses that treat the European Community as a quasi-federal system—"an obvious reference point for the European Community" in the words of one prominent analyst (Dehousse 1994c: 103)—are now quite common (Scharpf 1988; Majone 1992).

This is equally true within the ranks of comparativists who have turned their attention recently to the European Community (Sbragia 1992; Marks 1993; Anderson 1995; Pierson and Leibfried 1995). The principal reason for this new interest is revealing: students of a wide range of government activities, including industrial, regional, social, and environmental policies, have found that they can no longer understand the domestic processes and outcomes that interest them without addressing the role of the EC. These investigations also portray a complex and pluralistic political process, not firmly under the control of national governments and not explicable in terms of simple diplomatic bargaining. Coming from the detailed investigation of particular domestic policy arenas to address a strikingly new phenomenon, however, comparativists possessed few theoretical tools that appeared directly applicable. Like European analysts, they have tended to depict the Community as a quasi-federal, "multilevel" or "multitiered" political system. Yet these terms are used more to describe the current state of affairs than to explain it. Thus, if a growing body of detailed research reveals considerable unease about the dominant IR models of EC politics, critics have so far had little to offer as an alternative to intergovernmentalist accounts.

In practice, the critics of intergovernmentalism have tried to move forward in two ways. Some have continued to investigate particular policy areas, content to reveal the density and pluralism of actual policymaking while simply observing that the focus of international relations theory on grand diplomacy among sovereign member-states does not square with what is actually occurring "on the ground." However, it is almost always possible, ex post, to posit some set of government preferences that reconciles observed outcomes with the image of near-total COG control. Where policy outcomes do not conform to the expected preferences of national governments, they may be explained as part of a "nested game" or as an instance of side payments. Drawing on rational choice theory, intergovernmentalism possesses flexible conceptual tools that can "explain" why member-state governments would favor the observed outcomes (Green and Shapiro 1994).[1] Thus, absent a theoretically convincing explanation for the constraints on national governments, these detailed investigations will not persuade proponents of intergovernmentalism.

More theoretically oriented critics have drawn on aspects of the "neo-functionalist" tradition in international relations, showing how "spillover" processes and the autonomous actions of supranational actors (including the Commission and European Court of Justice) contribute to European policymaking. Recent efforts to update neofunctionalism have successfully highlighted important limitations in intergovernmentalist accounts, and I will rely in part on these arguments in developing my own analysis. Yet neofunctionalism has serious problems of its own. Given the strong institutional position of member-state governments in the EC, neofunctionalists seem to attribute greater autonomy to supranational actors than can plausibly be sustained. Although neofunctionalist arguments about the independent action of the Commission and Court of Justice have some merit, there is little doubt that the governments of member-states, acting together in the Council, remain the most powerful decision-makers. In most cases, it seems equally probable that these decision-makers act to secure their own interests, whatever those are deemed to be. Crucially, these "principals" retain the legal authority to rein in their "agents" if they find it in their interests to do so. Thus *at any given point in time* the key propositions of intergovernmentalist theory are likely to hold.

This chapter seeks to lay the foundation for a more persuasive account of member-state government constraint. My focus is on the reasons why gaps emerge in COG control over the evolution of European organizations and public policies, on why these gaps are difficult to close, and on how these openings both create room for actors other than member-state governments to influence the process of European integration while simultaneously constraining the room for maneuver of *all* political actors. The basis for this challenge to intergovernmentalism lies in insights from what I will term "historical institutionalism" (Steinmo and Thelen 1992; Ikenberry 1994). The label covers a diverse range of scholarship, much of it with little theoretical focus. Indeed, a principal goal of this chapter is to strengthen the theoretical foundations of historical institutionalism. There are, however, two unifying themes within this broad research orientation. This scholarship is *historical* because it recognizes that political development must be understood as a process that unfolds over time. It is *institutionalist* because it stresses that many of the contemporary implications of these temporal processes are embedded in institutions—whether these be formal rules, policy structures, or social norms.[2]

---

[1] A good example (among many possible ones) is Peter Lange's analysis of the Maastricht Social Protocol (Lange 1993). Lange may well be correct in arguing that the governments of poor member-states signed the Protocol because of side payments, but he provides no actual evidence that this was the case.

[2] Throughout, I rely on North's definition of institutions: "the rules of the game in a society or, more formally, . . . the humanly devised constraints that shape human interaction" (North 1990: 3).

The crucial claim I derive from historical institutionalism is that actors may be in a strong initial position, seek to maximize their interests, and nevertheless carry out institutional and policy reforms that fundamentally transform their own positions (or those of their successors) in ways that are unanticipated and/or undesired. Attempts to cut into ongoing social processes at a single point in time produce a "snapshot" view that is distorted in crucial respects. My analysis emphasizes temporal aspects of politics: the impact of actor's time-horizons, the lags between decisions and long-term consequences, and the constraints that emerge from societal adaptations and shifts in policy prefer-ences that occur during the interim. When European integration is examined over time, the gaps in member-state government control appear far more prominent than they do in intergovernmentalist accounts.

In contrast to the functional account of institutions which underpins inter-governmentalism, historical institutionalism stresses the difficulties of subject-ing institutional evolution to tight control. Two brief historical examples can illustrate the broad claim developed in this chapter. The first concerns the changing institutional position of state governments in the United States (Riker 1955). Because approval of the American constitution required state ratification, the interests of states received considerable attention in the process of institutional design. The framers intended the Senate to serve as a strong support of state interests. In an arrangement that partly echoes the EC's emphasis on the participation of member-state governments in collective deliberations, state legislatures were to appoint senators, who were expected to serve as delegates representing states in the formation of policy. Over time, however, Senators seeking greater autonomy were able to gradually free themselves from state oversight. By the early 1900s, the enactment of the 17th Amendment requiring popular election of Senators only ratified the result of a lengthy erosion of state legislative control.

The development of Canadian federalism provides another example (Watts 1987). The designers of the Canadian federation sought a highly centralized form of federalism—in part as a reaction to the ways in which decentralization contributed to the horrors of the American Civil War. Yet the Canadian federa-tion is now far less centralized than the American one. Among the reasons: the Canadian federation left to the provinces sole responsibility for many activities that were then considered trivial. With the growing role of government in social policy and economic management, however, these responsibilities turned out to be of tremendous importance.

In both these cases, the current functioning of institutions cannot be derived from the aspirations of the original designers. Processes evolving over time led to quite unexpected outcomes. Similarly, I will argue that what one makes of the EC depends on whether one examines a photograph or a moving picture. Just as a film often reveals meanings that cannot be discerned from a single photograph, a view of Europe's development over time gives us a richer sense of the nature of the emerging European polity. At any given time, the diplomatic maneuvering among national governments looms large, and an intergovernmentalist perspective makes considerable sense. Seen as a historical process, however, the authority of national governments appears far more circumscribed, and both the interventions of other actors and the cumulative constraints of rule-based governance more considerable.

My argument is developed in three stages. In the first, I review the main features of intergovernmentalist analyses of the EC. In the second, I develop a historical institutionalist critique. In section three, I briefly apply these historical institutionalist arguments to one aspect of European integration, the development of social policy. This application is hardly intended as a full test of my approach. Nonetheless, historical institutionalism's applicability in an area where intergovernmentalist analysis ought to be on strong ground provides further evidence of its theoretical promise.

1. Intergovernmentalist Theories and the Autonomy of Member-State Governments

The accelerated activity of the EC in the past decade coincided with a growing focus among international-relations scholars on international regimes, which were conceptualized as institutionalized forms of collective action among nation-states (Krasner 1983; Keohane 1984; Haggard and Simmons 1987). While some analysts of European integration have continued to echo the earlier international relations literature on neofunctionalism, the dominant intergovernmentalist perspective has treated the EC as a standard (albeit unusually well-developed and multifaceted) international regime. It would be unrealistic to attempt a thorough review of this diverse and sophisticated literature here. Instead, I focus on three core features of intergovernmentalism: the emphasis on national governments' preoccupation with sovereignty; the depiction of institutions as instruments; and the focus on "grand bargains" among member-state governments.

1.1. The centrality of sovereignty

Intergovernmentalism itself generally takes the preferences of member-state governments as given, focusing instead on how they seek to pursue those preferences.[3] Yet despite this apparent openness, intergovernmentalist accounts tend to stress the preoccupation of national governments with preserving sovereignty. As Keohane maintains, "governments put a high value on the maintenance of their own autonomy, [so] it is usually impossible to establish

---

[3] Moravcsik has outlined a "liberal intergovernmentalist" view in which "liberal" theories of COG preference formation are used to supplement intergovernmentalist theories of bargaining among national governments (Moravcsik 1993).

international institutions that exercise authority over states" (Keohane 1984: 88).

Of course, much of the writing on international regimes arose as a reaction against realist perspectives that were seen as putting *too much* weight on sovereignty concerns—suggesting that collective action among states should almost never be possible. Regime theorists have argued that in contexts where security concerns have diminished, nation-states may care about absolute gains as well as relative ones. Nonetheless, the realist focus on sovereignty carries over into intergovernmentalist treatments of the EC. Most intergovernmentalist analyses suggest that the preferences of member-state governments are heavily weighted toward preserving sovereignty, leading Chiefs of Government to be vigilant guardians of national autonomy in evaluating proposals for international cooperation. The issue is often posed in principal–agent terms (Garrett 1992). The principals (member-states) may delegate certain responsibilities to agents (international organizations), but only with the strictest oversight. The core calculation for member-states is whether the benefits of collective action outweigh any possible risk to autonomy. According to Moravcsik, "[i]n the intergovernmentalist view, the unique institutional structure of the EC is acceptable to national governments *only* insofar as it strengthens, rather than weakens, their control over domestic affairs" (Moravcsik 1993: 507, emphasis added).

1.2. The instrumentality of institutions

Work on international regimes has drawn heavily on the insights of Transaction Cost Economics (TCE), which analyzes institutions in functional terms (Williamson 1975; Keohane 1984; North 1990). As Moravcsik summarizes, "modern regime theory views international institutions as deliberate instruments to improve the efficiency of bargaining between states" (Moravcsik 1993: 507). Drawing on sophisticated work in game theory and economic theories of organizations, intergovernmentalists note that collective action among autonomous nation-states is often desired yet enormously difficult. A critical issue concerns problems of information. Uncertainty about the preferences, intentions, and reliability of other actors makes agreements difficult to execute and enforce. Institutions can help surmount these problems, reducing information asymmetries, monitoring compliance, and creating linkages across issues that diminish the likelihood of defection. According to Keohane:

Far from being threats to governments (in which case it would be hard to understand why they exist at all), they permit governments to attain objectives that would otherwise be unattainable. They do so in part by facilitating intergovernmental agreements. Regimes facilitate agreements by raising the anticipated costs of violating others' property rights, by altering transaction costs through the clustering of issues, and by providing reliable information to members. Regimes are relatively efficient institutions, compared with the alternative of having a myriad of unrelated agreements, since their principles, rules, and institutions create linkages among issues that give actors incentives to reach mutually beneficial agreements. (Keohane 1984: 97)

In intergovernmentalist accounts, self-conscious, maximizing actors (member-state governments) create institutions because these institutions help them surmount collective action problems and achieve gains from exchange. The best way to understand the development of international institutions is to identify the functions that they fulfill, especially the lowering of bargaining costs and the reduction of uncertainty through the provision of "a forum and vocabulary for the signalling of preferences and intentions" (Stone 1994a: 456).

1.3. The centrality of intergovernmental bargains

Students of the EC frequently distinguish between the intermittent "grand bargains" (e.g. the Treaty of Rome, the Single European Act, Maastricht) that establish basic features of institutional design and the "day-to-day" policy-making in the Community that occurs between these agreements. For intergovernmentalists, the grand bargains are where the action is. Since, as Moravcsik puts it, "functional regime theory view[s] . . . international institutions as passive, transaction-cost reducing sets of rules," it is the design of those rules that is central. The EC, he adds, "has developed through a series of celebrated intergovernmental bargains, each of which sets the agenda for an intervening period of *consolidation*. The most fundamental task facing a theoretical account of European integration is to explain these bargains" (Moravcsik 1993: 508, 473, emphasis added). The intergovernmentalist research agenda clearly reflects this line of thinking, focusing overwhelmingly on explaining aspects of two grand bargains: the Single European Act (Moravcsik 1991; Garrett 1992) and the Maastricht Treaty (Garrett 1993; Lange 1993; Martin 1993). Political developments during the periods between these bargains, or that concern matters that are not hotly contested during those bargains, have received almost no attention.

These three aspects of intergovernmentalist accounts are closely connected. The depiction of member-state governments as profoundly concerned about sovereignty contributes to a functional view of regimes. Given the preoccupation with sovereignty, the institutional underpinnings for cooperation will only be created or extended after a careful weighing of long-term costs and benefits. The "benefits" are the transaction-cost-reducing functions that regimes perform, while the costs often relate to any risk of lost autonomy. Similarly, the emphasis on grand bargains follows logically from the functional analysis of institutions. If the EC is an international regime in which member-state governments have carefully designed passive instruments to allow them to carry out collective goals, periods of "consolidation" are of little interest. It is the bargains themselves that create or change the rules of the game, and that therefore demand attention. The "post-bargain" period simply plays out the implications intended in the grand bargains. Together, these three positions have contributed to a powerful argument about the process of European integration. As I suggest in the next Section, however, all three are open to serious challenge.

2. A Historical-Institutionalist Critique

"Historical institutionalism" is a loose term covering a range of scholarship that has tried to combine social science concerns and methods with a recognition that social processes must be understood as historical phenomena (Steinmo and Thelen 1992; Ikenberry 1994). In my own usage, historical institutionalism cuts across the usual sharp dichotomy between rational choice and non-rational choice work, drawing instead on research within both traditions that emphasizes the significance of temporal processes. Thus it includes rational choice analyses that consider issues of institutional evolution and path-dependence crucial (North 1990; Knight 1992). It excludes much "historical" research in political science that uses history only as a technique for widening the universe of available cases.

The core arguments of historical institutionalism contrast with a more common view in the social sciences, which, as March and Olson observe, assumes (often implicitly) that "institutions and behavior . . . evolve through some form of efficient historical process. An efficient historical process . . . is one that moves rapidly to a unique solution, conditional on current environmental conditions, and is independent of the historical path" (March and Olson 1989: 5–6). Given this orientation, Theda Skocpol notes, "[a]nalysts typically look only for synchronic determinants of policies—for example, in current social interests or in existing political alliances. In addition, however, we must examine patterns unfolding over time" (Skocpol 1992: 58).

Recent research focusing on institutional evolution and path-dependence has challenged the expectation that institutions embody the long-term interests of those responsible for original institutional design (Krasner 1989; North 1990). Where the legal authority of the institutional designers is as unquestionable as that of member-state governments in the EC, I will argue that such a challenge must be based on two sets of claims. First, there must be an account of why "gaps"—by which I mean significant divergences between the institutional and policy preferences of member-state governments and the actual functioning of institutions and policies—would emerge. Second, critics must explain why, once such gaps emerge, they cannot reliably be closed. One can find scattered elements of such accounts in recent theoretical treatments of institutional change. When brought together, they provide a compelling response to the claim that institutional development in the European Union can be understood in functional terms.

I focus first on the factors which are likely to create considerable gaps in member-state government control. Four are of fundamental importance: the autonomous actions of European organizations, the restricted time-horizons of decision-makers, the large potential for unintended consequences, and the likelihood of changes in COG preferences over time. Each of these factors requires more detailed discussion.

2.1. **The partial autonomy of EC organizations**

The main contribution of recent neofunctionalist analysis has been to emphasize the autonomous role of supranational actors, especially the Commission and the Court (Sandholtz 1992*b*; Burley and Mattli 1993; Ross 1995). I begin by summarizing these arguments and suggesting why, by themselves, they constitute an inadequate response to intergovernmentalism.

The central objections raised by neofunctionalists can be cast in terms of the same principal–agent framework used in many intergovernmentalist accounts. The governments of member-states created the European Community, and they did so to serve their own purposes. In order to carry out collective tasks, however, these governments felt compelled to create new organizations. As Terry Moe has argued, the results are predictable:

A new public agency is literally a new actor on the political scene. It has its own interests, which may diverge from those of its creators, and it typically has resources—expertise, delegated authority—to strike out on its own should the opportunities arise. The political game is different now: there are more players and more interests to be accommodated. (Moe 1990: 121)

In the European context, the member-states' problem has been especially difficult. They have needed to create arrangements that would allow reasonably efficient decision-making and effective enforcement despite the involvement of a large number of governments with differing interests, and despite the need for decision-making, implementation, and oversight on a wide range of complex and tightly coupled policy arenas. These considerations generated pressure to grant those who run these organizations considerable authority. Thus, the political organs of the EC are not without resources; as a result, they are not simply passive tools of national governments.

Over time, EC organizations will seek to use grants of authority for their own purposes, and especially to increase their autonomy. They will try to expand the gaps in member-state government control, and they will use any accumulated political resources to resist efforts to curtail their authority. The result is an intricate, ongoing struggle that is well known to students of the European Union but would also be familiar to American observers of, say, relations between congressional committees and administrative agencies (McCubbins and Schwartz 1984; Moe 1987; Kiewiet and McCubbins 1991). National governments generally (but not always) seek to rein in EC organizations. They recognize, however, that these crucial collective organizations cannot function without significant power, and that the authority required must grow as the tasks addressed at the European level expand and become more complex.

For their part, actors in the principal European organizations—the Commission, the European Court of Justice, and the European Parliament—are always looking for opportunities to enhance their powers. Neofunctionalist analyses have emphasized the significant successes of these supranational actors. The Council, to be sure, continues to stand watch over proposed legislation, and actively protects member-state interests. Yet the Commission, Parliament, and Court possess considerable ability to advance their own interests. For the Commission, two assets are particularly important (Ross 1995). The first concerns the setting of agendas, a source of influence which it frequently shares with the European Parliament (Tsebelis 1994; Garrett and Tsebelis 1995). Choosing which proposals to consider is a tremendously important (if frequently unappreciated) aspect of politics, and here European organs often have primacy. Obviously, this power is far from unlimited; the Commission cannot expect to pass proposals that ignore the preferences of member-states. Usually, however, it will have some room for maneuver (Pollack 1995a, 1996b). Entrepreneurial European actors, such as the Delors Commission, may be able to frame issues, design packages, and structure the sequence of proposals in ways that maximize their room for independent initiative (Riker 1986). The expansion of qualified majority voting has widened the range of possible "winning coalitions," further increasing the agenda-setting powers of the Commission and Parliament. Neofunctionalists have argued persuasively that the Commission's effective use of agenda-setting powers has advanced European integration and increased its own role in policy reform (Ross 1995).

The Commission's second major asset is its role as what Volker Eichener calls "process manager" (Peters 1992; Eichener 1993). Policymaking at the EC level, as many have noted, is heavily tilted toward regulation—a type of policymaking with its own distinctive qualities (Lowi 1964; Majone 1992). The development of complex social regulations requires the assembly and coordination of dense networks of experts. This task falls to the Commission, and with it comes additional room for influence. Especially in the labyrinths of regulatory policymaking, this role may give the Commission significant power.

The political resources of the European Court are at least as significant. If the United States in the nineteenth century had a "state of courts and parties" (Skowronek 1982), the EC looks at times like a "state of courts and technocrats" (Leibfried 1992: 249). In the process of European integration, the European Court has taken an active, even forcing stance, gradually building a remarkable base of authority and effectively "constitutionalizing" the emerging European polity (Weiler 1991; Burley and Mattli 1993; Alter 1996). The Court has more extensive powers of judicial review than most of its national counterparts, and fewer impediments to action than other EC decision-making bodies. If the Council is prone to gridlock, the necessity of deciding cases inclines the ECJ to action. This inclination is strengthened by rules allowing simple majority decisions, and by a secrecy (neither actual votes nor dissenting views are made public) that shelters judges from member-state and popular pressures. ECJ judges also share a common professional background, legal culture (at least on the continent), and sense of mission that seems to effectively limit the influence of the member-states in judicial decision-making.

Neofunctionalist accounts of these supranational organizations have certainly demonstrated their prominent role in the EC, as even some intergovernmentalists have acknowledged.[4] Yet the true influence of the Court, Commission, and Parliament on policymaking and future institutional development remains uncertain. Do these supranational actors generate genuine gaps in member-state control, or do they simply act as agents, fulfilling monitoring, information-gathering, and implementation roles under the tight scrutiny of member-state governments? As Lisa Martin, among others, has suggested, autonomy may be more apparent than real:

> Politicians and academic observers often infer from such a pattern [of activity] autonomy of the Commission and/or of government leaders. However, consideration of institutional constraints leads us to examine delegation of authority. . . . because of the costs of exercising tight control over agents, an optimal structure of delegation may be one with little active oversight or overt interference in the negotiating process from principals. Agents rationally anticipate the responses of those they represent. The law of anticipated reactions suggests that we cannot infer a lack of political influence from a lack of observed oversight activity. (Martin 1993: 135)

Thus, what appears to be autonomy may simply reflect the principals' deft use of oversight. Relying on the disciplining power of anticipated reactions and the use of "fire alarms"—signals derived from reporting requirements or interest-group monitoring activity—to identify significant problems, national governments can stay in the background while remaining firmly in charge (McCubbins and Schwartz 1984).

Again, given the ease of assembling plausible ex post accounts of why given outcomes served COG interests, these arguments about delegation are difficult to refute, although they are equally difficult to demonstrate (Burley and Mattli 1995; Garrett 1995). To foreshadow a point pursued at length below, the intergovernmentalist claim that supranational actors are agents rather than autonomous actors is strengthened if we believe that the governments of member-states can react powerfully to observed losses of control. If the Commission, Court, and Parliament anticipate that their efforts to produce or exploit gaps will be detected, punished, and reversed, they are indeed unlikely to strike out on their own. Thus a crucial problem with neofunctionalism is that it lacks a coherent account of why the threat of such a reaction among national governments is not always credible. I address this problem in a moment.

Before proceeding to that issue, however, the case for constraints on member-state government control can be greatly strengthened if other sources of gaps can be identified. Here, the historical-institutionalist focus on the temporal dimension of politics is invaluable. It highlights three additional sources of gaps: the short time-horizons of decision-makers, the prevalence of

---

[4] Consider for instance Moravcsik's striking acknowledgment of the growing power of the ECJ: "the decisions of the Court clearly transcend what was initially foreseen and desired by most national governments. The 'constitutionalization' of the Treaty of Rome was unexpected. It is impossible, moreover, to argue that the current system is the one to which all national governments would currently consent, as recent explicit limitations on the Court in the Maastricht Treaty demonstrate" (Moravcsik 1993: 513).

unanticipated consequences, and the prospect of shifting policy preferences among national governments.

2.2. The restricted time-horizons of political decision-makers

A statement attributed to David Stockman, Ronald Reagan's budget director, is unusual among political decision-makers only for its candor. Asked by an adviser to consider pension reforms to combat social security's severe long-term financing problems, he dismissed the idea out of hand, exclaiming that he had no interest in wasting "a lot of political capital on some other guy's problem in [the year] 2010" (quoted in Greider 1982: 43).

Many of the implications of political decisions—especially complex policy interventions or major institutional reforms—only play out in the long run (Garrett and Lange 1994). Yet political decision-makers are frequently most interested in the short-term consequences of their actions; long-term effects are often heavily discounted. The principal reason is the logic of electoral politics. Keynes once noted that in the long run we are all dead; for politicians in democratic polities, electoral death can come much faster. Since the decisions of voters that determine political success are taken in the short run, politicians are likely to employ a high discount rate. They have a strong incentive to pay attention to long-term consequences only if these become politically salient, or when they have little reason to fear short-term electoral retribution.

The gap between short-term interests and long-term consequences is often ignored in arguments about institutional design and reform. As a number of critics have noted, choice-theoretic treatments of institutions often make an intentionalist or functionalist fallacy, arguing that the long-term effects of institutions explain why decision-makers introduce them (Bates 1987; Knight 1992; Hall and Taylor 1994). Instead, long-term institutional consequences are often the by-products of actions taken for short-term political reasons. The evolution of the Congressional committee system in the USA—a central institutional feature of contemporary American governance—is a good example. As Kenneth Shepsle notes, Henry Clay and his supporters introduced the system to further their immediate political goals without regard to long-term consequences: "The lasting effects of this institutional innovation could hardly have been anticipated, much less desired, by Clay. They were by-products (and proved to be the more enduring and important products) of self-interested leadership behavior" (Shepsle 1989: 141). In this case, the system's long-term functioning was not the goal of the actors who created it. By the same token, the reasons for the institution's invention cannot be derived from an analysis of its long-term effects.

Recognizing the importance of policymakers' high discount rates raises a challenge for intergovernmentalist theories of the European Community. As noted above, most international-relations approaches to European integration stress the tenacity with which nation-states cling to all aspects of national sovereignty. The design of collective institutions is assumed to reflect this preoccupation. Yet in democratic polities, sustained power requires electoral vindication. In many circumstances, the first concern of national governments is not with sovereignty per se, but with creating the conditions for continued domestic political success. By extension, where the time-horizons of decision-makers are restricted, *functional* arguments that are central to transaction-cost views of international regimes also come into question. Rather than being treated as the goals of policymakers in such circumstances, long-term institutional effects should often be seen as the *by-products* of their purposive behavior.

2.3. Unanticipated consequences

Gaps in member-state government control occur not only because long-term consequences tend to be heavily discounted. Even if policymakers *do* focus on long-term effects, unintended consequences are likely to be widespread. Complex social processes involving a large number of actors always generate elaborate feedback loops and significant interaction effects which decision-makers cannot hope to fully comprehend (Hirsch 1977; Schelling 1978; Van Parijs 1982; Perrow 1984; Jervis 1993). While social scientists possess limited tools for dealing with such outcomes, many models—such as core neoclassical arguments about the dynamics of market systems—are based on them.

Unanticipated consequences are likely to be of particular significance in the European Union because of the presence of high *issue density* (Pierson and Leibfried 1995). In sharp contrast to any existing international organization, the range of decisions made at the European level runs almost the full gamut of traditionally "domestic" issues, from the setting of agricultural prices to the regulation of auto emissions and fuel content to the review of proposed corporate mergers. In the past decade, there has been a massive expansion of EC decision-making, primarily because of the single-market project. The sheer scope of this decision-making limits the ability of member-states to firmly control the development of policy.

The profound implications of expanded policy activity need to be under-lined. As the number of decisions made and the number of actors involved grows, interactions—among actors and among policies—increase geometrically (Beer 1978). Fig. 2.1 offers a simple illustration. The connections between the points could represent either relationships among actors or among govern-mental activities. With two points (Fig. 2.1a), there is only one connection; with an expansion to four points (Fig. 2.1b), there are six connections; with an expansion to eight points (Fig. 2.1c), there are twenty-eight. This is the kind of process that has been underway in the EC.

Growing issue density has two distinct consequences. First, it generates problems of overload. As European-level decision-making becomes both more prevalent and more complex, it places growing demands on the "gatekeepers" of member-state sovereignty. In this context, time constraints, scarcities of information, and the need to delegate decisions to experts may promote

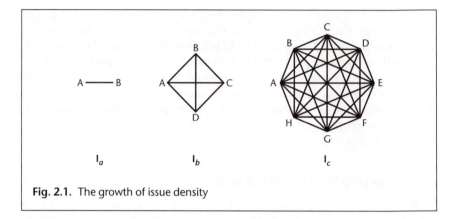

Fig. 2.1. The growth of issue density

unanticipated consequences and lead to considerable gaps in member-state control. Member-state scrutiny will usually be extensive in the formation of the grand interstate bargains which are the favorite subject for intergovernmentalists, such as the Treaty of Rome, the Single European Act, and the Maastricht Treaty. In the intervals between these agreements, however, flesh must be added to the skeletal frameworks. In this context, where much policy actually evolves, the ability of member-states to control the process is likely to be weaker. As Gary Marks has put it, "[b]eyond and beneath the highly visible politics of member state bargaining lies a dimly lit process of institutional formation" (Marks 1993: 403). Marks, for instance, has demonstrated how the Commission exploited its more detailed knowledge of the policy process and its manager role in policy formation to generate influence over the structural funds that the British government failed to anticipate.

As has already been discussed, problems of overload are especially consequential when member-state governments must contend with supranational organizations which are eager to extend their authority. In the development of complex regulatory judgments and the legal determination of what previous decisions actually require, essential policymaking authority is often in the hands of bodies of experts, where the Commission plays a crucial role, or in the hands of the Court. This is, of course, one of the central insights of principal–agent theory. Agents can use their greater information about their own activities and the requirements connected to their work to achieve autonomy from principals. *Asymmetrical access to information,* which is ubiquitous in complex decision-making processes, provides a foundation for influence (Moe 1984).

The second consequence of issue density is the oft-cited process of spillover: the tendency of tasks adopted to have important consequences for realms outside those originally intended, or to empower actors who generate new demands for extended intervention (Haas 1958). One of the key arguments in much writing on contemporary political economies stresses precisely the embeddedness of economic action within networks of tightly coupled social and political institutions (Hall 1986; North 1990; Garrett and Lange 1994). Efforts to integrate some aspects of complex modern societies without changing other components may prove problematic because the sectors to be integrated cannot be effectively isolated. The more "tightly coupled" government policies are, the more likely it is that actions in one realm will have unanticipated effects in others (Perrow 1984). McNamara, for example, has demonstrated the significance of such interaction effects in the cases of monetary and agricultural policies (McNamara 1993). Similar connections between the single-market initiative and social policy development have also been documented (Leibfried and Pierson 1995). As the density of EC policymaking increases, such inter-action effects become more prevalent, unintended consequences multiply, and the prospect of gaps in member-state control will grow.

2.4. Shifts in COG policy preferences

Intergovernmentalist theories tend to treat the institutional and policy preferences of the member-states as essentially fixed. This is one of a number of crucial respects in which intergovernmentalism involves a too-easy translation from the world of economic organizations to the world of politics. It may make some sense to assume stable preferences when studying firms, or even when one discusses the enduring issues of grand diplomacy. However, as one moves from traditional foreign policy issues such as national security toward the traditionally "domestic" concerns where the EC has become quite significant, this becomes a more dubious premise.

The policy preferences of member-state governments may shift for a number of reasons. Altered circumstances or new information may lead governments to question previous arrangements. Equally important, changes in govern-ment occur frequently, and governments of different partisan complexions often have quite distinct views on policy matters dealt with at the EC level. Governments come and go. Each inherits a set of arrangements from the past; each tries to place its own imprint on this heritage. The result, over time, is that evolving arrangements will diverge from the intentions of original designers, while any newly arriving COG is likely to find institutional and policy arrangements considerably out of sync with its own preferences.

Thus, there are a number of reasons why gaps in COG control are likely to emerge. Two general points about these sources of gaps deserve emphasis. First, most of these processes have a temporal quality that makes them invisible to a synchronic analysis of institutional and policy choice. The role of restricted time-horizons, unintended consequences, and shifting member-state prefer-ences will only be evident if we examine political processes over time. Second, most of the processes highlighted are much more likely to be prevalent in the European Community than in the more purely "international" settings which were the subject of original efforts to develop and refine regime theory. Because many of the more "domestic" issues which the EC considers have significant electoral implications, the time-horizons of decision-makers are likely to be shorter. Unanticipated consequences are also more prevalent, because unlike a typical international regime, the EC deals with many tightly coupled issues. Electoral turnover is more likely to cause shifts in COG preferences on the more domestic issues which the EC considers than on the traditional diplomatic agenda of most international regimes. In short, the EC's focus on core concerns of traditional domestic politics makes it more prone to all the sources of gaps in member-state control which historical institutionalism identifies.

At this point, however, the claim of member-state government constraint is incomplete. Transaction cost approaches are compatible with the possibility of at least some sorts of gaps, although these are rarely addressed in practice. After all, while it has not emphasized unanticipated consequences (Williamson 1993: 116), TCE is based in large part on how uncertainty about future events provokes particular organizational responses. It is not enough to demonstrate that gaps emerge; one must also show that once such losses of control take place they often cannot be corrected.

For intergovernmentalists, however, even where the possibility of gaps is acknowledged, these losses of control are considered theoretically unproblematic. Should outcomes occur which principals do not desire, TCE describes two routes to restored efficiency: competition and learning.[5] Competitive pressures in a market society mean that new organizations with more efficient structures will develop, eventually replacing suboptimal organizations. Learning processes among principals can also lead to correction. According to Williamson, one can rely on

[T]he 'far-sighted propensity' or 'rational spirit' that economics ascribes to economic actors . . . Once the unanticipated consequences are understood, these effects will thereafter be anticipated and the ramifications can be folded back into the organizational design. Unwanted costs will then be mitigated and unanticipated benefits will be enhanced. Better economic performance will ordinarily result. (Williamson 1993: 116–17)

Both these corrective mechanisms, however, are of limited applicability when one shifts from Williamson's focus on firms in private markets to the world of political organizations (Moe 1984, 1990). This is clearest for the mechanism of competition. Political organizations rarely confront a dense environment of competing organizations which will instantly capitalize on inefficient performance, swooping in to carry off an organization's "customers" and drive it into "bankruptcy." Political environments are typically more "permissive" (Krasner 1989; Powell and DiMaggio 1991). Within Europe, there is nothing like a marketplace for competition among international regimes, in which new

---

[5] Moravcsik has suggested to me that an alternative way to discount the significance of unintended effects would be to treat them as random "noise." Yet while this may be appropriate in studying mass populations (e.g. the dynamics of public opinion), it seems inappropriate when single unintended effects may be quite large and processes may be path-dependent (Pierson 1996). There is little reason to think that such effects will somehow "balance out," leaving an analyst free to study the "systematic" elements. To take an example discussed later in this chapter, it would be difficult to examine the dynamics of gender issues in Europe by treating the role of Art. 119 as "noise."

market entrants can demonstrate that their efficiency (however that might be defined and measured) is greater than the EC's.

While arguments based on competition are weak, learning arguments would appear to be more applicable to political environments. Indeed, Gary Marks, who has pointed to the significance of unanticipated consequences in limiting member-state control, concedes that the use of such arguments "is tricky in the context of ongoing political relationships where learning takes place" (Marks 1993: 403). The process through which actors "learn" about gaps in control and how to address them has received little attention (McCubbins and Schwartz 1984). However, at least on the biggest issues, intergovernmentalists can reasonably assert that national governments will gradually become aware of undesired or unanticipated outcomes, and will become more adept at developing effective responses over time. Learning thus seems to offer an effective mechanism for closing gaps and returning institutional and policy designs to an "efficient" (from the point of view of the member-states) path.

Yet the efficacy of learning argument depends crucially on the capacity of member-state governments to fold new understandings "back into the organizational design." Put differently, once gaps appear and are identified, how easy is it for principals to regain control? Here the distinction between economic and political organizations becomes crucial. In economic organizations, owners (or principals) may face few barriers to such efforts. In the *political* world, however (and the case of the EC in particular), incorporating new understandings into organizations and policies is no simple task The next stage of the argument, then, is to consider why gaps, even when identified, might be hard to close. There are three broad reasons: the resistance of EC organizational actors; the institutional obstacles to reform within the EC; and the sunk costs associated with previous actions. If these barriers are sufficiently high, learning will not provide a sufficient basis for correction, and member-state control will be constrained.

2.5. The resistance of supranational actors

To the extent that neofunctionalism has had an implicit argument about the difficulty of closing gaps, it has centered on supranational actors. The Court, Commission, and Parliament have accumulated significant political resources. They can be expected to use these resources to resist the efforts of national governments to exercise greater control over their activities. Yet neofunctionalism has failed to address the question of why, in an open confrontation between member-state governments and supranational actors, the latter could ever be expected to prevail. National governments, after all, have substantial oversight powers, along with control over budgets and appointments. More fundamentally, they possess the legal authority to determine (and alter) the basic rules of the game, including those affecting the very existence of the EC's supranational organizations. The resources of the Court, Commission, and Parliament, such as the capacity to play off one member-state against another in the agenda-setting process and perhaps exploit information asymmetries, are not trivial, but they are clearly modest by comparison. A persuasive account of member-state government constraint must draw on more than the political resources of supranational actors.

2.6. Institutional barriers to reform

The efforts of principals to reassert control will be facilitated if they can easily redesign policies and organizations. In the economic realm, principals are generally in a strong position to remake their organizations as they choose. Lines of authority are clear, and the relevant decision-makers are likely to share the same broad goal of maximizing profits. In politics, however, the temporal dimension raises distinct problems. Political decision-makers know that continuous organizational control is unlikely. This lack of continuous control has implications both for how organizations are designed and for the prospects of changing organizations once they are created. In particular, those designing organizations must consider the likelihood that future governments will be eager to overturn their designs, or to turn the organizations they create to other purposes. As Moe notes, the designers of organizations "do not want 'their' agencies to fall under the control of opponents. And given the way public authority is allocated and exercised in a democracy, they often can only shut out their opponents by shutting themselves out too. In many cases, then, they purposely create structures that even they cannot control" (Moe 1990: 125).

Thus, political organizations are often "sticky"—specifically designed to hinder the process of institutional and policy reform. This is, of course, far more true of some national polities than others (Weaver and Rockman 1993). Yet the barriers in most national political systems pale in comparison to the obstacles present in the EC. In principle, the governments of member-states decide: they have the authority, if they so choose, to reform or even abolish the Court, Commission, or Parliament. But in fact, the rules of the game within the Community were designed to inhibit even modest changes of course. The same requirements that makes initial decision-making difficult also makes previously enacted reforms hard to undo, even if those reforms turn out to be unexpectedly costly or to infringe on member-state sovereignty.

Efforts to employ the most radical vehicle of institutional redesign, a Treaty revision, face extremely high barriers: unanimous agreement among national governments, plus ratification by national parliaments and (in some cases) electorates. Given the chances for disagreements among COGs, let alone the problems connected to ratification, the chances of achieving such an extraordinary degree of consensus are generally quite low. Use of this process is now widely recognized to be extraordinarily difficult and unpredictable. As Mark Pollack notes, "the threat of Treaty revision is essentially the 'nuclear option'—exceedingly effective, but difficult to use—and is therefore a relatively ineffective and non-credible means of member state control" (Pollack 1995a: 30).

Efforts to produce more modest changes in course confront more modest hurdles, but these remain far tougher than the obstacles facing, for example, a Congressional committee trying to rein in a rogue federal agency. The governments of member-states will often be divided on significant issues, but in many policy areas change requires unanimous agreement. In other cases, qualified majority voting is the rule. This makes reform easier, but the standard—roughly 5/7ths of the weighted votes of member-states—still presents a threshold that is considerably tougher to cross than that required in most democratic institutions (Pollack 1994, 1995).

The extent to which these barriers constrain member-state governments has recently been questioned. Where it was once understood that participation in the EC was an all-or-nothing proposition, Maastricht has enhanced the prospects for a Europe "à la carte," or a Europe of "variable geometries." Britain and Denmark received opt-outs on monetary union; the eleven other member-states circumvented the British veto by opting "up and out" with the Social Protocol. As Jeff Anderson summarizes the new situation, "[Maastricht] and attached protocols established an important precedent, opening the door to a multitrack Europe in which the treaties and resulting secondary legislation do not apply uniformly to each member" (Anderson 1995: 449). This new flexibility, however, refers only to *additional* treaty obligations. Member-state governments may be able to obtain opt-outs from future treaty provisions. Unless they succeed in navigating the difficult EC decision rules for reversing course, however, they are not free to review and discard the commitments of previous governments, even if those earlier governments were preoccupied by short-term goals, had quite different policy preferences, or acted in ways that produced many unanticipated consequences. And as new policies are enacted, the scope of this restrictive *acquis communautaire* continues to grow.

The rules governing institutional and policy reform in the European Community create what Fritz Scharpf calls a "joint-decision trap," making the efforts of national governments to close gaps in control highly problematic (Scharpf 1988). The extent of the institutional obstacles will vary from issue to issue. Obviously, if the benefits of acting are high enough, member-state governments will be able to act. But often the benefits must be quite high. In shutting out their potential successors, COGs have indeed shut themselves out as well.

2.7. Sunk costs and the rising price of exit

The evolution of EC policy over time may constrain member-state governments not only because institutional arrangements make a reversal of course *difficult* when COGs discover unanticipated consequences or their policy preferences change. Individual and organizational adaptations to previous decisions may also generate massive sunk costs that make policy reversal *unattractive*. When actors adapt to the new rules of the game by making extensive commitments based on the expectation that these rules will continue, previous decisions may "lock-in" member-state governments to policy options that they would not now choose to initiate. Put another way, social adaptation to EC organizations and policies drastically increases the cost of exit from existing arrangements. Rather than reflecting the benefits of institutionalized exchange, continuing integration could easily reflect the rising costs of "non-Europe."

Recent work on path-dependence has emphasized the ways in which initial institutional or policy decisions—even suboptimal ones—can become self-reinforcing over time (Krasner 1989; North 1990). These initial choices encourage the emergence of elaborate social and economic networks, greatly increasing the cost of adopting once-possible alternatives and therefore inhibiting exit from a current policy path. Major initiatives have major social consequences. Individuals make important commitments in response to government actions. These commitments, in turn, may vastly increase the disruption caused by policy shifts or institutional reforms, effectively "locking in" previous decisions (Pierson 1992, 1993).

Work on technological change has revealed some of the circumstances conducive to path-dependence (David 1985; Arthur 1988, 1989). The crucial idea is the prevalence of increasing returns, which encourage a focus on a single alternative and continued movement down a particular path once initial steps are taken. *Large set-up or fixed costs* are likely to create increasing returns to further investment in a given technology, providing individuals with a strong incentive to identify and stick with a single option. Substantial *learning effects* connected to the operation of complex systems provide an additional source of increasing returns. *Coordination effects* occur when the individual receives increased benefits from a particular activity if others also adopt the same option. Finally, *adaptive expectations* occur when individuals feel a need to "pick the right horse" because options that fail to win broad acceptance will have drawbacks later on. Under these conditions, individual expectations about usage patterns may become self-fulfilling.

As North has argued, all of these arguments can be extended from studies of technological change to other social processes, making path-dependence a common feature of institutional evolution (North 1990: 93–5). Path-dependence may occur in policy development as well, since policies can also constitute crucial systems of rules, incentives, and constraints (Pierson 1993: 607–8). In contexts of complex social interdependence new organizations and policies will often generate high fixed costs, learning effects, coordination effects, and adaptive expectations. For example, housing and transportation policies in the USA after World War II encouraged massive investments in particular spatial patterns of work, consumption, and residence. Once in place, these patterns sharply constrained the alternatives available to policymakers on issues ranging from energy policy to school desegregation (Danielson 1976; Jackson 1985). Many of the commitments that locked in suburbanization were literally cast in concrete, but this need not be the case. Social Security in the USA became gradually locked-in through its financing system, which created a kind of rolling intergenerational contract (Pierson 1992). New policies may encourage individuals and organizations to develop particular skills, make certain invest-ments, purchase particular goods, or devote time and money to certain organ-izations. All these decisions generate sunk costs. That is to say, they create commitments. In many cases, initial actions push individual behavior onto paths that are hard to reverse.

Lock-in arguments have received relatively little attention within political science, in part because these processes have a tendency to depoliticize issues. By accelerating the momentum behind one path, they render previously viable alternatives implausible. The result is often not the kind of conflict over the forgone alternative that political scientists would quickly identify, but the absence of conflict. Lock-in leads to what Bachrach and Baratz (1962) called "non-decisions." This aspect of politics can probably be identified only through careful, theoretically grounded historical investigation of how social adaptations to institutional and policy constraints alter the context for future decision-making.

Over time, as social actors make commitments based on existing organiza-tions and policies, the cost of "exit" from existing arrangements rises. Within the European Community, dense networks of social, political, and economic activity have grown up around past institutional and policy decisions. In speculating about a hypothetical effort to stem the power of Court and Com-mission, member-state governments must ask themselves if this can be done without, for instance, jeopardizing the single-market project. Thus, sunk costs may dramatically reduce a member-state government's room for maneuver. In the EC, one can see this development in the growing implausibility of member-state "exit threats." While the governments of "sovereign" member-states remain free to tear up treaties and walk away at any time, the constantly in-creasing costs of exit in the densely integrated European polity have rendered this option virtually unthinkable.

Williamson's confident assertion that learning allows firms to adjust to unanticipated consequences applies far less well to an analysis of politics. Learning from past events may lead national governments, as it did at Maastricht, to impose greater restrictions on supranational actors in *new* in-itiatives (Dehousse 1994c). Recapturing ground in previously institutionalized fields of activity, however, will often be quite difficult. Member-state govern-ments do not inherit a blank slate that they can remake at will when their policy preferences shift or unintended consequences become visible. Decision rules hamper reform, while extensive adaptations to existing arrangements in-crease the associated costs. Thus a central fact of life for national governments is the *acquis communautaire*, the corpus of existing legislation and practice. As Michael Shackleton notes, "[h]owever much Member States might deplore certain aspects of Community policy, there is no question that all find them-selves locked into a system which narrows down the areas for possible change and obliges them to think of incremental revision of existing arrangements" (Shackleton 1993: 20). Just as has always been true in domestic politics, new governments in member-states now find that the dead weight of previous institutional and policy decisions at the European level seriously limits their room for maneuver.

The need to examine political processes over time is the crucial feature linking all the arguments presented in this section. None of these processes are likely to be captured by a "snapshot" view. Historical institutionalism provides a clear account of why gaps may emerge in member-state authority. Member-state governments are often preoccupied with short-term outcomes. Their decisions are certain to produce all sorts of unanticipated consequences. The preferences of national governments may also shift, leaving them with formal institutions and highly developed policies that do not fit their current needs.

At least as important, historical institutionalism provides a coherent account of why learning processes and "fire alarms" may not be sufficient to prompt member-state governments to reassert control. If member-state governments decide that their agents have captured too much authority, they may well seek to rein them in. Gaps, however, open possibilities for autonomous action by supranational actors, which may in turn produce political resources that make them more significant players in the next round of decision-making. Decision rules and the proliferation of sunk costs may make the price of reasserting control too high.

In short, historical-institutionalist analysis can incorporate key aspects of neofunctionalism while offering stronger and expanded analytical foundations for an account of the constraints on member-state governments. There are important points of compatibility between the two approaches. Both suggest that unintended consequences, including spillover, are likely to be significant for institutional development. Both point to the significance of supranational actors. A crucial difference is that neofunctionalism sees political control as a zero-sum phenomenon, with authority gradually transferred from member-state governments to supranational actors, while historical institutionalism emphasizes how the evolution of rules and policies along with social adaptations create an increasingly structured polity which restricts the options available to *all* political actors. What has been missing from neofunctionalism—and what historical-institutionalist arguments can supply—is a more convincing analysis of national government constraint. Intergovernmentalists challenge neofunctionalism with two key questions: why would member-state governments lose control, and even if they did why would they not subsequently reassert it? Historical institutionalism gives clear and plausible answers to both.

The crucial contrasts between an intergovernmentalist and a historical-institutionalist account can be seen in Fig. 2.2. While intergovernmentalists focus on the initial bargain at time T_0, historical institutionalism emphasizes the need to analyze the consequences of that bargain over time. Doing so reveals the potential for considerable gaps in member-state government control to emerge (T_1). When the time of the next "grand bargain" arrives (T_2), member-state governments will again be central actors, but in a considerably altered context. Member-state governments may dominate decision-making in these intergovernmental bargains, and actively pursue their interests, but they

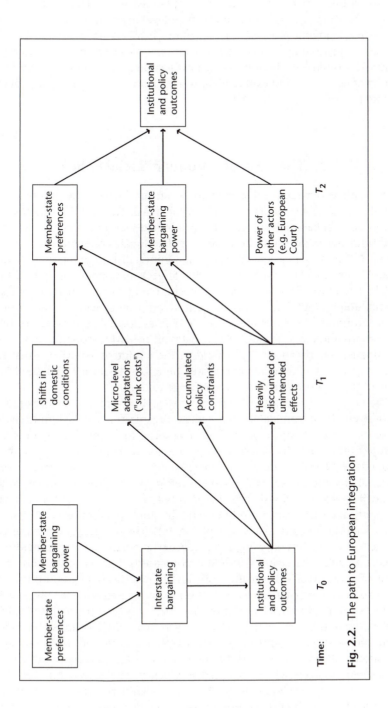

Fig. 2.2. The path to European integration

do so within constraints (frequently unplanned and often hardly visible) created by their predecessors and the microlevel reactions to those preceding decisions. Studying processes of policy and institutional change over time reveals that gaps may well be extensive and the prospects for recapturing lost control are often quite limited. As the next section demonstrates, this has been true in at least one significant (and unexpected) area of European policy development.

3. The Case of European Social Policy

Social policy is widely considered to be an area where the autonomy of member-state governments remains unchallenged. The need for action at the European level has not been self-evident, and national governments have been quite sensitive to intrusions on a core area of national sovereignty. Accounts of European social policy generally present a minimalist interpretation of European Union involvement (Mosley 1990; Streeck and Schmitter 1991; Lange 1992). The European Commission's direct attempt to construct a significant "social dimension"—areas of social policy competence where uniform or at least minimum standards are set at the EC level—has been a saga of high aspirations and modest results. The debates of the past few decades have been dominated by "cheap talk" produced in the confident knowledge that the requirements of unanimous European Council votes meant that ambitious blueprints would remain unexecuted (Lange 1992).

The obstacles to an activist role for Brussels in social policy development have always been formidable. As noted, EC organizations make it much easier to block reforms than to enact them. The social forces most sympathetic to European-level activity—labor unions and social democratic parties—have had relatively little influence in the past fifteen years. The member-state governments themselves, which serve as gatekeepers for initiatives that require Council approval, jealously protect social policy prerogatives. Economic and geopolitical changes since World War II have gradually diminished the scope of national sovereignty in a variety of domains. The welfare state remains one of the few key realms of policy competence where national governments still appear to reign supreme. Given the popularity of most social programs, national executives will usually resist losses of social policy authority. The agendas of member-state governments generally created only narrow, market-related openings for social legislation, and then only by super-majority vote.

Yet even in this area—where an intergovernmentalist account seems highly plausible—a historical-institutionalist perspective casts the development of European policy in quite a different light. Those seeking a more thorough analysis should look elsewhere (Leibfried and Pierson 1995). Here I discuss three aspects of policy development which point to significant initiatives that have extended beyond the firm control of national governments: (i) interventions on issues of gender equality; (ii) the expansion of health and safety regulations; and (iii) the recent enactment of the "Social Protocol." Each of these developments illustrates important aspects of an historical-institutionalist account.

3.1. The EC and gender equality

The European Community has assumed a central role in the development of policies to promote gender equality. It is clear that member-state governments did not seek this outcome. Rather, the EC's extensive role must be considered an unintended by-product of the Community's original institutional design. The key development was the inclusion of Art. 119 of the Treaty of Rome, requiring national governments to "ensure and maintain the application of the principle that men and women should receive equal pay for equal work." This provision grew out of a lengthy fight between Germany and France over the more general harmonization of social policy. The Germans, who rejected calls for harmonization, eventually won. Art. 119 was considered "merely hortatory"—a face-saving concession to France rather than a basis for policy (Hoskyns 1986: 305; Milward 1992: 209–16; Moravcsik 1994: 27). Indeed, the mandate to address pay inequities lay dormant for almost two decades.

Art. 119's broad wording, however, offered untapped potential. An opening occurred when the policy preferences of member-state governments shifted in the early 1970s—the high tide of social democratic sentiment in the EC and a time when women's movements were gathering strength in many countries. Politicians eagerly sought a symbolic response to these new demands. In this context, the Council agreed to several directives which gave the "equal treatment" provision some content. Catherine Hoskyns summarizes the atmosphere at the time:

[D]irectives were passed without much awareness of their consequences. Time and again interviews with national officials have shown that those who negotiated the original provisions had no idea what force they would prove to have or the legislative upheaval they would provoke. This is undoubtedly one of the reasons why governments have been so reluctant since 1978 to adopt new directives in this field. (Hoskyns 1986: 306)

This growing reluctance reflected both growing awareness of unintended consequences and yet another shift in COG policy preferences, this time accompanying the rightward drift in the ideological complexion of member-state governments after 1979.

If member-state governments soon became hesitant, however, their predecessors' initiatives had pushed the EC far down a path where national governments could no longer fully control the evolution of policy. The passage of the directives, backed by the now far from symbolic Art. 119, transferred considerable influence over gender policy to the ECJ. Over the past fifteen years, the European Court of Justice (ECJ) has played a crucial activist role, spurred on by women's groups which saw a significant opportunity to advance their agendas. The Court has turned Art. 119 and the directives into a broad set of requirements and prohibitions related to the treatment of women workers (Ostner and Lewis 1995).

The ECJ's expansive interpretations of Art. 119 and the various directives have required extensive national reforms of social security law and corporate employment practices. The impact on one member-state was described by Ireland's Joint Committee on Secondary Legislation of the EC:

The Community has brought about changes in employment practices which might otherwise have taken decades to achieve. Irish women have the Community to thank for the removal of the marriage bar in employment, the introduction of maternity leave, greater opportunities to train at a skilled trade, protection against dismissal on pregnancy, the disappearance of advertisements specifying the sex of an applicant for a job and greater equality in the social welfare code. After farmers, Irish women in employment have probably benefited most from entry to the EEC. (quoted in Mangan 1993: 72)

This conclusion may be generous, but few doubt the broad impact of EC interventions. To take just one important recent example, ECJ decisions have had a dramatic impact on public and private pension schemes. The Court's insistence on equal retirement ages in public pension schemes forced reform in a number of countries. When in *Barber* the ECJ made a similar ruling for occupational pensions, fear that the ruling might be applied retroactively to certain cases (at a cost to private insurers estimated at up to £40bn. in Britain and DM35bn. in Germany) fueled "what is probably the most intense lobbying campaign yet seen in Brussels" (Mazey and Richardson 1993: 15). In this instance, member-states acted to contain the potential damage, but it took a lot to do so: a unanimous agreement to add the so-called "Barber protocol" to the Maastricht Treaty. The protocol states that *Barber* is not to be applied retroactively. (In *Barber*, the Court itself had limited the retroactive effect of the decision, but somewhat ambiguously.) In recent decisions, the Court has not followed the strict letter of the protocol, but instead appears to be following the main tenets of its pre-*Barber* case law.[6] However this controversy is resolved, the prospective impact of the Court's ruling will be profound.

There continue to be considerable limits on EC gender policy (Ostner and Lewis 1995). As with much European regulation, a close connection to the "market-building" project restricts the range of possible interventions. Issues of gender equity which cannot be linked directly to the workplace remain out of bounds. Member-state implementation has been uneven. The point, however, is not to praise or criticize EC gender policies. Rather, it is to take note of their considerable impact and to demonstrate the historical processes through which this extension of supranational authority took place.

It is also true that member-state governments retain the capacity, as in the case of Barber, to modify outcomes when these are so unacceptable that they mobilize unanimous member-state opinion. Gaps, in other words, invariably have some limit (Pollack 1994). Such compensatory steps, however, are likely

---

[6] See Ch. 4 for a discussion of the impact of the protocol.

to be rare. National governments may well wish that the Community had never become active in pursuing issues of gender equality. It is quite another thing, however, to publicly stop or reverse such efforts once they have been enacted and incorporated in national laws, have motivated thousands of firms to adjust their labor market practices, and have enhanced the monitoring and mobilizing capacities of national and transnational interest groups.

The EC has thus come to play a major role in the development of gender policies, and it is the ECJ that now determines what the often vague EC rules require. This outcome cannot have been intended or desired by either the makers of the Treaty or the current COGs of member-states. Institutional designers, both in the 1950s and 1970s, were often preoccupied with the short-term and symbolic consequences of their actions; many long-term effects were either ignored or unanticipated. Changes in the preferences of national governments at later dates led to unexpected shifts in course that have proven hard to reverse. Other actors (notably the ECJ but also the Commission and European women's groups) were quick to seize these opportunities, and member-state governments have found it difficult to close the resulting gaps. Indeed, the case of gender equality reveals all of the features of institutional evolution stressed in Section 2 of this chapter.

3.2. Workplace health and safety

Another instance of gaps in member-state control can be seen in the development of health and safety regulations.[7] Openings for health and safety regulation came with the Single European Act, which allowed qualified majority voting on these issues. Policymakers were concerned that national restrictions could be trade barriers in disguise. The expansion of EC activity in this domain has been remarkable (Eichener 1993). By late 1994, twenty-nine new directives had been passed under the new procedures introduced with the SEA. Many of these were broad "framework" directives covering a range of more specific regulatory activity (Martin and Ross 1994).

Even more surprisingly, a very high level of standards has generally been achieved—often higher than that of any member-state. To be sure, the use of qualified majority voting has been crucial. Yet the outcome of very high harmonization seems difficult to explain in terms of simple intergovernmental bargaining. Constructing the single market might require harmonization of health and safety standards for *products*. There is, however, no clear need for harmonized standards for production *processes*. Here as well, however, the European Union has been highly interventionist. Nor is it clear why the governments of member-states with low standards should accede to significantly higher ones.

As Eichener's detailed investigation documents, the Commission's "process manager" role—a delegation of authority required to pursue complex

[7] The following account draws heavily on Eichener (1993). See also Martin and Ross (1994).

regulatory policies—appears to have been critical in this low-profile environment (Eichener 1993). Much of the crucial decision-making took place in committees composed of policy experts. Representatives within these committees were often interested in innovation, having gravitated toward Brussels because it seemed to be "where the action is" on regulatory issues. In this technocratic context, "best practices" from many member-states (and from countries then outside the EC, such as Sweden) were pieced together to form a quite interventionist structure of social regulation. At the same time, the Commission played a central part in joining together the work of different committees and incorporating concerns of other actors such as the European Parliament—all the while actively promoting particularly innovative proposals.

Throughout, national governments appear to have played only a loose supervisory role. This was especially true for the low-standard states of the EC's southern rim. These states had the most to lose from the enactment of high standards, since their adjustment costs would be highest (Lange 1993). Yet these governments found their limited supplies of specialists either co-opted in the "consensual" committee process or overwhelmed by the enormity of the regulatory task.

Health and safety policy reveals how the complexity of regulatory policy-making in a setting of high issue density may generate considerable gaps in control. Thus while the Commission, like other actors in the EC, operates under considerable constraints, it will often be able to advance its own agenda. As Eichener concludes, "[t]he complex, opaque and Commission-dominated decision-making process leads to results which would never be expected from simple intergovernmental bargaining within the Council" (Eichener 1993: 64).

3.3. The Maastricht Social Protocol

A final illustration of the historical dynamics of institutionalization can be seen in the Social Protocol enacted as part of the Maastricht Treaty negotiations. The Social Protocol grew out of continuing efforts to modestly enhance the capacity for activist social policy at the EC level. The Protocol itself allows qualified majority voting on a range of important issues, including working conditions, gender equality with regard to labor market opportunities and treatment at work, and the integration of persons excluded from the labor market. Already, the Commission has used the Social Protocol track to push through the long-stalled European Works Council Directive and is pursuing other initiatives (Falkner 1995).

While it is impossible to know at this stage how the Social Protocol will play out, this exercise in institutional reform again supports key parts of the historical-institutionalist argument. The enactment of the Social Protocol is very difficult to reconcile with a simple model of intergovernmentalist bargaining among sovereignty-focused member-state governments (Ross 1995: 191). The eleven national governments acceding to the Protocol were not introducing a carefully designed "instrument." The governments had in fact expected Britain to sign a much-watered-down clause on social policy, but the Major government rejected all proposed versions. Faced with the prospect that British intransigence would prompt a disastrous breakdown of the Maastricht conference, national governments rushed to adopt (at Delors' suggestion) a last-minute solution. The hastily cobbled together agreement, which excludes Britain, committed the other eleven member-states to a much more ambitious earlier draft on social policy. This version had been designed as a bargaining chip in the expectation that Britain would eventually accede to a contentless compromise. Member-state governments, which had exploited Britain's expected position to engage in cheap talk, suddenly found themselves exposed.

That Britain preferred to block any agreement rather than accept the largely symbolic alternative waiting in the wings is equally instructive. It illustrates how the long-term institutional consequences of the Protocol should be seen as the by-products of a decision made to meet various short-term domestic objectives. If Major had truly wished to preserve social policy autonomy, a solution was readily available. Britain's refusal to agree appears to have had less to do with some long-sighted views of sovereignty than with Major's need to placate right-wing Tories by taking a tough public stance.

Indeed, the Major government's strategy clearly created a greater long-term threat to British autonomy, in a way that could have been anticipated at the time. Choosing to opt out meant that Britain would not participate in decisions that it would have to abide by if a future government joined the Protocol.[8] While Conservatives resisted pressures to sign, the status quo could be maintained only if it was ratified at every British election. A single Labour victory would produce an institutional change that could not subsequently be reversed without provoking a constitutional crisis in Europe. Blair's victory in 1997 was in fact soon followed by a decision to join the Protocol. In short, the Major government accepted a considerable long-term threat to British sovereignty in the sphere of social policy in return for an important short-run symbolic victory which it needed for domestic political reasons.

Finally, one should note that the Social Protocol leaves tremendous room for unanticipated consequences (Rhodes 1995). Rather than being an example of Williamson's "far-sighted propensity" in institutional design, the arrangement clearly reflects a harried and desperate effort to keep the Maastricht negotiations from coming unraveled altogether. Legal ambiguities abound. Not only is the whole legal basis of the Protocol open to challenge, but, as Martin Rhodes notes, "the boundaries are blurred between areas subject to QMV, those subject to unanimity and those where the agreement eleven have no competence at all" (Rhodes 1995: 114). It is, of course, the ECJ that will determine how these ambiguities are resolved. Further uncertainties include whether and when Britain will "opt-in" to the agreement, and what the consequences will be if it remains on the outside. Even with several years hindsight, these uncertainties

---

[8] In this sense, the situation paralleled the development of the Common Agricultural Policy, where Britain's long absence from the development of policy left it in a weak position to pursue its goal of policy liberalization within the EC (Keeler 1996).

remain. They were clearly very much a part of the atmosphere in the short period during which the Protocol agreement was reached.

It is only now becoming possible to study the stream of consequences flowing from the Protocol's enactment—an important aspect of an historical-institutionalist investigation (Falkner 1995). Yet the process of institutional design itself appears to be quite in line with the general framework advanced in this chapter. Indeed, along with the earlier discussion of Art. 119, the case of the Social Protocol reveals that historical-institutionalist arguments are relevant not only during the day-to-day activities between the "grand bargains," but for understanding the grand bargains themselves.

3.4. The evolution of European social policy

A more complete review of social policy issues would reveal further constraints on member-state autonomy. Among the most important have been spillovers from the single-market project. Encouraging the mobility of labor has not been a high-profile issue in the EC, but it has gradually prompted an incremental expansion of Community regulations and, especially, court decisions that have seriously eroded national welfare state sovereignties (Leibfried and Pierson 1995). Social policy cases account for a growing share of the rapidly rising ECJ case load, increasing from 3.3 percent of total cases in 1968 to 8.1 percent in 1992 (Caporaso and Keeler 1993: table 1). Member-states are now prohibited from pursuing a range of social policy options because their actions would be incompatible with the single-market project. Furthermore, as individuals, firms, and non-profit organizations adapt to new opportunities made available by the single market (e.g. in private pensions and health services), these micro-level commitments will further restrict the policy options available to national welfare states. Member-state social policies are increasingly firmly embedded in a dense set of "hard" Community requirements and prohibitions, as well as "soft" incentives and disincentives.

Thus European integration has generated a partial but nonetheless significant development of European-level social policies. The processes that produced this outcome provide powerful illustrations of the institutional dynamics discussed in Section 2 of this chapter. In a number of instances, the short-term preoccupations of institutional designers have led them to make decisions that undermined the long-term control of member-state governments. Unanticipated consequences have been widespread, especially as the density of EC activity has grown. Shifts in member-state preferences led to unexpected exploitation of opportunities created earlier (e.g. Art. 119 in the 1970s) as well as growing frustration with previous commitments (the Gender Equality Directives in the 1980s). In short, even though social policy is widely seen as an area of member-state autonomy with a minimal EC role, a historical-institutionalist perspective highlights the growing significance of European policy, the influence of actors other than member-state governments, and the mounting constraints on the possibilities for initiatives by those governments.

4. Conclusion

The arguments advanced in this chapter present major challenges for an intergovernmentalist account of European integration. By providing explicit micro-foundations for an analysis that places much more emphasis on member-state government constraints, historical institutionalism increases the pressure on intergovernmentalists to offer convincing evidence that the causal processes they posit are actually at work. Rather than simply inferring preferences *post hoc* from an examination of outcomes, intergovernmentalists will need to show that the desire to achieve these functional outcomes actually motivated key decision-makers.[9]

In principle, important aspects of an historical-institutionalist analysis could be integrated with intergovernmentalism. Indeed, this chapter accepts the starting point of intergovernmentalism: that national governments are the most important institution-builders of the European Community, and that they do so to serve their own purposes. Although it has rarely been done in practice, many intergovernmentalist arguments could incorporate a temporal dimension. Keohane, for instance, has recognized the possibility that COGs might anticipate the potential for preference shifts in successor governments (Keohane 1984: 117). Other challenges, however, will not be so easy to reconcile, such as the possibility that COGs may employ a high discount rate in making decisions about institutional design, that unintended consequences are ubiquitous, and that gaps that emerge are difficult to close. It is hard to see how these factors could be systematically incorporated into intergovernmentalism without undermining the three pillars of that approach: the emphasis on sovereignty concerns, the treatment of institutions as instruments, and the nearly exclusive focus on grand bargains.

The challenge for those wishing to advance an historical-institutionalist account is also daunting. The temporal processes outlined here would have to be carefully specified to generate clear hypotheses concerning such matters as when we should expect policymakers to employ short time-horizons, when to expect that unintended consequences will be widespread, or how particular decision rules influence the prospects for closing gaps in control. As Mark Pollack has persuasively argued, such analyses should focus on the factors that can explain variation in outcomes across issues and among organizational arenas, as well as over time (Pollack 1995*a*, 1995*b*, 1996). To develop the historical-institutionalist line of argument will require difficult efforts to trace the motivations of political actors in order to separate the intended from the

---

[9] Moravcsik (1991) provides a good example of such an effort. Historical-institutionalist arguments, however, suggest the need to go beyond even Moravcsik's ambitious attempt to supplement intergovernmentalism with a "liberal" theory of COG preference formation. Moravcsik's account considers only the synchronic domestic sources of COG preferences, ignoring the possibility of significant feedback effects from previous rounds of institutionalization. For a critique of his interpretation along these lines see Cameron (1992).

unintended. Determining the impact of sunk costs on current decision-making also represents a considerable challenge. Studying political arenas in detail over long periods of time is arduous. The evidentiary requirements encourage a focus on detailed analyses of particular cases, rendering investigations vulnerable to the critique that the cases examined are unrepresentative. However, if one accepts the conclusion that intergovernmentalists must now show that the processes they hypothesize are actually at work, rather than simply inferring those processes from observed outcomes, it is not clear that their research tasks are any less formidable.

The purpose of the current investigation is not to pursue these difficult questions but to set an agenda by identifying plausible causal processes that can lead to growing constraints on COGs over time. While only the first step, such an effort can be a prelude to empirically grounded research, as demonstrated by the brief discussion of EC social policy. Indeed, this first step is a significant one. Historical-institutionalist arguments can provide a compelling account for a remarkable development that is widely accepted by European scholars and most Americans working in the field of comparative politics: the European Community is no longer simply a multilateral instrument, limited in scope and firmly under the control of individual member-states. Instead, the EC possesses characteristics of a supranational entity, including extensive bureaucratic competencies, unified judicial control, and significant capacities to develop or modify policies. Within Europe, a wide range of policies classically seen as "domestic" can no longer be understood without acknowledging the European Community's role within a highly fragmented but increasingly integrated polity. Historical institutionalism provides the analytical tools for thinking of the EC not as an international organization, but as the central level—albeit still a weak one—of an emergent multitiered system of governance. The power of national governments in this polity is not merely "pooled" but increasingly constrained.

It would be folly to suggest that member-state governments do not play a central part in policy development within the European Union. Rather, my point is that they do so in a context that they do not (even collectively) fully control. Arguments about intergovernmental bargaining exaggerate the power of national governments. In their focus on grand intergovernmental bargains, they fail to capture the gradually unfolding implications of a very complex and ambitious agenda of shared decision-making. While member-state governments remain extremely powerful, tracing the process of integration over time suggests that their influence is increasingly circumscribed. The path to European integration has embedded European nation-states in a dense institutional environment that cannot be understood in the language of interstate bargaining.

3

The Institutional Terrain of the European Union

NEIL FLIGSTEIN AND JASON MCNICHOL

THE European Union produced three large institution-building projects in the past fifteen years: the Single Market, the Single European Act, and the Treaty on European Union. The emergence of these projects has provoked scholars to reexamine the European Union (hereafter EU) as a political system (Keohane and Hoffman 1991; Sbragia 1992). Much of the speculation about the European Union concerns the nature of these political arrangements and their trajectories. The most common debate concerns whether or not the EU is most correctly characterized as an intergovernmental organization limited by the agendas of the member-state governments or if it acts as a supranational entity that restructures the politics of western Europe in such a way as to eventually result in a single European state or some more complex polity (Moravcsik 1991; Sbragia 1992; Schmitter 1992).

Stone Sweet and Sandholtz (Chapter 1) have proposed that one way to transcend this debate is to recognize that the policy domains in the EU can be viewed as a continuum from those domains that look more like an intergovernmental organization (for example, defense policy) to those that look more like a supranational organization (for example, the Single Market). They argue that three factors condition this process: the various Treaties which determine what policy domains can exist and the voting rules for that domain (rules), the existence of the supranational organizations of the EU (Council, Commission, Court, and Parliament) who push forward aspects of the integration project, and the existence of transnational actors who help constitute the policy domains.

The major purpose of this chapter is to explore these insights by considering how policy domains were actually constructed in the EU over time. Policy

This chapter was prepared for the collaborative project organized by Wayne Sandholtz and Alec Stone Sweet on Supranational Governance in the European Union. We would like to thank the members of that seminar for their input into this project over three very stimulating meetings at Laguna Beach. We would also like to thank Chris Ansell, Ernie Haas, Wayne Sandholtz, and Alec Stone Sweet for more detailed comments.

domains generally form when there exists a constitutional agreement to create legislation, a collective definition of what the issues are and who gets to be an actor, and organizational capacity and procedures to mobilize the production of new rules in the domain (i.e. legislation) (Laumann and Knoke 1989). Policy domains may be entirely constituted by government organizations or may also include non-governmental groups.

In the context of the EU, we want to explore two related themes. First, we demonstrate that the analytical concept of a policy domain is helpful and appropriate in describing the evolution of the EU as an institutional/legislative terrain. Here, we describe (i) what a policy domain is, and (ii) how the EU's institutional terrain does, indeed, appear to be constituted by policy domains. Second, we want to explore the evolution of these domains over time, looking for evidence of change from intergovernmental to supranationalist arrangements.

Our descriptive analysis traces the evolution of policy domains in the EU and concludes that their contours have been strongly shaped by the Treaty of Rome and its subsequent revisions with the Single European Act and the Treaty on European Union. We demonstrate that the Council and Commission are organized into units that directly mirror the policy domains articulated in the Treaty of Rome, the Single European Act, and the Treaty on European Union. The European Union also classifies legislation into these categories suggesting they function as shared meanings. We show how the Treaty revisions have altered the organization of the Council and Commission as the policy domains have been expanded. The Treaty expansions have directly effected the production of legislation. Legislation rose in the 1970s, dropped slightly around 1980, and rose steeply after 1986.

We document the relationship between the presence of transnational pressure groups in the EU and the production of legislation. Our analytic results show evidence for both intergovernmental and supranational accounts of the EU. Thirteen of seventeen policy domains had participants from pressure groups by 1990. The largest number of pressure groups existed in the Industry/Single Market domain giving some credence to the view that the Single Market Program had a built-in constituency in Brussels. Some domains (fisheries, financial/institutional affairs, regional policy, and development) remain firmly controlled by the nation-states. We have evidence that legislation grew in arenas where competencies of the EU were subsequently expanded or voting rules changed, such as the environment. But the states also agreed to expand competencies in arenas where there appeared to be no legislative or pressure group presence. And in every case, once competencies were expanded, legislation increased.

Our results imply that the EU is a complex organization with most of it resembling a supranational regime, but important parts firmly controlled by governmental actors. From the perspective of the continuum provided by Stone Sweet and Sandholtz (Chapter 1), the policy domains of the EU more resembles a supranational governance structure than an intergovernmental bargain in simple numerical terms. One could argue that the domains which remain under the control of the states, particularly the financial/institutional, allow them to retain control over the whole apparatus. We will consider this idea more closely in the conclusion.

This structure resulted partially from the planned purposes of the states. But it is clear that the production of policy domains was affected by the existence of transnational pressure groups which chose to go to Brussels to express their opinions to their governments.

1. Policy Domains and the Organization of the European Union

The goal of this section is to discuss both theoretically and empirically the issue of how many policy domains exist in the EU and how they are constituted. A policy domain implies that a group of actors are organized to participate in a collective debate with the goal of affecting the content of legislation or agreements. These actors include government organizations and might include organized interest groups, some of which might be other government organizations (Laumann and Knoke 1989). This view of policy domains is very broad and would include phenomena like intergovernmental organizations, supranational polities, and nation-states.

The construction of a policy domain requires a number of theoretical features, including agreement that the domain is a legitimate focus of policy-oriented actors (i.e. a constitutional agreement that allows actors to come to binding agreement on issues), a set of shared meanings that define that area as a "domain" and provide a way to understand who is a "player"; who has power, and why; a set of organized governmental actors who consider the domain their "turf," and if appropriate, other non-governmental actors who participate in policy construction in the domain. Institutionalization means that these organizations and meanings are shared and operate to structure subsequent cooperation.

The existence and stability of domains presents difficult empirical problems. Drawing the boundaries and tracking the effects of policy domains is quite problematic. So, if we have two pieces of legislation, how do we tell if they are in the same or different policy domains? Does every group in a given domain have to be equally involved in every piece of legislation? Or, alternatively, does every piece of legislation imply a new policy domain that comes together to pass that legislation?

We propose to address these difficult questions by viewing policy domains as broad sets of issue arenas that both state and non-state actors consider. These domains do not require every organized group to weigh in on every single issue. The domains evolve over time to specify which concerns are relevant to them and which are not. In this sense, policy domains become umbrella issue arenas. Indeed, there are likely to be turf wars between organized groups in different policy domains over jurisdiction over which particular issues belong in which domain. Part of the ongoing process is about who can control the agenda of a policy domain.

It is possible for groups of organized state and non-state actors to enter into an arena, exit, or remain inactive over a period of time. Nevertheless, once set into place, the domains act as powerful foci for collective action by defining where actors go to affect policy formation and what kind of language they use to engage in that process.

Actors in domains have different amounts of power. In the EU, for instance, we would expect because of the Treaty agreements that in some policy domains, like foreign and security policy, the nation-states would be the most important actors and these domains would remain intergovernmental in their structure. In others, where voting rules have shifted to qualified majority voting and transnational interest groups are present, like setting accounting rules for financial institutions, non-governmental organizations and the European Commission might be more powerful and those domains resemble supra-national arenas.

It is possible for groups to be members of more than one policy arena when groups maintain heterogeneous interests in different aspects of policy domains. So, the American Chamber of Commerce in Brussels participates in most policy domains reflecting the varied and broad interests of their membership (Philips 1994). The definitions and boundaries of certain policy domains which are well established before some groups come onto the scene, force these organizations to strategically attach their concerns to existing discussions of policy. Groups interested in environmental issues would be naturally led to Directorate-General XI, the Commission's directorate for the environment. But groups' interests might not so neatly fit into existing categories. This is likely to mean lobbying in more than one direction, particularly as groups try to increase their influence by discovering how their interests may be most usefully served (Mazey and Richardson 1993).

Organized groups from more than one policy domain might get involved in a particular policy issue. In the case of the EU, for instance, issues surrounding the internal market might intersect with issues concerning agricultural products. Organized groups from both policy arenas would become likely participants in both discussions. Members from both the Commission and the Council who deal with both sides of the issue are likely to be consulted by whomever is taking the initiative on any given issue. One could hypothesize that actors who were participants in both policy domains would be likely to have a great deal of power over potential outcomes by virtue of their being "polled" for their opinion twice, and by their standing in separate domains where they have networks of connections in both domains.

Early on, policy domains come into existence as the result of two major forces: a constitutional agreement and by the use of a common language to define how to think about the issue area (the latter is akin to what Geertz called "local knowledge" (1980)). These provide the tools for actors to engage in policy discussions. Once in place, these definitions both enable and constrain action. They enable actors by producing standard understandings about what are legitimate and illegitimate issues and how actors can frame their interests in terms of broader policy concerns. They constrain action in that they foreclose some sets of issues and methods of framing. They affect who can participate in issue area construction and what their roles are.

Institutionalization implies that actors from the nation-states, the organizations of the EU, and transnational pressure organizations, come to take advantage of constitutional openings to organize policy domains. Many of the chapters in this volume trace out these processes in detail (i.e. Chapters 5 and 8). The Council of Ministers, the Commission, the Court of Justice, the Parliament, and the Economic and Social Committee can be parties to policy domains. In practice, the major actors have been the Council of Ministers, the Commission, and the Court of Justice, although the Parliament has steadily increased its influence (Tsebelis 1994). The relative ability of these actors to organize policy domains comes from the various Treaties (which function as constitutions in the language used here) and the organizational capacity they muster. Organizational capacity implies having personnel, expertise, and money to bring to bear on any given policy domain.

We argue that rules (constitutions and shared meanings about how to interpret constitutions) and government organizational capacity (bureaucracies dedicated to acting in given arenas) have generally helped non-governmental organizations to organize to affect policy in the EU. Much of what actors in the EU apparatus do, is facilitate discussion among interested parties to any policy domain in order to broker some kind of new collective arrangement. The output of these organized domains is legislation. The purpose of the rest of the chapter is to take these insights about the constitution of policy domains and look at various kinds of measures of domain organization over time in order to flesh out a picture of how the EU has expanded.

2. The Constitution of Policy Domains in the EU

We first turn to the question of describing the number and scope of policy domains that exist in the EU. Following our earlier argument, it is possible to document how the Treaty of Rome, the Single European Act, and the Treaty on European Union expanded the possible policy domains. Table 3.1 describes the policy domains as they are defined by the three Treaties.[1]

Why are these the policy domains of the EU? The principal Treaties of the EU

---

[1] We think these categories are somewhat artificial and they overlap, but they are a good approximation to capture the major policy domains of the EU.

Table 3.1. Analytic categories that correspond to policy
domains from the various Treaties

Treaty of Rome (1957)

General, financial, and institutional matters
Customs Union and free movement of goods
Agriculture
Fisheries
Freedom of movement for workers and social policy
Right of establishment and freedom to provide services
Transport policy
Competition policy
External relations
Industrial policy and internal market
Economic and monetary policy and free movement of capital
Taxation
Energy
Regional policy and coordination of structural instruments
Science, information, education, and culture

Single European Act (1986)

Law relating to undertakings
Common, foreign, and security policy
Environment, consumers, and health protection
(Expanded) Economic and monetary policy and free movement of capital
(Expanded) Science, information, education, and culture
(Expanded) Industrial policy and internal market
(Expanded) Taxation
(Expanded) Energy
(Expanded) Right of establishment and freedom to provide services
(Expanded) Free movement of goods
(Expanded) Free movement of capital
(Expanded) Regional policy and coordination of structural instruments

Treaty on European Union (1992)

Cooperation in the fields of justice and home affairs
People's Europe
(Expanded) Freedom of movement of workers and social policy
(Expanded) Common, foreign, and security policy
(Expanded) Transport
(Expanded) Science, information, education, and culture
(Expanded) Economic and monetary policy and free movement of capital
(Expanded) Regional policy and coordination of structural instruments
(Expanded) Energy
(Expanded) Environment, consumers, and health protection

Note: See Appendix for details on coding.

use a certain kind of language to describe the purposes of the organization (what are called "competencies"). This language offers actors legitimate ways to organize. The foundations of the EU and its policy domains are laid out in Parts 2, 3, and 5 of the Treaty of Rome which produce fifteen potential arenas for policymaking in the original Treaty of Rome (CEC 1987a). The Single European Act modified the Treaty of Rome by adding three distinct policy domains (law relating to undertakings; common, foreign, and security policy; and environment, consumers, and health protection) and expanding EU organizational and institutional capacity in eight arenas that already existed (CEC 1987a: 1007–94). The Treaty on European Union added two new policy domains (cooperation in the fields of justice and home affairs; and "People's Europe") and substantially added institutional capacity in nine others (CEC 1992; see in particular 12–13). We note that fifteen of the twenty potential policy domains were specified in the Treaty of Rome.

These observations accord with our view of the formation of institutions in two ways. First, the big purposes of the EU were laid down in the original documents, particularly the Treaty of Rome. Second, this language became dominant in discussions of the EU and was embedded in all subsequent discussions of the EU. The largest amount of the expansion of institutional capacity came as the Treaties were modified mostly to change the institutional capacity of actors in existing arenas. These changes were of three varieties: opening new areas for discussion, changing the voting rules for the European Council of Ministers, and altering the procedures whereby legislation was produced.

We want to argue that these analytic categories were viewed by the organizations of the EU as potential arenas in which legislation could be written. If these arenas actually exist, it should be possible to document their organizational and legal reality. One of the most important empirical proofs of our argument is that these are the analytic categories that the EU uses to classify legislation (CEC 1995a: 13). In other words, policymakers follow these classifications as templates in their organization of legislative activity.

It is also the case that the European Commission and the European Council of Ministers used these categories to define their own organizational structure.[2] Table 3.2 presents the areas specified by the Treaty of Rome in one column and contains the names of the Directorates-General (hereafter DG) of the European Commission in 1970. There is a direct one-to-one mapping of the fifteen arenas defined by the Treaty of Rome to the organization of the European Commission. This implies that the competencies of the European Union as they were specified in the Treaty of Rome did not just serve as cognitive categories but also constituted organizational realities.

---

[2] The European Parliament committee structure has a similar set of domains defined. The annual report entitled *General Report of the Activities of the European Communities* contains a listing of the standing committees of the Parliament which parallel those of the Council and Commission. The Economic and Social Committee has a different organizational structure that is focused on dividing into firms, workers, and other organized groups. But it too has a committee structure that parallels the policy domains.

Table 3.2. Policy domains specified by the Treaty of Rome and the organization of the European Commission in 1970

Treaty of Rome	Directorate-General
External relations	I–External relations
Economic and monetary policy and free movement of capital	II–Economic and financial affairs
Customs Union and free movement of goods	III–Industry
Competition	IV–Competition
Free movement of labor and social policy	V–Social policy
Agriculture	VI–Agriculture
Fisheries	
Transport	VII–Transport
External relations	VIII–Development aid
	IX–Personnel
	X–Information
External relations	XI–External trade
Science, information, education, culture	XII–Research and technology
Right of establishment and freedom of services	XIII–Dissemination of information
Internal market and industrial policy	XIV–Internal market
Science, information, education, culture	XV–Research
Regional policy	XVI–Regional policy
Energy	XVII–Energy
	XVIII–Credit and investments
	XIX–Budgets
	XX–Financial control

Note: See Appendix for data sources and details on coding.

Table 3.3 documents how the structure of the European Commission changed between 1970 and 1993. In 1980, before either of the two large Treaty modifications, the structure of the Commission remained almost identical. The major change was moving DG XV (the Joint Research Centre) into DG XII (Research, Science, and Education). DG XV became oriented toward financial institutions and issues of taxation. This reflected the increased interest in monetary issues in the 1970s. The other major change was DG XIV (Internal Market) was combined into DG-III (previously, Industrial Affairs). DG XIV became the Fisheries Directorate, which was split off from DG VI (Agriculture). This reflected the expansion of fishery agreements in the 1970s.

The Single European Act expanded the institutional capacity of the European Community by increasing competencies. Many of these were related to the issue of completing the Single Market. Some of these changes can be linked to the purposes of the Single Market and the original purposes of the Treaty of Rome (for instance, regional policy, see Garrett (1992) for an argument about "side payments"), but many are more difficult to connect, i.e. foreign and security policy, science, and culture.

These changes are also reflected in the reorganization of the Commission. DG X changed from being concerned with issues of providing the public with

Table 3.3. Names of Directorates-General in 1970, 1980, and 1987 and 1993

1970	1980	1987	1993
I–External affairs	External affairs	External affairs	External affairs
II–Economic and social affairs	Economic and social affairs	Economic and financial affairs	Economic and financial affairs
III–Industry	Internal market and industrial affairs	Internal market and industrial affairs	Internal market and industrial affairs
IV–Competition	Competition	Competition	Competition
V–Social affairs	Employment and social affairs	Employment and social affairs	Employment, industrial relations, and social affairs
VI–Agriculture	Agriculture	Agriculture	Agriculture
VII–Transport	Transport	Transportation	Transportation
VIII–Development	Development	Development	Development
IX–Personnel and administration	Personnel and administration	Personnel and administration	Personnel and administration
X–Information	Information	Information, communication, and culture	Audiovisual media, information, communication, and culture
XI–External trade	External trade	Environment, consumer protection, and nuclear safety	Environment, nuclear safety, and consumer protection
XII–General research and technology	Research, science, and education	Science, research, and development	Science, research, and development
XIII–Dissemination of information	Information market and innovation	Telecommunications, information industries, and innovation	Telecommunications, information industries, and innovation
XIV–Internal market	Fisheries	Fisheries	Fisheries
XV–Joint research centre	Financial institutions and taxation	Financial institutions and Company Law	Financial institutions and Company Law
XVI–Regional policy	Regional policy	Regional policy	Regional policy
XVII–Energy	Energy	Energy	Energy
XVIII–Credit and investments	Credit and investments	Credit and investments	Credit and investments
XIX–Budgets	Budgets	Budgets	Budgets
XX–Financial control	Financial control	Financial control	Financial control
XXI–		Customs Union and indirect taxation	Customs and indirect taxation
XXII–		Coordination of structural policies	Coordination of structural policies
XXIII–			Enterprise policy, distributive trades, tourism, and cooperatives

Sources: See Appendix.

information about the activities of the Community to including issues of media and culture. DG XI in 1980 was concerned with issues of external trade. This group was moved over to DG VIII, Development. DG XI became Environment, Consumer Protection, and Nuclear Safety. DG XIII added Telecommunications to its activities, while DG XV added Company Law. Two new directorates were created: DG XXI, Customs Union and Indirect Taxation, and DG XXII, Co-ordination of Structural Policies. The former reflected moving functions from DG XV and DG III while the latter reflected changes made by the Single European Act.

The Treaty on European Union brought about more changes in the structure of the European Commission. The Treaty mainly expanded competencies by altering voting rules. The monetary and political union envisioned by the Treaty changed the issues confronted by the European Union. This expansion is reflected in the changes in the DGs. DG V expanded its purview to include issues of industrial relations as well as employment and social affairs as the social charter was expanded by the Treaty. DG X continued evolving more into a directorate concerned with media policy in the EU as well as providing member-state governments with information about the activities of the EU. A new DG was concerned with enterprise policy, distributive trades (services), tourism, and cooperatives.

Table 3.4 shows the relation between the original arenas defined by the Treaty of Rome and the structure of the European Council of Ministers. Each of the issues raised in the Treaty of Rome are represented in the organizational structure of the Council, mirroring the structure of the Commission. The

Table 3.4. The Treaty of Rome and the structure of the European Council of Ministers in 1970

Treaty of Rome	Directorate-General
External relations	DG-E
Economic and monetary policy affairs	DG-C
Customs Union and free movement of goods	DG-C
Competition	DG-C
Free movement of labor and social policy	DG-B
Agriculture	DG-B
Fisheries	DG-B
Transport	DG-C
External relations	DG-E
Science, information, education, culture	DG-B, DG-D
Right of establishment and freedom of services	DG-C
Internal market and industrial policy	DG-C
Regional policy	DG-B
Energy	DG-D
Budgets	DG-A

Source: *Guide to the Council of the European Communities*, annual publication.

Table 3.5. Structure of Directorates-General in the Council of Ministers 1980, 1987, 1993

	1980	1987	1993
DG-A	Administration	Administration	Administration
DG-B	Agriculture Regional policies Social policies Fisheries Education	Agriculture Fisheries	Agriculture Fisheries
DG-C	Free movement of goods Customs Union Competition Industrial policy Transportation Environment Consumer protection Company Law Right to establish services Banks/insurance Iron and steel Public contracts	Customs Union Internal market Competition Industrial policy Freedom of services Company Law Banks/insurance	Customs Union Internal market Competition Industrial policy Freedom of services Company Law Banks/insurance Tourism Broadcasting Telecommunications
DG-D	Science Technology Energy Nuclear safety	Science Research Energy Environment Transportation Consumer protection	Science Research Energy Environment Transportation Consumer protection
DG-E	External relations Development	External relations Development	External relations Development
DG-F	Relations to Parliament Economic and monetary affairs Tax harmonization Institutional affairs Information	Relations to Parliament Relations to ECSC Institutional affairs Budget	Relations to Parliament Relations to ECSC Institutional affairs Budget

DG-G		Economic and financial
		  affairs
		Social policy
		Health
		Education
		Regional policy
		Culture
		Tax harmonization
			Economic and financial
			  affairs
			Social policy
			Health
			Education
			Regional policy
			Culture
			Tax harmonization

Sources: See Table 3.4.

Council changed its organization with the Single European Act and the Treaty on European Union. Table 3.5 presents the organization of the Council of Ministers following these changes. The Single European Act caused the Council to reorganize its activities. DG-B became exclusively concerned with Agriculture and Fisheries, while DG-C focused on Single Market issues. The residual areas of the Treaty expansion (environment, consumer protection, education, health, and culture) were organized into a new directorate, G. The Treaty on European Union did not alter the organization structure of the Council very much. The expansion of competencies into tourism, broadcasting, and telecommunications were reflected in changes in DG-C.

One can observe that basic policy domains were given shape by the Treaty of Rome, the Single European Act, and the Treaty on European Union. These arenas were made concrete by providing organizational capacity in the European Commission and Council precisely as it was defined by these issues. As the Treaty of Rome was revised, the Commission's and Council's structure was changed.

There are other measures one can generate to index the development of policy domains. Table 3.6 presents a classification used by the Council of Ministers in their annual report on the topics of meetings. It was at these meetings that members of the Council of Ministers would discuss legislative issues. They index how the Council of Ministers spent its time. One can observe that between 1970 and 1980, there was an increase in the number of meetings from forty-three to fifty-nine and a similar increase to eighty in 1987. Over the period, the number of meetings of the Council of Ministers nearly doubled.

Table 3.6. Topics of meetings of the European Council of Ministers

	1970	1980	1987	1993
Agriculture	12	14	16	13
Foreign affairs	14	13	12	13
Finance	8	9	8	13
Internal market and industrial affairs	0	0	11	7
Budget	0	3	6	2
Fisheries	0	7	3	4
Transport	2	2	4	6
Environment	0	2	4	5
Development	0	1	3	3
Energy	0	2	2	3
Social affairs	2	2	2	3
Research	2	0	3	2
Consumer protection	0	0	3	1
Other	3	4	4	8
Total	43	59	80	83

Sources: See Appendix.

The topics of the meetings changed dramatically with the expansion of competencies of the EU. Agriculture, foreign affairs, and financial issues were always topics being considered by the Council. The largest change, which is not surprising given the Single Market Program, is in the category of the Internal Market and Industrial Affairs where the number of meetings rose from zero to eleven in 1987 and fell to seven in 1993. Fisheries became a big issue between 1970 and 1980, but it decreased in importance in the 1980s. Transportation, the environment, development, energy, and consumer protection became the focus of more and more Council meetings. The Treaty revisions in 1987 and 1993, which provided increased competencies in these arenas, expanded the number of meetings on these topics.

Another important measure of the ability to generate legislation in policy domains is the number of people who work in an issue area. Legislation in the EU comes from the European Commission. It follows that the more people working on a given set of topics, the more likely that the policy domain will produce legislation. Table 3.7 presents data on the number of people employed by the DGs of the Commission in 1989. The largest number of people worked for Translation, Personnel and Administration, and Science and Research. Most of the people employed in the Science and Research Directorate are employed in a research center and are not directly involved in the production of legislation.

The two next largest directorates are Agriculture and Development. Since these Directorates both administer large programs, this is sensible. Telecommunications and Information industries, Internal Market and Industrial Affairs and Energy follow in size. Many of the Directorates which have been the focus of a great deal of attention, the environment, financial institutions, and regional policies (where the structural funds are administered) are relatively small. The number of people employed to deal with these issues suggests that there are very few people who are writing new legislation in arenas recently expanded by the EU.

Another indicator of what the EU is doing is how it spends its money. Table 3.8 considers how the EU budget has grown from 1970 to 1993. The budget for the EU has expanded almost twenty-two times in twenty-three years. While the budget has increased across the board, the most dramatic shift has been away from agriculture and toward other concerns of the EU. In 1970, 91.2 percent of the EU's budget was spent on the Common Agricultural Policy. This decreased continuously until 1993 where it stood at 53.7 percent of the budget. The most dramatic increase in the budget occurred in the categories of structural funds. This category was on the rise from 1970 on and took 16.2 percent of the budget in 1987. This was right at the beginning of the Treaty revision that doubled the total of structural funds (Marks 1993). Funds spent on research increased more slowly over the period. Funds mostly for outside development issues (called "external action") increased from zero percent of the budget to 3.4 percent in 1993. Administrative costs of the EU were a relatively small part of the budget stabilizing from 1980 at about 4.5–5 percent of the budget. The "other"

Table 3.7. Number of employees in 1989 in the European Commission

	No. of Employees
Cabinets	294
Secretariat-General	335
Legal service	170
Spokesmen service	52
Consumer policy service	40
Task Force "Human Resources, Education, Training, and Youth"	55
Translation service	1678
Conference service	506
Statistical office	352
DG I–External relations	613
DG II–Economic and financial affairs	231
DG III–Internal market and industrial affairs	430
DG IV–Competition	309
DG V–Employment and social affairs	295
DG VI–Agriculture	826
DG VII–Transport	127
DG VIII–Development	766
DG IX–Personnel and administration	2536
DG X–Information, communication, and culture	369
DG XI–Environment and nuclear safety	119
DG XII–Science and research	2486
DG XIII–Telecommunications and information industries	492
DG XIV–Fisheries	164
DG XV–Financial institutions and Company Law	82
DG XVI–Regional policies	196
DG XVII–Energy	409
DG XVIII–Credit and investments	101
DG XIX–Budgets	260
DG XX–Financial Control	164
DG XXI–Customs Union and indirect taxation	229
DG XXII–Coordination of structural policies	60
DG XXIII–Enterprise policy, distributive trades, tourism	56
Euratom	23
Security Office	55

Source: R. Hay, *The European Commission and the Administration of the Community*. Luxembourg: Office for Official Publications of the European Communities, 1989: 60.

category of the budget includes all other programs of the EU including those focused on culture, education, and European networks.

The final indicator of institutional capacity is the total number of employees in each part of the EU. Table 3.9 shows that staffing at the EU has increased from about 9,000 people in 1970 to over 25,000 in 1993. These steady increases occurred as the budget increased over twentyfold. The bottom of the table shows that the European Commission started out as 84.8 percent of the total in

Table 3.8. Categories of budget expenditures

	1970	1980	1987	1993
	ECU (millions)			
Agriculture	3,108.1	11,291.9	22,950.1	35,052.0
Structural funds	95.4	1,808.5	5,859.6	20,709.8
Research	63.4	364.2	964.4	2,201.5
External action	1.4	603.9	809.2	2,997.3
Administration	115.3	829.9	1,696.9	3,400.9
Other	47.2	1,074.5	3,116.7	1,636.1
Total	3,385.2	15,857.3	35,088.0	65,522.6
	Percentages			
Agriculture	91.2	71.2	65.4	53.7
Structural funds	2.7	11.0	16.2	30.4
Research	1.8	2.2	2.7	3.2
External action	0.0	3.7	2.2	3.4
Administration	3.2	5.0	4.7	4.5
Other	1.3	6.5	8.6	3.6

Source: *The Community Budget: Facts and Figures.* Luxembourg: Official Publication of the European Communities, 1993: 19–24.

Table 3.9. The staff in the European Union

	1970	1980	1987	1993
	Numbers			
Parliament	532	2,573	3,360	3,686
Council	563	1,599	2,066	2,225
Commission	7,801	11,947	15,161	17,946
Court of Justice	114	363	646	800
Court of Auditors	26	259	366	396
ESC and Committee of the Regions	144	339	471	510
Total	9,235	17,080	22,070	25,561
	Percentages			
Parliament	5.7	14.8	15.1	14.4
Council	6.3	8.9	9.1	8.9
Commission	84.8	69.7	69.4	69.9
Court of Justice	1.3	2.2	3.1	3.1
Court of Auditors	0.3	1.7	1.8	1.6
ESC and Committee of the Regions	1.6	1.9	2.2	1.9

Source: *The Community Budget: Facts and Figures.* Luxembourg: Official Publication of the European Communities, 1995: 43.

1970, but dropped to about 70 percent from 1970 onward. The biggest increases in employment occurred at the European Parliament, particularly with the enlargement of the EU. The Council, Court of Justice, and Court of Auditors all grew as well.

What do these tables tell us about the organizational capacities of the EU? The EU is a relatively small organization. It manages a 65.5bn. ECU budget with a staff of 25,000. Eighty-four percent of the budget is tied up in two large programs: agricultural price supports and structural funds. The European Commission that is responsible for generating legislation has almost no regulatory capacity. It also has a relatively small number of people working for it who are directly engaged in producing legislation. This means that policy domains function not just as arenas to affect legislation through lobbying, but probably actually produce much of the legislation (Peters 1992; Mazey and Richardson 1993). This must be particularly true in arenas where the Commission has not grown rapidly such as transportation, the environment, and regional policy.

The picture of the EU emerging from our examination of its structure is that the Treaty of Rome, the Single European Act, and the Treaty on European Union strongly shaped the organization of the European Commission and Council of Ministers. The Treaty changes have mostly been couched in the language of the original Treaty of Rome. This shows the power of preexisting institutions and organizations as they have shaped the debate about what the EU can and should do.

The changes brought about by the two Treaty revisions have been substantial. They have altered the logic of the EU by changing from unanimous voting to qualified majority voting and opened up new arenas for possible cooperation. They have also shifted the activities of the EU away from agriculture and toward using the EU as a redistributive structure across western Europe (and indeed, to a smaller degree, the world). The Treaties have also plausibly helped define policy arenas by defining areas where negotiations would occur. These have been enshrined in the organizational structures of the Commission and Council.

The Treaty revisions did not occur in a vacuum. It is clear that changes in the organization of the Council and Commission and shifts in budget priorities were the end point of long-run discussions. So, for instance, negotiations over issues surrounding fishing rights eventually led to the formation of a separate DG to manage fishing. Similarly, discussions over coordinating monetary policies in the 1970s led to the founding of a directorate concerned with financial issues by 1980 and, eventually, the decision to begin a monetary union. Finally, the idea of structural funds and a regional and social policy to cope with dislocations due to economic development was already present in the Treaty of Rome.

We began this chapter by suggesting that studying the EU as a set of policy domains required considering three elements: the existence of a "constitutional" basis for interaction to define policy domains, organizational capacity that corresponded to organize those domains, and the existence of non-governmental organizations to affect legislation in those domains. The evidence so far has focused on demonstrating that the various Treaties have indeed defined domains and that there exists organizations that mirror those domains. It is useful to turn to how non-governmental organizations relate to the legislative output of policy domains.

3. The Evolution of Policy Domains

Haas, in his seminal work *The Uniting of Europe* (1958), argued that the expansion of the European Union would come through a process of "spillover." This implied that new areas of policy would come from the transnational organization of interests, the activism of the European Commission, and the pressures these groups brought to bear on the national governments that would lead to more cooperation and competencies for the European Community.

Our evidence shows that almost all of the expansion of competencies of the European Union occurred by Treaty modification in arenas already defined as relevant to common cooperation. The main new issue brought to the table by the Treaty revisions concerned military and security cooperation, although even here, there was precedent for this discussion. All of the other issues were in some way linked to the original purposes of the organization: i.e. the creation of a "single market" and cooperation in monetary and social policy necessary to attain it. Put another way, the "master frame" of the European Union was set by the Treaty of Rome and all other discussions have linked back to that frame.

Having said that, it is also clear that this "frame" has been used skillfully to make agreements that have substantially expanded the policy domains of the EU. After all, a vague agreement to discuss cooperation in some arena does not commit actors toward creating institutions. For instance, if one reads the original Treaty of Rome, there is a vague passage about cooperation on monetary issues. It would be absurd to argue that this passage led to the agreement on monetary union. The competencies of the European Union expanded along lines set in the original Treaty, but this does not answer the question of who acted, when, and why.

This question can be examined by looking at the timing of the Treaty revisions and the organization of policy domains. Did a flurry of legislation in policy arenas proceed the Treaty renegotiations? Did transnational groups expand their activities leading up to the Treaty revisions? Did gridlock caused by the unanimous voting rules of the European Union slow down the legislative process leading up to the Single European Act and only after that Act's passage did legislation flow? Did transnational groups precede or follow the openings presented to them by the Single European Act and the Maastricht Treaty? Finally, how many of the policy domains look like supranational politics?

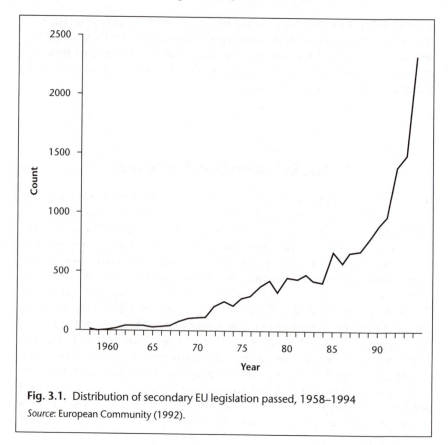

Fig. 3.1. Distribution of secondary EU legislation passed, 1958–1994

Source: European Community (1992).

Fig. 3.1 presents the frequency distribution of all forms of secondary legislation (directives, decisions, and regulations; see Appendix) from the beginning of the EU until 1994. The amount of legislation grew steadily in the 1960s and 1970s. It leveled off in the late 1970s and early 1980s. Starting in 1985, it rose rapidly, peaking in the early 1990s at over 1500 pieces of legislation a year.

Two patterns of change are worth highlighting here. First, the rate of growth in legislative output decreased markedly in the late 1970s and early 1980s coterminous with the political crisis of the EU (Moravcsik 1993). Second, once the Single European Act came on the agenda, the amount of legislation took off. This reflects the changes in the voting rules in the EU and the expansion of competencies for the EU. This evidence implies that the political crisis of the EU was being forced to some degree by pressure for more and more cooperation as evidenced by the increasing output of legislation in the 1970s. And when that pressure was relieved by the Single European Act, the legislative floodgates came open.

Fig. 3.2 traces the founding rates of the major transnational pressure groups

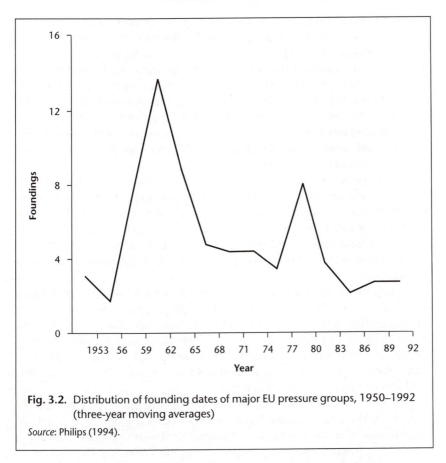

Fig. 3.2. Distribution of founding dates of major EU pressure groups, 1950–1992 (three-year moving averages)

Source: Philips (1994).

of the EU from 1950 to 1992.[3] The figure clearly shows that, following the formation of the EU, the number of transnational pressure groups took off. The formation of groups lessened after the "Empty Chair Crisis" and the Luxembourg Compromise. During the 1970s, as the legislative output of the EU began to rise, so did the founding of new transnational groups. The political crisis in the EU of the early 1980s saw a falloff in the formation of transnational pressure groups, although since 1986 there has been a renewed modest rise.[4]

There are several important conclusions to draw from these figures. First, we see solid evidence that the crisis of the early 1980s in the EU did not follow a

---

[3] The Appendix contains a discussion of the data source for this table and considers the question of the representativeness of this group of organizations.

[4] Anderson and Eliassen (1991) assert that as many as 2000 pressure groups exist in Brussels currently. Our examination of different lists of these groups led us to conclude that many of these groups are very small (one- or two-person offices) and that the major function of most of them is to provide a listening post for European-wide organizations. The largest pressure groups, not surprisingly, tend to be older, bigger, and much smaller in number.

moribund period from 1966, as measured by the amount of legislation and the number of transnational groups. Indeed, both legislative output and transnational pressure group representation increased during the 1970s. This suggests that expectations of continued and perhaps increased cooperation were brought to bear on the national governments by transnational pressure groups. The political crisis of the 1980s might best be characterized as a search for acceptable ways to get that cooperation. The slowdown in both legislative output and the formation of transnational groups around 1980 shows that the crisis was real, both in output terms for the EU and from the expectations of non-governmental organizations.

This is evidence for both intergovernmental and supranational accounts of the EU. There was pressure to produce more cooperation in the EU, as measured by the presence of transnational organizations (what Stone Sweet and Caporaso in Chapter 4 call transactors) and legislative output, but the problem was discovering how states would choose to deal with it. Once they changed the voting rules and expanded the competencies of the EU, a flood of legislation followed.

It is important to disaggregate these data in order to see what they imply about the nature of policy domains. Table 3.10 presents a breakdown of the total legislative output within the policy domains specified earlier over the period 1958–94 and the number of organizations that attach to each policy domain. Policy domains for organizations were coded by mapping the DGs with which organizations maintained regular contact onto corresponding legislative domains established in the EU.[5]

Table 3.10 does not present causal evidence regarding which came first, the domains or the organizations, but instead examines the degree to which organizations and legislation in domains correlate. The zero order correlation is 0.41, which indicates a strong positive association between the number of organizations in a policy domain and the corresponding amount of legislation.

Earlier, we argued that some of the policy domains could look more like intergovernmental bargaining while others might look closer to supranational regimes. The relatively high correlation between legislative outcomes and transnational pressure groups suggests that many of the domains of the EU either were or eventually became supranational. For instance, the policy domain of Industry/Internal Market has the third highest quantity of legislation and the largest number of transnational pressure groups.

On the other extreme, the Fisheries policy domain has 474 pieces of legislation and only one identifiable transnational pressure group. It is obvious that this domain more closely reflects intergovernmental bargaining. From Table

---

[5] We have already argued that the Commission was organized according to policy domains specified by the Treaties. It follows that groups interested in certain policies would locate the relevant people in the Commission and the Council in order to express their views, thus being participants in the policy domains. See the Appendix for details on how organizations were coded into policy domains.

Table 3.10. Comparison of total legislation and organization activity for European Union policy domains, 1958–1992

Domain	Legislation	Org. activity
Financial/Institutional	559	1
Customs/Taxation	1081	31
Agriculture	6939	92
Fisheries	474	1
Employment/Social policy	416	50
Right of establishment	331	42
Transport policy	589	26
Competition policy	770	46
Econ./Monetary policy	79	19
External relations	1620	83
Energy	251	10
Industry/Internal market	1226	185
Regional/Structural inst.	296	11
Environ./Consumer/Hlth.	741	49
Science/Information/Culture	202	92
Undertakings law	66	25
Coop. justice/Home affairs	1	0
People's Europe	2	0

Pearson's simple $r = 0.41$

Sources: European Community (1995); Philips (1994).

3.6, we note that the Council devoted a large number of meetings to the issue of fisheries in the 1970s and through the 1980s. The initiative to engage in a fisheries policy emerged in 1983. Many of the issues in this arena concerned fishing rights of various nations that related most directly to questions of national sovereignty (i.e. claims over coastal boundaries).

It is useful to explore these relationships in more detail. Table 3.11 presents the amount of secondary legislation passed in different historical periods by policy domain. The table contains the total amount of legislation, the average amount of legislation passed per year, and the percentage of legislation in that period in each domain.

Forty-four percent of the all legislation passed was in the domain of agriculture, with external relations accounting for the next highest amount (10.3 percent). All domains witnessed increases in the absolute amount of legislation over time. However, the mix of legislation changed somewhat between the 1960s and 1990s. The most dramatic increases in legislation occurred in the domains of fisheries, external relations, environment/consumer/health, science/ information/culture, and regional/structural policies. From the 1970s on, the largest relative decreases in the amount of overall legislation appeared in the domains of customs, employment/social policy, right of establishment of ser-

Table 3.11. Secondary European Union legislation passed between 1958 and 1994, by policy

Domain	1958–69			1970–9			1980–6
	N	/Yr	%	N	/Yr	%	N
Financial/Institutional	43	3.6	8.6	93	9.3	3.6	72
Customs	16	1.3	3.2	143	14.3	5.5	272
Agriculture	134	11.2	26.9	1067	106.7	40.9	1631
Fisheries	2	0.2	0.4	16	1.6	0.6	110
Employment/Soc. policy	18	1.5	3.6	108	10.8	4.1	112
Right of establishment	44	3.7	8.8	88	8.8	3.4	52
Transport policy	32	2.7	6.4	162	16.2	6.2	145
Competition policy	65	5.4	13.0	162	16.2	6.2	187
Taxation	9	0.8	1.8	35	3.5	1.3	39
Econ./Monetary policy	9	0.8	1.8	26	2.6	1.0	17
External relations	32	2.7	6.4	179	17.9	6.9	231
Energy	27	2.3	5.4	85	8.5	3.3	46
Industry/Internal market	54	4.5	10.8	307	30.7	11.8	267
Regional/Structural inst.	2	0.2	0.4	11	1.1	0.4	36
Environ./Consumer/Hlth.	5	0.4	1.0	86	8.6	3.3	144
Science/Information/Culture	4	0.3	0.8	30	3.0	1.2	37
Undertakings law	3	0.3	0.6	8	0.8	0.3	10
Common/Foreign/Security	0	0.0	0.0	0	0.0	0.0	0
Coop. justice/Home affairs	0	0.0	0.0	0	0.0	0.0	0
People's Europe	0	0.0	0.0	0	0.0	0.0	0
Totals	499	41.6	100.0	2606	260.6	100.0	3408

Source: European Community (1995).

vices, transport policy, competition policy, and energy (although the absolute level of legislation was increasing in most of these policy domains).

We can see that the Treaty revisions in the 1980s did result in an expansion of legislative activity. But, expansion of legislation after the Single European Act was not confined to the Industrial Policy/Internal Market arena (which already had a large amount of legislation and did not increase that dramatically). If we examine the increases in the average amount of legislation per year, we see that, during 1980–6, there were huge expansions of legislation before the Treaty revisions, particularly in customs, agriculture, fisheries, external relations, regional/structural policies, and environment/consumers/health. After the Treaty revisions, these policy domains continued their dramatic expansion. We conclude that while the Treaty revisions appear to have caused increases in competencies of the EU, there was pressure in several policy domains to increase these competencies.

One can see this more clearly if one examines Table 3.1. With the exception of agriculture and fisheries, those policy domains that experienced rapid legislative increases before the Single European Act and the Treaty on European Union were all arenas in which the competencies of the EU were expanded. To domain

/Yr	%	N	/Yr	%	N	/Yr	%	N	/Yr	%
		1987–91			1992–4			Totals		
10.3	2.1	156	31.2	3.9	195	65.0	3.8	559	15.1	3.6
38.9	8.0	318	63.6	8.0	165	55.0	3.2	914	24.7	5.8
233.0	47.9	1774	354.8	44.8	2333	777.7	45.1	6939	187.5	44.4
15.7	3.2	102	20.4	2.6	244	81.3	4.7	474	12.8	3.0
16.0	3.3	91	18.2	2.3	87	29.0	1.7	416	11.2	2.7
7.4	1.5	79	15.8	2.0	68	22.7	1.3	331	9.0	2.1
20.7	4.3	111	22.2	2.8	139	46.3	2.7	589	15.9	3.8
26.7	5.5	187	37.4	4.7	169	56.3	3.3	770	20.8	4.9
5.6	1.1	26	5.2	0.7	58	19.3	1.1	167	4.5	1.1
2.4	0.5	16	3.2	0.4	11	3.7	0.2	79	2.1	0.5
33.0	6.8	419	83.8	10.6	756	252.0	14.6	1617	43.7	10.3
6.6	1.3	39	7.8	1.0	54	18.0	1.0	251	6.8	1.6
38.1	7.8	280	56.0	7.1	318	106.0	6.1	1226	33.1	7.8
5.1	1.1	27	5.4	0.7	220	73.3	4.3	296	8.0	1.9
20.6	4.2	261	52.2	6.6	245	81.7	4.7	741	20.0	4.7
5.3	1.1	49	9.8	1.2	82	27.3	1.6	202	5.5	1.3
1.4	0.3	22	4.4	0.6	23	7.7	0.4	66	1.8	0.4
0.0	0.0	0	0.0	0.0	3	1.0	0.1	3	0.1	0.0
0.0	0.0	0	0.0	0.0	1	0.3	0.0	1	0.0	0.0
0.0	0.0	0	0.0	0.0	2	0.7	0.0	2	0.1	0.0
486.8	100.0	3957	791.4	100.0	5173	1724.3	100.0	15643	422.7	100.0

some degree, the Treaty revisions were a response to legislative pressure. There are exceptions to this result as changes in the Treaties also produced increases in legislative output in arenas where there this pressure did not exist.

Table 3.12 summarizes the formation dates of the major transnational pressure groups in the EU across policy domains. The greatest expansion of transnational pressure groups occurred between 1958–69, followed by 1970–9. The largest number of transnational pressure groups were formed in the Industry/Internal Market policy domain, followed by Agriculture, Science/Information/Technology, External Relations, Employment/Social Policy, and Environment/Consumer/Health.

The large number of transnational pressure groups present in the Industry/Internal Market domain suggests that, as the Single Market Program began to evolve in the early 1980s, there was an organized constituency that was mobilized to support it. It also suggests that the ability of actors in and around Brussels to drum up enthusiasm for the Single Market was probably high. While scholars have focused on the role of business in the production of the Single Market (Colchester and Buchan 1986; Ludlow 1988), they have generally focused on a small set of organizations like the European Roundtable. Our results

Table 3.12. Breakdown of major EU pressure groups by founding dates and domain activity

Founding	Unknown	<1958	1958–69	1970–9	1980–6	1987–91	Totals[a]
Domain[b]							
Customs/Taxation	4	1	17	6	2	1	31
row%	12.9	3.2	54.8	19.4	6.5	3.2	100.0
column%	6.0	1.1	4.8	4.3	2.8	2.5	
Agriculture	11	6	46	18	5	6	92
row%	12.0	6.5	50.0	19.6	5.4	6.5	100.0
column%	16.4	6.5	13.1	12.9	7.0	15.0	
Employment/Soc. policy	6	8	16	10	6	4	50
row%	12.0	16.0	32.0	20.0	12.0	8.0	100.0
column%	9.0	8.7	4.6	7.1	8.5	10.0	
Right of establish.	3	3	18	9	8	1	42
row%	7.1	7.1	42.9	21.4	19.0	2.4	99.9
column%	4.5	3.3	5.1	6.4	11.3	2.5	
Transport policy	2	3	14	2	2	3	26
row%	7.7	11.5	53.8	7.7	7.7	11.5	99.9
column%	3.0	3.3	4.0	1.4	2.8	7.5	
Competition policy	3	6	24	8	4	1	46
row%	6.5	13.0	52.2	17.4	8.7	2.2	100.0
column%	4.5	6.5	6.8	5.7	5.6	2.5	
Econ./Monetary policy	1	2	9	0	5	2	19
row%	5.3	10.5	47.4	0.0	26.3	10.5	100.0
column%	1.5	2.2	2.6	0.0	7.0	5.0	

External relations		4	14	35	18	10	2	83
	row%	4.8	16.9	42.2	21.7	12.0	2.4	100.0
	column%	6.0	15.2	10.0	12.9	14.1	5.0	
Energy		0	1	5	2	1	1	10
	row%	0.0	10.0	50.0	20.0	10.0	10.0	100.0
	column%	0.0	1.1	1.4	1.4	1.4	2.5	
Industry/Internal market		20	19	88	38	12	8	185
	row%	10.8	10.3	47.6	20.5	6.5	4.3	100.0
	column%	29.9	10.7	25.1	27.1	16.9	20.0	
Regional/Structural inst.		0	2	5	0	3	1	11
	row%	0.0	18.2	45.5	0.0	27.3	9.1	100.1
	column%	0.0	2.2	1.4	0.0	4.2	2.5	
Environ./Consumer/Hlth.		1	6	24	8	4	6	49
	row%	2.0	12.2	49.0	16.3	8.2	12.2	99.9
	column%	1.5	6.5	6.8	5.7	5.6	15.0	
Science/Information/Culture		12	17	40	12	7	4	92
	row%	13.0	18.5	43.5	13.0	7.6	4.4	100.0
	column%	17.9	18.5	11.4	8.6	9.9	10.0	
Undertakings law		0	4	10	9	2	0	25
	row%	0.0	16.0	40.0	36.0	8.0	0.0	100.0
	column%	0.0	4.3	2.9	6.4	2.8	0.0	
Totals[a]		67	92	351	140	71	40	761
		100.2	99.9	99.9	99.9	99.9	100.0	

[a] Row and column percents do not always add up to 100% due to rounding error.

[b] Financial/Institutional, Fisheries, Cooperation in Justice/Home Affairs, and People's Europe domains omitted due to low n ($n = 1, 1, 0, 0$ respectively).

Source: Philips (1994).

suggest that there was a wider range of organizations that had interests in the construction of the Single Market (Fligstein and Brantley 1995).

There are also policy domains where transnational group formation increased after 1980. This is seen most strikingly in the fields of employment/social policy, right of establishment of services, economic and monetary policy, and the environment. These were all policy domains that were expanded by the Single European Act and the Treaty on European Union (see Table 3.1). Most of these organizations were founded before the Single European Act.

Since the expectation that the EU was going to be relaunched was apparent by 1984, one could argue that people were just positioning themselves for the institutional openings. On the other hand, the presence of new organizations in arenas where new competencies were being prepared implies that the organizations might have played some role in lobbying their governments to accept Treaty revision. The clearest case of organizational founding after the Single Market initiative began, was in the field of the environment. Here, groups appeared to be responding to the political opportunity to organize.

The conclusion one can draw is that transnational pressure groups came to Brussels beginning in the 1950s. The 1970s witnessed a peak of organizational founding. The transnational pressure groups that attached themselves to the Industry/Internal Market policy domain was the largest contingent. There is evidence that growth in the number of organizations in a number of domains proceeded the Treaty openings. These transnational groups were either anticipating those openings or lobbying for them.

It is useful to consider which of the policy domains look the most dominated by transnational groups in the early 1990s. One rough index of this is to examine the ratio of the legislative output from 1992 to 1994 and divide it by the number of transnational pressure groups in the domain.[6] A large ratio indicates that there is substantial legislative output with few transnational groups. We take this as an indicator of domains dominated by states. A small ratio indicates the presence of more transnational groups and the possibility that the domain can be characterized as dominated by transnational groups.

This ratio has a bimodal distribution. Domains with a high ratio include financial/institutional matters, fisheries, taxation, and regional/structural funds. These domains are plausibly intergovernmental. The rest of the domains with low ratios include customs, agriculture, employment/social policy, right of establishment, transport policy, competition policy, economic/monetary policy, external relations, energy, industry/internal market, environment/consumer/health, science/information/culture, and law regarding undertakings. These domains look more dominated by transnational groups and are plausibly supranational.[7]

---

[6] We exclude the domains of Common/Foreign/Security policy, Justice/Home Affairs, and People's Europe because only six pieces of legislation were passed from 1992 to 1994.

[7] This ratio has several obvious problems. First, it depends on the amount of legislation in a domain. Domains with lots of pressure groups with little legislation could in fact be dominated by intergovernmentalism. That is, states are not allowing legislation to be passed. Second, it

This division is intriguing for several reasons. First, it shows that nation-state governments have kept control over the internal financial and institutional arrangements of the EU, issues regarding harmonization of taxes, the spending of structural funds, and fishing. Controlling the financial and institutional arrangements is an obvious way to exert leverage over the EU. Similarly, controlling taxation and the distribution of structural funds also seems to be sovereignty-enhancing. Nonetheless, nation-state governments have agreed to supranational cooperation over a wide range of important issues including monetary policy, agriculture, the internal market, and competition policy. This would seem evidence that some amount of sovereignty has indeed been transferred to Brussels.

4. Conclusion

It is useful to conclude this chapter by trying to capture the main outlines of the institutional terrain of the EU as it has shifted over the past forty years and then consider some implications for intergovernmentalism and supranationalism. The EU is an organization that has evolved in a path-dependent fashion. Most of the arenas in which the EU built competencies were laid down in the Treaty of Rome and the original language and definitions gave rise to organizational structures oriented toward producing legislation in those domains. We have evidence that the Commission and Council were organized around those domains, sifted and sorted information in those terms, and used those categories to classify legislation.

Most of the budget of the organization was originally devoted to agriculture, and, later, regional/structural funds and development. Most of the personnel worked for the European Commission. The organizations of the EU (the Council, Parliament, Commission, ESC, and the Court of Auditors) are relatively small. They have very little direct regulative capacity and they rely heavily on the nation-state bureaucracies to enforce directives. Besides managing the three large programs, most of what the Commission does is to try and broker agreements between states and non-governmental actors (Mazey and Richardson 1993).

Policy domains tend to be constituted with transnational groups, representatives of states, and the appropriate parts of the Commission. There also is a strong association between the presence of transnational pressure groups and the production of legislation. Most policy domains (thirteen of seventeen) are

does not adjust either for the importance of the legislation or the pressure groups. So, for instance, a small number of pressure groups might be very powerful and have a large legislative effect. The measure, however, has some face validity in two ways. The measure is bimodal in distribution implying that either domains have a high or low ratio. It is also the case that the domains that appear intergovernmental (taxation, financial/institutional matters, etc.) on the ratio are plausible candidates for remaining under the direct control of governments.

political arenas where there exist transnational pressure groups. But there remain policy domains (four of seventeen) that are mainly organized by and for the states.

Our most suggestive evidence was obtained by looking at the creation of transnational pressure groups and legislation over time. We showed that the 1970s witnessed an expansion in the amount of legislation and the growth of transnational pressure groups across the EU. Most intriguingly, transnational groups and legislation appeared in arenas where competencies were expanded by the Treaty revisions in the 1980s and 1990s. Yet, here there was some contradictory evidence as well. Some policy domains that witnessed openings by the Treaties did not experience increases in either transnational pressure groups or legislation before the Treaty openings. There was also a great increase in legislation across the board following the Treaty changes, particularly the Treaty on European Union where changes in the Council voting rules affected all policy domains.

Another important result was that the 1970s was a very active period in the EU both legislatively and in terms of the founding of transnational pressure groups. The Treaty revisions of the 1980s took place in the context of a demand for more cooperation at the European level. One can infer that the crisis of the 1980s was partially precipitated by the limits of the institutions and organizations of the EU to deal with these activities. Finally, the largest number of transnational groups were concentrated in the Industry/Internal Market policy domain before 1980. This implies that there were a great many organizations that were mobilized in favor of the Single Market initiative and this explains part of the attractiveness of that initiative.

It is useful to return to the intergovernmentalist–supranationalist debate over the EU. Our evidence could provide grist for both mills. Clearly, the Treaties and their revisions had a great deal of impact over what policy domains were possible, the organization of the EU, the production of legislation, and the way in which the budget was spent, giving support to the intergovernmentalist perspective. But equally clearly, some of the policy domains became organized by the Commission and transnational pressure groups from across the EU and this affected the output of legislation and produced pressure for increased cooperation in those domains. And the Treaties as often facilitated collective action as limited it. The Single Market initiative certainly gained greatly from the network of transnational pressure groups interested in that issue.

There is an obvious way to reconcile these theoretical traditions that is suggested by our data. "Spillover" (in the Haasian sense) mostly took the form of using competencies hinted at in the original Treaty of Rome to create supranational policy domains (i.e. organized arenas with state and non-state actors). In essence, the Commission and transnational actors were able to organize to put pressure on the nation-state governments to produce more legislation in policy domains hinted at in the Treaties. As a result, one can assume that nation-state actors found themselves being lobbied both in their home capitals, but also in Brussels.

Arguments from both the supranational perspective and the intergovernmentalist perspective imply that nation-state actors have interests and act on them (sometimes, intergovernmentalists want to deny this about supranational arguments). The main difference in the arguments is really about where transnational pressure groups, when they exist, lobby their governments, i.e. in their home capitals or Brussels.

Our data (consistent with the other chapters in this volume) imply that supranational arrangements are influenced by transnational pressure groups (indeed part of our definition of supranational policy domains is the existence of such groups). Those groups pressed their governments for more cooperation both at home and in Brussels. This means that intergovernmentalism, which emphasizes the interests of nation-state leaders as a cause of cooperation, is compatible with a supranationalism that emphasizes how the interests of nation-state leaders were affected by transnational pressure groups both at home and in Brussels. This leaves the issue of how the preferences of governments are formed somewhat open. Here, there is disagreement among scholars. It may be the case that those preferences changed as transnational interests groups pressured their governments toward embracing more cooperation as both intergovernmental and some supranational accounts would suggest.

But there is an alternative story one can tell. The leaders of the nation-states had to decide how to deal with pressure from transnational groups in the context of trying to preserve their national sovereignty. It may have been that the leaders of the governments were unsure about what to do in the early 1980s. Indeed, the EU was in multiple crises at that moment and the decision to cooperate more was not necessary or preordained. From the perspective of 1981, an observer could have easily concluded that the EU was caught in a bargaining trap from which there was no exit (Fligstein and Mara-Drita 1996).

Several scholars have argued (Ross 1995; Fligstein and Mara-Drita 1996; Pierson 1996) that the preferences of governments during this period were in fact reshaped by policy entrepreneurs in the Commission and this changed the terms of discussion so that there became momentum toward more cooperation.

But even this position is not diametrically opposed to either a intergovernmentalism or supranationalism based on preferences of governments. Nation-state leaders had to agree with whatever changes produced more supranational cooperation. While their conceptions of their interests were reorganized, their decisions on expanding those competencies were not inconsistent with the interests of their most organized transnational groups who were in Brussels.

One could argue that the nation-state governments realized that their sovereignty was already under attack in that governments found it difficult to make economic, and to a lesser degree, social and military policy independent of one another. The nation-states agreed to collectively bargain in Brussels and in many cases let transnational pressure groups and the Commission control the content of legislation. They accept the results of that bargaining as binding, even when they may have been outvoted by qualified majority voting. To the degree that their largest organizations are represented in these discussions, their "interests" can be served. By using their own regulatory apparatuses to enforce those agreements, they prevent Brussels from usurping the power of nation-state bureaucracies and at least keep those bureaucracies at work. In this somewhat roundabout way, more cooperation at the EU level could be thought to help preserve what is left of nation-state sovereignty.

The EU is an organization that has many faces as a result of its uneven institutional history and the complex nature of the Treaties that created it. In some policy domains, we observe transnational groups and Commission to be equal partners to the nation-state governments, and in others there remain situations that appear to reflect intergovernmental bargaining. If we are right, thirteen of the seventeen most important policy domains are now influenced by transnational groups. The creation of policy domains, the production of legislation, and the growth of transnational pressure groups have all contributed to the expansion of EU competencies in explicable ways.

METHODOLOGICAL APPENDIX

Table 3.1 is based on the Treaty of Rome and its two substantive revisions, the Single European Act, and the Treaty on European Union. The categories that appear in the first part of Table 3.1 come directly from the title and chapter headings from the Treaty of Rome (CEC 1987a: 209–11). The Single European Act modified the original Treaty of Rome by replacing certain passages and adding new ones to define new or expanded competencies for the European Union. The categories were considered "expanded" if the Single European Act explicitly changed the competencies in a particular arena. A new category was formed when a whole new chapter was added to the original Treaty (see CEC 1987a: 215–422). The Treaty on European Union specifies the competencies of the European Union by replacing Art. 3 of the Treaty of Rome with a new Art. 3, which specifies twenty separate domains in which the European Union has precedence (CEC 1992: 12). These include many of the domains already contained in the Treaty of Rome and the Single European Act. Wherever the competencies in the Treaty of Rome were substantially changed to increase the scope of the European Union (either by defining new responsibilities, changing the voting rules in the Council, or changing the procedures), the competence was counted as being "expanded."

Table 3.2 takes the original arenas specified by the Treaty of Rome and maps them onto the organization of the European Commission in 1970. One can observe that there is a one-to-one mapping between the titles and chapters of the Treaty of Rome and the DGs of the Commission in 1970. The structure of the Commission comes from the Directory of the Commission of the European Communities, a yearly publication of the Commission. Table 3.3 presents the titles of the DGs in 1970, 1980, 1987 (after the Single European Act) and 1993 (after the Treaty of European Union). These also come from the Directory of the Commission of the European Union.

Table 3.4 contains the topics considered at the meetings of the European Council of Ministers for 1970, 1980, 1987, and 1993. These are the categories reported by the Council. These appear in the yearly report of the European Council (*European Council of Ministers, Annual Review of the Council's Work*, Luxembourg: Official Publication of the European Communities, 1970, 1980, 1987, and 1993).

A.1. Legislation

Information for EU legislation passed between 1958 and 1994 was derived from the Directory of Community Legislation in Force (CEC 1995*a*). The Directory provides bibliographic summaries of all legislation broken down by twenty analytical sub-divisions defined by the EU. These subdivisions, listed in Table 3.11, are: general financial and institutional matters; customs union and free movement of goods; agriculture; fisheries; freedom of movement for workers and social policy; right of establishment and freedom to provide services; transport policy; competition policy; taxation; economic and monetary policy and free movement of capital; external relations; energy; industrial policy and internal market; regional policy and coordination of structural instruments; environment, consumers, and health protection; science, information, and culture; law relating to undertakings; common, foreign and security policy; cooperation in the fields of justice and home affairs; and People's Europe. As noted in the text, these subdivisions closely correspond to the policy domains of the DGs.

Our data include all legislation passed between 1958 and 1994 categorized by the EU as secondary legislation (CELEX documentary sector = 3), including amendments. Our dataset contains a total of 15,643 legislative events, composed principally of decisions, directives, and regulations. Of the total pieces of legislation coded, 43.4 percent are classified by the EU as regulations, 30.6 percent as decisions, 16.7 percent as directives, and the remainder composed of other acts. Listings for legislation passed in 1995 have not been included in the dataset, since the Directory only documents legislation passed through 1 December of that year. Including 1995 legislation in our dataset would have led to an undercount (when comparing to other full-year counts). The handful of legis-lation passed before 1957 (n = 29) was also omitted, as it occurred before the Treaty of Rome and thus might not be properly considered as Community legislation for the purposes of our analysis here.

A.2. Transnational Pressure Group Activity

Philips (1994) provides what remains one of the most comprehensive records of EU pressure group activity available to date. The compendium lists major attributes (e.g. staff size, purpose, budget, DG contacts) for approximately 800 pressure groups active in lobbying the European Community as of the early 1990s. Data provided by Philips were compiled from questionnaires sent in early 1991 to several hundred organizations, and were supplemented from a number of other sources available to the contributors. The compilation includes organizations that range in size from post office boxes with no full-time staff, on the one hand, to well-endowed international labor groups and trade unions with multiple offices (e.g. ETUC), on the other.

It is very likely that Philips (1994) is not an exhaustive inventory of organizations active in lobbying the European Commission. The contributors acknowledge that the recent growth in number of new voluntary organizations, combined with the absence of any central information source on lobbying activity in Brussels more generally, make the task of providing a comprehensive list difficult at best. Given these limitations and the methodology employed by the contributors, we can reasonably assume the organizations most likely to be missed by Philips (1994) are those that are either relatively small, were founded very recently, or that maintain such a low lobbying profile that they will not be familiar to an astute observer. To the degree that the list provided by Philips (ibid.) may be biased, then, it is likely to be skewed toward organizations that are larger, longer-established, and/or more prominent in discussions of EU policy. Nevertheless, for purposes of the current exercise, such a possible bias need not present a major problem.

We are concerned here with transnational pressure groups whose resources, institutional access, and lobbying efforts are significant enough to allow participation in the formation and evolution of policy domains in the EU. These are the groups for whom representation in Philips (1994) is likely to be most complete. Groups whose existence is mostly symbolic (e.g. no office or staff), or that have not been around long enough to muster a lobbying presence in Brussels, are not likely to be participants in a policy domain. Our use of Philips's book is therefore consonant with a focus on organizations that are active participants in policymaking at the EU level.

For purposes of data collection, we coded all organizations listed in the main body of Philips (1994) that provided information about contacts with one or more Directorates-General in the Commission. For each organization, information was recorded on all DGs associated with the group's activity as well as the organization's founding date (when available). A total of 245 organizations were coded, providing a total count of 761 "points of contact" between pressure groups and DGs. Most organizations listed one, two, or three DG contacts in the Commission; a handful listed six or more.

A.3. Mapping

For purposes of comparing pressure group and legislative activity across policy domains, we recoded information on DG lobbying activity to correspond with analytical classifications of legislation provided by the Commission. As we note in the text, there is a close correspondence between many of the DGs and the analytical categories used by the Commission to classify legislation. Table 3.A1 provides a listing of DG classifications and the analytical domain categories onto which they were mapped.

As can be seen in Table 3.A1, the majority of DGs map directly to a legislative domain. DGs that did not correspond in name to an analytical heading were mapped to the category closest in scope and content: Development was mapped to External Relations; Financial Institutions and Company Law was mapped to Law Relating to Undertakings; Credit and Investments was mapped to Economic and Monetary Policy and Free Movement of Capital; and Enterprise Policy and Small Businesses was mapped to Right of Establishment and Freedom to Provide Services. It should also be noted that two legislative categories were subsumed into other existing domains in order to more accurately correspond to the DG headings. Common, Foreign, and Security Policy was subsumed into External Relations; and, Taxation was subsumed under Customs Union and Free Movement of Goods.

Table 3A.1. Mapping of DG affiliations to domain categories for organizations

DG Category	Domain category(ies)
I External relations	External relations (Common, foreign, and security policy)[a]
II Economic and financial affairs	Economic and monetary policy and free movement of capital
III Industrial affairs and internal market	Industrial policy and internal market
IV Competition	Competition policy
V Employment, social affairs, and education	Freedom of movement for workers and social policy
VI Agriculture	Agriculture
VII Transport	Transport policy
VIII Development	External relations
IX Personnel and administration	General, financial and institutional matters
X Information and culture	Science, information, education, and culture
XI Environment, consumer affairs, and nuclear safety	Environment, consumers, and health protection
XII Science, research, and development	Science, information, education, and culture
XIII Telecommunications, information industries, and innovation	Science, information, education, and culture
XIV Fisheries	Fisheries
XV Financial institutions and Company Law	Law relating to undertakings
XVI Regional policy	Regional policy and coordination of structural instruments
XVII Energy	Energy
XVIII Credit and investments	Economic and monetary policy and free movement of capital
XIX Budgets	General, financial and institutional matters
XX Financial control	General, financial and institutional matters
XXI Customs Union and indirect taxation	Customs Union and free movement of goods (taxation)[a]
XXII Coordination of structural funds	Regional policy and coordination of structural instruments
XXIII Enterprise policy and small businesses	Right of establishment and freedom to provide services

[a] Domain in parenthesis subsumed in prior domain for mapping purposes.

4

From Free Trade to Supranational Polity: The European Court and Integration

ALEC STONE SWEET AND JAMES A. CAPORASO

I N this chapter, we propose and test a theory of legal integration, the process
by which a supranational legal system has been constructed in Europe; and
we develop the inherent connections between our theory, the empirical
evidence, and the arguments elaborated in Chapter 1. We argue that legal
integration has been driven by the emergence and consolidation of specific
causal linkages between three factors: transnational exchange, triadic dispute
resolution, and the production of legal rules. Once forged, these relationships
generate a self-sustaining dynamic that serves to expand the scope of supranational governance, and to accelerate the institutionalization of existing
supranational policy authority. Whereas intergovernmentalists argue that integration is produced by joint decisions taken by member-state governments,
we claim that transnational interactions, as shaped by EC organizations, are
the crucial catalysts. Whereas intergovernmentalists conceptualize the Commission and the ECJ as more-or-less faithful agents of the member-states, and
by extension of the Council of Ministers, we see them working in service of
transnational society.

One purpose of this research is to show that our differences with intergovernmentalists go beyond imagery and conceptualization, that they have an empirical content, and that empirical research can help us to evaluate competing
theoretical claims about how integration and institutionalization have proceeded. In Section 1, we contrast our theory with intergovernmentalist approaches. We adopt the theoretical language favored by intergovernmentalists
—derived from principal–agent (P–A) models of delegation—in order to organize, on a level playing field as it were, a discussion of the causal arguments of
each approach. The P–A heuristic, however, does not itself constitute a theory
of integration, least of all ours. In Section 2, we present our theory, derive
hypotheses, and then test these hypotheses quantitatively, with aggregate data
over the life of the Community. In Section 3, we cross-check our theory, by way

of process-tracing, exploring the dynamics of integration in two sectors: the free movement of goods and the Europeanization of social provisions. The data analysis and the case studies provide broad support for our explanation of how movement from intergovernmental politics (emphasizing bargaining among national executives) to politics constructed by and within supranational organizations (emphasizing transnational processes and rules) occurs.

1. Principals, Agents, and the European Court

In this section, we focus on the issue of autonomy of EC organizations, and especially the Court. The rationale for this focus is straightforward. Both intergovernmentalists and neofunctionalists recognize the existence and extensive scope of organizational capacities at the EC level. But there are fierce disagreements about the extent of the political autonomy exercised by these organizations. Neofunctionalists and the members of this project have stressed the importance of this autonomy, while intergovernmentalists emphasize the continuous control and mandate-setting powers of member-state governments.

The P–A approach provides an alternative language for the discussion of organizational autonomy. At its most abstract level, it is neutral with respect to intergovernmentalist and neofunctionalist claims. It takes no a priori stance with respect to organizational capacity, the degree of controversy in an issue area, the tightness with which member-states control institutions, or whether the issue in question represents high or low politics. Further, since the approach speaks in the idiom of rationality, it has a natural affinity with policy typologies based on explicit micro-foundations. In short, the approach is open-ended with regard to specific theoretical content, yet presents us with the relevant raw materials for fashioning theory and organizing empirical research.

In the P–A framework, political actors are divided initially between principals and agents. The principals hold constituent power, the locus of ultimate authority, and the latter are the agents—or servants—of constituent power. By assumption, principals are initially in control, in the sense that they have employed their resources to create the agent—the organization—in an explicit act of delegation. The reasons for delegation are various. Principals may be overloaded, or may lack the relevant expertise to govern in technical domains, or may not be able to make credible commitments with one another, or may desire the efficiency that arises from complex divisions of labor, and so on. The overriding idea of delegation is that, regardless of the specific reasons for its occurrence, the principals have an interest in establishing agents, and the task of these agents is to carry out the wishes of their creators.

The issue of agency autonomy—a critical dilemma for the principals—is built into the framework. Principals delegate governmental authority to agents, and expect agents to perform their tasks effectively. But agents are not automata, perfectly programmable by principals. Agents may face different incentives, have access to more, better, or different sources of information, be subject to different pressures, and be embedded in networks of personal influence that are distant from their principals. No contract between a principal and an agent is perfect; all contingencies cannot be spelled out in advance; and incentives are not perfectly compatible. Because of these differences, there are predictable, systematic gaps between what principals want and what agents do (Moe 1987; Kiewet and McCubbins 1991).

The P–A approach provides useful concepts for exploring questions relating to organizational autonomy, a phenomenon that is central to theoretical debates on European integration (Pollack 1995a; Pierson 1996). It reminds us that the member-states, the principals, have certain instruments of control. They can write precise mandates, rein in agents in various ways, set up oversight committees, demand periodic reports, and institute a variety of "fire alarms" to signal if agents are off course. Agents can develop special information sources, cultivate their own clients, exploit differences in preferences among principals, play dumb when called to account, and attempt to reverse the game by affecting the incentives of their principals.

The P–A framework is just that—a framework. It is not an explanatory theory that provides precise expectations about specific outcomes. States could develop institutional designs that effectively control agents, devising incentive structures that encourage some, and discourage other, forms of behavior or paths of organizational development. Or agents could manage to outmaneuver their principals by using privileged information or expertise, and by raising the costs to the principals of reining them in. How agents actually behave, with reference to the goals of principals, is always an open empirical question.

In one sense, the transition from delegation to integration is smooth. Member-states, after all, established the EC to achieve their purposes. The Treaty of Rome, the Single Act, and the Treaty of European Union were all exercises in institutional design and delegation. The member-states created the Community's organizations and fixed their roles and competences. The Council of Ministers embodies the interests of the member-states, and is constituted by the national ministers of the relevant issue area under discussion. The Council, and the bureaucracy attached to it (COREPER), has assumed the role of a principal in its relationship to the Commission in a variety of areas. The Commission mixes legislative, administrative, and even judicial functions. As a bureaucracy, it is expected to pursue the purposes announced in the Treaty. It is an agent from the standpoint of the member-states, but a principal from the standpoint of the administrative agencies that it oversees. The Court of Justice is charged with resolving legal disputes about the meaning of Community law. Our focus in this chapter is on the Court.

1.1. The European Court

The broad claim of the intergovernmentalists is that, while the ECJ has been involved in some important areas of litigation, it operates within well-defined boundaries established by the governments of the member-states, indeed by the most powerful governments. While the Court is quite active, this activity is restricted by a tight mandate constantly monitored and ultimately controlled by governments. In addition, the Court is a strategic actor that does not spin out its decisions in a political vacuum but instead anticipates the positions of key governments and takes these positions into account.

Intergovernmentalists explicitly adopt P–A imagery as the preferred mode of analyzing the institutional dynamics of European legal integration (e.g. Garrett 1992; Kilroy 1995; Moravcsik 1995). On balance, if not in each and every case, the Court faithfully serves the interests of its principals, the member-states. Indeed the argument goes, its case law tends to codify the policy preferences of the dominant states. "Decisions of the European Court," Garrett flatly declares, "are consistent with the preferences of France and Germany"; if it were not so, the member-states would have reined in the Court, and reconstructed the legal system (Garrett 1992: 556–9).[1]

The core of our theory, laid out in Section 2, is generally congruent with the neofunctionalist account elaborated by Burley and Mattli (1993; see also Mattli and Slaughter 1995).[2] We focus on the institutional effects of the constitutionalization of the Treaty system and, in particular, interactions between transnational social forces and EC organizations that—as a result of constitutionalization—take place beyond the direct control of member-state governments. As discussed below, governments can in principle reverse the Court's rulings, but reversal is often difficult and potentially costly. If governments calculate costs and benefits—and we agree with Garrett that they do—their decision-making is certainly not limited to consideration of market shares, the magnitude of absolute gains and losses, or pressure to protect endangered sectors. Politicians are also motivated to generate politically optimal distributions of rents and market freedoms, and in Europe these calculations are often strongly tied to electoral considerations. The consequences, electoral and economic, of protection and liberalization will be taken into account.

We distinguish our approach from intergovernmentalist approaches in two important ways. First, we expect to find far more organizational autonomy to be exercised by the Community's supranational organs, and the Court in particular. The ECJ, responding to demands made by those who are advantaged by EC rules and EC governance and disadvantaged by national rules and governance, will evolve its own distinctive rules and procedures. While this legal system is not cut off from politics, a certain amount of the driving force of

---

[1] Garrett writes about a "neorationalist" model, a term that confuses the debate. The argument between intergovernmentalism and neofunctionalism is in no sense about rationality or rational choice theories of politics.

[2] The emphasis on transnational society and the growth of an autonomous legal order is shared. Unlike Burley and Mattli, we do not stress the processes of socialization and cooptation that have taken place between the ECJ and national judiciaries, and we do not believe that legal integration has taken place surreptitiously (or at least not any more so than any other complex process of social construction).

legal integration comes from "the inside," i.e. from the law itself. Thus, we attribute relatively greater causality to transnational activity and to the dynamics of institutionalization than we do to the interactions between the governments of the member-states. In what is admittedly a system of mutual influence, our emphasis is more on the force of the connections between judicial activity and cross-national transactions, including the impact of these connections on the behavior and bargaining of governments.

A second difference stems directly from the first. Intergovernmentalists see governments in the driver's seat, making decisions that EC organizations implement. By contrast, we emphasize the extent to which transnational society, organizations, and processes of institutionalization structure the agenda of the national politician and the Council of Ministers. Much of the debate between intergovernmentalists and neofunctionalists turns on the question of the influence of transnational society and EC organizations in shaping the inter-governmental agenda. If one finds that governments have had a relatively free hand in defining the nature and scope of EC governance, then the intergovernmentalist position is buttressed. If private actors, working in complicity with supranational bodies have done so, the neofunctionalist position is strengthened.

At best, clear specifications of theories can identify the correct implications of arguments. But from here we must move to empirical research to adjudicate these differences. In this chapter, we challenge the intergovernmentalists on their own conceptual terrain. Accordingly, we need to specify, in terms of principal–agent theory, the mechanisms available to the member-states, as principals, to shape and control the exercise of authority that has been delegated to their agent, the Court.

We can sort these mechanisms into two broad categories: (i) direct controls; and (ii) indirect controls. The first set of controls is *formal*—the available mechanisms are institutionalized by explicit rules—and *negative*—they constitute the power to annul or authoritatively revise the Court's decisions. The operation of these mechanisms varies with reference to the nature—constitutional or legislative—of the Court's intervention. Thus: if, in resolving a dispute about the meaning of the Treaty (constitutional law), the ECJ produces an interpretation of a provision with which one or more member-states disagree, the member-states may overturn the Court's decision only by formally revising the Treaty. This act requires the unanimous vote of the member-states, assembled as a constitutional—or constituent—assembly, followed by ratification of the revision at the national level. The member-states could also alter the jurisdiction of the Court, or even abolish it, by the same means.

If, in resolving a dispute about the meaning of secondary legislation, such as a regulation or a directive, the Court produces an interpretation of a provision that is unacceptable to one or more member-states, the Council of Ministers may reverse the decision only by enacting new legislative provisions that counteract the dispositive effects of the Court's decision. The normal rules of the legislative process governing the production of secondary rules—variously:

unanimity, qualified majority, or simple majority—also govern reversal. In any effort to overturn an ECJ ruling on the scope and content of secondary legislation, the Commission and the European Parliament (EP) are fully involved. And the respective powers of the Council, the Commission, and the EP in this process too will be determined by legal basis and the rules establishing, depending on subject matter, a consultation, cooperation, or conciliation procedure, for example.[3]

Thus, to exercise control by direct means, a threshold number of states—a majority, a qualified majority, or all of them—must agree on whether, and on how, to respond to an act of the Court. Notice that our principal is not a unified actor, with preferences that are coherent across issue areas, but a composite of national governments. Some governments are nearly always pursuing objectives that are different from others; and hard-headed bargaining is the usual process through which collective solutions to common problems emerge. The rules of this bargaining process have consequences for our analysis. Intergovernmentalism has made much of the dynamics of Council voting, the logic of which favors minimum common-denominator integrative solutions. That is, where unanimity or qualified majority voting governs the production or revision of legal rules, one government or a minority of governments possesses a veto. These same decision-making dynamics make it difficult for governments to exercise effective direct control of the Court's work. If the Court expands the integrative effect of Community law in a given policy area, those member-states favoring higher levels of integration possess the veto.

The second set of potential controls is *informal* and *indirect*. These mechanisms are effective in as much as the agent internalizes the principal's interests (or alters its behavior to revealed preferences of the principal) and acts accordingly. The extent to which the agent does so is assumed, other things being equal, to be commensurate with the perception, on the part of the agent, of the credibility of the threat that the principal will activate direct controls (i.e. punish the agent). Indirect controls operate according to the logic of deterrence: the more credible the threat of punishment for transgression, the more the agent will constrain itself by behaving as if the principal's political preferences were its own. Applying the logic of the mechanism to our case is straightforward enough. The Court, like all agents, is concerned with its own survival, which partly depends upon how well it performs its delegated functions from the point of view of the principal. In performing inadequately, the agent risks being punished. Member-state challenges to the ECJ's authority might come in a variety of forms: governments may decide not to comply with a ruling; the member-states may seek to overrule a decision; and, one or more governments may move to politicize judicial appointments (or otherwise try

---

[3] Logically, in this situation, it is the Community legislator (the Commission, the Parliament, and the Council of Ministers interacting in fixed procedures) that constitutes the Court's principal, not the Council of Ministers. But, to the extent that the Council remains the crucial cog in the Community's legislative machinery, the view that the Council is itself the legislator, and therefore the principal, is only partly—if meaningfully—wrong.

to limit the Court's independence). Because the Court wishes to avoid such challenges, it evaluates all potential rulings in terms of probable member-state reactions. To the extent that the ECJ actually alters its decision-making as a result of such a calculus, member-states exert control over its agent. This control is registered as an anticipatory reaction that operates as a constraint on the Court's behavior.[4]

The intergovernmentalists have assumed that indirect controls have effectively constrained the Court. Empirical testing of the claim, however, poses fierce analytical difficulties. Anticipatory reactions are notoriously difficult to verify. We can all agree that the more the agent has internalized—or prioritized—the preferences and authority of the principal, the less likely it will be that agency problems will arise. But if we assume, in advance as Garrett has, that indirect controls are generally effective, we are left with no means to identify instances in which agents behave autonomously. As Moe argues (1987), to do so eviscerates the empirical domain and reduces the framework to a tautology (claims made are unfalsifiable). The agency dilemma, which the P–A construct organizes as the crucial empirical question to be studied, is assumed away.

To conclude, the formal, direct controls discussed above are maximally efficacious: the member-states possess the authority and the established procedures to rein in the Community's organizations. But the member-states can only do so by achieving a high degree of consensus. The efficacy of the informal controls discussed depends heavily on the perception, by the Court, of the credibility of the threat that it may be curbed, or its decisions reversed, by the member-states. Looking ahead, in Section 2 we lay out a theory of the institutional dynamics of European integration, employing at various points the P–A heuristic to draw out some of the implications of the theory. In Section 3, we engage the intergovernmentalists directly, assessing the empirical evidence of agency and the efficacy of member-state controls.

2. Theory of European Legal Integration

At best, the P–A framework provides a useful heuristic to evaluate competing claims about the sources and consequences of organizational autonomy for integration processes over time. But it does not constitute a positive theory of integration. That is, it can not answer the following question: what are the most important factors that drive the development of a system of supranational governance which, as it expands, gradually penetrates and even replaces modes

---

[4] Anticipatory reactions are part and parcel of any strategic context characterized by high levels of interdependence between two or more actors, such as that comprised by the principal–agent dyad.

of governance operating at the national level? This section of our chapter provides such a theory and an answer to this question from the standpoint of the legal system. After stating the theory in a relatively abstract manner, we test it quantitatively. As we proceed, we draw out the consequences of the theory for our understanding of the agency issues discussed above.

2.1. Exchange, third-party dispute resolution, rule-making

Reduced to bare essentials, our theory relies on three analytically independent factors that we expect to be interdependent in their effect on the construction of the European polity.[5]

The first factor is the growth of transnational exchange—cross-national interactions between individuals, firms, associations, etc.—within the territory of the EC. Such exchange generates a social demand for supranational organizations and for rules (see Chapter 1). We focus here on the demand for third-party dispute resolution—courts—and for legal rules. Increasing levels of cross-national exchange push, increasingly, for transnational rules and regulation that replace national rules and regulation, and for a stable mechanism of coordinating national and supranational legal frameworks. As trade increases, for example, national rules and practices that hinder trade will become increasingly costly to traders, who will seek to replace them with a set of transnational rules and practices that favor their activities.

Generally, transaction costs facing cross-national exchange are higher than costs faced by persons who contract with one another within a single member-state's jurisdiction, other things being equal, if: (i) such exchange is governed by a diverse (unharmonized) set of national rules; and (ii) there exists no effective system of supranational adjudication, comparable in its efficacy to national judicial systems, on which those who exchange can rely to pursue their legal interests.

The second factor therefore is the consolidation of a European system of adjudication capable of responding to the needs of transnational society. But courts do not simply respond to the functional demands of those who litigate. Because rule-making inheres in the dynamics of effective adjudication, judicial decision-making constitutes a powerful form of governance. Where judges are required, for legitimacy reasons, to provide legal reasons to support their decisions, the lawmaking impact of any decision is twofold. First, in settling the dispute at hand, the judge produces a legal act that is particular (it binds the two disputants) and retrospective (it resolves a preexisting dispute). Second, in justifying the decision, the judge signals how she will settle similar cases in the same way in the future; the legal act is a general and prospective one (it affects future potential disputants). Thus, judicial bodies with steady case loads adapt, continuously, abstract legal rules to concrete situations, thereby progressively

---

[5] The theory has been elaborated in a more complete and abstract form in Stone Sweet, forthcoming.

constructing and reconstructing the legal framework governing a given community or set of interactions.

The third factor is the elaboration of supranational rules. These rules replace the mosaic of idiosyncratic (from the point of view of transnational society) national rules. Legal rules structure exchange. Conceived in this way, the legislator serves a social function that is rather similar to that of the judge: both serve to reduce the transaction costs, enhance the legal certainty, and stabilize the expectations of those already engaged in, or contemplating, exchange. Legislating, of course, is a far more efficient means of coordinating activity than is case-by-case adjudication. But because legal norms are so efficacious—they bind broad classes of people and activities—their production poses a collective problem. In the EC, this problem is especially acute, since EC rules preempt national rules. Partly for this reason, and partly due to the dynamics of judicial lawmaking, we can expect that the European Court will at times legislate before the Community legislator. In any case, in all polities that possess a permanently constituted legislature and an independent judiciary, lawmaking powers are shared, and boundaries allegedly separating institutional functions blur. Thus, legislatures rely on the legal system to enforce their law, and the judiciary possesses broad capacity to generate legal rules where none existed prior to a given dispute, and to reconstruct legislative norms in interstitial processes of interpretation.

Viewed in dynamic relation to one another, transnational exchange, transnational litigation, and the production of Euro-rules can evolve interdependently and, in so doing, constitute and reconstitute the supranational polity. Thus, as the number of contracts rise, the legal system will increasingly be activated, not least, as those who exchange run up against national rules and practices that hinder their activities. To the extent that the legal system performs its dispute–resolution functions effectively, it reduces transaction costs, thus encouraging more exchange. As the scope of legislation widens and deepens, the conditions favoring the expansion of exchange are constructed, the potential for conflict between national rules and practices and the interests of transnational society increases, and the grounds available for judicial lawmaking expands. New collective decision-making problems are posed as older barriers to exchange are removed, and these problems push for normative solutions. Once constituted, the causal connections between social exchange, third-party dispute resolution, and rule-making generate a dynamic, expansive logic to the construction of the legal system and therefore of the supranational polity.

Components of the virtuous circle just described have been identified empirically and theorized by scholars working in diverse fields. North has argued that differential rates of national economic development are in large part explained by the relative effectiveness of legal systems to reduce the costs of exchange among strangers (1981, 1990). Although they did not focus on law and courts, Haas (1958, 1961) and Deutsch (1957) understood, somewhat differently, that sovereign states would respond to increasing levels of transnational interactions by integrating politically, that is, by creating common institutional and normative frameworks that would then take on lives of their own. Haas used the term "spillover" to capture the expansive logic of integration. Research on the birth and subsequent development of legal systems, has shown that highly structured linkages develop between self-interested litigants and judges, and that these interactions generate a self-sustaining dynamic that, by feeding back onto the greater political environment, can reconfigure the inner workings of the polity itself (Landfried 1984, 1992; Stone 1992, 1994*b*; Burley and Mattli 1993). These sorts of "policy feedbacks," and their political consequences, are also familiar to historical institutionalists, who give them pride of place (Steinmo *et al.* 1992; Pierson 1993).

2.2. Constructing a European constitution[6]

The transformation of the EC from a relatively traditional (albeit multifaceted) international organization into a transnational, indeed quasi-federal, rule-of-law governmental system needs to be explained. Our theory suggests that transnational exchange would be the crucial catalyst for such an event, generating a social demand for adjudication, revealing important collective action problems that beg for normative solutions (transnational rules), and thereby pushing for modes of supranational governance. The theory further suggests that once the causal connections between exchange, third-party dispute resolution, and rules are forged, the legal system will operate according to a self-sustaining and expansionary dynamic. But the development of these connections implies the existence of, respectively, some measure of individual property rights, some form of adjudication, and a lawgiver. For well-known reasons (e.g. Waltz 1979), these conditions have been notoriously difficult to achieve and sustain in the interstate system.

In Europe, the six states that signed the Treaty of Rome in 1958, establishing the European Economic Community, were able to overcome some of these difficulties, but only partly. The Rome Treaty contains important restrictions on state sovereignty, such as the prohibition, within the territory constituted by the EC, of tariffs, quantitative restrictions, and national measures "having equivalent effect" on trade after December 31, 1969. It enables the pooling of state sovereignty, by establishing legislative institutions and a process for elaborating common European policies. And it establishes "supranational" institutions, including the European Commission and the European Court of Justice, to help the Council of Ministers (the EC institution that is controlled by member-state governments), legislate and resolve disputes about the meaning of EC law. Nevertheless, despite these and other important innovations, the member-states founded an international organization—not a transnational, rule of law polity. Some Treaty provisions announced principles that, if interpreted and implemented in particular ways, would directly affect individuals

---

[6] This section is partly based on Stone Sweet and Brunell 1998.

(e.g. free movement of workers, equal pay for equal work among the sexes), but the Treaty was not meant to confer on individuals judicially enforceable rights.

In the next section, we briefly examine the European Court of Justice (ECJ) "constitutional" case law. These judgments recast the normative foundations of the Community, radically upgrading the capacity of the legal system to respond to the demands of transnational society. It bears emphasis that this case law underpins all of the causal models tested in this chapter.

2.2.1. The constitutionalization of the treaty system

The "constitutionalization of the treaty system" refers to the process by which the EC treaties have evolved from a set of legal arrangements binding upon sovereign states, into a vertically integrated legal regime conferring judicially enforceable rights and obligations on all legal persons and entities, public and private, within EC territory. The phrase captures the transformation of an intergovernmental organization governed by international law into a multi-tiered system of governance founded on higher-law constitutionalism. Today, legal scholars and judges conceptualize the EC as a constitutional polity, and this is the orthodox position (e.g. Weiler 1981, 1991; Lenaerts 1990; Mancini 1991). In its decisions, the ECJ has implicitly treated its terms of reference as a constitutional text since the 1960s and, today, explicitly refers to the treaties as a "constitutional charter," or as "the constitution of the Community" (Fernandez Esteban 1994).

The ECJ, the constitutional court of the Community, is the supreme interpreter of this constitution. Its functions are to enforce compliance with EC law, and to ensure that EC law is applied in a uniform manner across the Community. With constitutionalization, these two functions have become one and the same. Although the outcome was not anticipated, the vast bulk of the Court's case load is generated by preliminary references from national judges responding to claims made by private actors. This procedure is governed by Art. 177 of the 1958 EEC Treaty. According to that article, when EC law is material to the settlement of a legal dispute being heard in any national court, the presiding judge may—and in some cases must—ask the ECJ for a correct interpretation of that law. This interpretation, called a preliminary ruling, must then be applied by the national judge to settle the case. The procedure is designed to enable national courts to understand the nature and content of EC law, and to apply it correctly.

The constitutionalization process has been driven—almost entirely—by the relationship between private litigants, national judges, and the European Court, interacting within the framework provided by Art. 177 (Burley and Mattli 1993). The process has proceeded in two phases. In the 1962–79 period, the Court secured the core, constitutional principles of supremacy and direct effect. The doctrine of supremacy, announced in Costa (ECJ 1964), lays down the rule that in *any* conflict between an EC legal rule and a rule of national law, the former must be given primacy. Indeed, according to the Court, every EC-rule, from the moment of entry into force, "renders automatically inapplicable any conflicting provision of . . . national law" (*Simmenthal*, ECJ 1978). The doctrine of direct effect holds that provisions of EC law can confer on individuals legal rights that public authorities must respect, and which may be protected by national courts. During this period, the ECJ found that certain treaty provisions (*Van Gend en Loos*, ECJ 1963) and a class of secondary legislation, the directive (*Van Duyn*, ECJ 1974*a*), could be directly effective. The "regulation," the other major type of secondary legislation, is the only class of Euro-rule that the member-states meant to be directly applicable in national law.

These moves integrated national and supranational legal systems, establishing a decentralized enforcement mechanism for EC law. The mechanism relies on the initiative of self-interested private actors. The doctrine of direct effect empowers individuals and companies to sue member-state governments or other public authorities for either not conforming to obligations contained in the treaties or regulations, or for not properly transposing provisions of directives into national law. The doctrine of supremacy prohibits public authorities from relying on national law to justify their failure to comply with EC law, and requires national judges to resolve conflicts between national and EC law in favor of the latter.

In a second wave of constitutionalization, the Court supplied national courts with enhanced means of guaranteeing the effectiveness of EC law. In *Von Colson* (ECJ 1984), the doctrine of indirect effect was established, according to which national judges must interpret national law in conformity with EC law. In *Marleasing* (ECJ 1990*b*), the Court clarified the meaning of indirect effect, ruling that when a directive has either not been transposed or has been transposed incorrectly into national law, national judges are obliged to interpret national law as if it were in conformity with European law. The doctrine thus empowers national judges to rewrite national legislation—in processes of "principled construction"—in order to render EC law applicable, in the absence of implementing measures. Once national law has been so (re)constructed, EC law, in the guise of a de facto national rule, can be applied in legal disputes between private legal persons (i.e. non-governmental entities). Thus, indirect effect substantially reduces the problem that the Court's doctrine of direct effect only covers disputes between a private person and a governmental entity. Finally, in *Francovich* (ECJ 1991*a*), the Court declared the doctrine of governmental liability. According to this rule, a national court can hold a member-state liable for damages caused to individuals due to the failure on the part of the member-state properly to implement a directive. The national court may then require member-states to compensate such individuals for their financial losses.

In this case law, the ECJ has imagined a particular type of relationship between the European and national courts: a working partnership in the construction of a constitutional, rule-of-law Community. In that partnership, national judges become agents of the Community order—they become Community judges—whenever they resolve disputes governed by EC law. The Court obliges the national judge to uphold the supremacy of EC law, even against conflicting subsequent national law; encourages her to make references concerning the proper interpretation of EC law to the Court; and empowers her (even without a referral) to interpret national rules so that these rules will conform to EC law, and to refuse to apply national rules when they do not. The effectiveness of the EC legal system thus depends critically on the willingness of national judges to refer disputes about EC law to the ECJ and to settle those disputes in conformity with the Court's case law. Although national judges embraced the logic of supremacy with differing degrees of enthusiasm, by the end of the 1980s every national supreme court had formally accepted the doctrine (Stone Sweet forthcoming).

Fig. 4.1 plots the annual rate of Art. 177 references beginning with the first reference in 1961. It also temporally locates the leading constitutional decisions discussed here. The growth in the number of references is steady and dramatic. Without the doctrines of supremacy and direct effect, the level of preliminary references would surely have remained stable and low. In proclaiming supremacy and direct effect, the Court broadcasted the message that EC law could be used, by individuals, businesses, and interest groups, to obtain policy outcomes

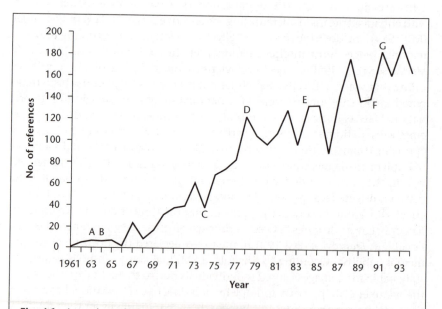

Fig. 4.1. Annual number of Art. 177 references to the European Court of Justice

Notes: The line plots the number of Art. 177 references to the ECJ. The following landmark decisions, discussed in the text, are indicated as follows: A: Doctrine of Direct Effect of Treaty Provisions (1963); B: Doctrine of Supremacy (1964); C: Doctrine of Direct Effect of Directives (1974); D: Simmenthal Doctrine (1978); E: Doctrine of Indirect Effect (1984); F: Marleasing Doctrine (1990); G: Doctrine of State Liability (1991).

Source: Source for Art. 177 references is data collected by the authors and the ECJ.

that might otherwise be impossible, or more costly, to obtain by way of national policy processes. It is evident from the graph that litigants and national judges heard this message and responded.

The constitutionalization of the Treaty, a political outcome of huge importance, defies a coherent, intergovernmentalist explanation. The member-states did not authorize the Court's moves. Indeed, the Treaty neither provides for supremacy nor the direct effect of treaty law and directives. Further, the member-states argued—in briefs to, and in oral arguments before, the Court—that the Treaty could not be interpreted so as to support either doctrine (Stein 1981). Nevertheless, the Court revised the Treaty, by authoritatively interpreting it, and these interpretations transformed the nature of Community governance. Member-state governments agreed to this transformation, but only after the fact, and only tacitly—by adjusting their behavior to the new rules of the game.

Our explanation, broadly consistent with the neofunctionalist account developed by Mattli and Slaughter (see Section 1), is twofold. First, we view the Court as generally working to enhance its own autonomy, which is then exercised to promote the interests of transnational society and to facilitate the construction of supranational governance. Stated differently, the Court does not work in the interests of member-state governments, except in the very loose sense in which those interests can be construed as being in conformity with the Treaty's purposes broadly—not narrowly—conceived. The move to supremacy and direct effect must be understood as audacious acts of agency. Second, the Court could afford to move aggressively to revise the Treaty on its own, because its formal relationship with its principals is a permissive one. The member-states could have blocked or reversed constitutionalization, but only by agreeing, unanimously, to revise the Treaty. Despite occasional threats to do so, the member-states have never reversed an ECJ decision by Treaty revision.

Most important for our purposes, constitutionalization effectively reconstructed the nature of the "Euro-law game." Simply put, the game is not a dyadic one, involving member-state governments on one side, and the Court on the other, but also involves national judges and private litigants. In consequence, as we will see in Section 3, the capacity of the member-state governments to control policy outcomes has been reduced, while the policy influence of supranational institutions, national judges, and private actors has been upgraded.

2.2.2. **Data analysis**[7]
Our model yields testable propositions. First, transnational exchange generates social demands for transnational TDR. Specifically, higher levels of cross-national activity will produce more conflicts between national and EC law, and therefore more Art. 177 references. Second, higher levels of transnational

---

[7] We are grateful to Thomas Brunell, a graduate student in political science at the University of California, Irvine, for his assistance in coding and analyzing these data.

activity will push for supranational rules to replace national rules. Third, to the extent that European judicial and legislative institutions function with minimal effectiveness, European integration—as evidenced by the rising tide of the ECJ's case law and of EC legislation—will feedback onto society. The consolidation and expansion of European governance will fuel more transnational activity, and provide the normative context for more Art. 177 references in an increasing number of domains. Fourth, to the extent that the above propositions hold, transnational activity, transnational TDR, and the production of European legislation will develop interdependently, and this interdependence will drive European integration in predictable ways. That is, once the causal linkages among these three factors have been constructed, a dynamic, self-reinforcing process will push for the progressive expansion of supranational governance. These propositions, of course, depend critically on the prior announcement, by the Court, of supremacy and direct effect.

We tested the theory with data collected in 1995, at the European Court of Justice in Luxembourg. With the help of the Court, we gathered information on Art. 177 reference activity from 1961 to mid-1995, for a total of 2978 references. We then coded each reference, among other things, by country of origin, year of referral, the national court making the reference, and the subject matter of the dispute.[8] These data had never before been compiled. We also compiled data on transnational exchange and the production of European legal rules; for the former, we make heavy use of data on intra-EC trade, because it is the only reasonable indicator of transnational exchange on which we have reliable data that are reported annually, partner-by-partner, for the life of the Community.[9]

We have argued that transnational exchange is fundamental to the construction of a legal system. To test the proposition, we confronted one of the deepest mysteries of European legal integration, namely what accounts for the wide cross-national variance in the number of Art. 177 references? The consensus scholarly position is that variance in the intensity of the ECJ–national court relationship is overdetermined, and/or explained by factors operating with different effects across the member-states (see Dehousse 1994*a*; Slaughter *et al.* 1997).

The mystery is solved. Fig. 4.2 depicts the correlation of the average level of intra-EC trade (a simple measure of transnational exchange for which we have

---

[8] Although most references are limited to a single subject matter of EC law, some references contain claims based on as many as five subject matters. This accounts for the difference between the total number of references and the total number of subject matters invoked in references in the data presented below.

[9] We are not arguing that intra-EC trade, one type of transnational activity, subsumes other important forms of exchange, such as labor and capital flows, and the formation of EC interest groups and social movements. Unfortunately, data on these and other forms of exchange are incomplete, and often unreliable. In any case, we had good reason to expect that trade would dominate the construction of Europe since, for most of the life of the Community, the core of the European integration project has been the creation of a common market for manufactures and agriculture.

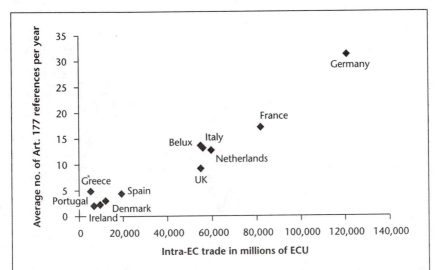

Fig. 4.2. Intra-EC trade and average number of Art. 177 references

Notes: For each member-state, the total number of Art. 177 references was divided by the number of years in which that member-state has been making references to the ECJ. Belux is Belgium and Luxembourg combined. Trade figures are the annual average of intra-EC imports and exports for each member-state, 1960–93. The regression equation is $y = 0.2105 + 0.0002247$ (Trade) + e. Adjusted $R^2 = 0.92$, $n = 11$, and the SEE = 2.46. The *t*-statistics are: 0.178 for the constant; and 10.8 for intra-EC trade.

Sources: Trade data are from *Eurostat: External Trade, 1958–93*, Brussels: EC Publications, 1995. Source for Art. 177 references is data collected by the authors and the ECJ.

solid data) over the years 1960–92 and the average number of Art. 177 references per year from the national courts of each of the twelve member-states. The linear relationship between intra-EC trade and references is nearly perfect, with countries that trade more with their partners in the EC generating higher levels of Art. 177 references (adj. R^2 is 0.92; SEE = 2.46; and $n = 11$). We also examined the impact on references on other plausible, quantifiable independent variables—including levels of diffuse support for the European legal system, GDP, population—but none came close to performing as well as intra-EC trade.

Fig. 4.2 depicts the relationship between intra-EC trade and Art. 177 references cross-nationally, with no time element. Fig. 4.3 depicts the relationship between the same two variables over time, since the first Art. 177 reference in 1961,[10] with no cross-national element. In this model, we include a dummy variable to account for (i) the constitutionalization of the Treaties, and (ii) the prohibition of national restrictions on intra-EC trade (Art. 30 EEC) that took

[10] In 1995, the Eurostat reporting service furnished annual intra-EC trade figures for the 1958–92 period. Because the service has not yet updated these figures, and because subsequent data are reported on different scales, we do not use post-1992 trade data here.

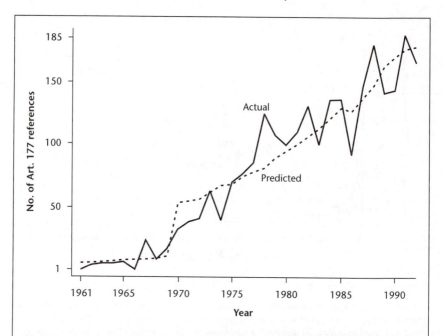

Fig. 4.3. Actual and predicted annual levels of Art. 177 references from intra-EC trade

Notes: The Actual line plots the yearly number of Art. 177 references by national courts to the ECJ, 1961–92. The Predicted line plots the number of annual references predicted by the regression analysis in which intra-EC trade and a post-1969 dummy variable (coded "0" from 1961 to 1969, and "1" from 1970 to 1992) are the independent variables, and the annual number of Art. 177 references for the EC as a whole is the dependent variable. Levels of aggregate trade begin with the original six member-states (Belgium, France, Germany, Italy, Luxembourg, and the Netherlands), and as new member-states join the EC, their trade figures are included. The regression equation is $y = 3.56 + 0.0000938$ (intra-EC trade) $+ 39.93$ (post-1969 dummy) $+ e$. The adjusted $R^2 = 0.91$, $n = 32$, SEE $= 17.92$, and the Durbin–Watson statistic for the regression equation $= 1.85$. The t-statistics are: 0.59 for the constant; 10.59 for intra-EC trade; and 4.52 for the post-1969 dummy.

Sources: See Fig. 4.2.

effect on January 1, 1970. The doctrines of supremacy and direct effect made it possible for individuals to have their rights under EC law protected before their own national courts; and, as of 1970, Art. 30—which proclaims the free movement of goods—provided the legal basis for traders to claim those rights. We coded the dummy variable "0" from 1961 to 1969, and "1" from 1970 to 1992 (the variable is hereafter referred to as the "post-1969 dummy"). The Predicted line—generated by a regression analysis in which the dependent variable is the yearly number of Art. 177 references, and the independent variables are annual intra-EC trade and the post-1969 dummy—plots the level of references predicted by the independent variables. The adj. $R^2 = 0.91$, SEE $= 17.92$, and $n = 32$.

Table 4.1. The impact of intra-EC trade on Art. 177 references: pooled, cross-sectional, time-series models

	Model 1	Model 2
Intra-EC trade	.000126[a]	.0000995[a]
	(18.89)	(13.29)
Post-1969 dummy		7.64[a]
		(6.25)
Adjusted R^2	.73	.77
SEE	6.19	5.74
N	246	246

[a] $p < .001$

Note: Entries are unstandardized regression coefficients, with t-statistics reported in parentheses. The dependent variable is annual Art. 177 references for each member-state, per year. The independent variable for model 1 is intra-EC trade, the value of both imports and exports for each member-state (Belgium and Luxembourg combined) with all other member-states, for each year. The independent variables for model 2 are intra-EC trade and a dummy variable coded "0" from 1961 to 1969, and "1" from 1970 to 1992. The model consists of 246 observations: Belgium–Luxembourg 1961–92; Denmark 1973–92; France 1961–92; Germany 1961–92; Greece 1981–92; Ireland 1973–92; Italy 1961–92; Netherlands 1961–92; Portugal 1986–92; Spain 1986–92; UK 1973–92. Econometric Views 2.0 was used to estimate a fixed effects model. See Stimson (1985) and Sayrs (1989) for a discussion of pooled models.

Sources: See Fig. 4.2.

The coefficients for both intra-EC trade and the dummy variable are positive and statistically significant.[11]

By using the time series and the cross-national data together, we increased the sample and provided a more stringent test of our hypothesis. Table 4.1 presents the results of two pooled models. The first examines the impact of intra-EC trade on Art. 177 references, cross-nationally and over time; the second examines this same relationship, but with the post-1969 dummy included as a second independent variable. The trade variable in both models is positive and highly statistically significant.[12] Thus, we have found overwhelming support for the claim that transnational exchange has been a crucial factor driving the construction of the EC's legal system.[13]

We also claimed that the emergence of an effective system of supranational dispute resolution is crucial to the emergence of supranational governance.

[11] The time-series data for intra-EC trade and Art. 177 references are non-stationary, a common problem for data containing a strong trend. The results are nevertheless valid: the data on intra-EC trade and Art. 177 references are cointegrated, indicating that a linear combination of the two variables is stationary; we checked for serial autocorrelation in the error terms, and found none.

[12] After estimating the models, we ensured that no serial autocorrelation of the errors existed.

[13] We expect that as the European polity matures, the litigation of EC legal disputes will increase. We do not expect that Art. 177 references will rise indefinitely. We predict that national judges themselves will increasingly resolve EC legal disputes on their own, without a prior reference, a topic that falls under the purview of stage 2 of this project.

The theory further suggests that the operation of TDR will produce powerful feedback effects, the most important of which are normative (rule-based). To test the claim, we analyzed the effects of EC legislation, alone and in combination with intra-EC trade. We found that the relationship between annual rates of EC regulations and directives promulgated and annual rates of Art. 177 references is positive and significant (adj. R^2 is .74) although less so than the relationship between intra-EC trade and Art. 177 references. We then analyzed the relationship, over time, between intra-EC trade and EC-rules, the independ-

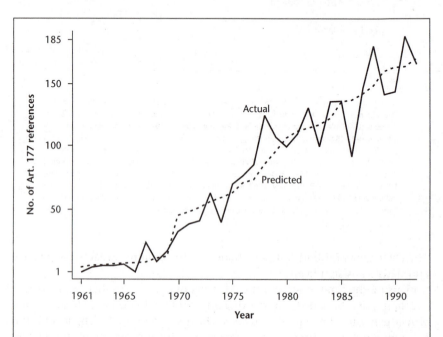

Fig. 4.4. Actual and predicted annual levels of Art. 177 references from intra-EC trade and Euro-rules

Notes: The Actual line plots the yearly number of Art. 177 references by national courts to the ECJ, 1961–92. The Predicted line plots the number of annual references predicted by the regression analysis in which intra-EC trade, Euro-rules, and a post-1969 dummy variable (coded "0" from 1961 to 1969, and "1" from 1970 to 1992) are the independent variables, and the annual number of Art. 177 references for the EC as a whole is the dependent variable. Levels of aggregate trade begin with the original six member-states (Belgium, France, Germany, Italy, Luxembourg, and the Netherlands), and as new member-states join the EC, their trade figures are included. The regression equation is $y = 2.84 + 0.0000731$ (intra-EC trade) $+ 2.04$ (Euro-rules) $+ 31.35$ (post-1969 dummy) $+ e$. The adjusted $R^2 = 0.92$, $n = 32$, SEE $= 17.01$, and the Durbin–Watson statistic for the regression equation $= 2.18$. The t-statistics are: 0.50 for the constant, 5.55 for intra-EC trade, 2.04 for Euro-rules, and 3.34 for the post-1969 dummy.

Sources: Trade data are from *Eurostat: External Trade, 1958–93*, Brussels: EC Publications, 1995. Euro-rules are the annual number of directives and regulations promulgated by the EC. The source for Art. 177 references is data collected by the authors and the ECJ.

ent variables, and Art. 177 references, the dependent variable. Fig. 4.4 plots the actual and predicted annual values of Art. 177 references. The predicted line—generated by a regression analysis in which the dependent variable is the yearly number of Art. 177 references, and the independent variables are annual intra-EC trade, the annual number of Euro-rules promulgated, and the post-1969 dummy—plots the level of references predicted by the independent variables. The adjusted $R^2 = 0.92$, SEE $= 17.01$, and $n = 32$. The coefficients for all three variables are positive and significant as expected.

Figure 4.5 depicts over time, the growth of international transactions (in the form of intra-EC trade), the development of the legal system (in the form of Art. 177 references), and the increase in the density of legal norms (in the form of Euro-rules). It thus depicts the development of the European polity from the standpoint of the theory developed here and in Chapter 1. The high inter-correlation among the three variables is another way of describing the virtuous circle at the core of the theory.

Finally, the theory posits an expansive logic to integration processes. According to this logic, the growing interdependence of transnational exchange, TDR,

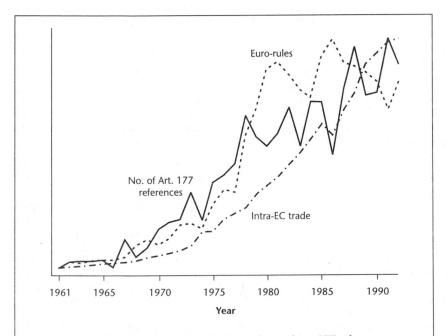

Fig. 4.5. Annual levels of intra-EC trade, Euro-rules, and Art. 177 references

Notes: The number of Art. 177 references line plots the yearly number of Art. 177 references for the EC as a whole, 1961–92. The Euro-rules line plots the annual number of directives and regulations promulgated by the EC. The intra-EC trade line plots levels of aggregate intra-EC trade for the EC as a whole. The graph has been rescaled since the variables are on different scales.

Alec Stone Sweet and James Caporaso

and the promulgation of Euro-rules drive the progressive construction of the supranational polity. By the construction of a supranational polity, we mean the process by which governmental competences, in an increasing number of domains, are gradually transferred from the national to the supranational level. Simply put, as barriers to transnational exchange are removed, and as supranational coordinative rules replace the kaleidoscope of disparate national rules, new obstacles to integration are revealed and become salient. These obstacles will be targeted by private litigants in the legal system, and pressure will be exerted on EC legislative institutions to widen the jurisdiction of EC into new domains.

The data provide some preliminary support for our contention. Table 4.2

Table 4.2. Distribution of legal claims by subject matter, Art. 177 references (percentages and number)

	1961–70	1971–5	1976–80	1981–5	1986–90	1991–5
Agriculture	20.4	30.9	25.1	20.3	19.6	12.5
	(30)	(109)	(176)	(153)	(160)	(135)
Free movement of goods	13.6	19.6	17.1	19.8	18.5	14.9
	(20)	(69)	(120)	(149)	(151)	(161)
Social security	19.7	12.5	10.3	8.4	9.1	10
	(29)	(44)	(72)	(63)	(74)	(108)
Taxes	11.6	2	4.6	4.8	8	8.5
	(17)	(7)	(32)	(36)	(65)	(92)
Competition	8.8	6.3	3.6	4.5	5	8.2
	(13)	(22)	(25)	(34)	(41)	(89)
Approximation of laws	2.8	0.3	1.9	4.9	3.8	5.1
	(4)	(1)	(13)	(37)	(31)	(55)
Transportation	2	0.6	1.4	1.3	1.5	2.9
	(3)	(2)	(10)	(10)	(12)	(31)
Establishment	0.7	2.6	2.3	2.7	5.6	6.6
	(1)	(9)	(16)	(20)	(46)	(72)
Social provisions	0.7	0.3	1.1	3.7	4.2	8.8
	(1)	(1)	(8)	(28)	(34)	(95)
External	0.7	2.8	1.7	2.4	0.9	1.5
	(1)	(10)	(11)	(18)	(7)	(16)
Free movement of workers	0.7	4.3	2	4.1	5	3.2
	(1)	(15)	(14)	(31)	(41)	(35)
Environment	0	0	0.4	1.6	0.9	2
			(3)	(12)	(7)	(22)
Commercial policy and dumping	0	0.6	1.4	0.9	0.9	1.8
		(2)	(10)	(7)	(7)	(19)
Total claims	147	352	702	754	816	1084
% of Total claims by period	3.8	9.1	18.2	19.6	21.2	28.1

Note: The table lists only the thirteen most important legal domains which, combined, comprise more than 80 percent of total claims.

Source: Constructed from data compiled by the authors with the help of the ECJ.

charts the evolution of the substantive content of Art. 177 references. Of the nearly 4000 EC subject matters implicated in references, more than 80 percent fall within the thirteen domains listed in Table 4.2. The table vividly records the extent to which the domain of EC law has expanded. The percentage of claims that national rules violate Euro-rules governing the exchange of goods directly—e.g. the free movement of goods and agriculture—has steadily declined, from over 50 percent in the 1971–5 period, to 27 percent in the 1991–5 period. At the same time, more indirect hindrances to trade—such as national rules governing equal pay for equal work (social provisions), environmental protection, and taxation policy—have become important sites of contestation.

Second, we assessed the relationship between trade and Art. 177 references over time by including a variable to capture the interaction of intra-EC trade and time. Table 4.3 presents the results of this model. Our a priori expectation about the interaction variable was that the coefficient would be negative, indicating a declining impact of trade on Art. 177 references over time. The coefficient for the interaction variable is indeed negative and statistically significant. We believe that the growing articulation and differentiation of the Euro-rules that constitute the EC's normative structure is—increasingly—generating Art. 177 references.

In the next section, we examine more closely our contention that the operation of the EC legal system both provokes and reinforces the spillover effects that partly drive the construction of supranational governance.

Table 4.3. The declining impact of intra-EC trade on Art. 177 references: pooled, cross-sectional, time-series models

Intra-EC trade	.000283
	(5.26)
Post-1969 dummy	4.62
	(3.11)
Trade interaction	–.00000554
	(–3.44)
Adjusted R^2	.78
SEE	5.61
N	246

Note: Entries are unstandardized regression coefficients, with *t*-statistics reported in parentheses. The dependent variable is annual Art. 177 references for each member-state, per year. The independent variables are intra-EC trade, the value of both imports and exports for each member-state (Belgium and Luxembourg combined) with all other member-states, for each year; a dummy variable coded "0" from 1961 to 1969, and "1" from 1970 to 1992; and an interaction variable which is intra-EC trade multiplied by year. The model consists of 246 observations: Belgium–Luxembourg 1961–92; Denmark 1973–92; France 1961–92; Germany 1961–92; Greece 1981–92; Ireland 1973–92; Italy 1961–92; Netherlands 1961–92; Portugal 1986–92; Spain 1986–92; UK 1973–92. Econometric Views 2.0 was used to estimate a fixed effects model. See Stimson (1985) and Sayrs (1989) for a discussion of pooled models.

Sources: Trade data are from *Eurostat: External Trade, 1958–1993*, Brussels, EC Publications, 1995. Source for Art. 177 references is data collected by the authors and the ECJ.

3. The Dynamics of Supranational Governance

We have argued that integration processes are generally driven by transnational activity, and by the autonomous behavior of supranational institutions that respond to this activity. Our model suggests that governments do not control the integration process in any determinative sense. We do not want to be misunderstood. Governments are hugely important actors in European politics. Their impact on integration is positive when they: (i) work to adopt, at the supranational level, Euro-rules, and (ii) faithfully transpose, on the national level, European directives into national law. Governments have a negative impact on integration when they: (i) block or dilute pro-integrative, secondary legislation (in their capacity as members of the Council), (ii) refuse to comply with Euro-rules that they do not like (in their capacity as national governments), and (iii) revise the Treaty to limit integration or reverse its effects (in their capacity as members of the EC's constituent assembly). The crucial empirical questions are: to what extent have the governments been able to block or reverse integration processes?; and to what extent have governments, acting as principals, used their authority to control their agents? These questions can only be answered by process-tracing, on a sector-by-sector basis.

In this section, we cross-check our model, examining concrete outcomes, over time, in two domains of European law: the free movement of goods and the Europeanization of social provisions. We therefore shift the focus from the broad relationships depicted in the statistical analysis to a more detailed examination of the institutional politics. Our choice of these two sectors, and not others, requires a defense.

Generally, case selection is defended in terms of representativeness and variance. While we can hardly claim a representative sample (it is a purposive sample based on only two cases), we do argue that free movement and social policy are quite distinct from one another. By avoiding two similar cases, we reduce the probability that the patterns we find are due to specific factors not likely to be replicated in other settings. While we make no claim that we can statistically generalize our results to all issue areas or sectors, we have taken the minimal steps to assure that our results are not completely idiosyncratic.

A second justification for our selection of cases has to do with robustness, defined as the persistence of uniformities in the face of theoretically extraneous variables. On the contrary, in specifying our theory in a certain way, we consciously open the door to other variables too. The free movement of goods domain is about the removal of national barriers to transnational exchange, where as the Europeanization of social provisions is about the construction of Euro-rules that replace national ones. Positive integration tends to generate more intergovernmental conflict than does negative integration (Scharpf 1988). The efficiency logic of the latter is often less obvious; and the development of common EC policies raises distributional issues, sets constituencies off against one another, and threatens the institutional interests of the national administrative state. Precisely because of these confounding influences, the design is stronger. Again, to the extent that patterns are invariant (or similar) across different conditions, the theory will be better supported.

The third justification relates to process-tracing in general. We thought it desirable to corroborate our statistical analysis with a microsectoral account of the operation of the legal system in two legal domains. This rationale does not imply the selection of specific cases. But by focusing on two sectors, we hope to understand better the mechanisms at work in the integration process. Detailed process-tracing will allow us to "see" the aggregate patterns in different and we hope complementary ways.

3.1. Process-tracing

Our differences with intergovernmentalists must begin with the challenge of explaining the constitutionalization phenomenon (for our explanation, see Section 2). Recall that references are triggered by litigants who claim that a rule or practice in place in a member-state is in non-compliance with EC law and re-quests, nevertheless, that a national judge enforce EC law. As discussed above, the Court, activated by these references, constructed the EC legal system: it worked to diffuse the doctrines of supremacy and direct effect, and to provide national judges with the means to respond to member-state decisions not to comply with Community law. Constitutionalization did not take place surrep-titiously (Stein 1981). Governments regularly file with the Court legal briefs—what are called "observations"—defending the legality of their own, or any other member-state's, rule, and instructing the Court on how it ought to re-solve the conflict at hand. In advance of any important decision, the ECJ is well informed of member-states' preferences. This dynamic would appear to belie intergovernmentalist assertions, although intergovernmentalists might be able to fashion a post hoc explanation to preserve their approach.

In moving from the dictates of our model to qualitative analysis, we can sharpen our differences with intergovernmentalists. Congruent with our the-ory, we expect Art. 177 litigation to be patterned in predictable ways. In stating these expectations as testable propositions, we further clarify our differences with intergovernmentalists. First, other things being equal, references will target—disproportionately—those national barriers to transnational activity which hinder access to larger markets relative to smaller markets. The hypo-thesis can be tested by examining the impact of litigation on negative integra-tion, the removal of barriers to trade and other activity. Second, other things being equal, references will target—disproportionately—those national rules and practices that operate to downgrade the effect and application of European secondary rules. The legal system will then operate to push policy outcomes issuing from intergovernmental bargaining in a progressive, pro-integrative direction. The hypothesis can be tested by examining the impact of litigation on positive integration, the production of harmonized European rules, and their transposition into national legal regimes. Our general claim is, therefore, that the EC legal system works to dismantle barriers to transnational activity in place in the dominant member-states, and to ratchet upwards lowest-common-denominator Euro-rules. If we are right, another proposition follows logically: member-state preferences will not have a significant impact on judicial outcomes. These claims and predictions conflict, fundamentally, with intergovernmentalist expectations. And they are testable.

3.1.1. Negative integration and the free movement of goods

The EEC Treaty fixed a timetable for the completion of the common market, and two political processes to achieve completion. The first process is known as negative integration: the obligation of all member-states to dismantle barriers to free movement within EC territory. It is negative because the member-states renounce their authority to regulate a range of economic transactions within their borders. Member-states were obliged by the Treaty to progressively reduce and ultimately eliminate (by 1969) all import tariffs and quotas, for example. The second process is known as positive integration: the creation of new rules, or coordinative norms, to regulate problems common to all member-states. Negative and positive integration were meant to proceed concurrently. Negative integration would erase whole classes of national rules and regulations, leaving important "holes" to be filled by EC legislation. The kaleidoscope of disparate national laws that functioned to hinder trade in 1958—such as taxes, duties, border inspections, and rules governing health, licensing, and environmental protection standards—would be replaced by uniform, "harmonized" Euro-rules. Beginning in 1966, some harmonization would proceed according to qualified majority voting rules.

This is not what happened. As the deadline approached, the French provoked a constitutional crisis which was resolved only by the "Luxembourg compromise" (January 1966). The compromise—an intergovernmental understanding among the member-states—enables any government to demand, after asserting that "very important interests are at stake," that legislation be approved by unanimity rather than by qualified majority voting. Thus, any member-state could veto secondary legislation that required Council approval. The Luxembourg compromise, in theory at least, shifted final lawmaking authority away from a qualified majority of states, and to the member-state(s) in favor of the least integrative outcome in any given domain.

Nevertheless, the ECJ sustained negative integration during the 1970–85 period. In its most important line of decisions, on the free movement of goods, the Court constructed a transnational legal framework capable of sustaining increasingly higher levels of cross-border trade. This case law generated a politics that ultimately resulted in the 1986 Single European Act (SEA). Among other things, the SEA reinstated qualified majority voting as the dominant legislative process for achieving the common market. Our argument is that—as the legal system systematically removed national rules and administrative practices that operated to restrict trade, and as transnational exchange soared—unanimity rules became increasingly costly to maintain. The Court and national judges were busily dismantling national rules; traders were busy pressing for Euro-rules; and the Council of Ministers was too often unable to produce those rules due to the unanimity requirement. In the end, governments adjusted their interests to the interests of transnational society. Governments, as the Court's principals, did not reverse the acts of their agent, nor did they succeed in maintaining the Luxembourg compromise. Instead, they ratified the Court's moves, and reduced the intergovernmental aspect of the Council of Ministers. We will briefly trace this historical process, from free trade to Treaty revision, beginning with the Treaty of Rome.

Arts. 30–6 of the EEC Treaty constitute the normative context for free movement. Art. 30 prohibits the member-states, after December 31, 1969, from maintaining "quantitative restrictions [quotas] on imports" as well as "all measures having equivalent effect"; Art. 33 empowers the Commission to adopt, on its own, secondary legislation to clarify and enforce Art. 30; and Art. 36 permits exceptions to the Art. 30 prohibition, on the grounds of public morality, public policy, public security, health, and cultural heritage. These provisions can be interpreted variously. What exactly are "effects" that are equivalent to quotas, and what types of national measures produce them? What national measures, otherwise prohibited by Art. 30, could not be justified with reference to an Art. 36 exception? For that matter, what exactly is a "public policy" exception? Pursuant to Art. 33, the Commission sought to resolve questions like these in a 1970 directive. The directive established a "dis-crimination test": national rules that treat national goods differently from imported goods are considered to be measures prohibited under Art. 30. Almost immediately, however, the Court's jurisprudence rendered the Council's directive obsolete.

The leading decision is *Dassonville* (ECJ 1974*b*). In 1970, Mr Dassonville im-ported Johnnie Walker Scotch Whiskey into Belgium, after having purchased it from a French supplier. When Dassonville put the scotch on the market, he was prosecuted by Belgian authorities for having violated customs rules. The rules prohibited the importation from an EC country, in this case France, of spirits that originated in a third country, in this case Britain, unless French customs rules were substantially similar to those in place in Belgium. Dassonville was also sued by a Belgian importer who possessed, under Belgian law, an exclusive right to market Johnnie Walker in the country. Dassonville argued that, under the Treaty, goods that had entered France legally must be allowed to enter Belgium freely, and exclusive rights to import and market goods were not legally valid.

The case provided the Court with its first real opportunity to consider the meaning of Art. 30. Dismissing the objections of the UK and Belgium, both of which argued that such rules were not prohibited under Art. 30, the Court found for Dassonville, declaring the following:

All trading rules enacted by the Member States, which are capable of hindering, directly or indirectly, actually or potentially, intra-Community trade are to be considered as measures having an effect equivalent to quantitative restrictions.

Thus the Court replaced the Commission's discrimination test with a rigorous "hindrance of trade" test (Gormley 1985: 22). National measures that negatively impact trade, even indirectly or potentially, are prohibited. If put to a vote, this Treaty interpretation—more expansively integrationist than any in circulation at the time—would certainly not have been accepted by the member-states.

The ruling posed a delicate policy problem for the Court. Ordering the wholesale removal of national regulations would strip away legal regimes serving otherwise legitimate public interests, such as the protection of public health, the environment, and the consumer. Further, given the Council's seeming inability to produce harmonized legislation in a timely fashion (partly a product of the Luxembourg compromise), this lack of protection could well become quasi-permanent. The ECJ resolved the problem by declaring that member-states could, within reason, continue to regulate the production and sale of goods in the public's interest, pending harmonization by EC legislation. The Court stressed that: (i) the burden of proof rests with the member-state to prove it has acted reasonably; (ii) such regulations—as with national measures justified under Art. 36 grounds—could not "constitute a disguised restriction on trade between member states"; and (iii) the European judiciary would review the legality of these exceptions to Art. 30 on a case-by-case basis. The decision thus laid the foundations of what became an ongoing, principled discourse about the relationship of Treaty law (and its inherent purposes) and national regulatory regimes.

The "Dassonville principles" have animated the Court's free movement jurisprudence to this day. They enable the EC legal system to monitor member-state behavior, but also to shape national law by progressively elaborating the permissible exceptions to Art. 30 (Gormley 1985; Oliver 1988). More generally, virtually every important domain of negative integration is today governed by judicially constructed rules resembling, in their broad outline and logic, the Dassonville principles. That is, the Court works to remove barriers to the movement of persons, or to the provision of services, while requiring member-states to justify such barriers on public interest grounds. The Court then controls the legality of these justifications in terms of the Community's, rather than the member-states', priorities.

The purely judicial construction of a common market on a case-by-case basis, although theoretically possible, would have been a slow and inefficient process. The (re)construction of the Treaty law governing free movement, however, exerted a profound impact—a feedback effect—on the European polity as a whole. In 1979, the Court ruled, in *Cassis de Dijon*, that Germany could not prohibit the sale of a French liqueur merely because that liqueur did not conform to German standards (ECJ 1979). While a seemingly straightforward application of the *Dassonville* principles, the Court also declared that it could not divine:

[any] valid reason why, provided that they have been lawfully produced or marketed in

one of the member states, alcoholic beverages should not be introduced into any other member states.

The Commission ran with the ruling. It immediately issued a *communiqué* abstracting from the decision a rule of general applicability, what is now called the principle of mutual recognition of national standards. The Court had shown the Commission how member-states might retain their own national rules, capable of being applied to the production and sale of domestic goods within the domestic market, while prohibiting member-states from applying these same rules to goods originating elsewhere in order to hinder trade.

After *Dassonville* and *Cassis de Dijon*, levels of free movement litigation rose sharply, rulings of non-compliance proliferated, and national regulatory frameworks were placed in a creeping "shadow of the law." At the same time, the Commission, in alliance with transnational business coalitions, worked to convert member-state governments to the idea that mutual recognition could constitute a general strategy for breaking intergovernmental deadlock. They were successful at doing so. The political science literature on the sources of the Single Act has sufficiently demonstrated the extent to which governments were dragged along in this process (Sandholtz and Zysman 1989; Alter and Meunier-Aitsahalia 1994; Dehousse 1994*b*; but Moravcsik 1995 disagrees). Governments acted, of course, in the form of a treaty that codified pro-integration solutions to their own collective action problems. But these solutions had already emerged, out of the structured interactions between transnational actors, the Court, and the Commission; and they were given urgency by globalization and the failure of "go-it-alone" policies to sustain economic growth.

We have argued that integration is an inherently dynamic, expansionary process which serves, among other things, to construct and reconstruct the contexts in which governmental choices and intergovernmental bargaining takes place. The impact of the Court's free movement case law on the European polity illustrates the point beautifully. Intergovernmentalists would presumably tell this story differently, highlighting the putatively proactive role of governments.

Leaving aside how best to interpret history, our confidence that we have got the story right is enhanced by our success at predicting outcomes in free movement cases. Table 4.4 depicts, quantitatively, cross-national patterns of litigation in the legal domains of free movement of goods and social provisions.[14] To compile the table, we separated Art. 177 references into categories corresponding to subject matter, assigning to each country the number of cases within each category that would be predicted by that country's total proportion of litigation expressed in percentage terms. We then subtracted, for each category and for each member-state, the predicted number of references from the actual number of references. The percentage highlighted in bold is the

[14] The table excerpts material reproduced in full in Table 4.A3 of the Appendix.

Table 4.4. Art. 177 references for free movement of goods and social provisions (percentage difference, actual number, and proportional share)

	Free movement of goods			Social provisions		
	Percentage difference	Actual number	Proportional share	Percentage difference	Actual number	Proportional share
Austria	−.05	0	.4	.55	1	.1
Belgium	−4.89	42	74.8	.22	19	18.36
Denmark	−.57	10	13.8	6.92	15	3.4
France	.23	116	114.3	−12.9	7	28.5
Germany	9.32	265	202.3	−6.28	40	50.3
Greece	−.73	3	7.9	−.58	1	2
Ireland	−.38	5	7.5	1.87	5	1.9
Italy	−.82	84	89.4	−7.97	9	22.2
Luxembourg	−.30	5	8.8	−.45	1	2.2
Netherlands	−1.43	86	95.5	2.50	28	23.8
Portugal	.51	7	3.6	−.54	0	.9
Spain	.27	11	9.2	−.77	1	2.3
Sweden	.19	2	.7	−.11	0	.1
UK	−1.34	34	42.9	17.54	40	10.7

Note: Excerpted from Table 4.A3, produced in the Appendix. The Percentage difference column indicates the positive or negative extent to which litigants are attacking the rules of a particular member-state in a particular legal domain relative to other member-states and other areas. The Actual number column indicates the number of Art. 177 references in that legal domain in each member-state. The Proportional share column indicates the number of references each member-state *would have registered* if there were no difference between overall litigation rates for each member-state and rates of litigation for each member-state in each policy area. Thus, if any member-state's legal system accounts for 10 percent of the references overall, we assigned a proportional share of 10 percent of the references in each policy area to that member-state. In other words, the proportional share entries are from the table of no association (the basis for the chi-squared test).

difference between the actual and predicted level of references for each country standardized, by percentage, in terms of the total number of cases in each column. Cell entries consist of positive and negative percentages: a high positive value indicates that litigants are attacking the rules of a particular country in a particular legal domain relative to other countries and other areas; a negative value indicates that a country is not being dragged to the ECJ as often as we might expect based on overall litigation rates relative to other member-states and policy areas.

Note that in the free movement of goods domain, accusations of German non-compliance dominate EC litigation. Of 670 references concerning the free movement of goods, 265 (40 percent) target German laws. This does not imply that Germany has been more protectionist than other member-states. It does mean that the German market is the key prize of free traders. Further, it means that the matrix of trade-relevant rules in place in Germany has provided the predominant context for the Court's construction of an integrative case law.

Does the Court, as an intergovernmentalist like Garrett has argued, defer to the revealed preferences of the dominant member-states, and especially Germany? Kilroy (1995), who explicitly adopts the intergovernmentalist framework and P–A imagery, analyzed 122 free-movement goods rulings, and assessed the relationship between observations—the briefs filed by the Commission and the member-states in pending cases—and the ECJ's rulings. She found that in eighty-one decisions (two-thirds of her pool), the Court struck down national rules as treaty violations, and that in forty-one cases (one-third of her pool), the Court upheld national rules as permissible under EC law. She further found that in ninety-eight of 114 cases in which the Commission intervened, the Court sided with the Commission. The Commission's position therefore predicted the Court's decision 86 percent of the time. Member-state interventions utterly failed to predict the Court's rulings, and German interventions were found to be particularly ineffectual in generating outcomes. Following the logic of Garrett, Kilroy found it "surprising that Germany has a relatively lower impact on the Court" (Kilroy 1995: 23). We are not surprised. In our model, for reasons clearly stated, the Community's supranational institutions—especially the Commission and the Court—function not to codify the preferences of dominant member-states, but to construct transnational society.

3.1.2. Positive integration: social provisions

Whereas negative integration results in the removal of barriers to integration, positive integration results in the construction of EC legal regimes that replace national ones. In positive integration processes, governments would seem to have enhanced means of controlling policy outcomes: a minority of Council members can veto secondary legislation; and, in consequence, lowest-common-denominator outcomes are common. If we restrict the empirical domain of positive integration to the process by which the Council of Ministers adopts secondary legislation, then governmental control of policy outcomes appears to be quite obvious. However, if we expand the empirical domain of positive integration to include what has gone on before and after Council intervention, then the Council's control of process and outcomes can only be an open empirical question. We will argue here, again, that the legal system both responds to and provokes the expansionary logic of integration processes. This dynamic undermines member-state control and enhances the power of private actors, national judges, and the EC's supranational institutions within policymaking processes.

The formal treaty basis for social provisions (Arts. 117–22) is thin: it establishes the competence of the Community's institutions to develop social policy, without laying down content-based duties binding on the member-states.[15] The great exception is Art. 119, which obliges the member-states to ensure that men and women receive "equal pay for equal work." In the negotiations lead-

---

[15] Other Treaty domains touching on social policy broadly conceived include rights of establishment (Arts. 52–8), free movement of workers (Arts. 48–51), and the European Social Fund (Arts. 123–8).

ing to the Treaty of Rome, France insisted on inclusion of Art. 119, in order to preserve its own equal pay for equal work rules, and to prevent social dumping. The rationale for Art. 119, therefore, was related to market integration: labor is treated as a commodity and a factor of production; and member-states should not be able to obtain productivity advantages by allowing wage discrimination.

Economic arguments taken as given, Art. 119 is also easily construed, as the Court did in *Defrenne II* (ECJ 1976), as forming "part of the social objectives of the Community, which is not merely an economic union, but is at the same time intended . . . to ensure social progress and seek the constant improvement of the living standards and working conditions of [its] peoples." The Court, through the window of Art. 119, envisioned a social Community. Three pieces of secondary legislation served to focus this vision: the Equal Pay Directive (1975), the Equal Treatment Directive (1976), and the Social Security Directive (1979). Each was adopted under unanimity voting rules. We note in advance that the operation of the legal system converted Art. 119 and the directives into expansive, judicially enforceable rights attaching to EC citizens, at a time when the concept of EC citizenship and EC rights was still in its infancy. Although we are examining the evolution of EC social provisions with other purposes in mind, this outcome marks an important shift in the complex relationship between market integration and the well-being of individuals that is now at the heart of EC politics.

We now turn to lawmaking and litigation in the area. It is a well-documented fact that the UK government has constituted the crucial veto point in Council deliberations on the three major pieces of legislation that have been adopted (e.g. Pillinger 1992: 85–101). Indeed, the UK government has never wavered in its intention, publicly declared, to veto any European proposal that would en-shrine, in EC law, rules not already present in existing UK parliamentary statutes. Table 4.4 shows that litigation originating in the UK judiciary has driven the ECJ's docket in this area of the law. Fully 24 percent (40/167) of all references in the sector have attacked, as inconsistent with EC law, legal rules and administrative practices in the UK. In this area, litigants have attacked, disproportionately, national legislation that represents the lowest-common-denominator position on EC secondary legislation adopted by the Council.

We then tested our predictions concerning outcomes and the impact of ob-servations made by the Commission and the member-state governments, by examining all of the Court's judgments pursuant to Art. 177 references in the social provisions area, from 1970 (the date of the first reference) through 1992.[16] Rulings were coded into one of two categories: either the Court had accepted a national rule or practice as consistent with EC law, or it had declared it to be in violation of EC law. We found that, in ninety-one judgments that

---

[16] We are grateful to Rachel Cichowski, a graduate student in political science at the Univer-sity of California, Irvine, for her invaluable research assistance. We were forced to exclude data that could otherwise have been collected from ECJ judgments rendered in 1993 (fourteen cases); as of August 1996, the European Court Reports for 1993 were unavailable, having been recalled to correct for errors.

could be unambiguously coded in this way, the Court made declarations of violation in forty-eight (53 percent). The ECJ considered the lawfulness of UK practices in twenty-four rulings, declaring violations in thirteen. Aggregating results from litigation involving the "big four"—France, Germany, Italy, and the UK—the Court declared violations in twenty-five of forty-three (58 percent) decisions. We also found, as Kilroy had in the free movement area, that the Commission's observations tracked results far better than did the observations filed by governments. The Commission's success rate is a whopping 88 percent: seventy-three of eighty-three observations predict the direction of the final ruling. The UK's rate of success was 58 percent (thirty-one of fifty-four observations tracked final results). These numbers (Tables 4.A1 and 4.A2 in the Appendix) refute claims that the preferences of the most powerful member-states constrain the Court in a systematic manner. The legal system functions to push the integration project forward, not to give legal comfort to member-state preferences.[17]

A large body of scholarship exists on litigation of equal pay and non-discrimination, much of it focusing, for reasons that are obvious from the numbers, on the impact of ECJ's case law on the British legal system (e.g. Prechal and Burrows 1990; Ellis 1991; Kenney 1992, 1994, 1996; and Pillinger 1992). This literature has shown that the ECJ has used its powers to expand the Community's jurisdiction over important areas of social policy, while shrinking member-state control. In the UK, British Conservative governments, who have staunchly opposed the Court's interpretation of the law in this area, have been forced by national court decisions to ask Parliament, on successive occasions over the past fifteen years, to amend British statutes to conform to the ECJ's evolving case law. As these adjustments have been well documented, it would be more tedious than illuminating to trace all of them here. Instead, we will focus on how the UK's efforts to contain the development of EU law in this field have failed.

The UK has pursued a clear and consistent strategy in the Council of Ministers, one designed to anticipate and then seal off pathways that might lead to the preemption of national by supranational authority. It has systematically refused to support any secondary legislation containing provisions that would innovate, when compared with the state of existing British law, in the area of equal pay and non-discrimination. And it has written into directives detailed "exceptions"—derogations to the proposed rules—the purpose of which is to permit practices which, although lawful under British law, would be rendered, in the absence of the exception, unlawful under the proposed directive.

---

[17] Relative to other European judiciaries, one would expect the UK courts to enforce EC law only with great difficulty (Stone Sweet 1998). The doctrine of parliamentary sovereignty formally prohibits judicial review of legislation, on any grounds, and doctrines governing the resolution of conflicts between treaty law and parliamentary statutes conflict with the ECJ's doctrine of supremacy. Both of these long-lived orthodoxies have been swept aside, in areas governed by EC law, as the UK judiciary has incorporated as national law the doctrines of supremacy, direct effect, and indirect effect (Craig 1991; Levitsky 1994).

Despite these efforts, the Court has consistently interpreted the directives progressively, virtually obliterating the fire-walls erected by the UK and other governments. A few examples will suffice to make the point. During Council negotiations on the Equal Pay Directive, the UK insisted on writing into the Council's minutes its understanding of the relationship between Art. 1 of the directive and British law, namely that the latter would conform to the former once the directive had been transposed into British law. Art. 1.1 of the Equal Pay Directive of 1975 calls for the "elimination of discrimination on grounds of sex" for "the same work" or "for work to which equal value is attributed." The provision employs language that is not contained in Art. 119 of the Treaty, which speaks only of "equal work," and not "equal work of equal value." The relevant UK rules then in place defined "equal work" restrictively, as "like work," as when a man and a woman perform essentially the same job. Art. 1 (2) then goes on to state that job classification schemes may be used to determine when "unlike work" might nonetheless be of equivalent value. British statutes on the matter recognized a woman's right to equal pay for work of "equal value," but only after, first, her employer had commissioned a study of the sources and effects of job classification in the workplace and, second, that this study had determined that women were being systematically segregated into lower-paying jobs. Under British law, however, women employees could not require their employers to commission such a study. In the Council, the UK worked to preserve this situation (pending changes in the British law that might be initiated by the British government itself).

In 1982, the Court ruled on the lawfulness of the UK rules (ECJ 1982). In its argument before the Court, the UK relied on a literal reading of the directive: according to Art. 1.1, "equal value" must be "attributed" by some means; the only means to attribute equal value that is recognized in the directive is that which is found in British practice—the evaluation of job classification practices; and, the directive does not confer a right on employees to demand—or an obligation on employers to commission—such an evaluation. Last, the UK argued that its support of the directive in the Council was contingent on the reading of the directive just given, and referenced the Council's minutes on the matter.

The Court rejected these arguments, stating that the situation under UK law "amount[ed] to a denial of the very existence of a right to equal pay for equal of equal value where no [evaluation of] classification has been made." The judges then declared that, in national law, "a worker must be entitled to claim . . . that his work has the same value as other work and, if that is the case, to have his rights under the Treaty and the Directive acknowledged by a binding decision." We need to emphasize that, in phrasing its ruling in this way, the Court had effectively: (i) conferred a judicially enforceable right on individuals (to have the value of their work evaluated for the purpose of determining the existence of discrimination in pay), *and* (ii) anchored that right in the Treaty (although the Treaty says nothing about equal pay for work of equal value). The "constitutionalization" of the provisions of the directive—interpreting the provisions of a directive in terms of Treaty law—is a common technique in this area of EC law (e.g. ECJ 1981). Among other things, this technique displaces the Council of Ministers as the site of reversal: to overturn this decision, and many others like it, member-state governments would have to reassemble as a constituent assembly, and then revise the Treaty. In this case, the impact of the Court was swiftly registered: the UK amended its law to conform with the Court's ruling (Ellis 1991: 99–101).

The Court has also found ways to bypass many of the more explicit fire-walls built into directives, including those exceptions which reflect important, and unambiguously stated, national interests. The Equal Treatment Directive, which laid down the principles of non-discrimination on the basis of sex in employment, promotions, and working conditions, but Art. 1.2 excluded from the purview of the directive pension and retirement schemes in the member-states, pending future EC secondary legislation on the matter. A series of decisions pursuant to Art. 177 references originating in Britain eroded the legal consequences of this exception. In *Marshall* (ECJ 1986a, discussed further below), the Court was faced with an alleged violation of Art. 5 of the directive, which extends equal treatment to "conditions governing dismissal." Ms. Marshall, a dietitian working for a British Health Authority, had been forced to retire at 60 years of age, whereas the mandatory retirement age for male employees was fixed at 65. The retirement deprived Marshall of certain pension benefits. In its decision, the Court announced that the provision excluding of "social security matters from the scope of [the] directive, must be interpreted strictly [i.e. narrowly], in view of the fundamental importance of the principle of equal treatment," thus relegating Art. 1.2 to a position of inferior status. The ECJ then grounded its decision on Art. 5: "the dismissal of a woman solely because she has attained the qualifying age for a state pension, which age is different under national legislation for men and women, constitutes discrimination on grounds of sex, contrary to [the] Directive."

In its post-Marshall case law, the Court went on to preempt the Council as the Community's legislator in this field. In 1990, in *Barber* (ECJ 1990a) the Court enacted, as a matter of Treaty interpretation, a directive designed to abrogate those provisions of the Equal Treatment Directive and the Social Security Directive which permitted the member-states to derogate from principles of equal treatment in the provision of old-age pensions. First proposed by the Commission in 1987, France and the UK had blocked its adoption in the Council (Curtin 1990). Ruling that certain types of pension benefits constituted pay, and that therefore the provision of these benefits must conform to the principle of non-discrimination proclaimed by Art. 119, the Court ordered the UK government to compensate Mr. Barber for pension payments lost due to discriminatory rules permitting women to retire earlier than men. In an extraordinary example of a court freely admitting the policy consequences of its own activism, the Court sought to mitigate what the member-states had characterized, at oral argument, as the "serious financial consequences" retrospective compensation for all victims of such policies would pose for national budgets. "The member states and other parties concerned," the Court declared, "were reasonably entitled to consider that Art. 119 did not apply to pensions" before its ruling, and that therefore only pending and future litigation would be subject to the new rules.

The preemption of the Council in *Barber* is not an isolated incident in the domain of equal pay and non-discrimination.[18] In *Dekker* (ECJ 1991*b*), the Court enacted, by judicial decision, the main elements of the pregnancy directive that had been opposed by the UK. The case, referred by a Dutch court, was brought by a woman who had been denied a teaching position at a youth training center. The center's hiring committee informed Ms. Dekker, three months pregnant at the time, that although she was the best candidate for the job, they could not hire her because its employment insurance did not cover sick leave for illnesses that (a) would occur during the first six months of employment, if (b) these illnesses could be anticipated at the time of hiring. At issue was the interpretation of Art. 2 of the Equal Treatment Directive prohibiting employment discrimination on the grounds of sex, marital, or family status. Dekker, supported by the Commission, argued that the center's decision constituted sex discrimination, since women but not men can become pregnant. In its observation to the Court, the UK argued that the directive requires only that men and women be treated equally when they "become unable to work" for health reasons. The ECJ agreed with the Commission, and ordered national judges to apply national laws as if they distinguished pregnancy from "illness." In 1992, the Council adopted the pregnancy directive, catching up to the Court.

Finally, we illustrate one of our core arguments, namely that the progressive elaboration of EU rules generates an expansionary dynamic tending to recast policy processes and outcomes at the national level of governance. Consider the combined impact of two very different sex discrimination cases on the work of British courts. As noted above, in 1986 the Court agreed that existing British law requiring women to retire earlier than men violated the Equal Treatment Directive, and ordered British judges not only to apply British law in conformity with the ECJ's equal treatment case law, but to compensate Marshall for her losses. Compensation, however, proved to be a difficult task. Although the British industrial tribunal assessed damages at £19,405 plus interest, the British sex discrimination act set a ceiling for such awards at £6,250, and excluded interest payments. Upon reference of the matter by the House of Lords, the Court ruled, in *Marshall II* (ECJ 1993*a*), that EC law requires "full and complete compensation" (including interest), and that national rules that did not meet this standard be set aside by national judges.

In the second case, *Webb* (ECJ 1994), the ECJ declared that provisions of the UK's Sex Discrimination Act of 1975 must be construed by British courts so that

---

[18] We are aware of yet another example. In *Hertz* (ECJ 1990*c*), the Court enacted the main terms of the "burden of proof" directive, proposed by the Commission, and designed to place the burden of proof on the member-states in certain cases involving maternity and sex discrimination. The directive had been blocked by a UK veto.

they would conform to *Dekker*. In 1987, Mrs. Webb was hired by an air cargo company to replace a female clerk who was scheduled for maternity leave. During her training period, Webb discovered that she was pregnant. The company dismissed her, on the grounds that she was no longer able to do the job for which she was hired. Webb lost a succession of appeals, including a unanimous judgment of the House of Lords. British courts distinguished between *Dekker*, which prohibited the dismissal of a woman simply because she was pregnant, and Webb's dismissal for being unable to fulfill her contract. Further, the Lords, backed in oral argument by the UK government, had determined that discrimination was not at issue, since if a male employee had been hired to replace a pregnant woman and then requested an extended leave of absence, he too would have been dismissed. The Lords nevertheless agreed to refer the matter to the ECJ. The European Court, in a terse decision, found for Webb, implying that her case had already been decided by *Dekker*.

The *Dekker* and *Webb* line of cases, coupled with the *Marshall II* requirement for full compensation, opened a floodgate of claims from women discharged from the British armed forces. In the 1978–90 period, some 5500 women were discharged on the grounds that pregnancy made them unable to perform their duties. Before Marshall, following the government's understanding of EC law on the matter,[19] the Defense Ministry began settling claims at £3,000 per woman. In settlements reached after Marshall, courts awarded one woman £33,000 plus pension rights, and an air force pilot £173,000. As of spring 1994, 1800 compensation claims were pending (Current Survey 1994: 221).

In summary, lowest-common-denominator outcomes in the social provisions field, as fixed by directives adopted by the Council of Ministers and by national legal regimes controlled by member-state governments and parliaments, do not stick. The ECJ has interpreted directives broadly, in terms of their effects on individuals, as bearers of rights guaranteed under EC law. Member-state interpretations of these directives, to the extent that they would reduce the effectiveness of individual rights, are pushed aside. More dramatically, the Court has supplanted the Council as the locus of lawmaking on more than one occasion, enacting legislative provisions that had stalled in the Council under unanimity voting. Lacking the unanimity necessary to reverse the Court in this area, the member-state governments have been forced to adjust to the Court's case law, by ratifying the ECJ's policy choices in Council directives and by revising national legal regimes.

This last point deserves to be nuanced somewhat. In response to the *Barber* decision, the member-states addressed themselves as a constituent assembly to a decision of the Court. In the so-called "Barber protocol," attached to the Maastricht Treaty on European Union, the member-states declared that:

[T]he direct effect of Art. 119 may not be relied upon in order to claim entitlement to a pension with effect from a date prior to that of this judgment [the ruling in *Barber*, May

---

[19] In *Marshall I* (ECJ 1986*a*), the UK government had argued that EC law required only that compensation be possible under national law, not that it be full and complete.

17, 1990], except in the case of workers . . . who have before that date initiated legal proceedings or raised an equivalent claim under the applicable national law.

The protocol does not reverse the Court's ruling. On the contrary, the protocol selects, from among several possible interpretations, one way to understand the temporal effects of its decision, and asserts that this is the correct interpretation. Simply stated, their preferred interpretation gives the member-states the longest period possible to adjust to the dictates of Art. 119 (as interpreted by the Court in *Barber*). As principals, the member-states have acted but, relative to the means at their disposal, only weakly. While a definitive evaluation of how effective the protocol will be in constraining the Court is premature,[20] a recent study of post-protocol judgments reveals that the member-states have *not* induced the Court to abandoned its pre-protocol case law (Whiteford 1996). Thus, again, we find that intergovernmental capacity to control judicial outcomes is limited, even when governments—unanimously—try to do so.

3.1.3. Assessment

We believe that the EC legal system operates according to a generalizable dynamic. Individuals ask national judges to void national rules in favor or Euro-rules within a particular domain of activity. The interaction between national courts and the ECJ recasts the law governing that domain of activity, and therefore recasts the policymaking environment. As new rules are generated and existing rules are reinterpreted, member-states, whose national rules are now out of step with EC rules, are placed "in the shadow of the law": they can expect to be the target of litigation until they act to comply with the dictates of the ECJ's case law. Further, that case law enhances the capacity of individuals to initiate future litigation, by providing potential litigants with more precise information about the content and scope of European law. In process-tracing, we have seen, again, the self-sustaining dynamic at the heart of our model.

In emphasizing regularities in how the legal system operates, we do not mean to imply that market integration and the Europeanization of social policy have proceeded at the same rate. On the contrary, we have argued that transnational activity drives integration processes. If we are right, it must be that the construction of supranational governance does not proceed evenly. Instead, it must be that levels of integration vary, across sectors, as a function of differential rates of transnational exchange. It follows that the competence to govern in areas in which exchange across borders is relatively low, compared to areas in which exchange across borders is relatively high, will be more resistant to being transferred to the supranational level. If this is so, the EC will tend to

---

[20] The legal status of the Barber Protocol is ambiguous. Even if we accept that the Protocol enjoys a rank equivalent to that of Treaty provision, the problem of how to resolve a potential conflict between the terms of the Protocol and conflicting Treaty provisions remains. The Court's ruling in *Barber* is based on an authoritative interpretation of Art. 119 of the Treaty, and the Protocol may well have been meant to enshrine rules that are contrary to Art. 119 (see Hervey 1994).

respond better to the interests of manufacturers and investors, especially to holders of mobile capital, rather than the interests of labor unions and welfare recipients. Because of this, the EC will continue to rely heavily on existing welfare state regimes, operating at the national level, to supply the bulk of what we normally mean by social policy.

That said, considerable controversy exists as to how far the EC has departed from its market-perfection project, whether that project is defined narrowly as exploiting opportunities for economic exchange, or more broadly to include devising the "correct" rules to facilitate not only economic but also political exchange. Unlike free movement, which raises the prospects of large collective gains, social policy implies redistribution and market limitations. We do not mean to say that free movement (of goods and productive factors) does not redistribute income, wealth, and jobs, among other things. But the efficiency logic of free movement is that a portion of the collective gains can be used to compensate the losers. The rationale for social policy rests partly on a logic of legitimation, which is tied more closely to merit goods or provision based on need. Market integration might only be tolerable to the extent that the social problems that it inevitably generates are mitigated by public policy.

4. Conclusion

To conclude, we revisit our points of departure and draw out the consequences of our research for the broad themes advanced by this volume.

The chapter lays out a theory of legal integration that does not itself rely on the P–A construct. We nevertheless chose to employ the framework for heuristic reasons, and because intergovernmentalists have used it to organize their research on institutional politics in the EC. Delegated mandates, agency discretion, degree and kind of oversight, and compatibility of incentives between principals and agents provide appropriate and useful points of departure. But judicial politics in the EC is not easily captured by P–A imagery. The Court's constitutionalization of the treaty system produced profound structural changes. Among other things, it reconstituted relationships among the ECJ, national judges, and private and public actors at the national and transnational levels. Often enough, the impact of the Court's rule-making is to effectively constrain member-state governments, both individually and collectively. The P–A framework is ill-equipped to capture these dynamics.

How do these findings relate to the collaborative project? We have shown that movement from intergovernmental to supranational politics has taken place in two quite different policy sectors; our explanation of why this movement takes place is compatible with the theory developed in Chapter 1; and we have tested our theory quantitatively, and cross-checked it with more intensive case studies. We have also demonstrated that intergovernmental theories of integration and institutionalization are of little, if any, value in explaining the evolution and impact of the EC legal system.

When we examine the judicial process in any detail, intergovernmentalism immediately runs into problems. The Court's work is constantly monitored by the member-state governments, and governments regularly intervene in the judicial process, in the form of observations. But litigation and the law, not the governments, generate the context for the Court's activities. As we have seen, the Court interprets the Treaty and, therefore the legal obligations of the member-states, expansively. Put differently, we found that the ECJ follows a "logic of rules," oriented toward constructing a transnational polity. While the scope of the mandate was initially larger in free movement, the Court's activity in social policy has been no less intense, nor less faithful to a pro-integrative interpretation of the Treaty.

The Court is not setting down a pattern of jurisprudence that follows (or reflects) the positions of the most powerful governments. Instead, the evidence provides broad support for our view that the legal system operates in favor of those individuals and firms who are advantaged by European rules and regulation, and disadvantaged by national rules and practices. As important, the Court operates to saturate supranational political arenas with rules, and with rule-oriented modes of deliberating, a process that proceeds gradually but inevitably in areas of sustained judicial activity. To the extent that private and public actors adapt to this process and to these rules, the Court has reinforced the move to supranational governance, making it all but impossible to reverse.

APPENDIX

Table 4.A1. Judicial outcomes pursuant to Art. 177 references in the field of social provisions

	Consistent	Inconsistent
Belgium	9	4
Denmark	7	3
France	0	1
Germany	5	10
Ireland	1	3
Italy	2	1
Netherlands	8	13
United Kingdom	11	13

Note: Outcomes were coded as "consistent" if the ECJ declares the national rule or practice giving rise to the reference as consistent, or not in non-compliance, with EC law, and "inconsistent" if the ECJ declares the rule or practice to be inconsistent with, or in violation of, EC law.

Source: Data compiled by Rachel Cichowski and Alec Stone Sweet from the *European Court Reports*. The pool consists of the ninety-one decisions taken in the social provisions area, 1970–92.

Table 4.A2. Member-state government observations and judicial outcomes pursuant to Art. 177 references in the field of social provisions

	Successful	Unsuccessful
Belgium	2	3
Denmark	9	3
France	6	1
Germany	8	8
Ireland	2	4
Italy	6	3
Netherlands	9	13
United Kingdom	31	23
European Commission	73	10

Note: An observation is coded as "successful" when the ECJ agrees with the claim made in the observation (to the effect that the national rule or practice in question is either consistent or inconsistent with EC law). An observation is coded as "unsuccessful" when the ECJ disagrees with the claim made in the observation (to the effect that the national rule or practice is either consistent or inconsistent with EC law).

Source: Data compiled by Rachel Cichowski and Alec Stone Sweet from the *European Court Reports*. The pool consists of the ninety-one decisions taken in the social provisions area, 1970–92.

Table 4.A3. Art. 177 references: actual number, proportional share, and percentage difference

	A	B	C	D	E	F
Austria	−0.05%	−0.05%	−0.05%	−0.05%	−0.05%	0.55%
Actual number	0	0	0	0	0	1
Proportional share	0.4	0.4	0.1	0.3	0.2	0.1
Belgium	−4.89%	−6.83%	1.79%	−3.22%	17.56%	0.22%
Actual number	42	33	29	5	112	19
Proportional share	74.8	85.1	25.0	7.0	43.5	18.4
Denmark	−0.57%	−0.10%	0.17%	−2.07%	−1.81%	6.92%
Actual number	10	15	5	0	1	15
Proportional share	13.8	15.7	4.6	1.3	8.0	3.4
France	0.23%	−3.72%	13.72%	−1.21%	−4.01%	−12.90%
Actual number	116	102	69	10	51	7
Proportional share	114.3	130.0	38.2	10.7	66.4	28.5
Germany	9.32%	13.54%	−11.03%	15.8%	−5.62%	−6.28%
Actual number	265	334	43	29	96	40
Proportional share	202.3	230.0	67.5	18.9	117.6	50.3
Greece	−0.73%	−0.26%	−0.29%	−1.18%	−0.67%	−0.58%
Actual number	3	7	2	0	2	1
Proportional share	7.9	8.9	2.6	0.8	4.6	2.0
Ireland	−0.38%	1.23%	0.66%	−1.13%	−0.61%	1.87%
Actual number	5	18	4	0	2	5
Proportional share	7.5	8.6	2.5	0.7	4.4	1.9
Italy	−0.82%	1.71%	2.27%	−0.66%	−11.82%	−7.97%
Actual number	84	115	35	8	6	9
Proportional share	89.4	101.6	29.9	8.4	51.9	22.2
Luxembourg	−0.30%	−0.39%	−0.60%	−1.05%	−0.28%	−0.45%
Actual number	5	5	1	0	3	1
Proportional share	8.8	10.0	2.9	0.8	5.1	2.2
Netherlands	−1.43%	−2.34%	−4.45%	0.02%	5.73%	2.50%
Actual number	86	91	22	9	78	28
Proportional share	95.5	108.6	31.9	8.9	55.5	23.8
Portugal	0.51%	−0.54%	1.25%	−0.54%	−0.28%	−0.54%
Actual number	7	0	4	0	1	0
Proportional share	3.6	4.1	1.2	0.3	2.1	0.9
Spain	0.27%	−1.11%	1.31%	−1.37%	−0.09%	−0.77%
Actual number	11	2	6	0	5	1
Proportional share	9.2	10.4	3.1	0.9	5.3	2.3
Sweden	0.19%	−0.11%	−0.11%	−0.11%	−0.11%	−0.11%
Actual number	2	0	0	0	0	0
Proportional share	0.7	0.8	0.2	0.1	0.4	0.1
UK	−1.34%	−1.04%	−4.63%	−3.24%	2.05%	17.54%
Actual number	34	41	4	2	33	40
Proportional share	42.9	48.8	14.3	4.0	24.9	10.7

A = Free movement of goods; B = Agriculture; C = Competition and dumping; D = External policy; E = Social security; F = Social provisions; G = Environment; H = Establishment; I = Free movement of workers; J = Taxes; K = Transportation; L = Common policy; M = Approximation of laws; N = Other. Actual number indicates the number of Art. 177 references in that legal domain for each member-state. Proportional share entries are the number of cases that each member-state *would have registered* in each legal domain if there were no difference between overall litigation rates for each member-state and rates of litigation for each member-state in each policy area. Thus, if Germany accounts for 30 percent of the references overall we by legal subject matter

G	H	I	J	K	L	M	N
-0.05%	**-0.05%**	**-0.05%**	**-0.05%**	**1.42%**	**-0.05%**	**-0.05%**	**-0.05%**
0	0	0	0	1	0	0	0
0.2	0.1	0.1	0.1	0.04	0.02	0.1	0.3
-6.61%	**5.91%**	**11.47%**	**-3.13%**	**7.96%**	**-8.94%**	**-0.52%**	**-0.21%**
2	28	31	20	13	1	15	66
4.9	18.3	15.3	27.8	7.6	5.0	16.8	67.3
0.21%	**-1.46%**	**-2.07%**	**4.36%**	**6.76%**	**0.16%**	**0.06%**	**-1.57%**
1	1	0	16	6	1	3	3
0.9	3.4	2.8	5.1	1.4	0.9	3.1	12.4
5.64%	**0.60%**	**-5.41%**	**-3.43%**	**-5.32%**	**-8.20%**	**-0.07%**	**8.95%**
10	29	16	34	8	4	24	157
7.5	27.9	23.3	42.4	11.6	7.7	25.7	102.7
-27.96%	**-14.99%**	**0.43%**	**-0.91%**	**-2.29%**	**9.77%**	**-9.66%**	**-11.49%**
1	25	42	73	19	18	29	113
13.3	49.4	41.3	75.1	20.5	13.6	45.5	181.8
-1.18%	**3.70%**	**-0.45%**	**-0.38%**	**-1.18%**	**-1.18%**	**-1.18%**	**-1.80%**
0	8	1	2	0	0	0	18
0.5	1.9	1.6	2.9	0.8	0.5	1.8	7.1
-1.13%	**0.09%**	**-0.40%**	**-1.13%**	**-1.13%**	**3.32%**	**-1.13%**	**-0.63%**
0	2	1	0	0	2	0	3
0.5	1.8	1.5	2.8	0.8	0.5	1.7	6.8
32.10%	**1.89%**	**-6.06%**	**2.30%**	**-7.48%**	**4.42%**	**10.05%**	**3.56%**
20	25	10	39	4	8	33	102
5.9	21.8	18.3	33.2	9.1	6.0	20.1	80.3
-1.05%	**1.39%**	**1.87%**	**-0.64%**	**0.42%**	**-1.05%**	**0.37%**	**0.94%**
0	4	4	1	1	0	2	12
0.6	2.2	1.8	3.3	0.9	0.6	1.9	7.9
1.64%	**-2.08%**	**-3.32%**	**3.00%**	**-2.51%**	**-0.94%**	**2.04%**	**1.65%**
7	20	15	43	8	6	23	96
6.3	23.3	19.5	35.4	9.7	6.4	21.5	85.8
-0.54%	**0.07%**	**-0.54%**	**0.67%**	**0.93%**	**1.69%**	**0.17%**	**-0.37%**
0	1	0	3	1	1	1	1
0.2	0.9	0.7	1.3	0.4	0.2	0.8	3.2
-1.37%	**4.73%**	**-0.64%**	**-0.16%**	**-1.37%**	**-1.37%**	**1.47%**	**-0.04%**
0	10	1	3	0	0	4	8
0.6	2.2	1.9	3.4	0.9	0.6	2.1	8.2
-0.11%	**0.50%**	**-0.11%**	**-0.11%**	**-0.11%**	**-0.11%**	**-0.11%**	**0.06%**
0	1	0	0	0	0	0	1
0.1	0.2	0.2	0.3	0.1	0.1	0.2	0.7
0.41%	**-0.31%**	**5.27%**	**-0.39%**	**3.88%**	**2.48%**	**-1.45%**	**-2.60%**
3	10	16	15	7	4	7	23
2.8	10.5	8.8	15.9	4.4	2.9	9.7	38.5

assigned a Proportional share of 30 percent of the references in each policy area to Germany. In other words Proportional share is the "table of no association" (the basis of the chi-squared test). Bold entries are "percentage differences," which are calculated the following way: (Actual number – Proportional share)/total number of references in the legal domain. These entries are indicative of the positive or negative extent to which litigants are attacking the rules of a particular member-state in a particular legal domain relative to other member-states and other areas.

5

The Emergence of a Supranational Telecommunications Regime

WAYNE SANDHOLTZ

TEN years ago, telecommunications in Europe was a patchwork of national systems, dominated in each country by a state monopoly, the PTT.[1] The Commission's efforts to bring telecommunications to Brussels had by 1986 yielded meager results. National governments possessed ample incentives for retaining control of the PTTs: they were frequently an instrument of industrial and employment policies, as well as a generator of revenues that could be siphoned off for other state purposes. Nevertheless, by 1996 new EU rules were abolishing the PTT monopolies and putting in place a regime for EU-wide markets for equipment, services, and infrastructure.[2] The aim of this chapter is to provide a theory-driven account of these developments.

The telecommunications case is an important one given the aims of this volume. We posit a causal connection between rising levels of cross-border transactions and European integration. In the modern economy, all of the relevant transactions—trade, finance, investment, production, distribution—occur via or require telecommunications networks. Markets are frequently not a physical location but rather a set of telecommunications links. Some transactions (payments, currency trades) exist only as electronic pulses carried over telecommunications networks. Telecommunications is thus the essential infrastructure of the modern economy. Increases in cross-border economic transactions strongly imply a mounting need for international telecommunications facilities. In other words, if transactions drive European integration, then

---

[1] The only exception being the UK, which liberalized telecommunications in 1981.

[2] "Equipment" refers both to network equipment (the lines and switches) and terminal equipment (devices connected to the network by users, including telephones, modems, faxes, local branch exchanges, and so on). "Services" refers to the various types of communications offered on a network (voice telephony, data communications, mobile communications, forwarding, paging, voice mail, databases, and so on). "Infrastructure" refers to the network itself, including the tasks of maintenance and management. The basic infrastructure historically consisted of the network of lines with copper wires running to each house or business. Today there are parallel and linked infrastructures: satellites, microwave transmission, cellular networks, and cable television networks (which can be used for telecommunications).

telecommunications is one policy domain where we should observe significant movement toward supranational governance. Such movement would be especially meaningful since the Treaty of Rome made no mention of an EC role in telecommunications. Indeed, at the founding of the EC, no one could have imagined anything but national monopolies.

This chapter also speaks to one of the central theoretical controversies in the study of integration. Intergovernmentalist theory holds that supranational organizations and transnational actors exercise no independent impact on EU politics. Governments, in this view, sometimes delegate certain functions to the Commission or the European Court of Justice, which remain on a short leash. EU outcomes are the result of bargaining among the member-states. Our theory of institutionalization denies these assertions. We argue that supranational organizations and transnational actors do exert an autonomous influence on EU politics. By tracing the process by which an EU telecommunications regime came into being, this chapter can determine the extent to which member-states controlled policy outcomes, versus the degree to which the Commission, the Court, and transnational actors drove developments.

The evidence is clear: the EU has created a supranational policy domain in telecommunications, and the initiative came primarily from the Commission, armed with legal precedents from the European Court of Justice and acting in alliance with societal groups that had a stake in efficient pan-European telecommunications. Movement toward supranational politics occurred along all three of our dimensions (rules, supranational organizations, transnational society). Furthermore, shifts toward supranationality in one dimension tended to produce or reinforce parallel shifts in the other two.

Section 1 summarizes the volume's theoretical framework as I will use it to structure the telecommunications case study. Section 2 looks at the "transactors" (societal groups), explaining why the PTT system harmed their interests and why European integration was their preferred solution. Section 3 describes the intergovernmental starting point, in terms of the PTT system and the nature of member-state preferences. Section 4 is an account of how the interested groups and the Commission exploited existing EC rules and institutions to integrate telecommunications policymaking. It documents movement along the dimensions in two phases of telecommunications policy integration. A brief conclusion closes the chapter.

1. Theory and Case

The core empirical proposition of this volume is that the European Union has transformed itself from a largely intergovernmental arrangement (the founding treaties) into a supranational polity. The intergovernmental–supranational continuum is a way to make that claim more nuanced by recognizing: (i) that the distinction invoked is not a dichotomy, and (ii) that specific policy domains can be located at different points along the continuum. The three dimensions (rules, supranational organizations, transnational society) offer ways of identifying and charting movement along the continuum. We suggested, for example, that as the EU becomes more supranational, we should expect to see more informal norms as well as formal rules (legislation, jurisprudence), more domains added to the competences of EU bodies, increasing autonomy of EU organizations, and the expansion of linkages among societal actors across borders and between EU bodies and societal actors.

We also suggested that there is a logic of institutionalization: once supranational rules, organizations, and transnational society have begun to emerge, they become important intervening or even causal variables. In some cases, because of "path-dependence" effects or the gaps in "principal" controls over "agents" (Chapters 2 and 8), national governments cannot pull policymaking back toward an intergovernmental or national mode. In other instances, supranational rules and organizations and transnational coalitions push the EU further toward the supranational pole. Supranational rules and organizations provide the context for determining interests and behaviors thereafter. Subsequent behaviors, policy debates, and disputes take place in a context in which the range of possibilities has been shaped by past practices, legislation, and judicial precedent.

What, then, initiates such a loop of institutional development? We argued, taking our cue from Deutsch and Haas, that societal actors engaged in cross-border communications and exchange ("transactors") are the motor driving integration. These are the people who need European standards, rules, or dispute-resolution mechanisms—who need integration. The causal mechanism is quite simple: increasing levels of cross-border transactions and communications by societal actors will increase the perceived need for supranational policymaking. In fact, the absence of European rules and coordination inhibits transactors from realizing their values. As Walter Mattli argues, state actors have their own interests; two fundamental ones are to maximize their own autonomy and to maximize the generation of wealth within their territory. In defense of their autonomy, states will frequently resist the shift toward supranational policymaking. But as they do so, they inhibit the generation of wealth within their territories by those actors that depend on European transactions. Maximizing autonomy therefore has its cost in prosperity. Since political leaders must generate prosperity to satisfy their constituencies, blocking integration for more than the short run is unsustainable (Mattli, forthcoming).

Thus, though states remain powerful actors in a supranational context, commanding important resources, they do not ultimately control the integration process. Societal transactors provide the impetus for integration. And once the dynamic logic of institutionalization is underway, it shapes the context in which actors—EU bodies, national governments, and non-state actors—define and pursue their interests. States, in fact, are embedded in supranational politics that they can influence but neither dictate nor control.

The integration of telecommunications policymaking in the EU provides a case in which the plausibility of most of these propositions can be probed. The role of societal transactors will be played by those groups whose well-being depends on cross-border communications and exchange within Europe: telecommunications users, and providers of equipment, services, and infrastructures. We would expect to find that rising levels of exchange across national borders (trade, finance, production, mergers, and acquisitions) increases the demand for state-of-the-art, pan-European telecommunications services, which in turn leads to demands by transactors for policy integration. We would expect transactors to exploit whatever opportunities European institutions afforded. We would further expect European organizations like the Commission and the Court to use existing rules in creative ways so as to advance integration. Member-states will frequently oppose or obstruct telecommunications policy integration, but they can be outflanked. The result should be movement toward supranational policymaking: new European rules, European organizations, and an expanding transnational society in telecommunications.

In fact, the telecommunications case confirms the expectations generated by our theory. By themselves, single cases do not make or break theories. They can, however, serve useful purposes in theory building and testing. Case studies are ideal for "process-tracing," which allows us to verify that the apparent empirical relationships we observe are not merely correlations. We find in the telecommunications case both the outcomes and the causal relationships that our theory posits.

2. The Transactors and Their Problem

An explanation of the transition from state monopolies to supranational policymaking begins with the societal actors for whom the PTT monopolies were increasingly costly and problematic. The key to the story in telecommunications is this: as the level of cross-border telecommunications rose, Europe's patchwork of national monopolies became increasingly dysfunctional. The expansion of intra-European economic activity—exchange of goods and services, finance and investment, management of multinational firms—entailed an increase in telecommunications traffic among EU countries.

Telecommunications networks are the essential infrastructure of the modern economy. Trade depends on communication between buyers and sellers. But the importance of telecommunications goes well beyond business people using their phones and faxes. Cross-border services—banking, investment, airline reservations systems—require constant, real-time data communication. Multinational firms coordinating and managing their affiliates in different member-states often need permanently open voice and data lines. Moreover, technological change has created new and more demanding *kinds* of communication: high-volume data and graphics, as well as various combinations of text,

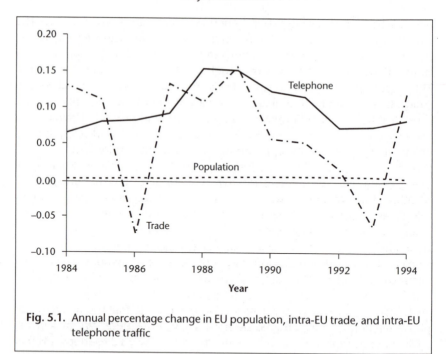

Fig. 5.1. Annual percentage change in EU population, intra-EU trade, and intra-EU telephone traffic

data, sound, and images. In other words, as economic integration progressed, Europe saw a steady increase in the number of actors who needed to communicate across borders and those actors required new and more demanding kinds of intra-European telecommunications.

Fig. 5.1 shows that cross-border calling in the EU has grown faster than both population and intra-EU trade for 1984–94 (telephone traffic data are unavailable for the period before 1983). Cross-border calling grew much faster than population. Growth in intra-EU calling seems to track the growth of trade, though usually at a higher rate and with less dramatic swings. If we take intra-EU trade as a rough measure of economic integration, my argument would imply a strong correlation between intra-Union commerce and intra-EU cross-border telecommunications traffic. As Table 5.1 shows, the correlation between trade and telecommunications for 1983–92 is very strong indeed (0.95), substantially stronger than the correlations between telecommunications and GDP or telecommunications and population (though both are also high). The analysis of panel data (see Table 5.2) with year-on-year change in telephone traffic as the dependent variable reinforces the close link between economic integration and cross-border telecommunications. In this multivariate regression, only the coefficient for "trade" achieves significance; the adjusted R^2 is 0.68 and the Durbin–Watson statistic is in the acceptable range (at 2.04). The data analysis is consistent with my proposition that economic integration in the EU leads to increased demand for cross-border telecommunications.

Table 5.1. Correlations between intra-EU
cross-border telephone traffic
and trade, GDP, and population

	Intra-EU cross-border telephone traffic
Intra-EU trade	.95
GDP	.85
Population	.76

Sources: Telephone data come from the International Telecommunications Union. Trade is the annual value of both imports and exports within the European Union. Trade data are from *Eurostat: External Trade, 1958–1993*. GDP data are from the *World Tables 1970–1994*, published by the World Bank. Population data are from the *World Tables of Economic and Social Indicators*, ICPSR 9300, the World Bank, second release. The years covered in the model are 1983–92. The countries are Belgium, Denmark, France, Germany, Greece, Ireland, Italy, Netherlands, Portugal, Spain, and the UK. N = 109.

Table 5.2. Pooled cross-sectional time-series analysis

	Intra-EU cross-border telephone traffic		
	Coefficient	*t*-statistic	Probability
Intra-EC trade	0.000587	2.4921	0.0147
GDP	0.003124	0.1682	0.8669
Population	0.011361	0.7128	0.4779
Adjusted R^2	0.68		
N	98		
Durbin–Watson	2.04		

Note: Coefficients are unstandardized. Each of the ninety-eight observations is for a particular country in a particular year. The model is a fixed-effects, pooled, cross-sectional time series, GLS regression model and was estimated using Econometric View 2.0. The dependent variable is the change from the previous year in telephone calls to other EU countries, in millions of minutes.

Sources: Telephone data come from the International Telecommunications Union. Trade is the annual value of both imports and exports within the European Union. Trade data are from *Eurostat: External Trade, 1958–1993*. GDP data are from the *World Tables 1970–1994*, published by the World Bank. Population data are from the *World Tables of Economic and Social Indicators*, ICPSR 9300, the World Bank, second release. The years covered in the model are 1983–92. The countries are Belgium, Denmark, France, Germany, Greece, Ireland, Italy, Netherlands, Portugal, Spain, and the UK. We are missing data for Denmark in 1992 and thus the total is ninety-eight.

In the following subsections, first, I briefly explain the technological revolution in telecommunications to show how it opened potentially vast markets for new services and equipment; and, second, describe those actors whose emerging telecommunications needs put them at odds with the PTT system.

2.1. Technological revolution

The telecommunications sector has been in an ongoing technological revolution for the past two decades. New transmission modes have created alternatives to the terrestrial network of copper wires. Microwave relays and satellites permit transmission without laying cable. Fiber-optic cable is now replacing coaxial cable on main lines, with enormous advantages: greater capacity (by at least ten times), greater immunity to electromagnetic interference, lower rates of signal attenuation, and declining prices (the primary material, silica, is abundant). By way of illustration: the first trans-Atlantic coaxial cable, which entered into operation in 1956, could carry thirty-six simultaneous conversations; the first trans-Atlantic fiber-optic cable, beginning service in 1988, could carry 40,000 calls simultaneously (Ungerer and Costello 1988: 64).

But the decisive revolution in telecommunications technologies began with the advent of the integrated circuit in the 1970s. Advances in microelectronics (faster, more powerful chips at steadily declining prices) were at the heart of the now-famous marriage of computing and telecommunications.[3] What emerged was the possibility of digitized, electronic telecommunications switching and transmission. The upshot of the microelectronics revolution is that computers can "talk" directly to each other without having to convert their digital information into analog signals for transmission through the telephone system. In fact, any form of information—text, images, moving pictures, music—can be digitized and sent directly through the phone lines in "packets" of electronic "1s" and "0s." The digital revolution, still underway, has transformed huge swathes of the economy that now rely on constant, reliable, high-volume data communications: banking, insurance, and securities; airlines and travel; publishing; medicine; design, engineering, and manufacturing; distribution; retailing; and more. There has been a similar proliferation of advanced telecommunications services available to consumers: paging, messaging, cellular phones, and online computer services.

The technological revolution led to an explosion of new telecommunications equipment and services, which meant upheaval in a vast range of markets. Producers of new devices and services wanted access to networks and customers. Existing businesses began to discover that their competitiveness depended on access to those new devices and services. For both sets of actors, the PTTs were too slow and inefficient.

2.2. The transactors

If societal transactors are ultimately driving integration, we must clearly specify who these actors were and why they would prefer telecommunications policymaking at the EC-level to the existing fragmentation. Four sets of actors

---

[3] A variety of neologisms capture the resulting hybrid: information technologies, telematics, *informatique*.

supported liberalization and coordination at the European level. The key societal actors involved in constructing an EC telecommunications regime were the principal equipment manufacturers, major business users,[4] new service providers, and potential operators of alternative infrastructures. This section briefly identifies their interests.

2.2.1. Equipment manufacturer

All of the major electronics firms in Europe produced a variety of telecommunications equipment, ranging from the large central exchanges (switches) to telephone handsets. Historically, each had cozy ties to its PTT. The PTTs purchased their network equipment from a privileged set (never more than three) of national producers. In Britain, for example, the British Post Office (which was the telecommunications operator until the 1980s) bought switches only from the so-called "ring" of domestic suppliers—GEC, Plessey, and STC—whose shares of BPO orders were respectively fixed at 40 percent, 40 percent, and 20 percent (Van Tulder and Junne 1984: 46). Telecommunications equipment procurement was commonly a tool of industrial policy, allowing governments to keep national champion electronics firms afloat and even to subsidize their research and development more broadly. Technical standards (again, set by the PTTs) reinforced the preference for domestic suppliers. Each national system operated on its own technical standards and it was prohibitively costly for a manufacturer to develop switches (the big ticket item) customized for each national standard. In any case, the PTTs would have ignored foreign bids.

Why did the equipment producers lose their taste for a system that had nourished them for so long? The technological revolution was again crucial. The first electronic switch entered the market in 1972. After that, the development costs of succeeding generations of faster and more capable digital switches soared. The R&D expense associated with developing a digital public exchange in the mid-1980s was as high as $1.4bn. (Dang-Nguyen 1986: 108). To recoup the development costs, a maker would have to sell some $14bn. to $16bn. worth of switches. The problem was that no single country had a switch market of that scale (Van Tulder and Junne 1984: 70). Makers of terminal equipment (telephones, modems, fax machines) also faced monopsony PTT buyers, which meant they were limited to producing and selling items that the PTT was willing to offer. Furthermore, the manufacturers were largely confined to producing for their domestic market, because of the differences in standards between countries and the preferential procurement practices of the PTTs.

2.2.2. Business users

Large firms with extensive cross-national transactions within Europe, as well as multinationals needing to coordinate subsidiaries and facilities in different EC

---

[4] "Users" refers to consumers of telecommunications equipment and services; many large enterprises are important consumers of advanced services and equipment.

countries, also found the PTT monopolies increasingly unable to meet their telecommunications needs. As intra-EC commerce expanded, and as the number of transnational mergers and acquisitions involving EC firms increased, business demand for cross-border telecommunications rose. Both trade and cross-national mergers and acquisitions received a boost from the Single Market program in the mid-1980s.

Equally important, major business users were also discovering that advanced telecommunications services were an element of competitive advantage. That is, low-cost, flexible, high-capacity telecommunications links could give firms specific advantages over their rivals (Bar and Borrus 1987: 4). Because the USA had deregulated telecommunications earlier and more completely than any other country, American companies had access to a greater variety of the latest equipment and services, all at lower prices. European firms feared that the telecommunications advantage gave US competitors an edge. In addition to needing a greater volume of cross-border communications, European companies also needed better access to the most advanced services.

Modernization of the networks was part of the problem—since the PTTs operated in a monopoly setting, the innovations came more slowly and at higher prices than in the USA. Liberalization (opening the market to competition) was also a piece of the problem. In fact, all of the PTTs were modernizing, and in the UK the public monopoly had been abolished and competition introduced in 1981. But the overarching difficulty, especially given the rising demand for state-of-the-art, cross-border communications, was the fragmented condition of Europe. Even when PTTs introduced new services, they did so without coordination. The new services on offer were incompatible from country to country, which meant that they didn't really exist for a user needing telecommunications links between, say, Copenhagen and Barcelona.[5] To establish a dedicated line linking those two cities (between for example a factory in one and a design center in the other) required separate arrangements with each PTT in between. Correcting malfunctions could become a nightmare. A policy paper published by the Roundtable of European Industrialists, whose membership includes many of Europe's largest multinationals, highlighted the problems caused for business by diverse national equipment approval rules, the incompatibility of services across borders, and the lack of coordinated planning for new services and networks (Roundtable of European Industrialists, 1986: 16–19).

Thus modernization and liberalization could, in theory, happen within each national telecommunications market and still not address the need to facilitate cross-border communications. As it turned out, major telecommunications users went to the Commission to push for both liberalization and EC-wide coordination.

---

[5] e.g. packet-switched data networks nominally using the X.25 standard could function at only 4.8 kilobits per second for trans-border traffic, compared to 48 kilobits per second domestically in the mid-1980s. See Roundtable of European Industrialists (1986: 9–12).

2.2.3. New service providers

Telecommunications has seen a proliferation in the number and variety of services that can be offered over the network. For decades, the telecommunications system was simply a medium for carrying telephone conversations. The possibility of data communications—the transmission of information from one computer to another via the telecommunications network—opened an immense new market for services geared toward businesses. It became possible to transmit voice, text, data, and images within and between firms. "Teleconferencing" (with video) became possible, as did computation services, the operation of "private" circuits (linking two or more sites within a firm), real-time tracking of inventory and distribution, and so on. An array of services for consumers also opened up, including message storage and forwarding; on-line information; "home" banking and travel reservations; paging and mobile telephony. The next stage will integrate voice, text, data, images, and moving pictures in a "multimedia" digital network serving households; it will be able to deliver ordinary telephony, online services, music, and movies on demand, and who knows what else.

The proliferation of potential services has attracted a variety of enterprises, large and small, hoping to offer new services via the telecommunications system. It is difficult to classify these newcomers. Some are established computer companies planning to offer various data services; others are media companies (publishing and entertainment, for example) preparing various online services. Many are "start-ups" hoping to exploit a particular niche. Service providers do not need to own or operate the network itself; they only need to be able to connect to it. The problem in Europe was that the PTTs controlled the approval process for connecting to the public network. In essence, companies hoping to offer services in competition with the PTT had to apply to the PTT for permission to do so. The PTTs began, of course, in a position of monopoly regarding the provision of telecommunications services, and only gradually began to license alternative services in specific niches. New entrants also wanted to meet the growing demand for advanced trans-border services within Europe. Naturally, they saw the incompatibilities among national systems as a major obstacle to offering pan-European services. Firms hoping to provide new services, or to compete with the PTTs in existing services, thus joined the band supporting liberalization and coordination at the EC level.

2.2.4. Alternative infrastructures

The ultimate potential competitors for the PTTs were actors who could build and operate telecommunications networks. The source of PTT power was their control of the infrastructure. The availability of alternative infrastructures would open competition in equipment and services. In recent years, a variety of industries have stepped forward with plans to build and operate telecommunications networks parallel to the existing monopolies. Railway operators were among the first to seek to build such networks. In each country, the railways own right-of-way linking the principal towns and cities—precisely the nodes for the "trunk lines" of a telecommunications network, as well as the most profitable markets. For instance, Mercury, the first company licensed to build infrastructure to compete with British Telecom, laid its fiber-optic cable along the tracks of British Railways.

Mobile (cellular) telephone operators (where these are not the PTTs) have generally been obliged to connect to the PTT's terrestrial network; they have pressed to be allowed to establish other terrestrial connections. The cable television (CATV) operators are natural competitors for the telecommunications monopolies. Cable TV networks own both distribution networks and links to individual households. Furthermore, television cables have greater capacity (bandwidth) than existing telephone lines and are therefore more immediately usable for the integrated multimedia telecommunications of the near future. Finally, water and electric utilities have also entered the fray. They too hope to piggyback on the widespread distribution networks that they already own.

For each of these groups—equipment manufacturers, major users, providers of new services, and owners of alternative infrastructures—domestic reforms were unacceptably slow and piecemeal. In any case, even domestic liberalization was not enough for transactors who needed markets of European scale (suppliers of equipment and services) or for those whose businesses required efficient communications across Europe (telecommunications users). These transactors consequently turned toward Brussels, for what they really needed was EC-level liberalization and harmonization. The Commission struck alliances with these various groups to push a liberalizing agenda under an emerging EC regulatory regime.

3. The Intergovernmental Starting Point

In this section I lay out the initial conditions in European telecommunications policymaking. The first part reviews the chronology of telecommunications reform in the member-states. The second part briefly examines the complete absence of telecommunications policymaking at the European level during the first few decades of the EC's existence.

3.1. The PTTs and the member-states

In European countries, the seemingly untouchable status of the PTTs had its roots in the longstanding conception of the telephone system as a natural monopoly and branch of the state. Since building the network (trunk lines, switching systems, and "local loops") entailed massive capital outlays, only a single provider could achieve the necessary economies of scale. Each additional user connected to the network reduced the average cost per line. Furthermore, the greater the number of households and businesses connected, the greater became the value of the system to each of them (because there was a greater number of telephone communications possible). Given the technological and economic realities, the case for natural monopolies was a logical one (indeed, competing networks became feasible only with the advent of alternative technologies).

In Europe, the telecommunications monopolies became a branch of the state. Governments wanted to ensure complete national coverage, with the obvious political pressure to have uniform pricing even for remote and rural areas (which, if charged on a cost basis, would pay vastly more for telephone service than the urban centers). Governments also took an interest in the national security implications of the networks. Finally, there was a deeper historical and institutional logic to the public monopolies. When countries undertook the building of telegraph systems, the postal service was the obvious agency to own and operate the lines. After all, the postal service had branch offices all over the country, and telegraph messages were seen as an alternative to letters. The military, of course, also perceived the importance of an efficient telegraph system under state control. When the telephone made its appearance, it was seen as an alternative to the telegraph. The postal service already had a network of wires, so the state added telephones to the post and telegraph service, creating the classic European PTT (post, telegraph, and telephone agency).

The PTTs, generally housed within a ministry of posts and telecommunications (MPT), maintained complete control over the national telecommunications systems. The employees of the PTT thus had civil servant status and could be expected to resist any changes that might affect their security of employment or government pensions. The PTTs owned the network infrastructure, provided all of the services, and supplied the terminal equipment (phones, modems, and so on). The ministries responsible for owning and operating the telecommunications network were also charged with regulating the sector (establishing standards and equipment approval procedures) and setting rates. Furthermore, governments siphoned the profits from the monopoly, frequently to offset losses in the unprofitable postal service, or to subsidize the high-technology electronics industries (as in France), or even to augment state revenues in the general budget. Furthermore, because the PTTs were major employers (frequently the largest single employer in a country, as in Germany), governments could use the posts and telecommunications administrations as a tool for employment policy.

Given the sacrosanct status of the PTTs, not to mention the concrete financial and policy benefits they provided to governments, it is not surprising that telecommunications liberalization has proceeded slowly in almost all EU member-states. In fact, the *timing* of telecommunications reforms has analytical significance. For the Commission to have acted merely as an agent of the member governments, it would have to be the case that the states had clear preferences that shaped and delimited the Commission's mandate. If the intergovernmentalist account is to be plausible, member-state preferences for the policies ultimately adopted had to exist *prior to* the emergence of Commission initiatives. In fact, however, European governments in the early 1980s were just beginning to grope for new models; there were no national telecommunications reform strategies in place (excepting Britain) until the latter half of the 1980s. The Commission had defined the key elements of its plan for EU-level liberalization and coordination as early as 1979, before states really knew what they wanted. The following paragraphs briefly review the timing of events in the member-states.

The *United Kingdom* is the only EU state where telecommunications reform occurred early, and thus the only state whose preferences for liberalization (if not an EU-level regime) were chronologically in step with the Commission's thinking. The Thatcher government separated British Telecom (BT) from the British Post Office in 1981 and privatized BT in 1984. The government authorized the first rival network operator, Mercury, in 1981 and created an independent regulator (Oftel) that same year. The terminal equipment market was opened to competition in 1984. The UK has been the lone state supporting the majority of the Commission's proposals to liberalize telecommunications markets. But given the deep ambivalence toward European integration in both the Thatcher and Major governments, the UK has not been a source of leadership and initiative for EU telecommunications reform.

Liberalization has been later and slower in *France*. The terminals market was partially open by the early 1980s; the Chirac government opened the market for value-added services (VANS) and licensed a second cellular provider in 1987. The Direction Générale des Télécommunications (DGT), an agency of the French government, was still the overwhelmingly dominant supplier (including cellular). Its operational arm was reorganized and renamed France Télécom in 1988. France Télécom remained under the ministry of posts and telecommunications, and was only separated from La Poste in 1990. It retained its monopoly in the basic domains (network provision, telephone, and telex). The French government in 1996 promised to establish a fully independent regulator and to privatize France Télécom; it has also signaled that it will introduce competition in the provision of networks and basic telephony as of January 1998, as required by EU rules (Noam 1992: 163–6; *Financial Times* 1996).

In *Germany*, the Bundespost was the entrenched monopoly. The European Commission compelled the Bundespost to end its monopoly of cordless telephones in 1985. Until 1986, the Bundespost was the sole supplier of modems, and even then it retained its monopoly on the provision of the first handset. The study of reform options did not begin until 1985 when the Witte Commission began its work. The Witte report in 1987 recommended reforms that fell short of full deregulation or privatization. Even those proposals were watered down in the government bill that passed in July 1989, separating a (renamed) Deutsche Telekom from the ministry of posts and telecommunications. The 1989 bill liberalized the terminals market (including first handsets). A second cellular operator did not begin service until 1990. The German government has promised to privatize Deutsche Telekom in advance of the full liberalization of networks and services that will take place, as required by the EU, at the beginning of 1998 (Noam 1992: 90–8; *Financial Times* 1995).

The *Netherlands* began to consider telecoms reform in 1981, but nothing happened until a telecommunications reform bill passed in 1986, converting the PTT into a state-owned holding company separate from the postal service. The reform liberalized the markets for terminals and "enhanced" services (VANS) starting in 1989. *Belgium* was more reluctant. The Belgian reform bill passed only in 1991, creating Belgacom as a state-owned enterprise with a monopoly on basic telephone service. Even then, the government imposed restrictive conditions on the licensing of new VANS and on the use of leased lines. In *Denmark*, the liberalization plan prepared in 1986 followed the guidelines emerging at the EC. Opening of the terminals market began in 1986 and was complete by 1990. A second cellular operator was authorized in 1990, but Denmark actually reduced internal competition in other telecommunications market segments to prepare for the increased European competition being mandated by the EU. Various restructuring plans emerged in *Italy* in the late 1980s, but liberalization was not on the agenda. A second cellular operator has been licensed but has made little headway against an obstructionist PTT (Noam 1992). Telecommunications liberalization was not on the agenda in *Greece*, *Ireland*, *Luxembourg*, and *Portugal* during the period in which the Commission was issuing its proposals.

For purposes of immediate comparison, and previewing the accounts to follow, we can briefly review what the Commission proposed and when. The Commission issued its first major policy statement in 1979. It declared that the overarching objective should be the creation of a European market for telecommunications equipment and services. Commission proposals in 1980, 1983, and 1984 fleshed out the goal of a Community-wide telecommunications market with specific measures. This brief chronological sketch of Commission and national telecommunications reform initiatives makes clear that the Commission was generally ahead of the member-states. Even the UK's liberalization of telecommunications followed the Commission's 1979 statement on pan-European markets by some two years. Most of the member-states did not begin contemplating domestic liberalization until the mid- and late-1980s or later.

3.2. The intergovernmental origins, 1957–77

The Treaty of the EEC makes no mention of telecommunications at all, not even as one of the domains for potential policy coordination in the indefinite future. It simply was not seen as a common market issue. Subsequent Council directives opening public procurement to competition in the EC excluded the public utilities, namely telecommunications, along with water, transport, and energy (Sauter 1995a: 188; Council Directives 71/305/EEC and 77/62/EEC). The telecommunications sector was also considered to be beyond the reach of EC competition rules. The PTTs were thought to be protected by Art. 90(2), justifying exemptions for the provision of public services, and Art. 222, regarding the special status of national laws on ownership (which indirectly sheltered state-owned telecommunications monopolies). As we will see, it took some key ECJ decisions and considerable creativity in interpreting the rules on the part of the Commission in order to establish an EC competence in telecommunications.

In 1957 the six member-states established a secretariat outside of the EEC to coordinate postal and telegraph policies. The six subsequently considered creating a European postal and telegraph union, either within the EEC (under Art. 235) or as an independent body. They chose neither option, deciding instead to form an organization outside of the EEC with broader European membership. The decision was due in part to French reluctance to increase supranational authorities in the EC, but also to a desire to include the UK, which was an important international telecommunications player. The result was the CEPT[6] (founded in 1959), a forum in which post and telecommunications administrations (not their governments) could set non-binding interconnection standards and tariff rules for cross-border traffic, leaving each PTT fully autonomous within its own national territory. The members of the CEPT were (and still are) the national PTTs. The PTT ministers of the EC met for the first time in 1964 (primarily to harmonize postal rates). They did not meet again until 1977. Meanwhile, in 1968, the Commission floated a proposal to form a postal and telecommunications committee to handle harmonization of technical standards (under Art. 100). It withdrew the proposal in 1973 because of a lack of member-state interest (Schneider and Werle 1990: 86–8).

4. Creating a Supranational Regime

The purpose of this section is to show how telecommunications moved from the intergovernmental pole toward the supranational one. By tracing the process by which that movement occurred, I show that the causal effects posited by our theory were in fact at work: transnational actors who needed European-level telecommunications reform exploited the political channels that EC institutions provided. Community organizations themselves became causal factors by establishing alliances with societal transactors (the Commission) and by interpreting EC rules in ways that allowed the Community to expand its domain into telecommunications (the Commission and the ECJ). In particular, the Commission and the ECJ exercised rule-making powers in ways that the member-states did not mandate, control, nor approve. I divide the process into two phases

4.1. Commission initiatives: the first phase

Telecommunications joined the EC agenda via industrial policy, the Commission's RACE program creating the breakthrough. Starting in the late 1970s, the Commission produced a stream of proposals for the telecommunications sector,

---

[6] Conférence européenne des administrations des postes et des télécommunications.

culminating in its comprehensive Green Paper of 1987. Though the legislation proposed by the Commission had to pass through the Council of Ministers, I will argue that the Commission had a substantial impact on the emergence of EU telecommunications policymaking during this period. Of course the need for Council approval of legislative proposals imposed constraints on the Commission; no one argues that the Commission is unconstrained. But for the member-states, the early 1980s were a period of substantial uncertainty regarding reform. Though the UK had liberalized rapidly, none of the other member-states had settled on a new model to replace the PTT system. Indeed, many states were unconvinced that they had to give up the PTT model, considering instead that the PTTs could be revamped to provide the new services that users demanded at reasonable prices. Because the national governments were in a mode of policy adaptation, their preferences were neither clear nor fixed. In this setting, the Commission could influence the formation of preferences and policies (Sandholtz 1992*b*: chs. 2, 8). The Commission: (i) had an impact on the ideas and models that shaped policymaking at both the national and the EU levels; (ii) supplied "focal points" for multilateral policymaking; and (iii) established alliances with important corporate players that in turn could lobby national governments. In short, though the legislative output for this period was intergovernmental in form, it was nevertheless shaped in significant ways by EU organizations and transnational society.

During the 1960s and 1970s, as the EC member-states were actively concocting technology policies, the Commission floated a series of proposals for EC industrial policies in the high-technology sectors. These plans produced meager results (Sandholtz 1992*b*: ch. 4; Sauter 1995*a*: 78–83). But by the late 1970s it was clear that the national champion strategies to promote high-tech industries had failed. The Commission began to find a more receptive audience for its industrial policy proposals, especially in electronics and telecommunications. The Commission also had an entrepreneurial figure in Etienne Davignon, who took a special interest in the information technologies. Davignon created the Information Technologies Task Force (ITTF) within the Commission, a small group that, aided by technical reports commissioned from outside consultancies, developed expertise in the sometimes arcane details of telecommunications technologies and regulation. The ITTF drafted the document that Davignon presented to the Council in November 1979: *European Society faced with the Challenge of new Information Technologies: A Community Response* (CEC 1979: 650). Four of the paper's six points related to telecommunications. The overarching goal was to be the creation of a European market for telecommunications equipment and services. The Council asked for specific proposals, and the Commission complied in 1980 with its first draft legislation in telecommunications. It would require that the PTTs open bidding to all EC manufacturers for "new" terminal equipment and for 10 percent of their annual purchases of network equipment. Even this modest proposal languished until November 1984, when the Council passed it as a non-enforceable recommendation.

But the Commission's objective—a liberalized EU market for telecommunications—had crystallized, and the next few years would see a series of Commission efforts to find politically feasible means of achieving that goal. Its case for an expanded Commission role in telecommunications had at its core the threat facing European manufacturers from the USA and Japan. For European firms to compete, they needed R&D support plus a home market of European proportions. The latter could only be achieved on the basis of common technical standards for future networks. These ideas came together in a set of "action lines" submitted to the Council in September 1983 (CEC 1983: 573). In addition, Davignon and the ITTF created a Senior Officials Group for Telecommunications (SOGT) in November 1979, with a mix of representatives from ministries of industry and economics and from the PTTs. The SOGT approved a program for the EC based on the Commission's action lines. It focused on creating a Community telecommunications market via standards, type approvals, and public procurement; coordinated planning of future networks, especially digital networks, mobile telephony, and broadband; and technology development through R&D cooperation (CEC 1984b: 277).

At this point, the Commission made its key move. Following a pattern it had successfully pioneered in the ESPRIT program, the Commission called on the twelve largest EC electronics firms to help it draft an R&D program (Sandholtz 1992a). Working through the summer of 1984, the companies produced a massive, detailed plan for collaborative R&D leading to the next generation of telecommunications technologies. This served as the basis for the Commission's proposal of a multi-year RACE program ("R&D in Advanced Communications technologies in Europe"). The program would fund specific projects involving companies, universities, or laboratories from at least two EC countries. The EC would pay half the costs; the participants would contribute the other half. With all of the national champions in the telecommunications equipment industry urging their governments to support the program, the Council approved the RACE Main Phase in 1987, with EC funding of ECU 550m. for five years. It similarly approved the Commission's proposed RACE Phase II in 1991 as well as a subsequent extension. RACE projects have involved some 350 organizations in 225 projects, with a total investment of about ECU 2.5bn. (CEC 1993d, 1995b).

RACE was an important breakthrough for several reasons. First, it established a significant Community role in telecommunications. Second, it marked the Commission's emergence as an actor in telecommunications, the Commission having designed and administered a complex Community R&D program with a substantial budget. Third, it cemented the Commission's ties with the most important firms in the equipment sector, thus constructing the core of a transnational coalition of actors supporting the Commission's objectives. Indeed, the Commission stood out as the political body with the most progressive agenda for telecommunications liberalization and EC-wide coordination. It therefore became the leader to which diverse liberalizing interests would rally. From an analytical point of view, RACE is important because it was not the product of member-state initiative or direction. The Commission and its industry partners designed RACE and sold it to the states.

Collaborative R&D, then, was the Commission's entry into telecommunications policymaking. Ironically, in telecommunications positive integration (common industrial policy) preceded negative integration (removing barriers to the common market); for the EC overall, the order has generally been exactly the reverse. The effort to open the EC's market started in earnest just as RACE commenced. It clearly drew energy from the broader "1992" program to complete the internal market. But one should bear in mind that creating a single market in telecommunications was not and is not at all the same sort of endeavor as opening a single market for beer or toys. In telecommunications, with the exception of the UK, it meant inventing competition, not just increasing it marginally. Opening an EC telecommunications market required terminating a deeply rooted system of state monopolies based on a public utility philosophy and a civil service ethic.

The effort to create a Community market in telecommunications included two main prongs. The first was to abolish monopolies by permitting new entrants to compete. The second was to establish EC standards; otherwise the result might be competition in national markets that remained unintegrated. The Commission's famous Green Paper on telecommunications mapped out an agenda for both dimensions (CEC 1987*b*: 290). The principal policy recommendations were:

(1) Open competition in a Community market for terminal equipment, with the possible exception of the first handset.
(2) Open competition in the provision of services, with the exception of voice telephony.
(3) Rules requiring the PTTs to grant fair network access to competing providers of services.
(4) European standards to ensure the "interoperability" of equipment and services anywhere in the Community.
(5) Splitting network operation and regulatory activities into separate administrations.
(6) Application of EC competition rules to the telecommunications sector, to prevent abuses of dominant position and other anti-competitive practices.

Ambitious as it was, the Green Paper did not propose abolishing the PTT monopolies in voice telephony and the provision of infrastructure. The Commission definitely recognized the limits of the feasible. Even so, the document foresaw the end of the PTTs' dominance.

Private-sector actors responded enthusiastically to the Commission's proposals. Major users weighed in with support for the Commission's liberalizing agenda. The International Telecommunications Users' Group (representing European national users' groups, in which large firms have a strong presence) endorsed all of the Green Paper recommendations. Its only reservations were that the Commission had sometimes not gone far enough, as in reserving the sale of the first handset for the PTTs (McKendrick 1987: 325–9). The Round-table of European Industrialists, whose members included many of Europe's largest multinationals, strongly supported the Commission's plans. "Among users," their report declared, "the will exists to bring the EEC's objectives to fruition" (Roundtable of European Industrialists 1986: 16–19). The policy proposals of the industrial association, UNICE, whose membership included both equipment manufacturers and large users, were also exactly parallel to the Commission's in the Green Paper (*La Tribune* 1987; *Financial Times* 1987). The liberalizing coalition forming around the Commission now included equipment makers and major telecommunications users. The Council passed a (non-binding) Resolution in June 1988 endorsing the Green Paper as a blueprint for EU telecommunications liberalization.

In addition to market opening, the Commission had early recognized EU standards as crucial to opening a European market in telecommunications. The Commission took advantage of the emerging new approach to harmonization, based on mutual recognition. The ECJ's *Cassis de Dijon* was a crucial underpinning for mutual recognition, which also became the heart of the 1992 single-market program. In telecommunications, terminal equipment has always required certification that it conformed to the relevant technical standards before it could be sold. The PTTs traditionally controlled this function. The Commission proposed applying the mutual recognition approach to "type approval" of terminal equipment. The Council agreed on a limited basis in 1986 and then approved a comprehensive directive on mutual recognition of type approval for terminal equipment in 1991.[7] The result is that a network of laboratories throughout the EC is now authorized to test equipment for conformity to EC standards. Once a device is approved by any one of the labs, the certification is valid throughout the EC.

The Commission also succeeded in altering the institutional arrangements for establishing European telecommunications standards. In the 1987 Green Paper the Commission had proposed establishing an independent European Telecommunications Standards Institute (ETSI). The move was designed to sidestep the CEPT, which the Commission regarded as too closed and dominated by the PTTs. After approval by the telecommunications ministers in 1988, ETSI came into being. Representatives of the network operators (still primarily the PTTs), equipment manufacturers, and telecommunications users participate in working groups to establish technical standards. Many of the standards so created are voluntary. But the Commission can also assign ETSI to prepare European standards. Once ETSI standards have been approved by the Commission and published in the *Official Journal*, they are binding in the EU. One of the most successful European standards has been the GSM standard for digital mobile telephony, which has become the dominant world standard.

---

[7] Council Directive *on the initial stage of the mutual recognition of type approval for telecommunications terminal equipment*, 86/361/EEC; Council Directive on the approximation of laws of the Member States concerning telecommunications terminal equipment, including the mutual recognition of their conformity, 91/263/EEC.

To summarize this section, beginning in 1978 (before even the British liberalization of telecommunications) the Commission articulated the goal of a Community-wide market for telecommunications equipment and services. By the late 1980s, a number of measures proposed by the Commission—in R&D, procurement, type approval, and standards—had taken shape in the form of legislation approved by the Council. The fact that the legislation took the form of intergovernmental agreements in the Council does not contradict a substantial, independent Commission role during this period. The Commission provided "focal points" for agreements among the states. It mobilized major equipment producers (RACE) and telecommunications users (the Green Paper) that supported its plans for Community-wide telecommunications markets. Perhaps most important, the Commission helped shape the ideas and models that influenced policymaking during a period when member-state preferences were unclear and in flux. Indeed, it seems plausible to argue that during this period, rather than taking directions and mandates from the member-states, Commission proposals influenced thinking and policymaking in the member-states. Though empirically validating that hypothesis would require detailed field research in the member countries, there is interesting confirming evidence from Germany.

The Witte Commission convened in 1985 to study the questions of telecommunications reform. Its deliberations were parallel to the Commission's work in preparing and drafting the 1987 Green Paper. The reforms proposed in the 1987 Witte report substantially mirrored the substance of the Green Paper. One analysis of the German process argues that important influences ran from the Commission to Germany. To begin, Herbert Ungerer, an official in DG XIII of the Commission and one of the principal architects of the Green Paper, was one of the experts reporting to the Witte Commission. In their analysis of German telecommunications policy networks, Schneider, Dang-Nguyen, and Werle identified communication links between the Commission and most of the major German actors, including ministries, political parties, interest groups, and telecommunications firms. Furthermore, 61 percent of policy actors in Germany rated Commission influence on German telecommunications reforms as strong or very strong, 17 percent considered it weak, and only 6 percent said the Commission had no influence (Schneider *et al.* 1994). I suspect that during a period of great uncertainty in the member-states, there were similar effects in other national policy processes.

4.2. The Court and Commission as rule-makers: the second phase

In the latest phase, beginning in 1988, the Commission clearly acted autonomously to push telecommunications liberalization faster than the member-states were prepared to go. Through a series of "consultations," the Commission has mobilized support for its program from a widening circle of influential societal actors. Relying on ECJ precedents, and supported after the fact by new ECJ rulings, the Commission has unilaterally legislated the breakup of PTT monopolies. The legal instrument for this effort has been Art. 90 of the Treaty. The salient features of Art. 90 directives are that they do not require Council assent and are enforceable in national and EU courts. If one could explain Commission behavior in terms of tracking the collective position of the member-states, there would be no need for procedures that bypassed the Council. The Commission turned to Art. 90 procedures precisely because the member-states were dragging their feet on implementing even the liberalization measures to which they agreed. But the extent of Commission autonomy is even greater than it immediately appears. After the ECJ affirmed the first pair of Art. 90 directives, the Commission leveraged the Council on later proposals by threatening further use of Art. 90. In other words, Council votes thereafter were in a purely formal sense intergovernmental bargains. But they were agreed in the shadow of the Commission's legal powers.

Enforcement of the Community's competition rules is one of the domains in which the Commission possesses substantial autonomy. The Treaty authorizes the Commission to police the internal market in order to prevent company practices that inhibit competition. What the Commission and the ECJ together have done is to extend the application of competition rules to state telecommunications monopolies. Art. 90(1) declares that member-states cannot allow state enterprises or undertakings to which the state has granted "special or exclusive rights" to engage in practices that violate the Treaty's competition rules (Arts. 6 and 85–94). But the treaty also contained clauses that had traditionally been interpreted as exempting the telecommunications monopolies: Art. 222, which states that the Treaty does not prejudice member-state laws concerning the ownership of property (indirectly shielding public monopolies); and Art. 90(2), which provides limited derogations from the competition rules for "services of general economic interest" and revenue-producing monopolies, as long as they were not harmful to the Community interest.

The European Court of Justice gradually expanded the application of competition rules to the public sector. A key decision for the telecommunications sector came in *Italy v. Commission* (ECJ 1985a), commonly referred to as the "British Telecom" case). Italy challenged a Commission decision directed against British Telecom, for anti-competitive pricing of telex services. The British government intervened on the Commission's side. The ECJ ruling supported the Commission's application of the competition rules (specifically, Art. 86 regarding use of dominant position), and denied a defense based on Arts. 222 and 90(2). The decision established that public undertakings must comply with competition rules and further noted that member-states did not possess discretion in the application of Art. 90(2) (Sauter 1995a: 101). The Court later confirmed the application of Art. 86 to state monopolies in its *Télé-Marketing* decision,[8] and extended this principle with its decision in *Macrotron*.[9]

---

[8] See ECJ 1985b.
[9] See ECJ 1991c, regarding a state employment agency.

In this case, the ECJ held that Arts. 86 and 90(1) applied "where undertaking in question, merely by exercising the exclusive rights granted to it, cannot avoid abusing its dominant position," and in addition ruled that a legal monopoly had a dominant position by definition. Finally, the Court established the direct effect of Art. 90 (which initially was held to apply only to states) in *ERT*[10] (Sauter 1995*a*: 169).

The Commission exploited this emerging jurisprudence by issuing two far-reaching directives under Art. 90 (which meant that Council agreement was not required). The Commission did so knowing that powerful private actors—manufacturers, service providers, and major users—fully supported their liberalizing agenda. These groups had been mobilized during the extensive consultations that the Commission initiated for the issuance of its 1987 Green Paper. The May 1988 Terminals Directive declared an end to monopolies in the provision of terminal equipment, opening the market to competition. It also required the member-states to establish bodies for type approval (certification) independent of the network operators. France (supported by Belgium, Germany, Greece, and Italy) challenged the directive in the ECJ. The Court affirmed the Commission's authority to issue Art. 90 directives, affirmed its power to apply Art. 90(1) in a general way vis-à-vis the states (rather than merely in regard to specific abuses), and affirmed the suppression of exclusive rights for state monopolies (following *Dassonville*).[11] The Commission has subsequently enforced the terminals directive against member-states reluctant to end monopolies, inducing Ireland to abolish the monopoly on the first handset and Denmark to open the market for private branch exchanges (*European Report* 1990*d*).

The Commission followed the terminals legislation in June 1989 with an extremely controversial directive opening the services market. The member-states were clearly not prepared to go as far as the Commission wanted, namely to liberalize all services except basic voice and telex. The Commission had been preparing an Art. 90 directive since 1988, but it nevertheless sought to minimize friction with the member-states. The Commission and the Council struck a compromise in December 1989. The Commission agreed to withhold formal issuance of the services directive until the Council had passed into law the Commission's proposed directive on Open Network Provision (ONP). The intent of ONP was to create common rules of access and technical interfaces, thus guaranteeing that equipment could connect and that services could operate anywhere in the EU. For its part, the Council reached political agreement on the ONP directive, with some details to be hammered out in the following months. Both directives took effect in June 1990 after some additional compromises between Commission and Council. The relationship between the two EU bodies in this episode was not simply one of member-states in control of a tightly reined Commission. Rather, Council and Commission each held

---

[10] See ECJ 1991*d*.
[11] See ECJ 1991*e*.

sources of leverage, and policies were the outcome of bargaining between the two—not just among the member-states. For instance, the Commission brandished its authority to issue (or delay) the Art. 90 services directive (to which several member-states objected) to push member-states to approve the ONP directive (under Art. 100a). In order to expedite passage of the ONP directive, the Commission could then agree to minor amendments (regarding the length of the transition period and conditions that states could attach to some service providers, subject to later Commission review) (*European Report* 1990a, 1990b). The resulting ONP directive was therefore the product of Council voting, but it was a Council voting under a Commission threat.

The Services Directive of June 1990 (Commission Directive 90/388/EEC) opened the market for enhanced or "value-added" services starting immediately and the market for basic data communications from January 1993. Basic voice telephony was reserved for the PTTs. Equally important, the Services Directive required the member-states to separate regulatory functions from the PTTs. Finally, the directive called for an assessment of the services markets with respect to the goals of the directive by 1992; this review would be the Commission's occasion to bring pressure to bear on the voice telephony monopoly reserved for the PTTs. Belgium, France, Italy, and Spain challenged the Services Directive in the ECJ. In its decision, the Court again affirmed the authority of the Commission to issue general regulations pursuant to Art. 90(3).[12]

Finally, in a handful of preliminary rulings on Art. 177 appeals, the ECJ has reinforced the implementation of the Art. 90 directives. The Belgian government had accused private parties of violating national rules by using or marketing devices that had not been approved by the national certification body. The accused parties sought enforcement of the Terminals Directive. The Court ruled against the Belgian government for failing to establish an independent agency for type approvals. In two cases from France, the Court ruled that the regulatory office established within the ministry of posts and telecommunications was not sufficiently independent. Both sets of cases[13] confirmed the direct effect of the Commission directives (Sauter 1995a: 105).

The movement toward supranational politics here can hardly be exaggerated. The Commission and the Court essentially created a Commission power to abolish state monopolies. These normative and institutional changes shaped subsequent politics. For instance, the review of the services markets called for in the Services Directive took place as scheduled in 1992. Again, the Commission invited responses to its October 1992 report on the telecommunications services market. In response, over eighty organizations submitted written comments and more than 110 offered oral responses at a series of hearings organized by the Commission. Groups providing input in the consultations included most of the PTTs, consumer and business user associations, telecommunications equipment manufacturers, service providers, potential suppliers

---

[12] See ECJ 1992.
[13] See ECJ 1993b, 1993c, 1993d.

of alternative infrastructures, consultancies, and individual companies not directly involved in the telecommunications sector (like Volkswagen). The Commission objective was clearly the complete liberalization of voice telephony in the EU (it had already drafted a directive on the application of ONP to voice telephony). Its report stressed the fragmentation of national markets as a competitive disadvantage for EC users and the price distortions resulting from the continuing monopolies in voice telephony (CEC 1993c: 159). However, the Commission recommended as politically feasible in the near term the opening of competition in international voice calls within the EU, with national calling to be liberalized later.

Naturally, the PTTs weighed in against competition in voice telephony. But the clear message from other groups was that liberalization of voice telephony should proceed as quickly as practicable. Furthermore, the ECJ in November 1992 (as the services consultation was underway) issued its ruling upholding the Commission's Art. 90 Services Directive. Emboldened by the court decision and by the support of the private groups, the Commission in the spring of 1993 dropped its cautious approach (to liberalize voice service only between, not within, member-states) and proposed full liberalization of voice telephony by January 1998 (*Eurecom* 1993). Given the array of forces in favor of liberalized voice telephony, the member-states could do little other than assent. Accordingly, they passed a July 1993 Council Resolution on full liberalization of all services (including voice telephony) by January 1998 (Council Resolution 93/C213/EEC). The Commission converted the Council's non-binding statement of principles into law with a new Art. 90 directive in December 1995 (*European Report* 1996).

Despite the legal breakthroughs, progress on liberalizing the service markets was uneven and unsatisfactory to the Commission and to many private actors. The PTTs (except in Britain) retained their monopolies of the telecommunications infrastructure—the network—and could therefore control access to the network by potential services competitors. Eliminating the network monopoly would liberalize services markets, as network operators would have to compete to attract service providers and customers. Liberalization of infrastructure became the next element in the Commission campaign. Art. 90 remained the instrument of choice because the member-states remained opposed to liberalization as the Commission envisioned it. For instance, as late as March 1993, the French were willing to consider the liberalization of telephone services—over a ten- to fifteen-year period. The French also believed that only some services should be deregulated and that, in any case, infrastructure should remain a monopoly (*European Report* 1993a).

The Commission set out its agenda for the liberalization of infrastructure in a series of Green Papers. Each of the Green Papers involved consultations like the earlier ones. The consultations thus served to inform and mobilize groups that supported liberalization. The first piece in this set was the 1990 *Satellite Green Paper*, which pointed out the link between infrastructure competition and services competition (CEC 1990; Council Resolution 19 December 1991). There existed considerable scope for liberalization in satellite communications (telephone, telex, data, and other services relayed by satellite). Only the UK had a completely liberal market, whereas in France and Italy satellite services were a PTT monopoly. Other member-states had restrictive licensing systems. All of the member-states maintained monopolies or quasi-monopolies with respect to terminals (dishes) capable of receiving and sending signals. A number of member-states, led by France and Belgium, strongly opposed the Commission's initial draft of the Green Paper on satellites, which proposed complete liberalization of satellite terminals and guarantees of fair access to satellites for service providers. Indeed, the Commission was forced to reconsider its initial proposals (*European Report* 1990c).

Nevertheless, the Commission eventually obtained its preferred policy, via an October 1994 Art. 90 directive on satellite terminals and services. Subsequent to the *Satellite Green Paper* and its poor reception, the ECJ affirmed the Commission's first two Art. 90 directives on terminals and services. Technically, the satellites directive amended the earlier two directives, which had already been upheld by the ECJ—another way of solidifying the new law (Commission Directives 94/46/EEC; 88/301/EEC; and 90/388/EEC). For the satellites directive, the Commission consulted with the member-states on its content and even obtained Council approval of the directive prior to issuing it (*European Report* 1994b). But again, the Council considered the satellite directive in the knowledge that the Commission had the power to issue it unilaterally and that the ECJ had already supported the Commission twice.

The second Green Paper was the April 1994 *Green Paper on Mobile and Personal Communications*, which emphasized the theme that infrastructure competition would promote the liberalization of services by neutralizing the PTT network monopoly. Mobile (cellular) networks would serve as an alternative to the monopoly ground-based networks (CEC 1994d: 145). The European standard for digital mobile telephony (GSM) was a world leader. The technology had the potential for users to operate their cellular phone anywhere in the EU. That potential had not been exploited because of national fragmentation. The Commission position was that member-states should license competing mobile networks in an open and non-discriminatory manner, and that mobile operators should be allowed to build their own terrestrial infrastructure, thus enabling them to connect to mobile or ground networks in other countries without having to go through their home PTT. The consultations following the release of the Green Paper drew written responses from over seventy associations and organizations; more than 100 organizations expressed their views orally at Commission hearings. The groups submitting comments covered the full range of telecommunications players: users, manufacturers, network operators, service providers, trade unions. Once again, though the PTTs opposed liberalization of mobile communications, the vast majority of other respondents fully supported the Commission's proposals.

By June 1995, the Commission had in hand a draft Art. 90 directive for liberalizing mobile communications. There was considerable scope for introducing competition: only the UK provided for open competition among mobile providers. In the rest of the EU, licensing of mobile networks was severely restricted, and mobile operators were frequently prohibited from utilizing any terrestrial infrastructure other than that supplied by the national telecommunications monopolies (*European Report* 1995*b*). Furthermore, most member-states—Italy, Belgium, Ireland, Spain, and Austria in particular—charged the second mobile operator an "entrance fee" that the state monopoly is not required to pay (*European Report* 1995*c*). As with satellites, the new law would amend the original services directive. It provided for liberal licensing of competing mobile operators and ensured that mobile networks could connect to each other and to the public network. The Commission adopted the Art. 90 directive liberalizing mobile communications in early 1996.

Completing the set of Green Papers was the 1994–5 *Green Paper on the Liberalisation of Telecommunications Infrastructure and Cable Television Networks*, issued in two parts. Even before the Green Paper was issued the member-states were voicing strong objections to the deregulation of alternative infrastructures. At the conclusion of a September 1994 Council meeting, a statement on alternative infrastructures was deleted from the final Conclusions because the member-states could not agree. Only Germany and the UK favored deregulation of infrastructures in 1998; Belgium, Denmark, Greece, and Portugal opposed the whole idea (*European Report* 1994*b*, 1994*c*).

But the Green Paper was extremely ambitious. It proposed full liberalization of infrastructures in 1998, which would mean permitting new entrants—cable TV operators, mobile operators, railroads, water and electric utilities—to build and operate telecommunications networks in direct competition with the PTTs. Services already liberalized (everything but voice telephony and telex) would be deregulated on alternative infrastructures in 1996 (CEC 1994*c*: 440; 1994*e*: 682). Consultations opened by the Commission in October 1994, and lasting through March 1995, drew inputs from an immense array of actors. Over 100 submitted written contributions and the hearings involved more than 125 groups. In addition to the usual players, the *Infrastructures* consultations attracted cable TV industry associations, broadcasters, filmmakers, and advertising industries. The interest of the latter groups stemmed from the Green Paper's proposal to permit the provision of telecommunications services via cable television networks. The attraction of cable TV networks for liberalizing telecommunications is that they already possess the crucial "local loop," that is, the connection to households. Furthermore, the greater bandwidth of TV cables (as compared to traditional telephone wires) would in principle be well suited for advanced telecommunications services (high-quality sound, images, moving pictures). As with the other consultations, aside from the PTTs, the various interested parties supported the Commission's objective of full infrastructure liberalization. In fact, the association of employers' federations, UNICE, released an additional endorsement of the Commission's agenda on the eve of the November 1994 Council meeting that was to discuss the first part of the Green Paper (*European Report* 1994*d*).

At that November meeting of the Council, the battle lines were clearly drawn. Four states supported the Commission's two-stage plan (France, Germany, Netherlands, and the UK, soon to be bolstered by Sweden and Finland). But the remaining eight states were absolutely opposed to the first stage (virtually immediate deregulation of infrastructures for services already liberalized). As a result, the Resolution issued at the conclusion of the Council mentioned only the 1998 deregulation of all infrastructures. In response, competition commissioner Karel van Miert, declared that the Council's reluctance would not stop him from considering an Art. 90 directive on the first stage (*European Report* 1994*d*).

In fact, even before it issued its *Green Paper on Infrastructures*, the Commission was holding out the possibility of leapfrogging a foot-dragging Council with an Art. 90 directive (*European Report* 1994*a*, 1994*c*). Immediately after the November 1994 Council meeting that debated the Green Paper the Commission prepared a draft Art. 90 directive that would open cable television networks for the provision of liberalized telecommunications services (*European Report* 1994*e*). At the time, only the UK had liberalized cable networks for the carrying of telecommunications services. But reaction from the Council in early 1995 was strongly negative: most of the delegations to the relevant working group opposed the early liberalization of cable TV for telecommunications (*European Report* 1995*a*). The Commission nevertheless pressed ahead, issuing the Art. 90 cable TV law (amending the 1990 services directive) in October 1995, to take effect as of January 1996 (*Eurecom* 1995).

The cable TV directive was only part of the infrastructure liberalization project. The Commission's ultimate objective was complete infrastructure liberalization, which was the subject of a February 1996 Art. 90 directive. The latest directive mandated that services liberalized already (in essence, all services except voice telephony and telex) could be offered on any infrastructure from July 1996, and that complete liberalization of all services and infrastructures would begin January 1998 (with limited transition periods for member-states with less developed networks). In addition, the directive set out basic principles for the regulatory framework that would govern the new regime of open competition, particularly in the sensitive areas of interconnection (conditions and fees for service providers to connect to existing networks), licensing (conditions for authorizing new market entrants), and provision of universal service (means of financing and guaranteeing access to some minimum level of service to all residents) (*European Report* 1996). The PTT monopoly on networks was coming to an end, as cable television operators, railroads, utility companies, mobile networks, and satellite systems were allowed to compete with the traditional telecommunications operators. In principle, service providers would not have to rely on the PTTs for access to customers (though in practice, there will be a lag before alternative networks are built and functioning).

5. Conclusion: An Emerging EC Regulatory Regime

A decade ago, telecommunications in the EU was a patchwork of state monopolies. Governments clearly preferred to retain control of the PTTs, for a
number of reasons: the historic public utility, natural monopoly ideology
surrounding telecommunications in Europe; the capacity to use the PTTs as instruments of industrial and employment policies; and the revenues generated
by the telecommunications monopolies. Furthermore, the Treaty made no
mention of telecommunications and there was a standing presumption that
certain articles protected the PTTs from EU competition rules. Yet today the liberalization of telecommunications is being driven primarily at the EU level. In
the language of our continuum, telecommunications policymaking has moved
substantially from the intergovernmental pole toward the supranational.

Intergovernmentalist theory cannot explain this movement. The intergovernmentalist account sees no independent role for the Commission, the
ECJ, and transnational groups. The EU telecommunications regime would
therefore be the result of a string of compromises each of which embodied the
preferences of the most reluctant state. But as the empirical record shows, the
key steps in liberalizing telecommunications at the EU level consisted of unilateral Art. 90 directives from the Commission. The Commission resorted to
Art. 90 precisely because the member-states were, with the UK being the only
regular exception, resisting liberalization. If liberalization were proceeding at
the pace of the slowest member-states, there is no question that reform would
be far less advanced than it is today.

In contrast, our theory of institutionalization explains the empirical record;
things happened as we would expect. The fragmented PTT system was increasingly costly both for the increasing number of transactors (users) who
relied on cross-border communications and for the new players who hoped to
meet their telecommunications needs. These groups—equipment manufacturers, service providers, business users, consumer groups, and providers of
alternative infrastructures—rallied to the Commission's cause in the series of
consultations. Those groups pressing for liberalization were the transnational
society of telecommunications.

Our theory also reserves a place for supranational organizations that can
have an independent effect on EU politics and policymaking. For a variety of
reasons—having to do with historical path-dependence, the costs of super-
vision, and formal EU law[14]—the member-states cannot always control EU
organizations like the Commission and the ECJ. In telecommunications, the
Court and the Commission were clearly not simply doing the bidding of either
the most powerful or the most reluctant member-states. As the empirical record
shows, Commission initiatives were almost invariably *more ambitious* (in terms

---

[14] See Chs. 1, 2, and 8 on these points.

of liberalizing) than most member-states were willing to contemplate. That is, the member-states could not have been dictating their preferences to the Commission because the Commission was always ahead of them. Even the British telecommunications reforms came two years after the Commission had formulated the objective of a pan-European market. The case for the Commission acting independently of member-state preferences is absolutely clear when the Commission utilized its rule-making powers under Art. 90 (liberalization of terminals, services, and infrastructures). But even in the first phase (from RACE to the first Green Paper) the Commission had an autonomous impact.

Of course it is true that the key legislative pieces in the first phase were voted by the Council of Ministers. But intergovernmental agreements can also be shaped substantially by supranational processes. As the empirical account showed, the Commission's initiatives in the first phase came before member-state preferences took shape. In fact, most of the member-states did not define their preferences regarding telecommunications reform until the latter half of the 1980s. The Commission's initiatives had an impact on member-state thinking and preference formation, by shaping ideas and models, providing focal points for EU decision-making, and mobilizing influential societal groups. The Commission's impact on policymaking was akin to education, or persuasion. More generally, if the interactions and discourses of the EU significantly shape state preferences, then interstate bargains are not what intergovernmentalists assume them to be.

The theoretical framework of this volume and its application in the telecommunications case suggest an answer to the puzzle of why liberalization in the EU has proceeded faster in some domains than in others. For instance, extensive EU liberalization in telecommunications contrasts with far more modest liberalization in the electricity sector (see Chapter 8; Schmidt 1996). Our theory suggests an explanation. In the case of telecommunications, there was a growing number of powerful business actors with a clear stake in up-to-date, cross-border telecommunications. Users needed advanced services that spanned borders, equipment and service providers wanted to meet that demand. The transactors in telecommunications have no counterpart in electricity. There is nothing inherently cross-border about energy consumption. The main rationale for electricity liberalization is that it would reduce energy costs in the Union and eliminate price differences across countries. A similar cost-reduction argument was at play in telecoms liberalization, but there existed in addition concrete business needs for advanced telecommunications services spanning the EU. The Commission could therefore ally with a variety of actors who needed pan-European telecommunications, but there was no similar constituency in electricity.

The factors frequently cited as making the difference between EU outcomes in telecommunications and electricity include favorable ECJ precedents and support among powerful non-state interests. There was a string of relevant ECJ cases in telecommunications, upon which the Commission could base its actions. There was no similar ECJ record in electricity. But this is no coincidence.

The ECJ had developed a jurisprudence relevant to telecommunications precisely because private actors had been taking telecommunications-related cases to the courts. The ECJ does not choose its policy domains; it can only respond to the cases that are being litigated and referred. Again, actors needing cross-border telecommunications were seeking remedies in the courts, which produced a body of cases, which in turn undergirded Commission activism. The absence of groups with a similarly compelling need for cross-border transactions in electricity explains the lack of ECJ precedents in the sector.

The telecommunications case shows the interactions among the three dimensions of our continuum: supranational rules, supranational organizations, and transnational society. EU law, driven in crucial instances by the autonomous rule-making powers of the Commission and the ECJ, has brought an end to the PTT era. The liberalization of telecommunications markets is underway. But a fully competitive EC telecommunications market poses broader challenges in a context of decentralized regulatory authority. Three main issues stand out:

(1) *Interconnection*, to ensure that the multiplying networks and services will be technically compatible everywhere, and that connection fees will not be a barrier to new entrants.
(2) *Licensing*, to guarantee that whatever procedures are used to license new providers are not discriminatory or anti-competitive.
(3) *Universal service*, to provide access to a minimum set of services to all users at affordable prices on an equal basis, to make sure that less profitable customer groups (like those in remote or rural areas) would not be abandoned or forced to pay radically higher tariffs.

The Commission has submitted directives (under Art. 100a, harmonization) in all three areas. There will be extended Council debates. There will be member-state foot-dragging. But to the extent that reluctant states inhibit the emergence of pan-EU telecommunications networks and services, they will impose costs on the increasing number of actors who rely on cross-border telecommunications in the EU. And those actors will respond as they have in the past, by pressing for more effective EU-level rules and coordination.

6

The Liberalization and European Reregulation of Air Transport

DOLORES O'REILLY AND **ALEC STONE SWEET**

As late as the mid-1980s, national governments still guarded virtually unchallenged authority to regulate air transport; today, nearly every significant aspect of that authority falls within the competence of the European Community. This remarkable transformation was not preordained. In writing the Treaty of Rome, the member-states had pointedly excluded air transport from provisions that otherwise obligated the Council of Ministers to develop common transportation policies. And at home, national executives faced powerful domestic constituencies, both public and private, who were advantaged by national control. Within a brief period, however, the Council did move to liberalize air transport and to reregulate the sector at the European level, exposing the state-owned monopoly airlines and their unionized workforces to competitive, commercial pressures for the first time.

In this chapter, we seek to explain the transfer of competence to govern, from national to supranational authorities, in this sector. We necessarily confront two big questions. First, how and why—through what process—did air transport come onto the European legislative agenda? Until the late 1970s, national control was not in dispute. Second, why did member-state governments agree to divest themselves of control at the national level? After all, the decision-making rule governing Council voting in the domain—unanimity—favored governments that prefer to maintain the status quo. In responding to these questions, we at times focus squarely on the Council of Ministers, and therefore on intergovernmental stages of the legislative process. Such a focus, however, need not entail adopting intergovernmentalist theories of integration. On the contrary, our case study broadly supports the theoretical claims developed in Chapter 1. We found that the increasing intensity of transnational exchange and the pro-integrative behavior of the EC's supranational organizations not only generated the context in which intergovernmental bargaining took place, but provoked the emergence of supranational governance.

The chapter is organized as follows. In Section 1, we discuss the ex ante status quo—the preference of member-state governments for national control over international air transport—and its consequences. In Section 2, we focus on the major forces—the activities of transnational actors and supranational organizations—that conspired to undermine the status quo. In Section 3, we examine the EC policymaking process, charting the response of governments to pressures for Europeanization of the sector.

1. National Protectionism and European Inertia

Historically, all modes of transport have experienced massive government regulation, not least because transportation policy has been critically implicated in state-building, market-building, and war-making. In the twentieth century, governments have regulated aviation more than any other mode (Lissitzyn 1968: 12). In the EC of the 1960s and 1970s, direct state control was the rule, in the form of publicly owned, national "flagship" carriers enjoying wide-ranging monopoly privileges within restricted markets. These carriers also functioned as important political instruments of their respective governments. Anxious to have the industry contribute to regional development, industrial policies, and full employment, governments obliged airlines to serve non-profitable routes, to purchase locally manufactured planes and parts regardless of relative costs and quality, and to maintain a large workforce. Public-sector unions, traditionally Europe's most powerful, flourished in the industry, and successfully pressed governments to provide employment security and relatively high pensions and other benefits. Carriers consistently operated at a loss, but governments tended to treat such losses as public policy expenditures. Even when the red ink was examined critically, the Commission stated in a 1984 memorandum, "the desire to avoid any increase in these deficits [enhanced] the reluctance of governments to expose their airlines to further competition" (CEC 1984a: 22). In effect, domestic structures had locked-in national control.

International regimes and EC law reflected the dominance of governments over the industry. The 1919 International Air Convention declared state sovereignty over the airspace above state territory. The 1944 Chicago Convention on International Civil Aviation characterized this sovereignty as "complete and exclusive," and then derived an obvious corollary: "No scheduled international air service may be operated over or into the territory of a contracting state, except with the special permission or other authorization of that state." At Chicago, negotiators proved unable to agree on a permanent, multilateral means of establishing routes, fares, limits on capacity, and the details of landing rights. In consequence, a vast network of bilateral treaties to coordinate international air traffic grew up, the details of which are today constantly being adjusted in intergovernmental processes of consultation and negotiation. In Europe, this system worked to reinforce the dominance of flagship carriers, all but eliminating meaningful competition between the public and private sectors (House of Lords 1980: 25; Doganis 1991: 29). For any intra-EC route, the two governments involved designated air carriers, fixed routes, fares, and capacity, and pooled the revenues received, normally splitting them 50:50. As Kassim (1996: 113–14) described the status quo: "the general pattern was one of protectionism, collusion and anti-competitive practice; [it was often] difficult to tell where the management of the airline ended and the state began."

Member-state governments did their best to write air transport out of Community law. In Title IV of the Treaty of Rome, the member-states promised to produce a *common transportation policy* but, significantly, they did not commit themselves to creating a *common market* for transport. Art. 84, which contains the final provisions of Title IV, states that "the provisions of this Title shall apply to transport by rail, road, and inland waterway," thus excluding sea and air transport from Title IV's reach. Art. 84 (2) provides the legal basis for legislating in the excluded sectors: "The Council may, acting unanimously, decide whether, to what extent, and by what procedure, appropriate provisions may be laid down for sea and air transport." In the first twenty-five years of the EEC, the Council did not adopt secondary legislation pursuant to Art. 84 (2), and it purposefully excluded transport from the application of competition (antitrust) rules. Although the Council adopted Regulation No. 17 implementing the Treaty rules on competition in 1962, Regulation No. 141, adopted the same year, exempted the transport sector from the reach of these same rules. (The Council, by virtue of Regulation No. 1017 of 1968, adopted competition rules for transport by rail, road, and inland waterway, but not by sea or air.) Thus, the member-states and the Council of Ministers had carefully insulated, from the purview of EC law, national control over civil aviation. Put simply, the discretion of national governments to regulate the domain as they saw fit was considered to be all but complete.

The first challenge to the status quo came from a European Court decision on the relationship between Treaty rules governing transport and the rest of the Treaty. In the French Merchant Seamen case (ECJ 1974c), the ECJ was asked to rule on the legality of a provision in the French *Code du Travail Maritime* enabling the administration to fix the percentage of French nationals that the crew of any ship operating in the merchant fleet must contain. In its observations to the Court, France argued that since Art. 84 (2) of the Treaty had excluded maritime transport from the rest of Title IV, it must be that the general provisions of the Treaty did not apply to the sector either. Treaty rules governing the creation and regulation of the common market, France reasoned, did not apply to merchant shipping unless specifically provided for by the Council in secondary legislation. Disagreeing, the Court ruled that the general rules of the Treaty—in this case those concerning the free movement of workers—applied to all economic activities in the Community except where there was specific provision to the contrary. Thus, although Art. 84 (2) made special provision for air and sea transport, they were both subject to the general rules of the Treaty on the same basis as other modes of transport.

The judgment prompted[1] the Council of Ministers in June 1977 to establish an air transport working party to "identify those areas of government activity which, with advantage, could be examined at Community level" (CEC 1979: 8). In 1978 the Council approved a list of nine priority areas but only three— competition, right of establishment, and possible improvements to inter- regional services—had any direct bearing on the economic regulation of the industry. The Commission then went to work on drafting reform proposals.

1.1. The Commission's first memorandum

In July 1979, the Commission issued a memorandum, *Air Transport: A Com- munity Approach* (CEC 1979), the purpose of which was to open debate among the Community institutions on liberalization. Emphasizing that change, although necessary, would only come gradually, the Commission outlined several actions that the EC could take to benefit consumers and the industry, as well as to "meet the demands of the Treaty of Rome" (ibid. 1979: 37). Measures proposed included: the removal of some restrictions on the introduction of new scheduled services between regional airports; broadening the range of fares available to consumers; protecting passengers from overbooking; establishing criteria for the granting of state-aids to publicly owned carriers; and application of the competition rules to air transport.

Reaction to the memorandum was overwhelmingly negative. The European Parliament—worried that liberalization would undermine the international competitiveness of the European industry, the public service mandate of the flagship carriers, and the position of public-sector unions—warned against tampering with the basic structure of the industry.[2] The Association of Euro- pean Airlines, an organization that represented the major airlines, considered the existing system adequate. Employee organizations "felt that the memor- andum . . . paid insufficient attention to . . . social problems." Publicly, at least, the Council of Ministers all but ignored the memorandum, inviting the Com- mission only to prepare draft legislation on frontier-crossing, interregional services (CEC 1984*a*: 3–8).

Despite this response, the Commission submitted three proposals to the Council in 1981–2. Two of these, a timid, draft directive proposing reform of the system for fixing tariffs and a draft regulation to extend certain competition rules (for a limited period) to air transport, were rejected by the Council. The third concerned interregional services, the aim of which was to give airlines new opportunities to operate outside the trunk routes (the main routes between city pairs, which were invariably operated by the flag-carriers of the

---

[1] Interviews with Commission officials.
[2] Two EP resolutions to this effect were adopted in 1980 (summarized in CEC 1984*a*: 3–4).

two countries concerned). Nearly three years later, the Council adopted a revised version of the Commission's draft, but, in the Commission's words, amendments had so diluted the measure that "it is questionable how much effect it will have in its modified version" (ibid. 15).[3]

As Table 6.1 shows, the directive impacted routes carrying less than 3 percent of all intra-Community scheduled traffic, as compared to the 37 percent that would have been affected had the Commission's initial draft been adopted. These services were to be operated by aircraft with no more than seventy seats, not by aircraft with up to 130 seats as the Commission had proposed, and the minimum route distance was fixed at 400, rather than the proposed 200, kilometers. Further, the directive extended the grounds on which a member-state government could refuse to license a new service, and limited the rights of carriers to obtain licenses. Thus, the directive's impact on both overall competition, and on competition on specific regional routes, was negligible.

Table 6.1. Limitations of regional services, 1985

Airport pair category	European scheduled international traffic	
	No. of city-pairs	% of total traffic
1-1	214	63.0
1-2	222	23.8
1-3	256	10.7
2-2	35	1.3
2-3	49	0.9
3-3	31	0.4
Total	807	100.0

Source: Association of European Airlines Yearbook 1985.

The first serious attempt at reform had left the status quo essentially intact. State-owned carriers continued to dominate the industry, barriers to market entry remained impermeable, and competition was practically non-existent. The directive was nevertheless the first piece of secondary legislation concerning air transport adopted under the legal basis of Art. 84 (2). Against this background, the Commission would present its second memorandum on Civil Aviation in 1984. What the memorandum proposed, and how member-state governments responded, is examined in detail in Section 3.

---

[3] The Council insisted on limiting the scope of the directive to services between regional airports, whereas the Commission had proposed that its reach extend to services from the regions to major, category 1 airports. See Table 6.A2 in the Appendix for the classification of EC airports.

2. Transnational Activity and Pressures for Europeanization

Although member-state governments had chosen to preserve the core elements of national authority, pressure for change was steadily building. As transnational activity expanded, business lobbies, air transport consumer groups, and some parts of the industry itself began calling for radical reform. Some registered their demands in Brussels, where they found sympathy and support within the Commission, others went to the courts. In this part, we examine the sources of the demand for the Europeanization of air transport policy, identify the motives of the societal actors involved, and discuss how European organizations responded to such pressures, focusing particularly on the ECJ and the Commission.

2.1. Transnational activity

One of the central claims of this volume is that as cross-national activity increases within a given sector governed by national authorities, those societal actors most adversely affected by state-centric control will press for European rules and governance to replace national rules and governance. We would expect, then, that an increase in the level of intra-EC air traffic will provoke demands from those societal actors whose prosperity is most dependent upon the continued expansion of intra-EC activity. These demands are crucial in that they help to construct the decision-making context in which supranational organizations operate, and in which intergovernmental bargaining takes place. To the extent that EC organs respond positively to these demands, supranational organizations help to construct rule-oriented arenas for politics; these arenas are then gradually institutionalized as societal actors, supranational organizations, and governments adapt to existing rules, and seek to influence the development of new ones.

Fig. 6.1 plots annual levels of freight and passenger traffic on intra-EC routes served by the flagship carriers of nine EC member-states beginning in 1977. As the graph shows, prior to the Commission's first memorandum in 1979, cargo and passenger use had risen sharply; in the 1979–83 period, traffic remained steady; and, in the 1983–92 period, levels shot upward. Fig. 6.2 traces the parallel growth of intra-EC commercial aviation and intra-EC trade. With one exception (1986), intra-EC trade rose every year, cutting through the 1979–83 plateau experienced in air transport.

We interpret these data in ways that are broadly consistent with the priorities of this volume,[4] and with certain elements of Haas's neofunctionalism. Even prior to the Commission's first memorandum, it was clear that large, joint gains

---

[4] See particularly Chs. 1, 3, 4, 5, and 7.

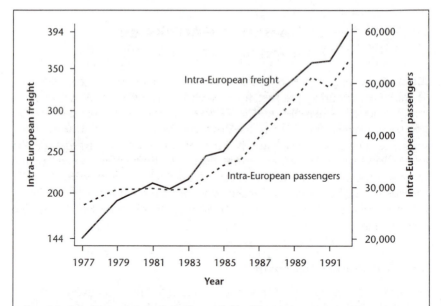

Fig. 6.1. Passenger and cargo traffic carried by flag-carriers on intra-EC routes, 1977–1992

Note: Intra-European passenger traffic = Revenue passengers carried (thousands); Intra-European freight traffic = Revenue freight tonnes (millions). The graph uses data for the nine flag-carriers of the EC, it does not include Greece, Portugal, and Spain.

Source: Data from *AEA Statistical Yearbooks*, 1977–1992.

from enhancing the efficiency of air transport were achievable. The demand for air services was rising, while inefficiencies in the industry were manifest and growing. Higher levels of intra-EC trade stoked this demand; and air services also facilitated more cross-national trade. Still, the existing, protectionist system of air transport was inadequate to the task of serving a common market that increasingly relied on that system. Services provided on existing routes were inefficient and costly, and the restrictions in the bilateral intergovernmental agreements often prevented airlines from meeting demands for new services. As the costs of maintaining existing arrangements became more salient to more users, so did the call for a more efficient and more responsive industry.

2.1.1. Transnational lobbying

In the eyes of European traders, passengers, and private airlines, the national regulation of air transport was a failure. Flagship carriers were slow or unable to adjust to the changing needs of business, who needed an efficient air transport system to develop and exploit the new European market. Other carriers were excluded from entering the market altogether, and charter airlines were not

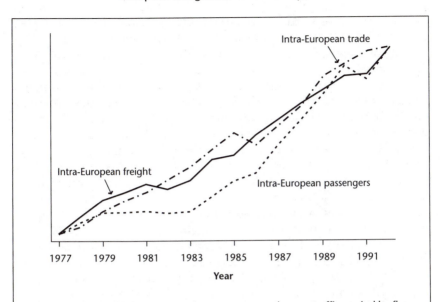

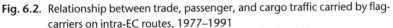

Fig. 6.2. Relationship between trade, passenger, and cargo traffic carried by flag-carriers on intra-EC routes, 1977–1991

Note: Intra-European passenger traffic = Revenue passengers carried (thousands); Intra-European freight traffic = Revenue freight tonnes (millions). The graph uses data for the nine flag-carriers of the EC, it does not include Greece, Portugal, and Spain.

Sources: Data from *AEA Statistical Yearbooks*, 1977–1991. Trade data are from *Eurostat: External Trade*, 1977–1991.

allowed to compete on a head-to-head basis with scheduled airlines for business traffic. Absent meaningful choice and competition, users paid a high price for the industry's inefficiency. They pressed both national governments and the Community for action, and the Commission used their demands to promote its own agenda.

The frustrations of major business users found expression both at national and European level. Joined by the International Chamber of Commerce, the Roundtable of European Industrialists was particularly active. A special Roundtable working group on transport infrastructure characterized the situation as "approaching . . . crisis," and argued that an efficient air transport system was essential for survival in an internationally competitive environment (European Roundtable of Industrialists 1986: 11).

Interest groups representing air passengers began to organize their activity at the supranational level.[5] Instigated (and now financially supported) by the Commission, a Brussels-based, transnational lobby, the Federation of Air

---

[5] Air transport user groups appeared in the UK in 1973, in Denmark in 1979, in Ireland and Italy in 1982, and in France and Belgium in 1983.

Transport User Representatives in the EC (FATUREC), was established in 1982. By 1984, FATUREC had constituents in all member-states and was holding regular consultations with the Commission's Directorate-General for Transport. General, non-specialized, transnational consumer organizations also became avid supporters of liberalization at this time. The European Consumer Unions Group adopted "an active and militant role in Community decisions on air transport" (Wheatcroft and Lipman 1986: 74), issuing a 1985 report urging competition among multiple airlines on all routes, an end to tariff consultations between airlines, and immediate application of the Treaty's competition rules to the sector. The UK-based, Consumers in the European Community Group was similarly critical, both of the existing regime and of legislative inertia. To take one more example, a commercial organization, the International Airline Passengers Association, also lobbied hard for change, as part of its "Freedom of the Skies" program. In 1985, the body created a non-profit foundation—the International Foundation of Airline Passengers Associations—to pursue the interests of passengers in any legislative package being formulated. It, too, campaigned vigorously for more choice in airlines, products, schedules, and fares.

Private airlines, the most important of which were represented by the Association of Independent Air Carriers in the European Community, called for the pure and simple abolition of national government management of the industry: "the industry [should] be allowed to evolve commercially in step with the changing pattern of demand for air transport services and . . . governments [should] refrain from obstructing that natural process" (House of Lords 1985: 270). Private carriers also criticized the Commission for its continual failure to implement the competition rules, making the telling point that the offending airlines and the Commission had a common "paymaster" in the member-states, each and every one "with a vested interest in the airline business" (ibid. 267).

The few scheduled carriers already operating in a liberalized environment, notably those in the UK, shared these views. British Caledonian argued that "it is absurd and unacceptable for European countries to call for and obtain increased freedom and competition in manufacturing and other industries while maintaining restrictive, protectionist postures towards civil aviation" (House of Lords 1985: 85). British Midland spoke of its satisfaction that the "groundswell of resentment and frustration at the lack of competition is beginning to impress itself on governments, regulators and, of course, on the EC itself" and it too appealed to the Commission to "enshrine the legal principles required for a genuinely free market" (Bishop 1993: 1).

It is not surprising that private actors who are adversely affected by existing policies will seek to have those policies replaced with new ones that are more favorable to them. It bears emphasis, however, that lobbying in the air transport sector was organized almost entirely at the national level before 1980. After 1980, new lobby groups appeared, and existing lobbies took up the demand for an EC air transport policy.

2.2. Revising the rules of the game: the ECJ and the applicability of Treaty law to air transport

In 1974 the European Court determined that although Art. 84 (2) had effect-ively excluded air and sea transport from the provisions of Title IV of the EEC Treaty, pending Council measures to the contrary, Art. 84 (2) could not on its own exclude the application of the "general rules" of the Treaty, specifically, rules governing the free movement of workers, to these sectors (discussed above). The judgment had vast potential to disturb the system of governance in place in the air transport sector, to the extent that Treaty provisions implic-ating the freedom to provide services, competition policies, and so on, might apply to the industry. In the 1980s, the Court rendered two more decisions bearing on transportation, each of which had the effect of "hardening" the law in this area. In the Common Transport Policy case (ECJ 1985c), the Court found that the Council, in failing to elaborate a common policy for transport, was in breach of its Treaty obligations.[6] The Court noted that the Treaty leaves it to the discretion of the Council to determine "the aims of and means for implement-ing [such] a . . . policy," and refused to order governments to produce a particular policy. Nevertheless, the judges reiterated their view that Treaty provisions on transport were obligatory, and not optional, for member-state governments.

The Nouvelles Frontières case (ECJ 1986b) directly challenged the legality of core elements of national control over the regulation of air transport. The dispute arose from criminal proceedings brought against a number of private airlines, charter companies, and travel agencies operating in France in the early 1980s. French prosecutors had charged the accused with violating provisions of the Civil Aviation Code making it a crime to sell tickets at tariffs which had not been preapproved by the French Minister of Civil Aviation. The fares offered by the defendants on intra-EC and other international routes undercut the pre-approved tariffs of the national airlines. The defendants—private carriers selling cheap charter flights in complicity with French "bucket shops"—were overtly working to usurp the price-fixing arrangements issuing from inter-governmental agreements in place. Exercising its Art. 177 (EEC) prerogatives, the criminal court of first instance (the *Tribunal de police*), stayed the trial, pend-ing a ruling of the European Court on the conformity of the relevant sections of the Civil Aviation Code with Community law. In referring the matter to the ECJ, the trial judge stated the following: "those provisions [of the Civil Aviation Code] that call for a concerted practice between airlines, undoubtedly have as their effect the prevention, restriction, or distortion of competition within the Common Market. Those practices are therefore incompatible with Art. 85 of the EEC Treaty." Art. 85 lays down the general principles of competition law in the common market.[7] Even more assertively, the judge declared that "Art. 84

---

[6] The European Parliament brought the case against the Council of Ministers.

[7] In particular, Art. 85 prohibits "agreements," "decisions," and "concerted practices"

(2) of the EEC Treaty [cannot] be raised as an objection to the immediate application of Art. 85" (ibid. 1427–8).

The case turned on two linked questions. First, did competition rules contained in the Treaty apply to the air transport sector? Second, if they did apply, which authority was competent to assure the implementation, monitoring, and enforcement of these rules? In their observations to the Court (ECJ 1986*b*: 1432–6, 1442–9), the defendants, the Commission, the UK, the Netherlands, and the Advocate-General argued that the answer to the first question was "yes," despite the exclusion of air transport from the matrix of European rules on other modes of transport, and despite the fact that the Council had rejected the Commission's proposals to implement competition rules in the sector. They derived as much from the Court's judgment in the French Merchant Seamen case. France, Air France, and KLM argued that the Court did not mean to make the entire Treaty applicable to transport, but only that portion (Part II) on the "Foundations of the Community." Interpreting the Court's case law in this way would exclude the provisions, such as competition rules (contained in Part III), from application to air transport.

The second question concerned the legal consequences of a finding to the effect that competition rules applied to the management of the industry. Simplifying, France, Italy, the Netherlands, KLM, and Air France argued that the French practices at issue, and the practice of tariff coordination more generally, were permitted by the Treaty, while the Commission, the Advocate-General, and the defendants disagreed. Further, all of the member-state governments submitting observations agreed that—because the competition rules are aimed primarily at undertakings and not national laws and administration, and in the absence of secondary legislation giving competition rules a more specific content—each member-state government possessed, within its territory, the primary responsibility for ensuring compliance. The Commission and the Advocate-General agreed, but stressed that governments were not thereby empowered to "introduce or maintain in force measures . . . which may render ineffective the competition rules applicable to undertakings." The Commission and the Advocate-General insisted that national courts—and especially those courts charged with reviewing the legality of administrative acts—must be positioned to ensure that governments comply with treaty obligations

The Commission possesses broad supervisory powers in antitrust, by virtue of Arts. 89 and 90 (see Chapter 8). According to the terms of Art. 89, the Commission "shall . . . ensure the application of the principles" of competition law, such as those contained in Art. 85, and "shall propose appropriate measures to bring [infringements] to an end"; Art. 90 gives to the Commission the authority to verify that member-states do not operate nationalized companies in ways that conflict with competition rules, and to take "appropriate directives or

---

which "have as their effect the prevention, restriction or distortion of competition within the common market, and in particular those which directly or indirectly fix purchase or selling prices or any other trading conditions."

decisions" against member-states that infringe these rules. Prior to these proceedings, the Commission had never used these powers in the air transport domain, due partly to the controversy surrounding the status of the competition rules. Although France had cited Commission inactivity as evidence that the rules were not applicable in the sector, the Advocate-General disagreed:

The only consequence of the fact that the Council has not adopted the "appropriate regulations or directives in this sector" is that the Commission does not have at present the means of investigating or punishing infringements of Art. 85 . . . in air transport as such. . . . The provisions of Art. 85 . . . of the Treaty are, therefore, not suspended; the member-state [governments] have merely retained their competence and the obligation to ensure compliance with them.

At stake, then, was not just the applicability of the Treaty rules to air transport, but if, how and by what authority governments might be placed under legal surveillance.

In its judgment, the ECJ, referencing its decision in the French Merchant Seamen case, declared that Art. 84 (2) merely restricts the scope of Title IV, and does not bar the application of competition rules to air transport. Specifically, the Court ruled that national rules requiring air fares to be preapproved effectively "deprived [the provisions of Art. 85] of their effectiveness," and therefore constituted a breach of Treaty law entailing the legal responsibility of that member-state (ECJ 1986*b*: 1471). In such cases, "the competent national authorities"—in particular, those authorized to review the legality of administrative acts, such as administrative courts—and the Commission, acting under Art. 89 authority, had to ensure that competition rules were respected. In the present case, the Court declared, the referring court (a criminal law court):

does not in itself have jurisdiction to hold that [a] concerted action in question is incompatible with Art. 85. It should be pointed out, however, [that] if such a ruling or recording has been made, either on the initiative of the national authorities . . . or on that of the Commission . . . , [all] national courts must draw . . . the necessary conclusions therefrom and in particular conclude that . . . the concerted action . . . is automatically void under Art. 85. (ECJ 1986*b*: 1470)

The judgment made immediate what had previously been only a distant threat, namely that the Commission might make use of its powers under Art. 89 to investigate infringements of Art. 85 in the aviation sector, and to propose "appropriate measures" to bring any such infringements to an end. The litigation in the Nouvelles Frontières case had begun before the Commission produced its second memorandum; and the ECJ announced its decision as the Council was debating the Commission's new proposals. Thus, in 1986 governments faced a choice, which the decision made urgent. Governments could either establish an air transport policy for the Community; or they could seek to maintain national authority, but this time under the constant threat of legal action, and in the face of rising pressure from increasingly militant and better organized lobbies.

3. From National to Supranational Governance

The liberalization of air transport and the reregulation of the sector at the European level was achieved in a series of decisions taken by the Council of Ministers beginning in December 1987. In this section, we trace the package of reforms proposed by the Commission in its second memorandum through the EC legislative process.[8] We begin by outlining the Commission's proposals, before turning to the dynamics of intergovernmental bargaining. We then describe and assess the significance of the legislation adopted.

3.1. The Commission's second memorandum

The Commission presented the *Civil Aviation Memorandum No. 2* (CEC 1984*a*) to the Council in March 1984 knowing full well that a great majority of governments remained strongly opposed to any significant change in management of the industry. The Commission documented the pressing reasons for embarking on such a reform, among them: a huge increase in consumer criticism of the existing regime since the publication of the first memorandum; the poor economic health and long-term prospects for most European airlines; the apparent success of deregulation in the USA which had given consumers greater choice and had resulted in lower fares since its advent in 1978; and, the memorandum stressed, growing doubts as to whether "the present system is compatible with the Treaty of Rome," citing the French Merchant Seamen case (ibid. 12, 17).

Contrasting its preferred, evolutionary approach to American deregulation, the Commission asserted that "American-style deregulation would not work in the present European context." The American air transport industry differed in many respects from that of the EC. The USA comprised a large and unified market reserved to private US carriers, and it was American government policy to radically reduce federal intervention in the market and to accept its social and economic effects. The USA had twenty major carriers, all operating on a commercial basis, and therefore "the [Federal] Government can take a relaxed view on the fate of any one of them." By contrast, the major European airlines were owned, financed, or otherwise supported by their governments and "most, if not all, member-state governments would regard it as unthinkable that their airline should go out of business." Thus, the Commission would progressively introduce changes to the basic structure of the existing regime, in order to "increase airline efficiency, allow the efficient and innovative airline to benefit, encourage expansion and thus employment, and better meet consumer needs" (CEC 1984*a*: i, 22, 27).

The Commission laid out four concrete proposals, which it insisted should

---

[8] This section is heavily based on information obtained in interviews with national civil servants and Commission officials who were involved in the negotiations. The interviews were conducted by Dolores O'Reilly Parr between October 1996 and January 1997. To our knowledge, no source material on these negotiations has yet been published.

Table 6.2. Actors and preferences regarding regulatory reform of EC air transport (1984)

Actors	Actor preferences	
	Maintain status quo	Regulatory reform
European Commission		X
"Liberal" MS		UK, Netherlands
"Illiberal" MS[a]	B, D, Dk, F, Gr, Irl, I, L, P, S	
State-owned airlines[b]	AF, AZ, EI, IB, LH, LG, OA, SN, SK, TAP	BA, KLM
Non-state-owned airlines[c]		BC, BM, VA
Potential new entrants[d]		ACE
Major businesses[e]		CC, ICC, REI
Consumer groups[f]		FATUREC, BEUC, CECG, IFAPA
Industry trade unions[g]	IFT	

[a] B = Belgium, D = Federal Republic of Germany, Dk = Denmark, F = France, Gr = Greece, Irl = Ireland, I = Italy, L = Luxembourg, P = Portugal, S = Spain

[b] AF = Air France, AZ = Alitalia, BA = British Airways, EI = Aer Lingus, IB = Iberia, KLM = Royal Dutch Airlines, LH = Lufthansa, LG = Luxair, OA = Olympic, SN = Sabena, SK = SAS, TAP = TAP-Air Portugal

[c] BC = British Caledonian, BM = British Midland, VA = Virgin Atlantic

[d] ACE = Association of Independent Air Carriers in the European Community

[e] CC = National Chambers of Commerce, ICC = International Chambers of Commerce, REI = Roundtable of European Industrialists

[f] FATUREC = Federation of Air Transport User Representatives in the European Community, BEUC = European Bureau of Consumer Unions, CECG = Consumers in the EC Group, IFAPA = International Airline Passengers Association

[g] IFT = International Transport Workers Federation

Source: Compiled by the author using material from submissions made to DG VII and various published sources.

be adopted and implemented as a package. These proposals dealt with the following matters: the capacity and revenue-sharing rules in bilateral agreements between member-states; fares for scheduled air transport between member-states; the application of the competition rules to EC airlines; and the Commission's powers to grant block exemptions from these rules for certain categories of inter-airline cooperation. Table 6.2 summarizes the attitudes of the principal actors to these proposals.

3.2. Intergovernmental deliberations

The Council established a High Level Working Group, comprised of senior civil servants, directors-general of civil aviation in each member-state, and representatives of the Commission, to assess the proposals. Prospects for achieving consensus were not good. In the interval since publication of the Commission's first memorandum, there had been a marked shift in the position of the UK government, following from the election in 1979 of a Conservative Party committed to privatization and market liberalization. A similar shift had occurred in the Netherlands. These two governments thought the proposals did not go far enough. The other eight member-state governments considered that they had gone too far, "and of these five or six thought that they had gone far too far" (House of Lords 1985: 133). Although it met eight times during the second half of 1984, the Working Group's report did no more than restate existing positions along with a set of guidelines, reflecting majority views, for any future action.

Meanwhile, the UK, whose intra-EC passenger traffic activity had increased the most since 1979 (see Table 6.3 below) embarked on negotiations to liberalize international air services with other governments best positioned to gain from reform. The breakthrough agreement, signed by the UK and the Netherlands in 1984, permitted any airline in either country to operate between the two without the need to seek further government approval, while substantially relaxing restrictions on scheduling, capacity, and fares. The Commission "encouraged and supported" this strategy, recognizing it as a means of opening up the intra-EC market without obtaining the formal agreement of the Council of Ministers.[9] There followed a series of similar agreements between the UK and Ireland, the UK and Belgium, and the UK and Germany.

Through mid-1986, the Council of Ministers deadlocked on the Commission proposal, a situation that, being coincident with the Dutch and UK presidencies of the European Council, shifted the site of debate to summitry. Although unable to get agreement on specific proposals before passing the torch to the British, the Dutch succeeded in incorporating the following paragraph into the conclusions of the European Council held at The Hague on June 26–7, 1986:

The European Council concluded that the Council of Ministers (Transport) should make a further effort to overcome the difficulties which have recently appeared in relation to the liberalization and harmonization of land, sea and air transport, in light of the relevant judgments of the European Court of Justice. With regard to air transport, the Council of Ministers should without delay adopt the appropriate decisions on air tariffs, capacity and access to markets, in accordance with the rules of the Treaty.[10]

Working closely with the Commission throughout its Presidency, the UK government deliberately devised a "stick and carrot" strategy to persuade the reluctant governments of the need to do a deal. The British had concluded that the Commission's proposals would have little practical effect unless the package contained greater provision for new airlines to enter the market and also provided existing airlines with the opportunity to fly new routes. They recog-

---

[9] Interview with a senior Commission official.
[10] European Council 34th Meeting, (1986) *Presidency Conclusions*, internal EC documentation.

nized, on the other hand, that the inclusion of such provisions would radically alter the impact of the package and would make it harder for unwilling member-state governments to accept. In consequence, they deliberately set out to rebalance the package in two respects, first, by reducing the scope of the original proposals on fares and capacity-sharing arrangements and, second, by putting greater emphasis on the Commission's right to exempt certain types of inter-airline cooperation from the application of the competition rules. The aim was to make the texts on fares and capacity more closely resemble existing arrangements through a critical transition period, and at the same time to give assurances that various cooperative arrangements between carriers would be safe from legal action under Art. 85 of the Treaty.[11]

3.3. Exploiting ECJ decisions

Armed with the ECJ's ruling in Nouvelles Frontières, the Commission became more militant in its interactions with member-states. In June 1986, the Commission formally apprised the major European airlines of activities that it considered to be contrary to Art. 85, demanding modification or abandonment of these activities within two months (Wheatcroft and Lipman 1986: 60). The Commission knew full well that the airlines would find it impossible to disengage so quickly from commercial and operational relationships developed over many years. The threats, in reality, were directed at governments. As the Commissioner for Competition put it at the time:

The decision . . . will . . . clarify the obligation under the Treaty of governments and airline companies—a recognition that there can be no standing still on liberalization. We shall continue pressing the Commission reform plans for air transport, but the Court decision should force governments to action. (Reported in Wheatcroft and Lipman 1986)

Although it is difficult to verify with certainty the full extent to which these threats were instrumental in breaking the deadlock, some have argued that they were crucial (e.g. Berlin 1992). There are very good reasons to believe that the French government, at least, altered its position after receiving its letter.[12] The letter may also have made it easier for the German government to respond favorably to intense lobbying by the country's Chambers of Commerce. As Table 6.3 shows, German business had come to depend heavily on intra-EC air services: passenger traffic had grown by 18 percent between 1979 and 1987, while freight traffic increased by 30 percent, significantly more than in any other member-state. By the autumn of 1986 the balance of forces within the Council had dramatically changed. The UK, the Netherlands, Germany, and France agreed, in principle, on the need for reform, and Belgium, Ireland, Luxembourg, and Portugal had softened their opposition.

On the other side, Italy, Greece, Denmark, and Spain remained firmly

---

[11] Interviews with a former British civil servant.
[12] Interviews with Commission officials.

Table 6.3. Flag-carrier airlines' passenger and freight traffic increases, 1979–1987

Flag-carrier	Passenger increases (%)	Freight increases (%)
Aer Lingus/Ireland	3.28	−3.45
Air France/France	17.41	18.74
Alitalia/Italy	12.56	19.15
British Airways/UK	23.07	14.55
Iberia/Spain	6.60	21.34
KLM/Netherlands	10.22	23.36
Lufthansa/Germany	18.06	30.75
Luxair/Luxembourg	0.85	n/a
Olympic/Greece	5.35	14.55
Sabena/Belgium	1.82	3.56
SAS/Denmark	16.34	2.02
TAP-Air Portugal/Portugal	2.57	5.83

n/a Data not available.

Source: Compiled by author using data from AEA Statistical Yearbooks, 1979 and 1988.

opposed. The opposition of this latter group focused on a proposal that had been introduced by the UK presidency, and was similar to a Commission proposal that the Council had rejected in the 1984 directive on interregional services: Community air carriers should have a right, under certain conditions, to operate services between Category 1 airports in one country and regional airports in another. This innovation would both provide market opportunities to airlines previously frustrated by bilateral restrictions and facilitate the development of new business across national boundaries. Italy and Spain based their objections on the inadequacy of existing infrastructure to cope with the increased air traffic that this reform would surely generate. They intimated, however, that they might be able to agree once air traffic control systems and facilities at their regional airports had been improved. The Danes feared that the proposals would undermine regional-development policies: to allow airlines from other member-states to operate directly to Danish regions would, for reasons related to a complex system of determining fares and schedules, destabilize policies designed to promote uniform economic development in the country. The Greek government argued that there was no capacity at its two main airports to take additional traffic, although like Italy it admitted that developments already planned would make this a comparatively short-term problem. Its other objection was more fundamental. The country's economic development depended largely on the provision of year-round air services between the mainland and the Greek Islands, yet this traffic was seasonal. If airlines other than the national flag-carrier were allowed to cream off the lucrative summer traffic, heavy losses would be incurred during winter months.

Since at that time, Art. 84 (2) of the Treaty required Council decisions on air transport to be taken by unanimity, the deadlock could only be broken by flexibility and compromise. The Commission continued to insist that its proposals, including the regional airports provision, made a single package and that the granting of block exemptions from the competition rules was dependent on an overall solution. The other governments looked to make a side deal. The Commission brokered the compromise: all the airports cited by these four governments would be excluded from the regional airports arrangement during the first stage of liberalization (or in the case of the Greek Islands indefinitely), on the understanding that further measures would be adopted not later than mid-1990 and the internal market for air transport completed by 1992.

It was on this basis that agreement was finally reached in December 1987.

3.4. What the negotiations achieved

The package finally adopted consisted of four measures: two regulations concerning the application of the competition rules to air transport; a decision on capacity-sharing between EC airlines on scheduled intra-Community services and on market access to intra-Community routes; and a directive on fares for scheduled air services between member-states.[13]

The main features of the measures are set out in the following subsections.

3.4.1. Fares

(i) "Reference fares"[14] were to remain subject to approval by the competent authorities of the member-states concerned. However, the directive allowed for consultation and, if necessary, arbitration if disagreements occurred. Initially, the Commission saw no necessity to provide for arbitration but those governments which saw it as the best available means of blocking opposition to the introduction of lower fares insisted upon its inclusion.

(ii) Carriers were given freedom to charge less than the reference fare (45–65 percent) to passengers satisfying certain restrictive conditions deliberately designed to make it difficult for business travelers to obtain a cheaper fare, for instance by requiring a minimum stay of six nights or over a Saturday night.

3.4.2. The sharing of capacity and access to routes

(i) In any bilateral relationship, the carriers of one of the states concerned should be allowed to increase their share of the total capacity offered to 55 percent and to 60 percent after October 1, 1989. The carriers of the other state should have the right to bring their capacity into line. The whole process could occur twice.

(ii) However, if the initial move to a 55:45 split led to serious financial damage for the carriers providing the lesser share, the Commission has the power to

---

[13] For full texts, see the *Official Journal of the EC*, no. L374 of 31 Dec. 1987: 1–26.
[14] In nearly every case the "reference fare" was the normal economy fare.

veto any further movement, although such a decision could be reversed by the Council acting unanimously.

(iii) Each member-state must accept the designation of more than one airline by any other member-state to operate between the two countries, but need not do so on any one route, except where the number of passengers carried on that route exceeded a certain threshold (250,000 in the first year, reducing in each of the next two years to 180,000 in year three).

(iv) Subject to the foregoing provisions, EC carriers would be allowed to introduce services between Category 1 airports in their own home state and a regional airport in another—or vice versa. In such cases, a carrier from the other member-state concerned could claim reciprocal rights. Capacity provided by aircraft with fewer than seventy seats would not be taken into account for the calculations made under points (i) and (ii). These provisions were qualified by the exemptions outlined in the preceding section.

(v) In certain carefully defined circumstances, carriers might operate fifth freedom services[15] (i.e. services between two member-states other than their state of registration) but only where such services were operated as an extension of a service from, or a preliminary to a service to, their home state.

(vi) The rights conferred under points (iii), (iv), and (v) could be refused by a member-state in cases where the airports concerned had insufficient facilities to accommodate the proposed services or where navigational aids were inadequate.

3.4.3. Application of the competition rules

The Council adopted two regulations. One outlined the procedures for applying the competition rules to the air transport sector (but only in respect of intra-EC transport). The second provided for the Commission to grant time-limited block exemptions from these rules to certain categories of inter-airline agreements and concerted practices.

To a large extent, the first regulation followed the model established for the other sectors of the EC economy, but three points are noteworthy:

(i) It was for the undertakings themselves to ensure that their practices conformed to the rules and that notification to the Commission "need not be compulsory."

(ii) An annex to the regulation included a non-exhaustive list of inter-airline practices which, insofar as their sole objective was to achieve "technical improvements or cooperation," were excluded from the prohibitions in Art. 85 (1) of the Treaty.

(iii) The Commission was given the right to fine airlines up to 10 percent of their annual turnover for intentional and negligent infringements of the competition rules or for breach of conditions attached to any block exemptions which it had granted.

---

[15] See Table 6.A1 in the Appendix for a full list of the freedoms of the air.

There was much dispute as to what should go into the second regulation. The Commission insisted that it alone had the right to define what types of activity should be given block exemptions. Member-state governments, wanting time for the industry to adapt to more competitive conditions, disagreed. They demanded that the regulation should list the types of inter-airline agreement to be exempted. Eventually, a compromise was reached whereby the Commission agreed to the inclusion of a list, but the member-states accepted that the Commission alone should define the terms on which the exemptions would be granted.

The list specified types of activity, including: consultations on tariffs and conditions of contract; the joint planning and coordination of capacity; revenue-sharing arrangements; and the allocation of landing and take-off slots at congested airports.

3.5. The end of national control

The 1987 package of legislation began the transfer of authority to manage the market for air services from national governments to the EC. Under the decision-making rule of qualified majority introduced by the Single European Act, subsequent packages were adopted in July 1990 and in July 1992, and the last internal barriers were removed on April 1, 1997 (see Appendix). A series of complementary measures have also been adopted, the most important of which concern consumer services (common rules for the operation of computer reservations systems and for the payment of denied boarding compensation to victims of overbooking). With the exception of air traffic control, every aspect of the industry's activity is now within the competence of the European Community.

4. Conclusion

We began with an empirical question. In 1984, a large majority of member-state governments were content with a protectionist, bilateral system for regulating civil aviation, a system that had existed almost as long as the industry itself. National control of air transport provided public services and employment, helped to maintain state security, and facilitated industrial and trade policies. Twice in the previous five years, the Commission had faced strong government opposition to what were in fact cautious initiatives. Three years later, governments voted to Europeanize the sector, expanding the domain of supranational governance, and enhancing the policymaking capacity of supranational organizations. Why?

Our answer to this question begins, but does not end, with activities of transnational actors and supranational organizations. As cross-border exchanges (trade, passenger, and freight traffic) grew, so did the costs of a rigid, inefficient, and necessarily patchwork regulatory system for those (major business users, private consumers, cargo shippers, and ultimately governments) who bore them. Interest groups organized at European level, forged alliances with the Commission, and lobbied national governments for change. The Commission, at first timidly then ever more aggressively, pursued an increasingly comprehensive agenda for full-scale reregulation of the industry at the European level. Activated by an Art. 177 reference from a national court (itself faced with litigation involving a private carrier offering intra-EC flights against the wishes of a member-state government), the ECJ rewrote the rules governing national rule-making in the sector, placing member-state governments in the shadow of the law (see Chapter 4). This shadow deepened considerably in 1986 when the Commission used the Court's judgment to leverage recalcitrant governments. In sum, governments, faced with declining benefits and rising costs of maintaining national governance structures, reacted by constructing supranational governance.

In important respects, the air transport case resembles the telecommunications case examined by Sandholtz (Chapter 5). Like Sandholtz, we found that a combination of transnational forces and supranational initiative overcame the commitment of governments to national control, which we take to support the transaction-based theory of integration laid out in Chapter 1. Intergovernmentalists would presumably conceptualize and understand these factors differently. They might insist that supranational organizations are performing their assigned tasks when they deal with private actors and interest groups, propose reforms, and work to clarify and enforce EC law. In doing so, the argument might go, the Commission and the Court lower the costs of information and transactions that face governments, facilitating agreements that allow governments to enhance their own control over a given sector. It is impossible to refute this kind of argument, when applied on an ex post facto basis to explain an intergovernmental decision. On our own theoretical terms, we recognize that there is no magic process for translating societal demands into European legislation; that is, we expect intergovernmental decision-making to be a crucial stage in the legislative process. To the extent that the factors that we have emphasized shape these contexts, intergovernmental bargaining is analytically secondary. Last, we expect that transnational actors and supranational organizations will work to sustain the consolidation of supranational control over air transport and that, in consequence, no member-state government will ever again possess as much authority to determine outcomes as it did in 1987.

APPENDIX

Table 6.A1. Freedoms of the air

First freedom	The right to fly over another country without landing.
Second freedom	The right to make a landing for technical reasons (e.g. refueling) in another country without picking up/setting down revenue traffic.
Third freedom	The right to carry revenue traffic from your own country (A) to the country (B) of your treaty partner.
Fourth freedom	The right to carry traffic from country B back to your own country A.
Fifth freedom	The right to carry traffic between two other countries other than its own.
Sixth freedom	The use by an airline of country A of two sets of third and fourth freedom rights to carry traffic between two other countries but using its base at A as a transit point.
Seventh freedom	These rights are also known as cabotage rights. The right of airline of country A to carry revenue passengers between two points in country B that is to say to provide domestic services in a country that is not your own.

Source: Adapted from Doganis 1991: 346.

Table 6.A2. EC classification of airports open to scheduled international traffic

State	Airport	Airport category
Belgium	Bruxelles-Zaventem	1
Denmark	København-Kastrup/Roskihde	1
West Germany	Frankfurt/Rhein-Main	1
	Dusseldorf-Lohausen	1
	München-Riem	1
	Hamburg-Fuhlsbuttel	2
	Stuttgart-Echterdingen	2
	Köln/Bonn	2
Greece	Atina-Hellinikon	1
	Thessaloniki-Micra	1
Spain	Palma-Mallorca	1
	Madrid-Barajas	1
	Málaga	1
	Las Palmas	1
	Tenerife-Sur	2
	Barcelona; Ibiza; Alicante; and Gerona	2
France	Paris-Charles de Gaulle/Orly	1
	Marseilles-Marignane	2
	Nice-Côte d'Azur	2
	Lyon-Satolas	2
	Basle-Mulhouse	2
Republic of Ireland	Dublin	1
	Shannon	1
Italy	Roma-Fiumicino/Ciampino	1
	Milano-Linate/Malpensa	1
	Nàpoli-Capodichino	2
	Venèzia-Tessera	2
	Catania-Fontanarossa	2
Luxembourg	Luxembourg-Findel	2
Netherlands	Amsterdam-Schiphol	1
Portugal	Lisbon	1
	Faro	1
	Funchal	2
	Oporto	2
UK	London-Heathrow/Gatwick/Standstead/Luton	1
	Manchester-Ringway	2
	Birmingham-Elmdon	2
	Glasgow-Abbotsinch	2
All other airports open to scheduled international traffic		3

Source: EC Decision on Capacity Sharing and Market Access No. 602/87.

Table 6.A3. Liberalization of the EC aviation industry

Deregulatory action	Inter-regional services 1983	1st package 1987	2nd package 1990	3rd package 1992
Geographical scope				
Regional airports	X	X	X	X
Regional/main airports		X	X	X
Main airports			X	X
Domestic				X
Traffic rights				
Multiple designation		X	X	X
3–4 Freedoms	X	X	X	X
5 Freedom		X	X	X
6 Freedom			X	X
7 Freedom				X[a]
Tariffs				
Close relatedness	X	X	X	
Flexibility zones		X	X	
Double disapproval			X	
Matching		X	X	
Free pricing				X
Capacity				
60-40		X		
60-40+			X	
Free	X			X
Air carrier licensing				
Economic fitness				X
Technical fitness				X
Ownership				X
Leasing rules				X

[a] From April 1, 1997

Source: Present author's table using data from the "three packages" of aviation liberalization.

7

Creating Supranational Authority in Monetary and Exchange-Rate Policy: The Sources and Effects of EMU

DAVID R. CAMERON

BY the Treaty on European Union, the member-states of the European Union committed themselves to moving to the third and final stage of Economic and Monetary Union by January 1, 1999 at the latest.[1] In 1995, the heads of state and government of the EU, meeting as the European Council, agreed that the third stage would in fact commence on the first day of 1999.[2] On that day, a European System of Central Banks, consisting of a new European Central Bank and the existing national central banks of the member-states of the EU, will assume full responsibility for defining and implementing the monetary policy of the participating member-states, conducting foreign exchange operations, holding and managing the officials reserves of the participating states, and promoting the smooth operation of international payments.[3] At the

[1] Art. 109j (3) of the Treaty committed the member-states to decide by the end of 1996 whether a majority fulfilled the necessary conditions for the adoption of a single currency, whether it was appropriate for the Community to enter the third stage, and, if so, when that stage would start. Art. 109j (4) states that if, by the end of 1997, a date for the beginning of the third stage has not been set, it will start on January 1, 1999. On the negotiation of the Treaty's provisions for EMU, see, among many, Kenen (1992, 1995), Sandholtz (1993a, 1993b), Dyson (1994), Eichengreen and Frieden (1994), Padoa-Schioppa (1994), and Cameron (1995b). For the text of the Treaty, see CEC (1992).

[2] At Cannes in June 1995, after the Finance Ministers had agreed that the earliest possible date for the third stage—January 1, 1997—was "not realistic," the heads of state and government restated their "firm resolve" to move to the third and final stage by January 1, 1999 at the latest, in strict accordance with the convergence criteria, timetable, protocols, and procedures laid down by the Treaty. At Madrid six months later, they attached a precise date to the commitment, "confirming unequivocally that stage three of economic and monetary union will commence on 1 January 1999." See CEC (1995c, 1995d).

[3] Art. 109l of the Treaty stipulates that the ESCB and ECB will be created prior to the start of the third stage, immediately following the appointment of the Executive Board of the ECB, which is to occur immediately after the identity of the member-states participating in the third stage becomes known. As soon as it is established, the ECB will take over the tasks of the European Monetary Institute, which will be liquidated. It will begin exercising its full powers and responsibilities on the day the third stage begins.

same time, the conversion rates of the currencies of the participating member-states will be irrevocably fixed against each other and against a new currency, the euro, that will come into existence and eventually will become the single currency of those member-states.[4]

The decision to assign responsibility for defining and implementing monetary policy within a group of member-states to a single central bank, and to cede all responsibility in the domain of exchange-rate policy to the institutions of the EU, undoubtedly represents one of the most significant extensions of supranational authority in the four decades since the Treaty of Rome. Indeed, given the likelihood that—notwithstanding the considerable difficulties most of the member-states had in meeting the criteria by which the "high degree of sustainable convergence" necessary for adoption of a single currency would be judged—a large number of member-states, possibly as many as ten or eleven, will be deemed eligible for participation in the third stage, the decision may well constitute the *most* significant extension of supranational authority since the agreement in Rome four decades ago to create the European Economic Community.[5]

This chapter seeks to understand why the member-states of the EC sought, intermittently but, eventually, successfully, over the past three decades to extend supranational authority in the domain of monetary and exchange-rate policy, and to understand, also, some of the likely consequences of the extension of supranational authority in those domains of policy. It considers, first, why the member-states of the EC concluded several decades ago, and, for the most part, have persisted in believing, that their national interest is best served by extending the authority of existing supranational institutions and creating

[4] At Madrid in 1995, the European Council adopted the "reference scenario" for the change-over to the single currency proposed by the European Monetary Institute (1995*b*), according to which the national currencies of the participating member-states and the euro would circulate as "different expressions of the same money" until the first half of 2002, at which time the national currencies would be withdrawn from circulation and the euro would become the sole legal tender, and single currency, of the participating states.

[5] The four criteria, described in Art. 109j (1) and Protocol 6 of the Treaty, are: (i) a "high degree of price stability," apparent from a rate of inflation which is "close" to, and does not exceed by more than 1.5 percentage points, that of, at most, the three best performing states; (ii) an average nominal interest rate on long-term government bonds or comparable securities that does not exceed by more than 2 percentage points that of the three best performing states in terms of price stability; (iii) observance of the "normal" fluctuation margins of the exchange rate mechanism of the European Monetary System for at least two years without "severe tensions" or a devaluation "on its own initiative"; and (iv) a government budgetary position such that the state is not the subject of a decision by the Council under Art. 104c (6) that an "excessive deficit" exists. Of the eleven member-states likely to satisfy the convergence criteria pertaining to inflation, interest rates, and participation in the ERM (Belgium, Denmark, Germany, Spain, France, Ireland, Luxembourg, the Netherlands, Austria, Portugal, and Finland), as of early 1998 only five (Denmark, Ireland, Luxembourg, the Netherlands, and Finland) had been judged not to have an "excessive deficit"—and one of those (Denmark) had already given notice, at Edinburgh in 1992, that it would not participate in the third stage. Nevertheless, the other ten, plus Italy, were deemed eligible for the third stage when the final decision was made in May 1998. For a discussion of the criteria and their likely application, see Cameron (1998).

new ones in the domains of monetary and exchange-rate policy. We suggest the answer lies in the fact that EMU represents, and has represented since its conception three decades ago, a means of resolving the inherent tension that occurs when states that retain such essential attributes of sovereignty as national currencies and pursue distinctive monetary and exchange-rate policies seek to create and extend a single internal market among their increasingly interdependent economies.

After considering the imperatives posed by increased economic interdependence, the progressive extension of the single internal market, and the need to address and resolve tensions and conflicts among the member-states over monetary and exchange-rate policy, the chapter turns to a consideration of some of the economic, political, and institutional uncertainties and dilemmas that are likely to confront the member-states participating in the third stage. Concentrating on the issues of growth and employment, and political control of macroeconomic policy, we consider whether EMU will provide a remedy for the low growth and high unemployment that now afflict much of the EU. And we consider whether, as some have argued, it will be necessary to create an "economic government," a "political counterweight" to the ECB, in the third stage and perhaps further extend the authority and capacity of existing and new supranational institutions in the domain of macroeconomic governance.

1. Why EMU? The Underlying Imperatives

Considerable skepticism exists throughout the EU about the feasibility and desirability of moving to the third stage of EMU in 1999. Several member-states—most notably, Britain, Denmark, and Sweden—decided, at varying times, not to join the third stage in 1999.[6] And in the wake of the economic, political, and human costs of meeting the Treaty's "reference value" of 3 percent of gross domestic product for the 1997 budget deficit, several others appeared increasingly uncertain about their commitment to enter the third stage in 1999, notwithstanding the unambiguous language of Art. 109j (4).[7] Despite the skepticism

---

[6] Britain negotiated an "opt-out" at Maastricht by which, according to the terms of Protocol 11, it is not obliged or committed to moving to the third stage without a separate decision to do so by its government and parliament. (And in any event, it has not participated in the ERM of the EMS since September 1992.) Denmark negotiated an "opt-out" from the third stage which appears in Protocol 12 of the Treaty and gave notice at the Edinburgh meeting of the European Council in 1992 that it would not participate in the third stage. Sweden announced in June 1997 that it would not enter the third stage in 1999 and that it would hold an election or referendum on the issue in the event it decided to recommend entry. (In any event, however, Sweden, like the UK, would not qualify since it remains outside the ERM.) In addition to these three, a fourth, Greece, will not participate—because it did not meet any of the convergence criteria in 1997.

[7] Of these, perhaps the most consequential is France, where, after its triumph in the May–June 1997 elections, the Socialist-dominated government brought to office a set of "conditions," inscribed in the Socialist Party's program and election manifesto, that were necessary

and equivocation, however, most if not all of the member-states have maintained a commitment to EMU for much of the time over the past three decades. Why is that? And why is it that, almost without exception, governments have been willing in recent years to impose considerable costs on their economies and their citizens—and upon themselves in the form of lost support—in order to qualify for the third and final stage of EMU?

One possible explanation for the continuing commitment to EMU is that it reflects a commitment to the ongoing process of European integration. Another is that it reflects not so much a commitment to integration as a recognition that the process of integration has a life and history of its own covering a half-century, that individual governments for the most part are no more than brief participants in the larger drama, and that they are therefore, for better or worse, bound by the commitments of their predecessors. Still another is that none of the member-states, not even the ones which are most skeptical about the creation of supranational authority, wishes to be left behind and on the margins as the EU embarks on perhaps the most consequential institutional innovation in its history.

As plausible as each of these may be, there is an alternative explanation for why most of the governments of the EU member-states have so single-mindedly pursued the objective of qualifying for the third stage of EMU. We shall argue that, as paradoxical as it may seem, the continued commitment to EMU and the willingness to pursue policies that are, in certain respects, costly to their citizens, their economies, and in some instances, to themselves, reflects a belief that the extension of supranational authority associated with EMU will serve their national interest. In particular, the extension of existing and creation of new supranational authority in the domains of monetary and exchange-rate policy will, they believe, enable them to resolve tensions posed by the juxtaposition of political sovereignty and economic interdependence. Problems and conflicts inevitably arise among states that, on the one hand, retain control of their national currencies and are able to pursue different monetary and exchange-rate policies and, on the other, have economies that are not only highly interdependent but are being reconstituted into a single internal market. Unable to escape from economic interdependence, one remedy, when policies conflict and either impose costs on others or impede the development and maintenance of the single market (or both), is to increase the

---

if France were to enter the third stage—(i) that Italy and Spain be among the states entering the third stage in 1999; (ii) that a pact of "solidarity and growth," emphasizing employment, be negotiated; (iii) that a "European economic government" be created to provide a "political counterweight" to the ECB; and (iv) that the euro not be overvalued vis-à-vis the dollar and yen. In addition, it stipulated that no new austerity measures be taken to reduce the deficit—despite the fact that the deficit was expected to exceed 3% of GDP. The Socialists' leader, Lionel Jospin, repeated the "conditions" immediately after having been named Prime Minister. The equivocation in the government's support for entry into the third stage in 1999 was underscored by the fact that, in the absence of a Socialist majority in the Assembly, the new government depended on the support of the Communist Party, which was implacably opposed to EMU. On the "conditions," see *The Economist*, May 10, 1997: 46; and *Le Monde*, June 7, 1997: 1, 2.

congruence between the scope of political authority and the domain of economic activity. For states that are embedded in a densely institutionalized supranational organization, that in all likelihood means extending the domain of responsibility and institutional capacity of that organization.

In short, resolving the tension between political sovereignty and economic interdependence, between control of policy by the member-states and creation of a single integrated market, has constituted the underlying imperative driving the quest for EMU intermittently over the past three decades. We shall illustrate several aspects of the argument, first by noting the extent and degree of economic interdependence among the member-states of the EC and the "spillover" effects of the progressive development of the single internal market. Then we shall note how both in the late 1960s, when the idea of EMU was first broached, and the late 1980s, when the idea was resurrected, the extension of supranational authority into the domains of monetary and exchange-rate policy provided a means by which states in conflict over exchange-rate policy—in particular, France and Germany—could secure and defend their interests.

2. Trade, Interdependence, and EMU

Although its popularity has fluctuated over time, the assumptions underlying EMU have remained largely unchanged over the three decades since the concept was first articulated in the late 1960s. It is predicated on the assumptions that the attainment of an internal market among the member-states requires stability among the currencies of the member-states, that currency instability can be eliminated by irrevocably fixing the exchange rates among the member-states' currencies, and that maintaining irrevocably fixed exchange rates requires the creation of a common currency and an institution at the supranational level charged with responsibility for monetary policy. Resting on those foundations, the idea of EMU, and of extending supranational authority in the domains of exchange-rate and monetary policy, appeared as a credible remedy to an enduring problem—how to create a single internal market for goods and services among member-states with highly interdependent economies in a world with multiple currencies, volatile exchange rates, and fragile exchange-rate regimes.

Tables 7.1 and 7.2 provide an indication of the extent of interdependence among the member-states of the Community and Union, and the extent to which their interdependence has increased over time.[8] Table 7.1 presents a measure of trade dependence—the ratio of all exports to gross domestic product (GDP)—for each of the EU member-states at different times over the period 1958–95. (For the sake of comparison, it also includes comparable data for the USA and Japan.) Table 7.2 presents a measure of the concentration of

---

[8] On interdependence, see, among many, Kenen (1995).

Table 7.1. Trade dependence of the EU member-
states, 1958–1995

	Exports as a % of GDP			
	1958	1973	1986	1995
Belgium	31.9	55.6	70.5	72.6
Luxembourg	77.3	88.1	98.3	91.8
Netherlands	48.3	46.0	50.7	53.3
France	12.3	17.6	21.2	23.5
Germany	22.1	21.8	30.2	23.6
Italy	12.5	17.4	20.2	27.6
UK		23.7	25.7	28.4
Ireland		36.2	52.7	74.6
Denmark		28.5	32.0	34.5
Greece			17.0	16.5
Spain			19.9	23.7
Portugal			29.5	33.3
Austria				37.7
Sweden				40.9
Finland				38.0
EU[a]	34.1	37.2	39.0	41.3
Japan	11.0	10.0	11.4	9.4
USA	5.0	6.9	7.4	11.4

[a] Average of ratios for EU member-states.

Source: Organization for Economic Co-operation and Development (1997, and earlier).

trade within the Community—the ratio of exports to other member-states
relative to all exports—for each of the member-states over the period 1958–95.
These data demonstrate that the degree of trade dependence in the EU has been
and remains far greater than in the USA or Japan. Thus, whereas exports now
constitute roughly 10 percent of the GDP of the USA and Japan, they constitute, on average, roughly 40 percent of the GDP of the fifteen member-states
of the EU. (Even if the EU is treated as a single entity and the ratio is calculated
by dividing the combined exports of all fifteen members by their combined
GDP, the figure—about 30 percent in 1995—exceeds those of the USA and
Japan by a factor of three.) And for some of the member-states—most notably,
the smaller ones with unusually "open" economies such as Luxembourg,
Ireland, Belgium, and the Netherlands—exports constitute a far larger share of
GDP.[9] Finally, and perhaps most important, while the data in Table 7.1 suggest

---

[9] De Grauwe (1994: 55, 76) notes that the benefits of monetary union increase, and the costs
decrease, with increasing trade dependence and interdependence. Seen in that light, it is not
surprising that, as will be seen later, support for EMU has been unusually strong in these four
member-states.

Table 7.2. The concentration of EU trade within the EU,
1958–1995

	% of all exports to other EC/EU member-states			
	1958	1973	1986	1995
Belgium–Luxembourg[a]	45.1	73.1	73.2	71.6
Netherlands	41.6	72.6	74.9	75.7
France	22.2	54.7	55.3	62.8
Germany	27.3	47.1	50.8	57.0
Italy	23.6	50.1	53.7	56.8
UK		31.8	48.0	53.9
Ireland		76.0	72.0	72.2
Denmark		45.3	47.0	61.6
Greece			63.7	55.5
Spain			60.3	72.3
Portugal			68.3	80.3
Austria				59.3
Sweden				56.9
Finland				56.7

[a] Following IMF conventions, Belgium and Luxembourg are treated as one country.

Source: Calculated from data in International Monetary Fund (1996, and earlier).

that the degree of dependence on trade has tended to increase over time in most of the member-states and in the EU as a whole, the data in Table 7.2 suggest that very significant increases occurred in almost every member-state in the extent to which trade was redirected from markets outside the EC and EU to markets in the other member-states.

Recognition of the implications of interdependence for monetary and exchange-rate policy first occurred in the late 1960s—most consequentially, when Pierre Werner, the Prime Minister and Minister of Finance of Luxembourg, proposed that the Community create a European unit of account, lock irrevocably exchange rates among the currencies of its member-states, and create a European Monetary Fund with sufficient resources to intervene in exchange markets in order to maintain the fixed exchange rates. Obviously, Werner was not responding mechanistically to changes in the extent of trade dependence and concentration within the EC.[10] Nevertheless, the data in

---

[10] It goes without saying, but is nevertheless worth noting, that Werner's proposal to lock irrevocably the exchange rates of the member-states' currencies would have seemed eminently reasonable to the Prime Minister and Minister of Finance of a country whose currency had been irrevocably locked with that of a neighbor (Belgium) at a 1 : 1 ratio without margins, and which had accepted that neighbor's central bank as the arbiter of monetary policy for the two coun-

Tables 7.1 and 7.2 for the period 1958–73 *do* suggest that at the time he made his proposal all of the member-states had experienced a marked and dramatic redirection in trade toward other member-states. Thus, whereas roughly one-fifth to one-quarter of the exports of Germany, France, and Italy were sold in other member-states in 1958, by 1973 approximately one-*half* were. And whereas slightly more than two-fifths of the exports of Belgium, the Netherlands, and Luxembourg were sold in other member-states in 1958, nearly *three-quarters* were fifteen years later. Indeed, the data in Table 7.2 suggest that the extent to which trade was redirected toward other member-states may have been greater in the first fifteen years of the European Economic Community (EEC) than at any later time. Obviously, the increasing dependence on trade and increasing concentration of trade within the EC—in short, the increasing economic interdependence of the member-states—could only have raised the salience of currency relations among them.

2.1. The progressive extension of the internal market and EMU

If a high and rising level of interdependence among the economies of the member-states of the EC constituted the context for Werner's proposal (and later ones as well) to form an Economic and Monetary Union, an important feature of that context that gave additional impetus to the idea of EMU was the fact that the member-states' economies were not only highly interdependent but were the subject of an effort undertaken after the creation of the EEC in 1958 to create a single internal market. Thus, one of the reasons Werner put forward his initial proposal in January 1968 was the fact that the Six faced imminent deadlines in regard to internal tariffs and the pricing of agricultural commodities that would make them even more sensitive to fluctuations in the exchange rates among their currencies. In particular, the Community faced the imminent elimination, on July 1, 1968, of internal tariffs, which would reduce the ability of governments to affect, to their advantage, the prices of foreign-produced goods in domestic markets and, presumably, would make relative prices, and trade, dependent exclusively on costs, profits, and exchange rates. And the first phase in the establishment of common agricultural prices was scheduled to begin on that same date as well—and common prices for commodities would, of course, require stable exchange rates among the

tries, for nearly five decades, since the advent of the Belgium–Luxembourg Economic Union in 1922.

A month after Werner put forward his proposal, Raymond Barre, the vice-president of the Commission and the member responsible for monetary affairs, responded with a memorandum to the Council that, while not advocating that exchange rates be locked and a European Fund be created, nevertheless called for the progressive elimination of margins of fluctuation among the currencies of the member-states, the creation of a notional unit of account, multilateral negotiation of realignments, the development of a mechanism of mutual assistance to fund interventions in currency markets, and possible adoption of a joint external fluctuation range vis-à-vis non-Community currencies. On Werner's proposal and Barre's rejoinder, see Magnifico (1973), Tsoukalis (1977), and Kruse (1980).

member-states' currencies.[11] Although the imminent elimination of tariffs and establishment of common agricultural prices may not have "spilled over" automatically into the domain of exchange-rate policy and made the introduction of EMU a necessity, there can be no doubt that, at a time when the vast bulk of the EC budget was devoted to agriculture and the EC was about to establish common prices in one agricultural commodity after another, the Six (and their farmers and consumers) were highly sensitive to, and concerned about dampening, fluctuations over time in the values of their currencies.

If a functionalist "spillover" from the progressive extension of the single internal market to EMU was largely limited to one sector, and largely implicit, in the late 1960s, the subsequent effort in the 1980s to complete the internal market broadened the linkages between that effort and EMU and made them more explicit. Indeed, the Single European Act (SEA) explicitly put EMU back on the agenda of the Community, claiming in its Preamble that one of its objectives was the "progressive realization of economic and monetary union." And the Act itself contained a chapter with the somewhat ambiguous title of "Co-operation in Economic and Monetary Policy (Economic and Monetary Union)." Soon after the formal signing of the SEA, Jacques Delors, the President of the Commission, sought to marshal support for monetary reform by commissioning a group of economists and other experts, headed by Tommaso Padoa-Schioppa, to investigate the economic consequences of the decision to create a single internal market by 1992. Although they did not explicitly call for a new variant of EMU, Padoa-Schioppa and his colleagues (1987) did foresee the need for greater coordination of monetary policy and a strengthening of the European Monetary System (EMS) as the internal market became a reality, noting the incompatibility of nationally determined monetary policies with EC-wide free trade, free movement of capital, and fixed exchange rates.

No less important than the language of the SEA and the analyses of experts in moving EMU back onto the agenda of the EC were the actual policies undertaken in pursuit of the internal market. Of those, undoubtedly the most important was the decision taken in June 1988 to remove all exchange controls that impeded the movement of capital. Indeed, Colchester and Buchan (1990: 45) claim that decision was "arguably the most important single directive in the 1992 programme." Involving an agreement by eight member-states—including, most notably, France and Italy, where such controls were most pervasive—to remove all controls by mid-1990 and by four others to remove them by 1995,[12] it created at least the hypothetical possibility that, henceforth, capital could, in response to divergent economic performances, move across borders unfettered by national regulatory controls. The result of that free movement, of course, could be greater variability in the relative value of cur-

---

[11] On the role these Community actions played in prompting the proposal for EMU, see Kruse (1980).

[12] In addition to the eight which agreed to end capital controls in 1990, Spain and Ireland were allowed to retain their controls until 1992, and Portugal and Greece until 1995.

rencies, thereby amplifying and exacerbating whatever tendencies might exist for exchange rates to be volatile and unstable. Such a prospect, coming just as the EC was about to achieve its longstanding objective of creating a single internal market, could only reinforce the view that the creation of a single internal market among interdependent economies would require—eventually if not immediately—the creation of a single currency. As Eichengreen and Frieden (1994: 7–8) argue:

A truly integrated European market for capital as well as labor and commodities cannot exist in the presence of exchange controls. The efficiency gains of the Single Market thus require the removal of capital controls. The removal of controls, according to this thesis, renders infeasible all monetary arrangements but a single European currency . . . [since] periods of exchange-rate stability punctuated by occasional realignments were possible only because capital controls protected central bank reserves against speculative attacks motivated by anticipations of realignment. . . . In this sense, then, the Single European Act forced the issue. It required the removal of capital controls, which undermined the viability of the EMS and confronted the Community with the choice of reverting to floating or moving forward to monetary unification.

2.2. Franco-German exchange rate conflicts and EMU

If the high and increasing interdependence of the European economies and the progressive extension of the single internal market made it increasingly necessary for the member-states of the EC to contemplate some institutional means by which exchange-rate policy could be coordinated so as to reduce the potential fluctuation over time in the values of their currencies and the exchange rates among them, it was tension and conflict between certain member-states—in particular, between France and Germany—over exchange-rate policy that in large part provoked the original commitment to EMU in the 1960s and then again in the 1980s the renewal of that commitment. In both instances, the member-states concluded, paradoxically, that their national interests could best be served by extending the authority of existing and new supranational institutions in that domain of policy along the lines first suggested by Werner in 1968.

Not long after Werner first articulated his vision of EMU, a dispute developed in the fall of 1968 between France and Germany over the appropriate exchange rate between the franc and the mark. Prompted in large part by a growing divergence in monetary policy and rates of inflation in the two countries—the result of Germany's successful effort to stabilize prices (an effort aided by the country's first post-War recession in 1966–7), on one hand, and a spiraling rate of inflation in France, on the other[13]—the dispute resulted in a year-long

---

[13] In order to settle the widespread strikes of May–June 1968, the French government had accepted labor union demands for a sharp increase in wages which soon resulted in an increase in demand and consumption, including the consumption of imported goods, an increase in costs and prices, including the price of exports, and a deterioration in the balance of trade and an acceleration in the rate of inflation.

standoff between the two governments as to whether the mark should be revalued, the franc devalued, or both. Despite downward pressure on the franc, in anticipation of a devaluation, the French government refused to devalue and called upon Germany to revalue the mark. But the German government, fearing the effects of a revaluation on its export sector and on the prices its farmers would receive through the Common Agricultural Policy, and believing, in any event, that the source of the problem was France's higher rate of inflation rather than undervaluation of the mark, refused.[14] Still refusing to devalue, the French government instituted exchange controls and a deflationary macroeconomic policy.

The standoff continued through the winter and into the spring and summer of 1969. Funds continued to flow out of France, in anticipation of a devaluation, and into Germany, in anticipation of a revaluation, but the French government refused to devalue and the German government refused to revalue (despite being urged to do so by, among others, the Bundesbank President and the Minister of Economics.)[15] Eventually, in August 1969, the French government decided to devalue. But underlining the continued lack of cooperation between the two countries, the devaluation was instituted without prior consultation between the two governments and was large enough—11.1 percent —to threaten whatever advantage German producers had in French markets or vis-à-vis French producers in the German market. In Germany, meanwhile, the mark remained undervalued in the view of many, notwithstanding the devaluation of the franc, and funds continued to flow into the country in anticipation of a revaluation after the impending election. Indeed, the inflows were so great that in late September, several days before the election, the government closed the foreign exchange markets. After opening them again several days later, the mark was allowed to float, which it did for several weeks until being revalued by 9.3 percent.[16]

The year-long tension over exchange-rate policy between the two governments, followed by a realignment of the magnitude that occurred between August and October 1969, shattered any illusion that the Bretton Woods exchange-rate regime, even if it remained intact (something that was beginning to appear increasingly improbable by then), was sufficient to assure the stability of exchange rates among the currencies of the EC that was necessary for the creation and maintenance of a single internal market for goods and services.[17] For even if the external exchange-rate regime remained stable, as long as multiple currencies existed within the Community and as long as they

---

[14] On the Franco-German currency dispute of 1968–9, see Tsoukalis (1977: 70–6) and De Grauwe (1989: 30–40). On the German central bank's position, see Marsh (1992: 188).

[15] On the positions taken within the German government and the Bundesbank, see Tsoukalis (1977: 73–80).

[16] For discussion of the French devaluation and German revaluation, see Magnifico (1973), Tsoukalis (1977: 76–80), and Kruse (1980).

[17] On the last years of the Bretton Woods exchange-rate regime, see, among many, De Grauwe (1989).

could move in different directions, in response to the different economic performances and prospects of the member-states, the potential for exchange-rate instability of the kind witnessed in 1968 and 1969 would remain. And just as that instability had led the two governments to introduce barriers to trade within the Community—France had introduced capital controls rather than devaluing in 1968 and border taxes to keep agricultural prices down in 1969, while Germany had provided its farmers with price supplements to offset the lower prices they received through the Common Agricultural Policy (CAP) after the revaluation of the mark—so, too, any such instability in the future might disrupt trade and impede the development of the single internal market that would soon, upon completion of a twelve-year transition period, come into being.

The dispute in exchange-rate policy, the side effects of that dispute for the internal market, and the adverse effects of the final resolution of the dispute for both France and Germany—for France an acceleration in the price of imported goods because of the large devaluation, for Germany a substantial erosion in the price competitiveness of its exports in the French market and other markets as well—led the newly elected leaders of the two countries to propose that the EC create an Economic and Monetary Union. Based largely on the earlier proposals of Werner and Barre, and put forward at the December 1969 summit meeting of the leaders of the Six by Willy Brandt, the Chancellor in the newly elected Social Democratic-Free Democratic government, with the support of Georges Pompidou, de Gaulle's successor as President, the proposal was endorsed by the leaders, who called upon the Council to prepare a plan to move in stages to Economic and Monetary Union.[18] The Council established a working group, chaired by Werner, that recommended the creation of an EMU in three stages over a period of ten years, culminating in a monetary union marked by irrevocably fixed exchange rates without margins of fluctuation, complete liberalization of capital movements, agreement on budget aggregates and deficits, and centralization of all decisions regarding monetary policy.[19]

The EC did not, of course, succeed in implementing the Werner committee's plan. No sooner had the Council endorsed the proposal than the Bretton Woods exchange-rate regime entered the last phase of its existence.[20] The effort to create a common European monetary and exchange-rate policy soon foundered on the shoals of the new floating exchange-rate regime that replaced Bretton Woods, and as the European currencies lost their anchor to gold via the dollar, the ambition to irrevocably lock exchange rates and create a single currency gave way to a more pressing and less ambitious concern—how, in a world of

---

[18] The first stage was to be marked by coordination and harmonization of economic policy and a second stage by the creation of a reserve fund and completion of EMU. On the contents of the proposal and the fact that it was put forward by Brandt, see Tsoukalis (1977: 83).

[19] For the report of the Werner committee, see European Communities (1970). For a discussion of the committee's deliberations, see Tsoukalis (1977: 83–105). Its recommendations were accepted by the Council in February 1971.

[20] On the last years of the Bretton Woods regime, see, among many, De Grauwe (1989).

flexible exchange rates, to confine the fluctuations over time in the values of the EC currencies to a narrow range so as to maintain the internal market. Eventually, after the failure of the first such effort, the "snake," in the mid-1970s and a resurgence of inflation and exchange-rate instability, a new, improved version of the "snake," the European Monetary System, came into being in March 1979.[21]

Despite the difference in contexts between the late 1960s, when the idea of EMU was first articulated, and the late 1980s, when it was resurrected—most notably, the demise of the Bretton Woods regime and the development of the EMS—an important commonality exists in the antecedents of the two proposals, in addition to the continuing impact of high and increasing economic interdependence and the progressive extension of the single market. In the late 1980s, as in the late 1960s, EMU came onto the agenda of the EC because of a dispute between France and Germany over exchange-rate policy. And as was the case in the 1968-9 dispute, EMU came onto the agenda because at least one of the governments believed an extension of supranational authority in that domain of policy would serve the national interest.

The EMS was designed to create a "zone of monetary stability" in Europe but as it evolved it became not only a zone of monetary stability but a zone of exchange-rate stability as well. As inflation rates in the EC began to drop in the early 1980s and converged at historically low levels in the mid-1980s, exchange rates likewise became increasingly stable, a by-product of that deceleration and convergence in rates of inflation (as well as the serendipitous sharp upward movement in the value of the dollar vis-à-vis the European currencies that occurred in the first half of the 1980s). Table 7.3 provides some summary indicators of the extent to which the EMS evolved over time into a highly stable exchange rate system. The data indicate that the frequency and magnitude of realignments decreased sharply over time, to such an extent that by the late 1980s the EMS appeared to have become a quasi-fixed exchange-rate regime. Thus, while seven realignments occurred in the first four years of the EMS, through March 1983, of which five involved two or more currencies and four involved the franc and/or the mark, in the next four years, from April 1983 through April 1987, there were only four realignments, only three that involved two or more currencies, and only three that involved the franc and/or the mark. And in the five and one-half years between April 1987 and September 1992, there was only *one* realignment, involving one currency, and that involved only a technical adjustment when the lira shifted from its wider ±6 percent band to the narrower ±2.25 percent band. In retrospect, it is perhaps

---

[21] While retaining several features of the "snake," such as its bilateral parity grid of currencies and its fluctuation range of ±2.25 percent, unlike its predecessor the EMS had a mechanism for joint interventions in currency markets and for negotiating realignments among exchange rates. For the definitive account of the creation of the EMS, see Ludlow (1982). On the performance of the EMS, see, among many, Van Ypersele and Koeune (1985), Giavazzi *et al.* (1988), Giavazzi and Giovannini (1989), De Grauwe and Papademos (1990), Ungerer *et al.* (1990), and Cameron (1992).

Table 7.3. Realignments in the European Monetary System, March 1979–August 1992

	No. of realignments	No. of realignments involving two or more currencies	No. of revaluations of the mark	No. of devaluations of the franc
March 1979 through March 1983	7	5	4	3
April 1983 through April 1987	4	3	3	1
May 1987 through August 1992	1	0	0	0

Sources: Ungerer *et al.* (1990: 95) and Cameron (1992: 46).

understandable that the member-states could imagine, as their currencies re-mained within the narrow bands for long periods of time without realignment, that fixing their rates irrevocably would be little more than the logical next step in the evolution of the EMS.[22]

As inflation rates decelerated and exchange rates became increasingly stable, a consensus about macroeconomic policy began to take shape that emphasized the desirability and even necessity of price stability, exchange rate stability, and fiscal and monetary austerity.[23] The emerging macroeconomic consensus in Europe (and elsewhere) in the 1980s implied, for the member-states of the EC, emulation, above all, of the economic and monetary policy pursued in Germany and the Netherlands—the countries with the lowest rates of inflation and the only ones never to devalue their currencies within the EMS. The German Bundesbank came to be perceived as the institutional embodiment of "wise" policy and the mark increasingly took on the role of "anchor" currency within the EMS. The Bundesbank came to be recognized as the body that shaped monetary policy in Europe by, in effect, setting the floor with its interest rates for rates in the other member-states participating in the exchange rate mechan-ism of the EMS; as Colchester and Buchan (1990: 160–1) put it, "The Bundes-bank in Frankfurt has become Europe's de facto central bank. Other EMS

[22] It is interesting to note how the increasing stability in exchange rates came to be viewed, perhaps erroneously, as indicative of good exchange-rate policy. Indeed, this presumption was incorporated into the Treaty as one of the "convergence criteria" to be satisfied in order to enter the third and final stage of EMU, when it was stipulated that one measure of a "high degree of sustainable convergence" was the observance of the normal fluctuation margins of the ERM for at least two years without "severe tensions" or a devaluation "on its own initiative."

[23] Of central importance in the development of that consensus was the French Socialist government's decision in 1982–3 to remain in the EMS and negotiate a series of modest devalu-ations that were accompanied by increasingly tight fiscal and monetary policy. See Cameron (1995a, 1996a).

participants have to ape a German monetary policy in which they have no formal say." As that happened—as the Bundesbank appeared increasingly to be the body that shaped monetary policy in Europe, it was inevitable that the idea of EMU would return, for if it were true that the German central bank had become "Europe's de facto central bank," how long could it be before other member-states concluded that, if the EC *did* in fact already have a national central bank that was playing a role analogous to that of a single European central bank, and a national currency that had in some respects taken on a role analogous to that of a single European currency, their interests might best be served by having a share of control over that bank and currency?

The growing perceptions of asymmetries in power and influence in the EMS in the mid-to-late 1980s were compounded by growing perceptions that asymmetries existed as well in responsibilities for adjustment within the EMS and in the distribution of the gains from trade. When the EMS was founded, it was assumed that the burdens of adjustment would be distributed symmetrically between both the strong- and weak-currency countries. But as the system evolved, adjustment came to be seen as ultimately the responsibility of the weak-currency countries whose policies diverged from those of Germany (and its close associate, the Netherlands). And not only was the responsibility for adjustment borne largely by the weak-currency countries but, as exchange rates became increasingly stable in the EMS and less responsive to overvaluations (or undervaluations) of currencies, adjustment by the weak-currency countries inevitably came to rely to a greater extent on domestic contraction—that is, adjusting relative prices downward by contracting domestic demand through some combination of tight fiscal policy, high interest rates, and wage restraint.

Just as the burdens of adjustment were asymmetrically distributed, so too the distribution of material benefits from intra-EC trade became distinctly *asymmetric* as the EMS evolved in the 1980s. For example, the greater degree of price stabilization in the strong-currency countries, when coupled with the decreasing frequency of realignments of exchange rates in the EMS, caused the strong currencies to become increasingly undervalued over time and thereby provided the countries with those currencies a competitive advantage in export markets. As a result, they tended to earn increasingly large surpluses from their international transactions, both within the EC and globally. Conversely, the countries with higher rates of inflation and weaker currencies found, as realignments became less frequent, that their currencies became increasingly *overvalued* and their exports thus *less* competitive. Thus, as the data in Table 7.4 indicate, over the first dozen years of the EMS, from 1979 through 1990, Germany earned a cumulative surplus in its trade with other members of the EC of more than $275bn., and the Netherlands a cumulative surplus of more than $150bn. France and Italy, on the other hand, experienced large cumulative *deficits* during the period—more than $40bn. for Italy and more than $85bn. for France.

Those asymmetries in influence and gain provided the backdrop for a new round of Franco-German tension over exchange-rate policy that, very much

Table 7.4. The balance of trade within the European Community, 1973–1990: Cumulative surplus (+) or deficit (–) with other EC member-states (in $bn.)

	1973–8	1979–84	1985–90	1979–90
Germany	27.6	49.4	227.8	277.2
Netherlands	26.2	71.9	86.2	158.1
Belgium–Luxembourg	–0.6	1.5	5.1	6.6
Italy	–4.0	–13.0	–32.5	–45.5
France	–9.2	–37.3	–51.6	–88.9
UK	–26.2	–23.0	–114.3	–137.3
Ireland	–2.4	6.2	16.4	22.6
Denmark	–8.1	–5.4	–1.2	–6.6
Greece	–7.3	–13.9	–26.6	–40.5
Spain	–9.2	2.7	–40.9	–38.2
Portugal	–4.9	–7.5	–15.2	–22.7

Source: International Monetary Fund (1996, and earlier).

like the experience in 1968–9, led to the resurrection of the idea of EMU. In January 1987, the franc was overvalued (as it had been throughout most of the 1980s) and was increasingly under pressure in the currency markets as the American dollar dropped sharply from its 1985 high and the German mark increased in value.[24] As the franc moved toward its floor in the EMS, Edouard Balladur, the Minister of Finance in the conservative "cohabitation" government headed by Jacques Chirac, deliberately let it fall through its floor in order to force the Bundesbank to intervene in the markets in support of the franc. The French position reflected a view similar to that of the government nearly two decades earlier in the 1968–9 dispute—that, rather than the franc being overvalued and deserving devaluation, the mark was undervalued and should be revalued. To that was added the belief (supported by trade statistics) that, as a result of the mark's undervaluation, Germany enjoyed an unfair advantage in intra-EC trade while the weaker-currency countries not only suffered in trade but were increasingly required to bear a disproportionate share of the costs of adjustment.

Eventually, the German government agreed, reluctantly, to revalue the mark by a modest amount (3 percent). Balladur's gambit had a modest, but measurable, effect on French growth, employment, and trade. Nevertheless, he remained dissatisfied with the operation of the EMS, and in July 1987 he called upon the Community to strengthen the EMS and alleviate the asymmetry that existed between Germany and its partners. That call, reiterated in August, led to

[24] Between 1980 and the first quarter of 1985, the dollar increased in value, relative to the currencies of its trading partners, by about 60%. During the next two years, it dropped in value by almost one-third. For a discussion of the overvaluation of the franc, despite the three devaluations of 1981–3, see Cameron (1995*a*, 1996*a*).

the Basle–Nyborg Agreements of September 1987, in which the Committee of Central Bank Governors and the Finance Ministers agreed to create a credit facility to support intramarginal interventions in currency markets.[25]

Balladur continued to call for alterations in the EMS. In December 1987, he publicly called for reform of the EMS and prepared a set of proposals for his colleagues in the Finance Ministries of the Community designed to improve the functioning of the EMS and promote greater exchange-rate stability. Prepared in the wake of renewed attacks on the franc at the end of 1987—prompted by a rise in the mark as the American dollar dropped in value—that had forced several increases in French interest rates, just as the French presidential campaign was getting underway (in which Chirac would be a candidate), Balladur's proposals sought to introduce a greater degree of symmetry in the operation of the EMS—especially in the obligation to defend currencies under attack.[26] Among other things, he called for a strengthening of the European Monetary Cooperation Fund to assist central bank intervention in markets. And he proposed that, in order to present a common European posture vis-à-vis the dollar and the yen, a common currency be created that would be managed by a single central bank. In effect, he called for a new EMU!

Several of Balladur's colleagues—for the most part, ministers in weak-currency countries—endorsed his proposals. Giuliano Amato, the Italian Finance Minister, was the first to do so publicly. And in a paper circulated to his Community colleagues, Amato (1988) criticized the EMS for enabling Germany to systematically undervalue the mark—and thereby accumulate huge trade surpluses at the expense of its partners in the Community—while generating a deflationary bias throughout the Community through its tight money policy. For Amato, the political cost of an "agreed loss of autonomy" through the creation of a European central bank was preferable to the unilateral loss of autonomy to Germany that existed in the EMS and the economic costs suffered in that system.[27]

Not surprisingly, the Balladur initiative was criticized by German leaders and officials. Helmut Kohl registered his "coolness" toward the plan almost immediately, and Gerhard Stoltenberg, the Finance Minister, and Karl-Otto Pöhl, the Bundesbank President, voiced their skepticism as well.[28] They disputed France's claim that it was disadvantaged by the operation of the EMS, urged Britain to enter the EMS as a first step in a process that might eventually lead to a single central bank and common currency, and called for the elimination of all capital controls in the Community. However, Balladur's proposals *did* receive the endorsement of one important German official—Hans-Dietrich

[25] On the Basle–Nyborg agreements, see Colchester and Buchan (1990: 163).
[26] On the Balladur proposals, see Colchester and Buchan (1990: 166) as well as *Financial Times*, January 7, 1988: 2; January 8, 1988: 2; and January 25, 1988: 3. The proposals themselves were presented to the Council in Balladur (1988).
[27] See Colchester and Buchan (1990: 167).
[28] See *Financial Times*, January 15, 1988: 2, which reports Kohl's comments at a press luncheon. On the German finance ministry's views, see *Financial Times*, January 25, 1988: 3. Stoltenberg's views were presented to the Council in Stoltenberg (1988).

Genscher, the Foreign Minister.[29] And because Germany held the Council presidency in the first half of 1988, and because the task of preparing the agenda of the meeting of the European Council during the German presidency fell to Genscher, the proposals, and the issue of EMU, appeared on the agenda of the European Council in Hanover in June 1988. The result, of course, was the creation of the committee chaired by Delors—and, ultimately, the negotiation of the Treaty on European Union.[30]

3. EMU after 1999: Third-Stage Dilemmas

At Madrid in 1995, the heads of state and government of the EU confirmed "unequivocally" that the third and final stage of EMU would begin on January 1, 1999. Despite the difficulties that many of the member-states have encountered since then in satisfying the criteria for entry to the third stage—especially the criterion pertaining to "excessive deficits"—the commitment remains intact and there is little reason to think the EU will not in fact move to the third and final stage of EMU on the first day of 1999. Indeed, as noted earlier, not only is it very likely that the final stage of EMU will commence on January 1, 1999 but it is very likely, as well, that a large number of member-states—possibly as many as ten or eleven—will be judged worthy of entry to the third stage at that time.

If it is the case, then, that, armed with the European Monetary Institute's "reference scenario," the EU is clearly on a course that will carry most of its member-states into the third and final stage of EMU in 1999, it is nevertheless also true that considerable uncertainty exists as to how EMU will function *after* 1999 and, in particular, how participation in the third stage will affect the member-states that adopt the euro and participate in the Governing Council of the ECB. Of special concern, no doubt, will be the effect of EMU on the economic performance of the participating member-states—in particular, the extent to which (if at all) EMU will enable them to redress the longstanding problems of low rates of economic growth and high levels of unemployment that afflict so much of the EU. No less important will be issues pertaining to institutional design and governance—specifically, how (if at all) economic policy

---

[29] See Colchester and Buchan (1990: 167–8) and, for Genscher's views, his speech to the European Parliament, reported in *Financial Times*, January 21, 1988: 2; and Genscher (1988).

[30] At Hanover, the leaders created the Committee for the Study of Economic and Monetary Union to "study and propose concrete stages leading to the progressive realization of economic and monetary union." The committee, chaired by Delors and consisting largely of the central bank governors, issued its report in April 1989, and at Madrid in June 1989 the European Council accepted it as defining a process leading to EMU, agreed that the first stage would begin on July 1, 1990, and agreed, also, that an Intergovernmental Conference would be convened sometime after the start of the first stage to negotiate the Treaty amendments necessary for the later stages of EMU. The IGC began in December 1990 and concluded at Maastricht a year later. For the Committee's report, see Committee for the Study of Economic and Monetary Union (1989).

will be coordinated and conducted among the governments of the member-states participating in the third stage of EMU and whether (if at all) those governments, finding themselves no longer able to control the exchange rate, monetary policy, and, to a large degree, fiscal policy, will be able to exercise collective control of their economies. In this section, we consider some of the economic, political, and institutional issues that are likely to confront the third-stage participants in EMU, and the EU in general, *after* 1999.

3.1. Growth and employment after 1999

Art. 2 of the Treaty on European Union commits all of the member-states to promoting "a harmonious and balanced development of economic activities, sustainable and non-inflationary growth respecting the environment, a high degree of convergence of economic performance, a high level of employment and of social protection." The countries moving to the third stage are likely to find it difficult, with exchange rates irrevocably fixed, monetary policy under the control of the ECB, and fiscal policy constrained by both the "excessive deficits" criterion of the Treaty and the sanctions on such deficits stipulated in the "Stability and Growth Pact" negotiated in 1996–7,[31] to respond to asymmetric shocks that may affect particular regions and/or countries more than others and that could jeopardize their attainment of such objectives as "balanced development," "sustainable growth," a "convergence of economic performance," a "high level of employment," etc. They are likely to find it even more difficult to respond to a larger, more intractable problem—the sclerotic performance of their economies over the long term.

With few exceptions (Ireland in terms of growth, Luxembourg in terms of unemployment), the EU has become, during the 1990s, and is likely to remain, after 1999, an area of low economic growth and high unemployment. Thus, even when the rate of growth recovers after cyclical downturns (as it did in 1997), the level of unemployment remains at high levels—a reflection of the fact that employment has, to some extent, become uncoupled from the rate of growth. As a result, most of the member-states of the EU, and, in particular, those which are most likely to move to the third stage of EMU in 1999, appear

---

[31] The subject of protracted negotiation, the leaders of the EU informally agreed to the "Pact" at their meeting in Dublin in December 1996, and formally agreed to it at their meeting in Amsterdam six months later. The "Pact" stipulates the conditions under which penalties and/or fines may be assessed on member-states participating in the third stage of EMU that have budget deficits in excess of 3% of GDP. In the first year, they will be required to make a non-interest bearing deposit equal to 0.2% of GDP plus an additional deposit equal to 0.1% of GDP for each percentage point by which the deficit:GDP ratio exceeds 3%. Thereafter, an additional deposit will be required equal to 0.1% for each percentage point difference between the deficit:GDP ratio and 3%. After two years, if no corrective action has been taken, each deposit will be translated into fines, up to a maximum of 0.5% of GDP per year. The sanctions will be automatically waived if the member-state had suffered a drop in GDP greater than 2%. If the decline in GDP is between 0.75% and 2.0%, the Commission will prepare a report, on whether the decline was the result of "exceptional and temporary circumstances," that will provide the basis for a Council decision as to whether the sanction should be waived.

Table 7.5. Growth and unemployment in the European Union, 1995–1997

	% Change in "real" GDP			% Unemployed (commonly used measures)		
	1995	1996	1997	1995	1996	1997
Belgium	1.9	1.4	2.3	9.9	9.8	9.5
Denmark	2.7	2.4	3.0	7.1	6.0	5.1
Germany	1.9	1.4	2.3	8.2	9.0	8.9
Greece	2.0	2.6	3.1	9.1	9.0	8.9
Spain	2.8	2.2	2.8	22.9	22.2	21.3
France	2.2	1.3	2.3	11.6	12.3	12.5
Ireland	10.7	8.4	7.2	12.4	12.7	11.7
Italy	2.9	0.7	1.2	11.9	12.0	12.0
Luxembourg	3.8	3.6	3.7	2.9	3.1	3.3
Netherlands	2.1	2.8	3.1	7.0	6.6	6.8
Austria	1.4	1.0	1.6	3.8	4.1	4.2
Portugal	2.3	3.0	3.2	7.3	7.3	7.0
Finland	4.5	3.3	4.4	16.6	15.7	14.0
Sweden	3.6	1.1	2.1	9.2	10.0	9.9
UK	2.5	2.1	2.8	8.8	8.2	6.8
EU	2.4	1.6	2.4	10.9	11.0	10.6

Source: European Commission (1997*b*: 68–9, 82–3).

locked in to historically high rates of unemployment. Thus, as the data in Table 7.5 suggest, France, Belgium, Ireland, Finland, and Spain—all likely participants in the third stage of EMU—had unemployment rates of 12 percent or more in 1997. In France, for example, the unemployment rate during the spring of 1997 was 12.8 percent, the highest level in the post-World War II period. And in Germany, where the rate of unemployment was above 10 percent for 1997 as a whole, the seasonally unadjusted rate of unemployment soared above 12 percent in the first month of the year and remained near that level throughout the year.[32]

Some have assumed that eliminating exchange-rate uncertainty through the creation of a single currency will reduce transaction costs within the single market and increase the risk-adjusted rate of return on investment, thereby stimulating higher levels of investment, which in turn will raise the rate of growth, thereby contributing to a reduction of the rate of unemployment. Moreover, the existence of low rates of inflation in the member-states participating in

[32] In February, the "headline" (seasonally unadjusted) unemployment rate remained at 12.2%, thereafter dropping slightly to 11.7% in March, 11.3% in April, and 11.1% in May. In May, the seasonally adjusted rate was 11.4%, representing a total of 4,358,000, a post-World War II record. See *Financial Times*, February 2, 1997: 1; March 7, 1997: 16; April 9, 1997: 1; June 7–8, 1997: 1.

EMU, the improvement in their public finances, and the credibility of their commitment to maintain those policies for the foreseeable future are assumed to allow interest rates to be maintained at lower levels than at present, thereby further stimulating investment, growth, and employment.[33]

As plausible as such assumptions may be, it is by no means obvious that participation in the third stage of EMU will in fact have those salutary effects on investment, growth, and employment. The notion that use of a single currency will eliminate transaction costs that otherwise would prevent investment seems implausible given that most if not all major investors have long since learned the fine art of hedging as a means of reducing the uncertainty associated with transactions in multiple currencies, and the fact that most major international economic actors—including, almost certainly, those accounting for the vast bulk of investment in the EU—routinely conduct transactions in the various EU currencies. Although it would be difficult to demonstrate, since it would require information about all possible investments that were never made, it is probably the case that very few potential investments, if any, within the likely "euro-zone" in recent decades have failed to occur only because of the costs involved in operating in multiple currencies.

Regarding the putative beneficial effects on interest rates of moving to the third stage of EMU, it is possible, of course, that low rates of inflation, small public deficits, and public commitment to those policies will enable the EMU participants to enjoy lower interest rates. But it is also the case that monetary policy will be under the control of a central bank that is free of political instruction, singularly committed to maintaining price stability, and—especially in its early years when the credibility of its commitment to maintain the value of the new currency will, to a large extent, be contingent upon its behavior—likely to maintain rates sufficient to prevent inflationary increases in the money supply (even at the cost of low growth and high unemployment) and depreciation of the value of the euro. It is possible, certainly, that interest rates under the aegis of the ECB could be lower than a weighted average of the current rates in the member-states that participate in the third stage. However, it is probably more reasonable to anticipate that a central bank that is, by its founding statute (Protocol 3 of the Treaty), politically independent and committed to maintaining stable prices will maintain rates sufficiently high to prevent inflationary increases in the money supply, even at the cost of low growth and high unemployment—especially in the early years of EMU when it will be concerned with establishing its credibility as the guardian of the value of the euro not only with the markets but with the national publics which, with some considerable skepticism, agreed to give up their national currencies.

One means by which the EMU participants might seek to alleviate the pattern of relatively low rates of economic growth and high levels of unemployment would involve manipulating the external exchange rate of the euro

---

[33] The most extensive analysis of the putative benefits of EMU is the one prepared by the Commission that appears, in published form, as Emerson *et al.* (1992).

vis-à-vis other currencies.[34] For example, by stabilizing the external exchange rate or otherwise keeping it from appreciating vis-à-vis other currencies such as the dollar and the yen, they might conceivably provide a price advantage for "euro-zone" exports and make externally produced goods less competitive *within* the "euro-zone"—both of which would boost growth and presumably create or maintain jobs within the zone. Art. 109.1 of the Treaty on European Union, it should be noted, stipulates that the Council can conclude formal agreements on an exchange-rate system with non-EU currencies, and it can adjust or abandon the rate of the euro in such systems. And in the absence of such an exchange-rate system, Art. 109.2 gives the Council the power to formulate "general orientations" for exchange-rate policy with non-EU currencies.

The strength of the euro vis-à-vis non-EU currencies and, conversely, the propensity of the EU to pursue an aggressive external exchange-rate policy that would give its exporters a competitive advantage in world markets, may, of course, depend on the membership of the "euro-zone." Presumably, a larger "euro-zone," including such member-states as France, Italy, Spain, and Portugal among others, might be somewhat less inclined, all else equal, to pursue a "strong euro" policy than a "euro-zone" with fewer members and in which the member-states with the "hardest" national currencies (e.g. Germany and the Netherlands) might have marginally more influence. Given the likelihood that a relatively large number of member-states—possibly as many as eleven, and including France, Spain, Portugal, and Italy—will be judged as having achieved the high degree of sustainable convergence necessary for adoption of the single currency, therefore, it is quite possible that the member-states of the "euro-zone" will in fact pursue an aggressive external exchange-rate policy that seeks competitive advantage in world markets for EU producers by stabilizing and/or undervaluing the euro relative to non-EU currencies. The likelihood of that happening has, of course, undoubtedly been further increased by some unknown amount because of the commitment of the Socialist-dominated government in France to support, as one of its conditions for entry to the third stage, an external exchange-rate policy that aids growth and employment.

However, while it is conceivable that the external exchange rate of the euro may be manipulated by the Council in such a way as to improve the competitive position of the "euro-zone" countries in global markets, it is important to note that the Treaty places certain constraints on the Council in regard to the external exchange rate. Art. 109.1 stipulates that the Council must act unanimously, that it must act upon a recommendation from the ECB or the Commission, and that it must consult with the ECB "in an endeavor to reach a consensus consistent with the objective of price stability." In regard to the formulation of "general orientations," the Treaty stipulates that the Council must act, by qualified majority, upon the recommendation of the Commission,

---

[34] The nature of the relationship between the euro and the major non-EU currencies has received surprisingly little attention. Among the few works that examine the relationship in detail, see Kenen (1995: 108–12) and Henning (1996).

followed by consultation with the ECB, or upon the recommendation of the ECB. And as with the agreements described in Art. 109.1, these "orientations" must be "without prejudice to the primary objective of the ESCB to maintain price stability."

Given the constraints specified in Art. 109, the consultative role provided the ECB in exchange-rate policy, and the admonition to adhere to the objective of price stability, it is more likely the case that the participating member-states will obtain little or no relief from their condition of low growth and high unemployment via manipulation of the exchange rate of the euro than that they will be able to achieve higher rates of growth and employment through an aggressive external exchange-rate policy. For rather than pursuing the latter policy, it is probably more likely, given the constraints introduced in Art. 109, that the Council would allow the euro to float within a large and imprecisely defined range, just as the mark and the other European currencies have floated in a large range in recent years, subject only to the occasional efforts of the G7 to "manage" the system when one currency or another goes well outside the largely implicit "target range." And just as the mark and the European currencies that track it closely have appreciated vis-à-vis non-EU currencies in recent years,[35] so too such an arrangement could very well cause the euro to appreciate in value relative to the dollar and the yen, something that would erode the competitive position of "euro-zone" producers both in export markets and vis-à-vis imports from non-"euro-zone" states in their home markets—which, in turn, could erode the rate of growth, employment, and income at home. Lest there be doubt about the likelihood that the euro will be allowed to float (even at the cost of domestic growth and employment) rather than stabilized and undervalued (at the cost of a higher rate of inflation), it is useful to note what one of the principal architects of EMU has to say about the relative importance of domestic price stability and exchange-rate stability:

> The Bundesbank always decided in favor of domestic price stability and sacrificed exchange-rate stability if necessary. . . . The Bundesbank, I assume, is much happier [after the 1992–3 ERM crisis] living with a de facto floating system, with practically no intervention obligations for the time being, than with a system of fixed but adjustable exchange rates, which [has been] accurately called 'half-baked' because adjustments never take place at the right moment. . . . The mandate of the ECB must be to maintain stability of the value of money as the prime objective of European monetary policy . . . Domestic stability of the value of money must take precedence over exchange-rate stability.[36]

If the preference for domestic price stability to exchange-rate stability that Karl-Otto Pöhl describes is in some sense the generic preference ordering of all central bankers, it is probably also the case that the Governing Council of the

---

[35] See the chart accompanying Samuel Brittan, "Right rate for the franc," *Financial Times*, September 12, 1996: 12. Kenen (1995: 111–12) notes that until the single currency replaces the national currencies (by July 2002 at the latest), foreign-exchange traders are likely to use the mark as a proxy for all of the currencies that are, as of January 1, 1999, irrevocably locked.

[36] Karl Otto Pöhl, in Gaidar and Pöhl (1995: 61, 67, 109).

new ECB will be especially sensitive to that lexical ordering of priorities in its early years, as it attempts to establish credibility for itself and for the euro by demonstrating its commitment to maintaining stable prices. To the extent that is the case, then, one would expect the euro, like its predecessors that remained in the ERM after 1992–3, to be a strong currency relative to others such as the dollar and the yen—even if as many as eleven member-states enter the third stage of EMU in 1999. Thus, one would expect that it will be allowed to float and to appreciate, even at the cost of continued losses of export markets and, in turn, of production, jobs, and income at home. That is especially likely to be the case since the EU has gone to such lengths to immunize the ECB from those actors—exporters, workers, governments—who might conceivably prefer an undervalued currency that would give exports a competitive advantage to the alternative of maintaining stable prices.

Whatever the salutary consequences of moving to the third stage of EMU and irrevocably locking exchange—and there no doubt *will* be such consequences, most notably, perhaps, the elimination of the instability and fluctuation among the European currencies that occurred every time the mark increased in value against the dollar—then, the move to the third stage in 1999 will, in all likelihood, do little to improve the competitive position of the "euro-zone" in the world and provide an export-based boost to growth and employment. Indeed, if anything, the likely constraints operating on the external exchange rate of the euro may contribute to a *deterioration* in the competitive position of the economies of those participating member-states in global markets, thereby accentuating the pattern of low growth and high unemployment at home that already characterizes so much of Europe.

The possibility that the low growth and high unemployment that now characterize most of the EU will continue within most of the member-states that move to the third stage of EMU poses more than an economic challenge for them. It is likely to pose a *political* problem as well, and not just for the citizens who suffer the immediate consequences of low growth and high unemployment and the national governments that, by failing to alleviate the problem, risk incurring the wrath of the citizens in elections. There is some evidence that, just as the poor performance of an economy tends, all else being equal, to cause a diminution of electoral support for the government, so too low growth and high unemployment diminish the extent of public support for the EU.[37] And if that is the case with support for the EU in general, it is likely to be especially true for EMU, to which, rightfully or wrongly, the policies resulting in low growth and high unemployment can be attributed.

The possible adverse effect of low growth and high unemployment on support for EMU may be of particular concern because of the low levels of support for EMU already evident in several of the member-states. Table 7.6 presents

[37] e.g. Cameron (1996*b*: table 13.4) reports a consistently strong relationship across the member-states of the EU between the magnitude of the increase in unemployment since 1991 and the magnitude of the *de*crease since then in the net proportion of the public saying that membership is a good thing and that their country benefits from membership.

Table 7.6. Public support in the EU for introduction of a single currency, October–November 1996

	% Favoring/Opposed to introduction of single European currency[a]		
	Yes	No	Net
Italy	73	11	62
Netherlands	69	26	43
Luxembourg	66	23	43
Spain	65	18	47
Ireland	64	18	46
Greece	63	19	44
Portugal	57	23	34
Belgium	56	24	32
France	55	30	25
Germany	39	42	–3
Austria	35	41	–6
Denmark	33	61	–28
Sweden	32	55	–23
UK	31	57	–26
Finland	29	56	–27
All EU	51	33	18

[a] Full wording: "Are you for or against the European Union having one European currency in all member-states, including (respondent's country)? That is, replacing the (name of currency) by the European currency? Are you very much for, somewhat for, somewhat against, very much against, neither for nor against, or don't know?" Yes = % saying "very much for" and "somewhat for." No = % saying "very much against" and "somewhat against."

Source: European Commission (1997*a*: 33).

the degree of support registered in Eurobarometer surveys conducted in the member-states in the fall of 1996 for introduction of the single currency. The data reveal a substantial degree of opposition to what is undoubtedly the most salient aspect of EMU for the European public. Thus, although slightly more than 50 percent of the EU public supported introduction of the single currency at that time, a substantial minority—33 percent—did not. And while substantially larger portions of the publics favored introduction than opposed it in most member-states, in at least six the proportion opposed to introduction of the single currency exceeded the proportion favoring introduction. In four of the six—Britain, Denmark, Sweden, and Finland—more than one-half of the public opposed introduction (which, of course, may help explain why governments in three of the four decided not to participate in the third stage when it commences in 1999). In two others—Austria and, most significantly, Germany —substantial pluralities were opposed to introduction. Thus, if the distribution of support observed in 1996 were to remain unchanged, at least three member-states—Germany, Austria, and Finland—that are likely to enter the third stage of EMU in 1999 would do so with publics that are, on balance, opposed to introduction of the single currency.

3.2. Economic policymaking in the third stage

The discussion in the preceding section raises a larger issue of institutional design and governance that confronts the EU in regard to EMU and that will continue to confront the member-states which participate in the third stage. Whether the member-states participating in the third stage of EMU will be capable of addressing the enduring problems of low growth and high un-employment is likely to depend on whether they have available to them the institutional capacity and authority to conduct economic policy. The Treaty on European Union is far from encouraging in that regard. Art. 102a commits all of the member-states, including those participating in the third and final stage of EMU, to conducting their economic policies with a view to achieving the objectives of the Community as described in Art. 2. Art. 103.1 stipulates that the member-states will regard their economic policies as a matter of "common concern" and shall "co-ordinate them within the Council." Art. 103.2 stipulates that the Council, acting by qualified majority on a recommendation from the Commission, shall "formulate a draft for the broad guidelines of the economic policies of the member-states and the Community," and that the European Council will then "discuss a conclusion on the broad guidelines" that will, in turn, become the basis for a Council "recommendation setting out these broad guidelines."

The language of these Articles—the use of such phrases as "common concern," "co-ordinate . . . within the Council," "formulate a draft," "broad guidelines," "discuss a conclusion," and "recommendations setting out these broad guidelines"—makes it apparent that the Treaty creates no new authority or competence in the field of economic policy. No new institutional body is established in the area of economic policy that would include only the member-states participating in the third and final stage of EMU, and no new competencies or policy instruments are created for use by those participating member-states in the realm of economic policy. Instead, the Councils, composed of the representatives of all of the EU member-states, will simply formulate guidelines, discuss conclusions, and make recommendations based on those guidelines and conclusions.

The extent to which the Treaty fails to create the authority and institutional capacity by which member-states participating in the third stage of EMU could act collectively in the domain of economic policy becomes most obvious when the cursory language of Art. 103 is juxtaposed with the extensive discussion in Arts. 105–9 and Protocols 3 and 4 pertaining to monetary policy, the ESCB, and the ECB. In the single-minded effort to create a strong independent central bank, the authors of the Treaty ignored a simple and obvious fact of political life—that no central bank, independent or otherwise, has ever operated, or could ever operate, without a political counterpart that is responsible for shaping the overall contours of economic policy.[38]

Some voices within the EU have recognized the need for such a counterpart once the third stage of EMU has commenced. Most notably, French political figures both on the Right and the Left have argued for some form of "political counterweight" or "economic government" to balance the power and autonomy of the ECB in the third stage. Thus, for example, at his meeting with Chancellor Helmut Kohl in Nuremberg before the December 1996 meeting of the European Council in Dublin, President Jacques Chirac called (not for the first time) for a political force to offset the power of the ECB, for precisely such a "political counterpart." A short while later, the French Minister of Finance Jean Arthuis repeated the French call for the creation of some institutional form—perhaps, he suggested, a council for stability and growth composed of the representatives of the member-states participating in the third stage of EMU—to act as a political counterweight to the ECB. Not surprisingly, the central bankers reacted negatively to these proposals, as when Hans Tietmeyer, the President of the German Bundesbank, denounced the effort to create a *pouvoir politique* and warned that such an effort did not conform to the Treaty. Nevertheless, the French government continued to advocate creation of such a council, and in February 1997 it received the endorsement of Jacques Delors, who suggested that a protocol be added to the Treaty allowing for the creation of a council to coordinate macroeconomic policy.[39]

At a meeting of the Finance Ministers and heads of the central banks of France and Germany in Lyon in March 1997, the German officials appeared to shift their position to one of qualified support for the French proposal for a "stability and growth" council, composed of the Finance Ministers of the member-states participating in the third stage, which would coordinate economic policy. That occurred, apparently, after the French officials had assured the Germans that the proposed council would be informal, would concern itself with economic policy and not monetary policy, and would not intrude upon the independence of the ECB.[40] However, several days later, at a meeting of the fifteen Finance Ministers, the Council, while accepting the idea in principle, indicated the proposed body would have little power, would *not* act as a "political counterweight" to the ECB, and would not possess responsibility for exchange-rate policy (which would remain in the hands of the full Council).[41]

Potentially the most influential endorsement of the ambition to create a "political counterweight" to the ECB came when the French Socialist Party, which had committed itself to the creation of a "gouvernement économique"

---

[38] The failure to create a political counterpart to the ECB is hardly surprising, of course, since the central bank governors themselves played a major role in authoring the EMU provisions of the Treaty. For a discussion that emphasizes the role of the central bankers in the preparation of the Treaty, see Cameron (1995*b*).

[39] On the comments by Chirac, Arthuis, Tietmeyer, and Delors, see, respectively, *Financial Times*, December 10, 1996: 16; December 17, 1996: 1; January 20, 1997: 1; and February 28, 1997: 2.

[40] See *Financial Times*, March 13, 1997: 16.   [41] See *Financial Times*, March 19, 1997: 2.

in the third stage, returned to office with its allies, the Communists, the Citizens' Movement, and the *Verts*, after the Assembly elections of May–June 1997. Seeing such a "gouvernement" as a necessity for assuring the promotion of jobs and growth in the third stage, the Socialist-dominated government insisted, as the price of its acquiescence in approving the "Stability and Growth Pact," that the leaders meeting at Amsterdam in June 1997 commit themselves, among other things, to issuing a resolution elaborating existing provisions supporting greater coordination of macroeconomic policy by the Finance Ministers and the development of new language in the Treaty to give the ministers a role in the formulation of external exchange-rate policy vis-à-vis the dollar and yen.[42]

Whether the Amsterdam resolution will cause the EU to elaborate the language of Arts. 102a and 103 into actual institutional capacity for control of macroeconomic policy by the Council is, of course, one of several important unknowns about the third stage. Notwithstanding the various efforts to water down that and previous French proposals, the likely presence in office for at least the first several years of the third stage of a government committed to the creation of such a "counterweight" to the ECB will presumably keep that issue on the agenda—and perhaps even insure that the commitment made at Amsterdam will, in time, become something more than rhetoric! But if it does not, if it remains only rhetoric, it is quite likely that, as low growth and high unemployment continue to characterize economic life in the EU after 1999, the European public will almost certainly ask, more frequently and more sharply than it does now, why the EU is unable to achieve higher rates of growth and reduce the high levels of unemployment, why the popularly elected national governments do not control macroeconomic policy—in short, the question with which we began, why EMU? The asking of those questions may, in time, lead to something more than rhetoric—perhaps to a further extension of supranational governance of macroeconomic policy.

4. Conclusion

On January 1, 1999, the third and final stage of Economic and Monetary Union will begin. On that day, a new European Central Bank will assume full responsibility for defining the monetary policy of the member-states that have moved to the third stage, and on that date, also, the conversion rates of the currencies

---

[42] In a flurry of negotiations between the time the Socialist-dominated government came to power and the Amsterdam meeting of the European Council less than two weeks later, the government also obtained the following commitments supporting growth and employment, in exchange for its support of the "Pact": (i) a special meeting of the European Council (to be held in November 1997); (ii) encouragement to the European Investment Bank to broaden its lending to infrastructure projects and small and medium-sized businesses in order to increase job creation and to take on a venture capitalist role; and (iii) a somewhat beefed-up employment chapter in the revised Treaty. See *Financial Times*, June 12, 1997: 1; June 14–15, 1997: 1; June 16, 1997: 3; and June 17, 1997: 1, 3.

of those member-states will be irrevocably fixed against each other and against a new currency, the euro. As that happens, the EU will be launched in the final stage of what must be regarded as the most ambitious, far-reaching, and consequential institutional innovation yet undertaken by the member-states of the European Community and Union, one that will in time greatly extend both the supranational authority of the EU and its institutional capacity for supranational governance in the domains of monetary, exchange-rate, and perhaps even economic, policy.

This chapter has examined some of the underlying imperatives and third-stage dilemmas of EMU. It began by considering, briefly, some of the reasons why the member-states of the EC concluded several decades ago, and have persisted in the belief, that their national self-interest was best served by an extension of the authority of existing and new supranational institutions in the domains of monetary and exchange-rate policy. It then turned to a consideration of the economic, political, and institutional issues and dilemmas that are likely to confront the participating member-states in the third stage.

In regard to the imperatives driving the three-decade quest for EMU, the chapter suggests that EMU has represented, since its conception in the late 1960s, a means of resolving the inherent tension that occurs when states that retain such essential attributes of sovereignty as national currencies and pursue distinctive monetary and exchange-rate policies seek to create and extend a single internal market among their increasingly interdependent economies.

Consideration of the resurrection of the idea of EMU in the late 1980s suggested that many of the features which had generated the idea two decades earlier remained salient and were reinforced both by the extension of, and ambition to complete, the single internal market and the evolution of the EMS into a highly stable exchange-rate regime in which influence over monetary and exchange-rate policy, and gains from trade, were distributed asymmetrically.

After considering why the member-states of the EC concluded that their interests would be served by creating new institutions and responsibilities at the supranational level in the domains of monetary and exchange-rate policy, the discussion turned to a consideration of some of the economic and institutional uncertainties and dilemmas that are likely to confront the member-states participating in the third stage of EMU *after* January 1999. That discussion suggested that, whatever the salutary effects of assigning responsibility for monetary and exchange-rate policy to supranational institutions, the problems of low growth and high unemployment that exist in so many of the member-states are likely to endure, largely because the new European Central Bank is unlikely to allow those problems to influence monetary and exchange-rate policy and because the Treaty on European Union creates little new institutional capacity for addressing such problems. If that turns out to be the case, the discovery that EMU has done little to alleviate those problems, and possibly has even exacerbated them, may open yet another chapter in the still-unfolding story of supranational Europe.

8

The Engines of Integration? Supranational Autonomy and Influence in the European Union

MARK A. POLLACK

THE notion that the EC's supranational organizations might act as the "engines" of the integration process is not a new one.[1] Indeed, the phrase derives from the neofunctionalist literature of the 1950s and the early 1960s, which predicted that the EC's supranational organizations—the Commission, the Court of Justice, and the European Parliament—would act as a sort of vanguard, nudging the member governments of the Community toward deeper and deeper integration. Later, however, during the late 1960s and 1970s, intergovernmentalists argued that the member governments of the Community remained very much in control of the process of integration through its intergovernmental bodies, namely the Council of Ministers and the European Council, thereby limiting the ability of supranational organizations to drive forward the integration process. During this period, neofunctionalist predictions about the causal importance of supranational organizations seemed to have been falsified, and students of the EC turned their attention to the process of intergovernmental bargaining in the Council.

Since the relaunching of European integration in the 1980s, however, the debate on the causal role of these organizations has been reopened with regard to all three major EC organizations: the Commission (Sandholtz 1992a; Moravcsik 1995); the European Court of Justice (Stein 1981; Weiler 1991; Burley and Mattli 1993; Stone 1995; Mattli and Slaughter 1995; and Alter 1996), and the European Parliament (Tsebelis 1994, 1995; Tsebelis and Kreppel 1995; Garrett and Tsebelis 1996). In this chapter, I explore the autonomy and the influence

The author would like to thank the members of the Laguna Beach Group for comments on an earlier draft of this chapter, Michael Mosser for invaluable research assistance, and the World Affairs and the Global Economy (WAGE) initiative of the University of Wisconsin for research support.

[1] Throughout this chapter, I distinguish between EC *institutions*, which establish the general decision rules for policymaking and institutional change, and EC supranational *organizations*, which are collective actors operating within the Community's institutional system. For a good discussion, see North (1990: esp. p. 5).

of the EC's supranational organizations, and the extent to which they can indeed act as engines of the integration process, focusing in particular on the executive activities of the European Commission. In terms of the larger project of this volume, my primary emphasis is on supranational organizations and the extent to which they can drive the integration process along the continuum between an intergovernmental and a supranational polity. In addition, as we shall see, two of the other aspects of the project's continuum, namely rules and transnational actors, turn out to be important determinants of the autonomy and influence of supranational actors like the Commission.

I begin in the first section with a theoretical discussion of the role of supra-national organizations in the integration process, examining both the prefer-ences of supranational organizations, and their autonomy and independent causal influence, which I argue is best understood in terms of principal–agent analysis (for a similar analysis of the Court, see Chapter 4). I then generate some basic hypotheses about the variables which may explain variation in the autonomy and influence of supranational agents such as the Commission, Court of Justice, and European Parliament. I also discuss the difficulties of em-pirically testing these hypotheses, arguing that superficial quantitative studies are unlikely to capture the nuances of variation in the autonomy and influence of supranational organizations, and that careful case-study analysis is therefore imperative. In the second, third, and fourth sections of the chapter, I turn to the empirical record of the Commission's activities in the areas of structural policy, competition policy, and external trade policy, respectively, in order to illustrate the complex interaction among the Commission and the member governments, as well as with the other supranational organizations and trans-national constituencies which establish the context for Commission autonomy and influence. I conclude by arguing that the EC's supranational organizations can serve, and have served, as the engines of the integration process, but only within the limits established by the preferences of the member governments, by the decision rules governing their conduct, by their possession of informa-tion, and by their ability to manipulate transnational coalitions. Supranational autonomy and influence, I argue, is not a simple binary matter of "obedient servants" or "runaway Eurocracies," but rather varies along a continuum be-tween the two points, as we shall see below.

1. Theorizing Supranational Preferences, Autonomy, and Influence

1.1. The preferences of supranational organizations

In retrospect, the neofunctionalist concept of the EC's supranational organiza-tions as engines of the integration process relied on two fundamental assump-tions. The first of these assumptions concerns the *preferences of supranational organizations*. As a first approximation of supranational preferences, a number of theorists have adopted the assumption of supranational organizations as "competence-maximizers" which seek to increase both their own competences and more generally the competences of the European Community (Cram 1993; Majone 1994; Pollack 1994); and a similar view of supranational preferences was implicit or explicit in much of the neofunctionalist literature. Ross puts it most succinctly, arguing that supranational organizations like the Delors Commission seek "more Europe" (Ross 1995: 14). There are a number of reasons why such organizations might adopt a pro-integration or competence-maximizing agenda, including self-selection of personnel for the European organizations, socialization of members within the organizations, or simply bureaucratic politics. Whatever the source of their pro-integration preferences, however, it seems clear that the Commission, the Court of Justice, and the European Parliament have indeed pursued a broadly pro-integrationist agenda throughout the history of the EC.

As Hix and others point out, however, actor preferences are multi-dimensional, concerning not simply the question of integration but also other dimensions such as environmental protection, consumer protection, and the neoliberalism vs. interventionism cleavage that has characterized much of the Community's history (Hix 1994). On these issues, the preferences of supranational organizations like the Commission are less consistent and less predictable than along the integration dimension. The reason, as a number of authors point out, is that the Commission itself is not a monolithic actor, but a complex "multi-organization," consisting of (a) an essentially political college of Commissioners headed by a President as "first among equals" and (b) an essentially administrative civil service divided up into Directorates-General (DGs) and Services, which possess differing and often contradictory preferences on various issues (Cram 1994; Ross 1995). As we shall see below, for example, the Commission is frequently split between the relatively interventionist Commissioners and DGs responsible for industrial and technology policies, and the more laissez-faire Commissioners and DGs responsible for competition and commercial policy. Under these circumstances, the substantive preferences of the Commission, and of other supranational organizations, is the result of the internal politics of each organization. Hence, theorizing deductively about the preferences of supranational organizations outside the integration dimension is exceedingly difficult, and most case studies have simply treated these preferences as an object of empirical study rather than theoretical prediction, as I will do in the case studies presented below.

1.2. Delegation and agency

The second assumption underlying the concept of supranational organizations as the engines of integration is the claim that supranational organizations are actually autonomous in the pursuit of their preferences, and can exert an independent causal influence on policy outcomes. My central argument in this chapter is that the autonomy and influence of supranational organizations can best be understood in terms of rational choice models of principal–agent interaction.

In the standard principal–agent model of delegation, an actor or set of actors, known as the *principals*, may choose to delegate certain functions to another actor or actors, known as *agents*. However, this initial delegation of authority immediately raises a problem for the principals: what if the agent behaves in ways that diverge from the preferences of the principals? Agents might behave in this way, the literature suggests, for two reasons. First, the agent may use its delegated powers to pursue its own preferences at the expense of the principals, a process known as "shirking." Second, the agent may, as a result of the structure of delegation, be subject to perverse incentives to behave in ways contrary to the aims of the principals, a process known as "slippage." Although both shirking and slippage are likely to create losses for the principals, the principal–agent literature in political science has focused primarily on the problem of shirking, which in the case of the EC would consist of pro-integration, competence-maximizing behavior by supranational agents.

Agency shirking is a problem because, and insofar as, an agent has the ability to pursue its own preferences at the expense of those of the principals. In particular, the literature suggests, the agent possesses better information than the principal regarding its area of expertise, its budgetary needs, and its own activities, and this asymmetrical distribution of information may make it difficult for the principals to control agency shirking.

The principals are not, however, helpless in the face of this dilemma. Rather, when delegating authority to an agent, principals can also adopt various administrative and oversight procedures to limit the scope of agency activity and the possibility of agency shirking. Administrative procedures define ex ante the scope of agency activity, the legal instruments available to the agency, and the procedures to be followed by it. Such administrative procedures may be more or less restrictive, and they may be altered in response to shirking or slippage, but only at a cost to the flexibility and comprehensiveness of the agent's activities (McCubbins and Page 1987; McCubbins *et al.* 1987, 1989). In the case of the EC, both the Commission and the Court of Justice have generally been given a broad mandate, while the European Parliament was restricted to a limited institutional role prior to the Single European Act.

Oversight procedures, on the other hand, allow principals ex post to (a) monitor agency behavior, thereby mitigating the inherently asymmetrical distribution of information in favor of the agent, and (b) influence agency behavior through the application of positive and negative sanctions. With regard to monitoring, for example, McCubbins and Schwartz (1984) suggest that principals may use any one of a number of oversight mechanisms, including the "police-patrol" method of standing oversight committees, and the "fire-alarm" oversight offered by individual constituency complaints and judicial review of agency behavior. As for sanctioning, the literature points out that principals enjoy a formidable array of sanctions, including control over budgets, control over appointments, overriding of agency behavior through new legislation, and revision of the agency's mandate. Through the use of such monitoring and the application of sanctions, much of the literature argues, both shirking and slippage by agents can be minimized, if not eliminated (McCubbins and Page 1987; Kiewiet and McCubbins 1991).

As Moe (1987) points out, however, both administrative and oversight procedures can be quite costly to principals as well as agents, and these difficulties can create some limited room for agency autonomy from principals—indeed, much of principal–agent analysis is given over to the study of when, and under what conditions, agents can acquire such autonomy from, and influence over, their principals. More specifically, I have argued elsewhere (Pollack 1997) that four primary factors or independent variables explain the autonomy and influence of supranational agents like the Commission. The first of these, familiar from Moravcsik's intergovernmentalism, is the distribution of *preferences* among the member governments and their supranational agents. Put simply, supranational organizations always act within the constraints of member-government preferences, which must be taken into account by such agents in carrying out their delegated powers. As we shall see, however, supranational agents may also exploit weak or conflicting preferences among member governments, to avoid the imposition of sanctions against shirking, and to push through legislative proposals via their agenda-setting powers.

Second, the autonomy and influence of supranational organizations depends crucially on the *institutional decision rules* governing the delegation of powers to a supranational agent, as well as the sanctioning of that agent in the event of shirking. Thus, as we shall see below, EC-decision rules establish differing thresholds for the overruling and sanctioning of supranational agents like the Commission, and these decision rules directly affect the autonomy of agents from member governments.

A third factor is the distribution of *information*, or uncertainty, among the organizations and the member governments, respectively. Put simply, the autonomy of a supranational organization is greatest where information is asymmetrically distributed in favor of the organization, and where the member governments have difficulty monitoring its activities.

Fourth and finally, the influence of supranational agents is greatest where those agents possess clear *transnational constituencies* of subnational organizations, interest groups, or individuals within the member-states, which can act to bypass the member governments, and/or to place pressure directly on them. Indeed, I would argue, all three EC supranational organizations possess such transnational constituencies: interest groups and multinational firms in the case of the Commission, national courts in the case of the European Court of Justice, and national electorates in the case of the European Parliament. In all three of these cases, national constituencies act both as a constraint on the freedom of action of the supranational organizations (the European Court of Justice, for example, must rely on national courts to accept its jurisprudence), but also as a counterbalance to the influence of the member governments (once national courts accept ECJ jurisprudence, the costs of noncompliance for member governments rise considerably). In other words, all three supranational organizations navigate constantly between two sets of constituents: the inter-governmental principals that created them and may still alter their mandates, and the transnational constituencies that act both as constraint and resource in the organizations' efforts to establish their autonomy and strive for "more Europe."

1.3. The perils of empirical analysis

Unfortunately, testing such hypotheses empirically is far more difficult than it might appear at first blush, and the principal–agent literature is replete with methodological warnings about the difficulties of distinguishing between obedient servants and runaway bureaucracies. In essence, the problem is that agents such as the Commission may *rationally anticipate* the reactions of their principals, as well as the possibility of sanctions, and adjust their behavior in order to avoid the costly imposition of sanctions. If this is so, then agency be-havior which at first glance seems autonomous may in fact be subtly influenced by the preferences of the principals, *even in the absence of any overt sanctions*. Indeed, as Weingast and Moran (1983) point out, the more effective the con-trol mechanisms employed by the principal, the less overt sanctioning we should see, since agents rationally anticipate the preferences of the principals and incorporate these preferences into their behavior. In this view, sanctions should take place only rarely, when an agent miscalculates the likely reactions of its principals, or the likelihood of sanctions in response to its actions.

The relevance of these observations becomes clear when we examine the literature on supranational organizations in the European Community. For example, in response to Mattli and Slaughter's (1993) claims that the European Court of Justice has independently fostered the development of a supranational constitution for the EC, Garrett has argued that the Court's independence was only apparent, and that the judges actually rationally anticipated the responses of the most powerful member governments and adjusted their rulings accord-ingly. Similarly, analysts have differed in their interpretation of the comitology system of committees overseeing the Commission, and the remarkable rarity of negative opinions by these committees. According to Gerus (1991), for ex-ample, the management and regulatory committees for agriculture issued some 1,894 opinions on Commission actions during 1990—not a single one of which was negative! At first glance, the remarkably low rate of committee refer-rals to the Council would seem to suggest that committee oversight is perfunc-tory, and the Commission largely independent in its actions. However, as Gerus points out, rational anticipation of committee action by the Commission may mean that the Commission is effectively controlled by the member gov-ernments, despite the startling rarity of sanctions against it.

The point here is not that the Commission and other supranational organ-izations enjoy no autonomy from the member governments, but rather that such autonomy cannot be easily ascertained from the apparently independent behavior of supranational organizations, and that quantitative measures of comitology votes or legislative sanctions are unlikely to capture the nuances of agency autonomy from, and influence on, member governments. Instead of focusing on such broad aggregate data, I would argue, testing of the above hypotheses should rely on three particular research strategies. The first of these, and perhaps the most important, is to conduct systematic *case studies* and engage in careful *process-tracing* in order to establish the respective preferences of the member governments and supranational organizations, and the subtle influences that these actors may exert upon each other. Process-tracing may also, as Pierson points out in this volume, reveal the path-dependent effects of early decisions (on the delegation of powers and on administrative and oversight procedures, for example) which become "locked-in" and affect the outcome of later principal–agent interactions.

A second method, recently advocated by Moravcsik (1995) for the study of informal agenda setting, is *counterfactual analysis*, asking what would likely have happened if the Commission, the Court, or the Parliament had not behaved as they did in a given case. If it seems likely that a member government, or some interest group, would have stepped in to fill the breach, Moravcsik argues, then the independent causal role of the supranational organization is clearly less significant.

A third and final way to study the nature, and the limits, of supranational agency is to examine cases of open *conflict* between supranational organizations and one or more member governments, which may or may not result in sanctioning of the organization and a change in its behavior. The risk of focusing on such conflicts is that they are, after all, extremely rare, since agents like the Commission typically avoid open conflict with, and sanctioning by, their principals. Despite this risk, focusing on conflicts between member governments and their supranational agents has the advantage of revealing the conflicting preferences among the various actors, and illuminating the conditions under which member governments are able—or unable—to rein in their supranational agents, limiting their autonomy and their influence on policy outcomes. Such incidents of open conflict are, furthermore, hard or critical cases for the principal–agent model presented above, according to which agents like the Commission should enjoy autonomy only within the confines of member-government preferences, and not directly against the member governments. Hence, if we find that agents like the Commission enjoy some independent causal influence in cases of open conflict, it is likely that such agents should enjoy as much or greater influence in other, less high-profile cases where member governments have little information or only weak preferences.

In keeping with these rough guidelines, I devote the rest of this chapter to a preliminary testing and illustration of the above hypotheses, focusing upon the executive actions of the European Commission in three issue-areas: the administration of the EC's Structural Funds, the conduct of EC competition policy, and the representation of the common EC position in the Community's external trade policy. Within each issue-area, I focus in some detail on a particular instance of conflict between the Commission and the member governments, namely the RECHAR controversy in the Structural Funds, the use of Art. 90 and the debate over the Merger Regulation in competition policy, and the treatment of agriculture in the Uruguay Round of the GATT. The overall research design, therefore, is one of "comparative statics," examining Commission activities across a range of policy areas, in an effort to explain the observed differences among them. In addition, however, I also discuss, albeit briefly, the temporal development of the various policies, and the extent to which Commission influence does, or does not, become institutionalized in each policy area.

In all three areas, I argue, member governments have delegated significant powers to the Commission, which the Commission has exploited to pursue its own preferences for "more Europe." By the same token, however, I shall demonstrate how the Commission's efforts in these areas have been constrained in particular by the preferences of the member governments, by the varying possibilities for sanctioning available to dissatisfied member governments, by the information available to the Commission and the member governments at different points in time, and by the Commission's varying ability to strike up alliances with transnational actors and with other supranational organizations such as the European Court of Justice. I begin with the Commission's high-profile role in the administration of the Structural Funds.

2. The Commission and Structural Policy

In EC parlance, "structural policy" refers to the administration of the Community's Structural Funds—the European Regional Development Fund, the Social Fund, and the European Agricultural Guidance and Guarantee Fund Guidance Section—created primarily to reduce regional disparities in the Community.[2] In the 1970s and the early 1980s, these Funds were essentially a redistributive share-out, agreed as side-payments in larger intergovernmental bargains, and the Commission's executive role in implementing the Structural Funds was a minor one.

By the mid-1980s, however, the largest contributing member-states had become concerned with the efficient expenditure of the increasingly large Structural Funds, especially in the new southern member-states of Greece, Spain, and Portugal, and they began pressing for greater control over, and monitoring of, the use of EC funds. In Kingdon's (1984) terms, these calls for greater control created a "window of opportunity" for a new and more ambitious structural policy, with a greater role for the Commission. And it was in this context that an entrepreneurial Delors Commission seized the initiative, proposing a series

---

[2] This section draws largely on Pollack (1995c).

of Structural Fund Regulations which simultaneously increased Community monitoring of Fund expenditures to include "value for money," while at the same time substantially increasing the Commission's role in both the planning and implementation of the Funds, which would henceforth take on a genuine Community dimension.

The Commission's reforms, which were adopted with very few amendments by the member governments, were based on four principles: (i) concentration of the Funds' resources in the neediest areas; (ii) partnership among the Commission, the member governments, and regional authorities in the planning and implementation of the Funds; (iii) programming, whereby member governments would be required to submit comprehensive development programs for each region, rather than individual development projects as in the past; and (iv) additionality, the principle that any Community funds should be additional to, rather than replace, national development funds in a given area.

Under the 1988 reforms, roughly 90 percent of the Structural Fund budget goes to finance measures proposed by the member governments under the Community Support Frameworks (CSFs) devised in partnership by the member governments, the Commission, and the regional authorities designated by the member governments. The remaining 10 percent of the Funds are allocated to Community Initiatives, which are Community-wide programs designed by the Commission to focus on a particular problem or type of region. It is these Community Initiatives which provide the Commission with its most important source of power vis-à-vis both the member governments and regional authorities. Put simply, with Community Initiatives the Commission may, with or without the cooperation of regional governments, present member governments with a given sum of Community funding, for a given purpose, and on a take-it-or-leave-it basis. In 1989, for example, the Commission created the Envireg program, which directed 500 mecus at Objective 1 regions for environmental protection measures "which had not always received sufficient consideration within the development plans of some Member States" (CEC 1993*b*).

2.1. The Commission exploits its new powers: the RECHAR controversy

Between 1988 and 1993, the Commission exercised its new powers vigorously, building strong networks to subnational regions; launching Community Initiatives which reflected the policy agendas of the Commission rather than the member governments; and insisting that all member-states satisfy the Funds' criteria for additionality, the principle that all EC funds should be additional to, rather than replacement for, national regional funding. In the most famous case of conflict under the 1988 reforms, the Commission's insistence on additionality in the granting of aid brought it into direct conflict with the British government of Prime Minister John Major. In that case, the Commission designed a Community Initiative program, dubbed RECHAR, the benefits of which would accrue largely to coalmining regions in Scotland. In order to secure these benefits, however, the UK government would have to accept the Commission's definition of additionality, as laid down in Art. 9 of the new Framework Regulation for the Structural Funds. When the UK government refused to do so, Commissioner Bruce Millan froze the UK funds. Finally, in response to pressure from the Commission above and regional governments below, and with a general election looming, Major's government backed down and agreed to the Commission's demands in return for its share of RECHAR funding. For many analysts, this RECHAR incident became emblematic of the Commission's renewed power and influence vis-à-vis even the most powerful member governments (McAleavey 1993; Marks 1993). In the RECHAR case, as in Envireg and other Community Initiatives, member governments complained that the Commission was either interfering in internal affairs or duplicating efforts already underway within the CSFs; but, faced with the possible loss of EC funding, member governments gave in and participated in these programs on the Commission's terms.

2.2. The Commission reigned in: the 1993 Structural Fund reforms

The Commission's position, however, was fundamentally weakened by the fact that the 1988 Fund Regulations, and hence its own executive powers, were set to expire at the end of 1993, and required a unanimous vote from the member governments for reauthorization. In Scharpf's (1988) terms, the "default condition" for the Commission's powers in the event of no agreement among the member governments was not the status quo but expiration, meaning that a positive decision would be required to reauthorize the Commission's powers under the 1988 Fund Regulations. Under the rules of the Single European Act, moreover, the unanimous agreement of the Council would be required for the most important of the new Fund Regulations. These decision rules considerably strengthened the position of member governments—including but not solely the British government—seeking to clip the Commission's wings by demanding substantial changes in the Fund Regulations. In particular, many member governments had expressed irritation with the Community. Most governments, for example, argued that there were too many CIs, and that each of these individual CIs spread a small amount of EC funding across a wide area, decreasing their effectiveness. The bureaucratic requirements for these initiatives, moreover, remained equally onerous for the member governments regardless of the size of the programs, with the result that a large proportion of these funds were spent on administration. Most importantly, however,

policy-makers believe strongly that there is too little consultation with Member States regarding the introduction of CIs. Indeed, the negotiation process has been described as a "complete sham" with the predominance of self-interest. Member States say that they are often taken completely by surprise when new CIs are launched. However, Member States and regions have a vested interest in receiving as much EC finance as possible, and it is difficult for them to object constructively to Commission proposals without harming their changes of obtaining funding. Policy-makers are frequently under political pressure, especially at regional levels, to apply for and use CI funds regardless of whether the money is limited and the measures are inappropriate or undesirable. (Yuill *et al.* 1993: 74)

Thus the member governments, if not the Commission, had a clear incentive to reassert control over this least predictable and controllable aspect of the 1988 reforms.

In response to these concerns, and to the imminent expiration of the 1988 Fund Regulations, the Commission in early 1993 submitted proposals for the new Fund Regulations, which were described by the Commission as largely a continuation of the principles of the 1988 reforms, with several administrative changes to improve the efficiency of the Funds. Put simply, the Commission proposed to retain the four basic principles of the 1988 reforms, while proposing slight changes to each of these. The concentration of the funds on the neediest areas, for example, would be increased, while the "partnership" provisions of the 1988 reforms would be modestly expanded to include consultation of the so-called "social partners" (organized labor and industry), and the programming procedure would be simplified from the Byzantine three-step procedure laid down in the 1988 Regulations. The proposed Regulations would also spell out more clearly than the 1988 Regulations the precise obligations of the member governments regarding the "additionality" of EC funding. Finally, with regard to the Community Initiatives, the Commission had proposed in its initial communications that 15 percent of the Funds' resources go to the CIs. In December 1992, however, the Edinburgh European Council indicated that the CIs should comprise between 5 percent and 10 percent of the Funds, and the Commission, predictably, proposed the high end of this range, 10 percent for the CIs from 1994 to 1999. With regard to the working of CIs, the Commission suggested that these would be fewer in number, and organized around a specific set of priorities in response to member-government concern about excessive dispersion of funds.

2.3. The Council clips the Commission's wings

Now, many of these proposals, with the obvious exception of the last, were intended to address the concerns of various member governments with the operation of the 1988 Fund Regulations. In the event, however, these Commission proposals did not go far enough to address the concerns of the member governments—which proceeded to change the substance of the Commission's proposals in several non-trivial ways, so as to respond to concerns about the distribution of funds, efficiency, and member-state control of the Funds' operation. The effect of these changes on the Commission were mixed. For example, the Council actually *increased* the Commission's role in the monitoring of Fund expenditures, at the insistence of net-contributing member governments concerned about the efficient use of the Funds in the poorer member-states; but the Council also *decreased* the role of the Commission in the designation of eligible areas, and weakened the Commission's proposed language on additionality.

Perhaps most importantly, the Council amended the Commission's provisions regarding the Community Initiatives. Thus, for example, the amount to be devoted to the CIs was reduced from 10 percent to 9 percent of the total Structural Fund budget. More importantly, the Council created de novo, in a new Art. 29a of the Coordination Regulation, a Management Committee for the Community Initiatives. Under the Management Committee procedure, the Commission would adopt Community Initiatives which would apply immediately, but these initiatives would have to be submitted to the Management Committee, which would approve or reject these by a qualified majority; if this committee rejected the Commission's proposals, the Council could, acting within a month of the committee vote, take a different decision by qualified majority. Predictably, therefore, the Commission openly "deplored" the creation of the new Management Committee (*European Report* 1993*b*; *Agence Europe* 1993). In the event, the new Management Committee approved the Commission's proposals for new CIs, but the existence of such a committee meant that the Commission could stray only so far from the wishes of the member governments without risking having its decision overturned by the Council of Ministers.

As a result of these changes, the Community Initiatives which were adopted for the period 1994–9 under the new Fund Regulations were subject to an extended consultation with the member governments, the EP, and other interested actors such as regional and local authorities and the social partners. By contrast with the striking independence of the Commission in the selection of the early CIs, the Commission in June of 1993 published a Green Paper on the future of the Community Initiatives, which proposed a trimmed-down series of initiatives concentrated in five priority areas: cross-border and interregional cooperation, rural development, outermost regions, employment and vocational training, and adaptation to industrial change. This initial list of objectives and programs was then modified, however, after consultation with the member-states and the EP, to include new initiatives on fishing (PESCA), on urban problems (URBAN), and—in response to the intergovernmental bargain struck over GATT ratification in December 1993—on a 400 mecu aid program for the Portuguese textiles industry (CEC 1994*a*). These revised proposals, for thirteen initiatives spread over seven priority areas, were then approved by the new Management Committee, and formally adopted by the Commission in June 1994 (CEC 1994*b*).

Summing up the Structural Funds case, then, the Commission was able in 1988 to capitalize on widespread member-state concerns about "value for money" to receive significant new powers to draw up Community Initiatives, to play a central role in drawing up Community Support Frameworks with the member governments and the regions concerned, and to police the expenditure and the additionality of EC funds. During the five-year lifespan of the 1988 Fund Regulations, Millan and the Commission used its delegated powers aggressively, funding Community Initiatives in line with the Commission's own policy agenda, and coming into direct conflict with the United Kingdom over the issue of additionality. By 1993, however, the Commission's delegated powers for structural policy were scheduled to expire, and the unanimity voting rule favored reformers like the UK, which successfully insisted on changes to the 1993 Fund Regulations in line with their own preferences.

The story of Commission autonomy and influence does not end with the 1993 reforms, however. As Marks (1996) has pointed out, the 1993 Fund reforms still left the Commission with considerable, and in some cases increased, powers in both the planning and implementation of Community Support Frameworks and Community Initiatives. Principal–agent interaction, therefore, is not a one-shot but an iterated game, in which the Commission exploits loopholes in Council legislation, the Council responds (if possible) by sanctioning the Commission, and the Commission begins the cycle again by making the most of its new mandate. The 1993 Fund reforms are merely the latest cycle in this ongoing principal–agent interaction.

3. The Commission and Competition Policy

In the area of competition policy, a number of analysts have correctly identified the Commission's powers on antitrust and state aids issues as "the first supranational policy" in the EC.[3] The drafters of the EEC Treaty had foreseen the possibility that certain actions by either private industry or by national governments might distort competition within the common market, and accordingly included in the Treaty a chapter on competition policy (Arts. 85–94), which laid down the basic competition rules for the Community, and empowered the Commission to enforce these rules. The rules themselves fall into two broad groups: the first, laid down primarily in Arts. 85 and 86 and elaborated in Regulation 17 of 1962, concern anticompetitive practices by firms, such as cartels and abuse of dominant positions, while the second, laid down in Arts. 92–4, concern the compatibility of state aids with the common market. In each of these areas, the Commission has acted as the Community's competition authority, supervised only by advisory committees, limiting member governments' ability to overturn the Commission's competition decisions through the comitology process.

During the 1970s, a period of both economic crisis and a sclerotic integration process, the Commission's enforcement of its competition powers is widely considered to have been lax, as the Commission tolerated cartels in sectors

---

[3] For good general discussions of EC competition policy, see Allen (1983, 1996); Montagnon (1990); Goyder (1993); and McGowan and Wilks (1995).

such as sugar, steel, and shipbuilding, and routinely approved sizable state aids to declining industries. In the 1980s, however, under Competition Commissioners Peter Sutherland and Sir Leon Brittan, the Commission took advantage of the neoliberal preferences of the member governments and the completion of the internal market to make greater use of its existing powers, cracking down on both cartels and anticompetitive practices, imposing larger fines on firms found to have violated EC rules, and specifying conditions for state aids to industry. We should be cautious, however, about assigning great causal importance to Sutherland's and Brittan's activism in this area. While both Commissioners were indeed determined to apply Community competition rules with renewed vigor, their efforts also coincided with the neoliberal turn toward the market among member governments, making the causal roles of the member governments and the Commission exceedingly difficult to disentangle.

Rather than focusing on the Commission's activities in the traditional areas of competition policy, therefore, I focus on the Commission's recent activities in two new policy areas. During the late 1980s and early 1990s, the Commission aggressively exploited its long-dormant Treaty power to liberalize state monopolies under Art. 90, and conducted a long campaign, ultimately successful, to acquire the power to review mergers and acquisitions of Community-level importance. In both of these areas, the Commission has come into conflict with various member governments which have limited its influence, but has nevertheless expanded the scope of Community and Commission competence, and contributed to the completion of the internal market. Let us, very briefly, consider each of these two cases in turn.

3.1. Article 90 and national monopolies

The Commission's aggressive use of Art. 90 to liberalize the telecommunications sector in the 1990s is one of the most spectacular and conflictual examples of Commission activity in any area of policy, and has been analyzed at some length by many scholars of European integration (Montagnon 1990; Fuchs 1995; Schmidt 1996; Sandholtz, Chapter 5). Put simply, Art. 90 deals with public undertakings, such as state monopolies in telecommunications and energy. Under Art. 222 of the Treaty, member-states are free to determine the public or private nature of such utilities, and the Commission cannot force member-states, for example, to privatize their telecommunications industries. However, at the insistence of Germany and the Benelux countries, which feared possible trade distortions resulting from the extensive public monopolies in France and Italy, the framers of the Treaty inserted Art. 90, which allows the Commission to enforce EC competition rules vis-à-vis national monopolies. Furthermore, Art. 90 (3) contains an extraordinary clause allowing the Commission to issue directives binding on the member-states, without the approval of the Council of Ministers.

Prior to the 1980s, Art. 90 had been invoked only rarely by the Commission. In the late 1980s and early 1990s, however, the Commission began to use Art.

90 as a key instrument in its drive to liberalize the telecommunications sector in the EC. The Commission's initiative in this regard began in 1987, when it issued a *Green Paper on the Development of a Common Market for Telecommunications Services and Equipment*, laying out its plans for the liberalization of the telecommunications sector, and calling for input from both member governments and from interest groups representing the users of telecommunications services, who promptly mobilized in favor of the Commission's actions. In its communication, moreover, the Commission pointed to the 1985 *British Telecoms* case in the European Court of Justice, in which the Court ruled that telecommunications was a regular economic activity under the Treaty, and that EC competition law was applicable in the telecommunications sector. This and other rulings, according to Schmidt (1996), presented the Commission with a crucial "window of opportunity" to apply the long-dormant provisions of Art. 90 to a sector which it was keen to liberalize despite some member-government opposition.

For its first telecommunications directive under Art. 90 (3), the Commission chose a relatively uncontroversial directive in terms of substance, much as the European Court of Justice had chosen small and uncontroversial cases to establish major points of European law in the 1960s. This Terminals Directive, adopted by the Commission without the approval of the Council in May 1988, would liberalize the market for terminal equipment, a move which few member governments opposed and which certain member governments, such as the UK, strongly supported on substantive grounds. Nevertheless, the Commission's use of Art. 90 to adopt liberalizing directives without the approval of the Council would set a dangerous precedent which could be exploited in the future, and so a number of member governments (France, Italy, Belgium, Germany, and Greece) challenged the directive before the European Court of Justice, arguing that the Commission should have proceeded under Art. 100A, with the Council taking the final decision. In early 1991, the Court ruled in favor of the Commission, upholding the directive and legitimating the Commission's use of Art. 90 (3) to issue directives.

Having established with the Terminals Directive its right to issue directives under Art. 90 (3), the Commission then turned to the more controversial problem of opening the market for telecommunication services, including data services. Unlike the terminals case, the liberalization of data services was disputed by member governments such as France, which relied on such services to underwrite other telecommunications costs, such as the provision of service to outlying areas. The Commission therefore agreed to negotiate with the Council on a package deal comprising both the Services Directive adopted under Art. 90 (3), and a framework Directive on Open Network Provision which was adopted by the Council. The final version of the Services Directive would open up the market for enhanced telecommunications services, including data transmission, from January 1993. This directive was again challenged by France, this time with the support of Belgium, France, Italy, and Spain, but the European Court once again upheld both the directive and the Commission's use of

Art. 90 (3). The adoption of telecommunications directives under Art. 90 (3), moreover, has continued into the 1990s, with new Commission directives on satellite services and equipment in 1994, the liberalization of cable TV networks in 1995, and the liberalization of mobile communications networks in 1996.

However, as Schmidt (1996) has persuasively argued, the telecommunications case presents a particularly favorable setting for the aggressive use of Art. 90, featuring a string of favorable ECJ decisions, strong support among powerful interests within the member-states, and a clear preference for liberalization among large member governments such as the UK and Germany. Hence, while the Commission did enjoy extraordinary success with its use of Art. 90 in the telecommunications sector, this initial success should not be taken as a sign that the Commission enjoys carte blanche to apply Art. 90 in all sectors and regardless of the preferences of member governments. Indeed, as Schmidt demonstrates, the Commission has proceeded much more tentatively in its liberalization of another national monopoly, electricity.

In the case of the electricity sector, the Commission began with a similar approach to the liberalization of the sector, adopting a report on *The Internal Market for Energy*, in 1988, and following this up with a number of specific proposals in subsequent years. In contrast to the telecommunications case, however, the Commission could not rely on a clear ECJ ruling that the rules of competition applied to electric utilities. Furthermore, in the electricity case the Commission faced strong opposition from many of the member governments, from the utilities, and from the European Parliament as well, leading the Commission to withdraw its plans for liberalization of the Community's energy market under Art. 90 (3). Instead, the Commission proceeded under Art. 100A, requiring an agreement within the Council of Ministers, which took years to reach the awkward compromise contained in the final directive adopted in June of 1996.

In sum, the Commission was able to use its Treaty powers, conflicting preferences among the member governments, and above all the support of interest groups and the European Court of Justice, to force the pace of telecommunications liberalization, which has been more rapid and more far-reaching than would likely have been the case if the various directives had had to wind their way through tortuous Council bargaining. However, as the electricity case demonstrates, the Commission has been considerably less successful in its application of Art. 90 in those areas where it lacked the support of interest groups, member governments, and the Court of Justice. The Commission, therefore, acted "alone" under Art. 90 only in the narrow legal sense. More broadly, it relied on the support of a variety of national, transnational, and supranational actors in liberalizing the telecommunications sector.

3.2. The adoption of the 1989 Merger Regulation

The adoption of the 1989 Merger Regulation differs in the details from the Commission's use of Art. 90, but here once again the Commission was able to achieve a major victory by rallying and relying upon the support of some member governments, a large number of transnational interest groups, and the supranational Court of Justice (Hölzer 1990; Goyder 1993; Bulmer 1994*b*; Allen 1996). In order to understand the nature of the Commission's victory in this area, it is important to note that the Commission's competition powers under the Treaty of Rome, although far-reaching, did *not* include the power to vet mergers and acquisitions, even under Art. 86 on the abuse of a dominant position. Nevertheless, the absence of any direct control over mergers and acquisitions was seen as a great weakness by the Commission and its Directorate-General IV in charge of competition, and so the Commission decided in the early 1970s to apply Art. 86 to prevent a merger which would strengthen the preexisting dominance of a firm within a particular market.

In its 1972 decision, the Commission prohibited the Continental Can group from acquiring a Dutch packaging company, TDV, arguing that such a merger would increase the already large market share of the Continental Can in the Benelux countries and in Germany, and thus constitute an abuse of the company's dominant position. Continental Can, however, appealed against the Commission decision in the European Court of Justice, whose landmark 1973 ruling supported the Commission's interpretation of Art. 86, ruling that the Commission could indeed use Art. 86 to prevent a firm which already enjoyed a dominant position within a given market from expanding its market share through mergers and acquisitions.

Continental Can was a landmark ruling in terms of its expansive reading of the Commission's powers under the Treaty of Rome, but from the Commission's perspective it was not a satisfactory legal basis for exercising control over mergers within the EC, since the impact of the Court's decision was limited to mergers and acquisitions by firms which *already* enjoyed a dominant position, and not to mergers which would *create* such a dominant position. The Court's decision, moreover, would give the Commission only post hoc jurisdiction over mergers, not the prior notification or control of mergers which it sought. In 1973, the Commission therefore proposed to the Council a Merger Regulation that would give the Commission the power to review Community mergers and acquisitions in all cases where the joint turnover of the undertakings concerned exceeded a threshold of one billion units of account (later ecus). Unfortunately for the Commission, the Commission's proposed regulation remained deadlocked in the Council of Ministers for sixteen years, stymied by fundamental member-government opposition to any increase in the Commission's supranational powers.

A major step forward was taken, however, with the 1987 *Philip Morris* ruling of the European Court of Justice. In the *Philip Morris* case, the Court of Justice ruled that Art. 85, which deals with cartels and other anticompetitive practices, could apply to agreements between two or more companies that allowed one of the companies to obtain legal or de facto control over the other. The practical effect of the Court's decision was to provide the Commission with a back-door means of reviewing mergers and acquisitions, and the Commission, which had not sought the Court ruling, responded by successfully applying Art. 85 to a number of high-profile mergers, applying conditions to the takeover by British Airways of British Caledonian, and blocking the acquisition of Irish Distillers by GC and C Brands. As a result, the European business community was left uncertain as to its legal responsibilities, which would emerge only in the incremental case law of the Court of Justice, and began lobbying for an EC Merger Regulation which would spell out clearly the powers of the Commission and the responsibilities of business. As Allen writes:

From the Commission's perspective the great advantage of this merger regime, using Article 85, was the uncertainty it generated. This served to put pressure on the doubting member states to settle for a better worked-out and potentially more limited merger regulation. By a combination of luck and skill the Commission had managed to create a problem which the Council felt could be eased only by passing the legislation it had previously refused to consider. (Allen 1996: 171)

In March of 1988, therefore, the Commission introduced a new, amended version of its 1973 proposal for an EC Merger Regulation, which was adopted by the Council in December 1989. Within the Council, negotiations focused on two provisions of the Commission's proposed regulation. The first of these concerned the thresholds above which a merger would become subject to the jurisdiction of the Commission. In this area, the Commission, with the support of some of the smaller member governments, proposed that EC jurisdiction apply in all cases in which the combined world turnover of the undertakings involved was one billion ecus, with a Community turnover of 50m. ecus for each of the undertakings. These thresholds were resisted, however, by Britain, France, and Germany, all of which proposed a threshold of 10bn. ecus in joint world turnover. In early 1989, the Commission proposed a compromise proposal, specifying thresholds of 5bn. ecus in world turnover, and 250bn. ecus in aggregate Community turnover for each company; these thresholds, however, would be subject to later review and amendment by a qualified majority vote in the Council of Ministers. The member governments, including Britain, France, and Germany, agreed to this proposal.

The second contentious issue concerned the balancing of competition and other social and industrial-policy criteria, which split the member governments into neoliberal and interventionist camps. The first camp, led by Germany and Great Britain, argued for the criteria to be strictly limited to competitive issues, in line with their own approach to mergers and acquisitions, while the second group, led by France, wanted to include social and industrial policies among the criteria which the Commission could apply in assessing proposed mergers. The Commission's initial draft had included social and industrial policy issues among the criteria to be considered, but the Council's final version was closer to the German and British position, emphasizing the strict application of competition rules. Nevertheless, Art. 2 (1) of the Regulation does contain a brief reference allowing the Commission to consider in its decisions "development of technical and economic progress provided that it is to consumers' advantage and does not form an obstacle to competition" (Goyder 1993: 398). How the Commission would interpret and apply these criteria, however, would become clear only after the Merger Regulation had come into effect, in September 1990.

3.3. **The Merger Regulation since 1990**

A complete discussion of the Commission's implementation of the Merger Regulation is, of course, beyond the scope of this chapter, but a brief discussion is nevertheless in order. Under the 1989 Regulation, the Commission must respond to all prior notifications within one month, at which time it may indicate either that the merger is approved, or that a second-stage investigation is being held into the specifics of the merger. By and large, the Commission has lived up to these deadlines, closing the vast majority of cases within the specified periods (Allen 1996: 174).

Despite its procedural promptness, the Commission has nevertheless come under assault for its administration of the Merger Regulation, in particular from Germany, which has a tradition of strict competition enforcement by the *Bundeskartellamt* (Federal Cartel Office). As Wilks and McGowan (1995) point out in their excellent review, the criticisms have been threefold. First, it is often argued, the Commission's implementation of the Regulation lacks transparency, with the Commission frequently striking up informal agreements with the companies it is regulating. Second, the Commission is often accused of violating the principle of subsidiarity, by refusing to refer competition cases to national competition authorities which request the right to handle specific cases.

Third, and perhaps most importantly, the *Bundeskartellamt*, supported by the German government, has argued that the Commission's enforcement of the Merger Regulation is excessively lax and "politicized," with the Commission approving mergers which should have been blocked, and improperly applying social and industrial policy criteria to merger decisions. The heart of the problem, in this view, lies in the nature of the Commission's decision-making structure. By and large, DG IV and the Commissioner in charge of competition policy tend to take a hard line on competition policy issues, including mergers as well as state aids and other competition cases. The final decision on mergers cases, however, lies not with DG IV but with the full Commission, where the competition criteria spelled out in the Regulation can be watered down by Commissioners who have either (*a*) national sympathies for the companies involved, or (*b*) a functional interest in other policy areas, such as social or industrial policy.

The nature of the problem is illustrated vividly by Ross's (1995) depiction of the Commission's decision to block the merger of the acquisition of the

Canadian aircraft manufacturer de Havilland by ATR, a Franco-Italian con-
sortium—the first merger rejected by the Commission under the Merger
Regulation. According to Ross, Brittan took a hard line on the de Havilland
case, writing to Delors that "we must *not* allow this merger to proceed,"
and planning to make the de Havilland merger a test case. Within the full
Commission, however, Brittan was opposed by Delors, by the other French
and Italian Commissioners, and by Industrial Policy Commissioner Martin
Bangemann, who argued that the merger would give European aircraft manufacturers the economies of scale they needed to compete on world markets.
Finally, after days of lobbying within the Commission by Brittan and his
cabinet, the Commission voted narrowly, by nine votes to seven, to block the
de Havilland merger. At the end of the day, the merger had been blocked,
leading to tremendous controversy in France and in Italy, but the de Havilland
case had made clear how haphazard the Commission's decision-making process was in the area of competition policy, and it provided grist for the mill of
the Commission's critics in Germany and elsewhere.

3.4. The future of the Merger Regulation

The years since the de Havilland merger have witnessed a double stalemate,
with Germany attempting vainly to create a European Cartel Office (ECO)
which would enforce EC merger rules in place of the Commission, while the
Commission has attempted, equally vainly, to increase the scope of its competition powers by lowering the thresholds established by the 1989 Regulation.
With regard to the former, the *Bundeskartellamt*, supported by the German
Economics Ministry, has pressed for the creation of an ECO independent of the
Commission, which would decide merger cases on the basis of narrowly defined competition criteria, thus insulating the decision-making process from
the twofold politicization found in the college of Commissioners. The creation
of such a new agency, however, would almost certainly require an amendment
to the Treaties, and hence a unanimous agreement from the member governments (Wilks and McGowan 1995). In recent months, the German
government has pressed its case for an ECO within the 1996 intergovernmental
conference, attracting the support of Italy, but Germany seems unlikely to gain
a unanimous consensus in favor of its proposals from other member governments, such as France, which have traditionally been more sympathetic to
social and industrial policy concerns (Buckley 1996).

However, while Germany has thus far been unsuccessful in its efforts to
transfer the Commission's merger powers to a new ECO, the Commission has
been equally unsuccessful in its attempts to expand its powers by lowering the
thresholds for Commission jurisdiction. In keeping with the provisions of the
Merger Regulation, the Commission proposed in 1989 to lower the thresholds
from 5bn. ecus for worldwide turnover and 250m. ecus for Community turnover, to 2bn. and 100m., respectively. According to the rules laid down in the

Regulation, the Commission would require only a qualified majority vote in the Council to approve the new thresholds, an easier target than the unanimous vote required to adopt the initial Merger Regulation. Furthermore, the Commission's proposal was broadly backed by European business, including the peak employers' association UNICE, which was eager to expand the "one-stop shop" provided by the Regulation for European-level mergers (*European Report* 1993c). An initial survey of member-government positions, however, revealed fundamental opposition to the Commission's proposal from Germany and the UK (which found the Commission's enforcement too lax), and from France (which found it too strict), and so in August of 1993 the new Commission Commissioner, Karel van Miert, withdrew the Commission's proposal, bluntly asking, "what is the point of proposing something if you know it won't be accepted?"[4] Instead, Van Miert proposed to continue with the existing thresholds for three more years, and propose new thresholds in the light of experience in 1996.

Accordingly, in January 1996, the Commission published a Green Paper on the review of the Merger Regulation, renewing its case for a lowering of the thresholds to 2bn. and 100m. ecus, respectively, and this was followed by formal proposals in July. Once again, however, the Commission has encountered entrenched resistance from the member governments, and in particular from Germany, which has linked any lowering of the thresholds to the creation of an independent ECO (Buckley 1996). The result is likely to be a continued stalemate, in which the Commission maintains its powers and discretion in merger control, despite dissatisfaction in Germany and others, but is unable to expand these powers due to the entrenched opposition of several member governments.

In sum, the record of Commission autonomy and influence in the case of competition policy, as in the case of structural policy, is mixed. On the one hand, the Commission succeeded, through its use of strong Treaty powers and transnational support, in pushing through the liberalization of telecommunications and the Merger Regulation, more rapidly and more thoroughly than the member governments would likely have done in the absence of Commission initiatives. On the other hand, we have also seen clear limits to the Commission's ability to overcome determined resistance among the member governments. In the case of national monopolies, for example, the Commission was unwilling to force through the liberalization of energy markets under Art. 90 (3) in the face of opposition from both member governments and transnational interest groups, and without the explicit support of the ECJ. Similarly, in the area of merger control, the Commission enjoyed a triumph with the adoption of the Merger Regulation in 1989, but has since been unsuccessful in its attempt to have the thresholds of the Regulation lowered in the face of firm opposition from the member governments.

---

[4] Quoted in *International Securities Regulation Report*, 10 Aug. 1993. See also *Agence Europe*, 29 July 1993.

4. The Commission and External Trade Policy

The Commission's delegated authority in the area of external trade policy constitutes, alongside competition policy, some of its oldest and most important
powers, specified directly in the body of the 1957 EEC Treaty. Under Art. 113 of
the Treaty, the Community possess exclusive competence in the area of commercial policy, and the Commission is designated as the sole and exclusive
negotiator for the Community for all international trade negotiations, at
which the member governments are forbidden to negotiate independently
with third parties. The Commission, however, is not given a free hand to
negotiate whatever agreements it likes at the international level. Rather, the
Commission begins the process by proposing a negotiating mandate to the
member governments, who may amend and adopt the Commission's mandate
within the so-called "Art. 113 Committee," a committee of senior national
officials who approve, by a qualified majority, the Commission's negotiating
mandate. The Art. 113 Committee also monitors the Commission's conduct of
the negotiations, and may, in response to a request from the Commission,
amend the Commission's negotiating mandate, again by qualified majority.
Furthermore, the final agreement negotiated by the Commission must be ratified by the General Affairs Council on behalf of the member-states, imposing a
final check on the Commission's negotiating authority (Woolcock and Hodges
1996).

In theoretical terms, the Commission's role in external trade policy is closely
analogous to the position of the chief negotiator in Putnam's two-level games
model (Putnam 1988; Evans *et al.* 1993). In Putnam's model, all international
negotiations take place simultaneously at two levels: at the international level,
or Level 1, chief negotiators bargain with their foreign counterparts in an effort
to reach a mutually beneficial agreement; at the domestic level, or Level 2, the
same chief negotiator engages in bargaining with her domestic constituencies,
or principals, who must ultimately ratify the contents of any agreement struck
at Level 1.

Perhaps most importantly for our purposes, Putnam examines the role of the
chief negotiator, whose preferences (like those of any agent) may diverge from
those of her domestic principals, and who may be able to influence the substance of an agreement by virtue of her dual role at both the international and
the domestic bargaining tables. More specifically, a chief negotiator may employ international pressures, and her own strategic position at both boards, to
manipulate her own domestic constituencies. A chief negotiator may, for example, be eager to effect some domestic policies or reforms, but be unable to do
so because of resistance from a coalition of domestic interests. In a two-level
negotiation, however, the chief negotiator may plausibly argue to her own domestic constituents that her preferred policies are in fact necessary in order to
reach agreement at the international level, and must therefore be accepted in
order to enjoy the benefits of the overall agreement. The chief negotiator's

domestic position may be further strengthened if, as in the case of the US "fast track" authority, the resulting international agreement must be ratified according to a straight up-or-down vote, thus providing the chief negotiator with formal agenda setting power and increasing the likelihood of ratification at the domestic level. In sum, the chief negotiator's central position at both the international and the domestic tables may strengthen her bargaining leverage at both tables simultaneously.

In his liberal intergovernmentalism model, Moravcsik (1994) has adapted Putnam's two-level games approach to the study of the European Community, in which EC member governments act as chief negotiators between their domestic polities and parliaments on the one hand, and their fellow member governments on the other hand. According to Moravcsik, this privileged position has allowed member governments to increase their own autonomy vis-à-vis their domestic constituencies, by concentrating resources—initiative, information, institutions, and ideas—in the hands of the member governments negotiating in Brussels. In Moravcsik's model, national parliaments and other domestic constituencies are simply left to rubber-stamp the decisions taken by member governments in Council, and the net effect of the Community's two-level game has been to strengthen, rather than weaken, the member governments of the EC.

Applying Putnam's model to the external relations of the Community, however, reveals that EC trade negotiations are not a two-level but a three-level game: at Level 1, the Commission negotiates with representatives of the USA and other trading partners, in order to reach international trade agreements. These agreements must then be ratified at Level 2, representing the intergovernmental Art. 113 Committee and the Council of Ministers. Finally, at Level 3, national governments seek domestic ratification of decisions taken at Community level (see e.g. Dusek 1995; Pan 1996).

In this three-level game, the Commission as chief negotiator should theoretically enjoy many of the advantages of Putnam's COG, manipulating and misrepresenting its own win-set to increase its bargaining leverage at the international level, and using external pressures to increase its "domestic" bargaining leverage vis-à-vis both the member governments at Level 2 and national interest groups at Level 3. The possibilities of the Commission's role as COG in external trade policy, and its limits, are well illustrated by the negotiation of the Uruguay Round and its most contentious element, agriculture.

4.1. The Uruguay Round, the CAP, and the Commission

Convened in 1986 in the Uruguayan capital of Punta del Este, the Uruguay Round of the GATT was to address a number of new issues in the area of international trade, including most notably trade in services, trade-related intellectual property issues (or TRIPs), trade-related investment issues (or TRIMs), and the creation of a new World Trading Organization to encompass the existing GATT. In each of these areas, the Uruguay Round attempted to establish rules for issues which had previously been outside the domain of multilateral international trade negotiations. Indeed, both services and TRIPs involved areas of so-called "mixed competence," for which the member-states agreed to negotiate with one voice, and appointed the Commission as their sole negotiator, but without prejudice to the ultimate distribution of competences between the member-states and the Community (Woolcock and Hodges 1996; Sbragia, Chapter 10).

Undoubtedly the most difficult issue, however, and one in which the Community had clear and exclusive competence as a result of the Common Agricultural Policy, was agriculture.[5] Agriculture had been included in previous rounds of the GATT, but various exemptions to GATT rules meant that states were in effect free to adopt national (or Community) systems for subsidizing and protecting national production, and for export subsidies as well. By the late 1980s, however, the Reagan administration was determined to secure a substantial reduction in agricultural subsidies, especially in the EC, where both subsidies and exports had grown rapidly in the course of the previous decade. Indeed, it was largely American concerns about agricultural subsidies which led the Reagan administration to press in 1985 for the opening of the Uruguay Round.

Not surprisingly, the initial US and EC negotiating positions were far apart. For its part, the Reagan administration put forward a radical proposal, often called the "zero option," calling for the complete elimination of agricultural subsidies by the year 2000. To the Commission and the member governments of the Community, on the other hand, such an approach was anathema, as it would threaten the fundamental principles of the Common Agricultural Policy. The Uruguay Round therefore presented the Delors Commission with both challenges and opportunities. On the one hand, as chief negotiator for the Community, the Commission would face the challenge of reconciling the far-reaching demands of the USA and other states at the international level with the entrenched resistance to any reform of the CAP among EC farmers and among their representatives in the Council of Agriculture Ministers and the Art. 113 Committee. On the other hand, as Putnam points out, the Commission's presence at both negotiating tables (the EC and the international) also provided it with the possibility of using external pressure to strengthen its negotiating position internally, and vice versa. The Commission, and in particular President Jacques Delors and Agriculture Commissioner Ray MacSharry, therefore established a dual strategy, with two central goals. First, Delors and MacSharry would design and steer through the Council a far-reaching reform of the bankrupted CAP, designed to make the CAP sustainable through the long term and avoiding any possible bankruptcy or renationalization of the

[5] The account of the Uruguay Round negotiations and the 1992 CAP reform presented here is necessarily brief, focusing primarily on the role of the Commission. For more complete discussions, see the excellent account by Eric Pan (which also applies a three-level analysis to the negotiations), and the accounts by Stewart (1993); Preeg (1995); Ross (1995); Meunier (1996); and Woolcock and Hodges (1996).

system, while at the same time making the CAP compatible with the minimum demands of the Community's trading partners. Second, and equally important, the Commission would present the newly reformed CAP to its trading partners as the Community's bottom-line offer, beyond which the Commission could argue that its hands were tied. Ross, although eschewing the language of two-level games, nevertheless sums up the Commission strategy perfectly in his account of the actions of Delors *cabinet* official, Jean-Luc Lamarty:

> Once on the table, Jean-Luc thought, the reform would almost certainly grant the Commission more maneuvering room on the Uruguay Round front, both internally and externally. The fact that CAP reform was in progress would set limits on external pressures while the need for CAP reform to succeed in the Uruguay Round would work internally. (Ross 1995: 113)

This is indeed what took place, but the process was to take several years, leading to open conflicts between the Commission and the USA, the Commission and the EC member governments, and within the Commission itself.

4.2. Internal bargaining: the 1992 CAP reform

The long-stalemated negotiations on agriculture between the USA and the EC had made clear, at least to the Commission, the need for substantial CAP reform in order to unblock the GATT negotiations, providing the Commission with a strong external incentive to press for CAP reform. In addition, however, the CAP in the early 1990s faced an internal crisis, with rising stocks of agricultural surplus and a spiraling budget which, according to Commission estimates, was expected to increase by some 30 percent in 1991. Such expenditures would, if left unchecked, lead to the breaching of the Community's agricultural guidelines established by the European Council in 1988, and could well create pressures for the renationalization of agricultural policy in the Community. Fearing the collapse and possible renationalization of the CAP, Directorate-General VI (Agriculture) began work in late 1990 on a series of proposals for a radical reform of the CAP designed to bring spending under control (*Agra Europe* 1991). In February 1991, after an extended "seminar" and debate, the full Commission approved a general communication to the Council on the need for reform, followed in August by a detailed reform plan, often referred to as the MacSharry reforms.

In response to the crisis, MacSharry proposed a sweeping set of reforms, the heart of which consisted of a shift from price support to direct payments to farmers. More specifically, the prices of a number of agricultural products would be cut severely, most notably for wheat, which would be cut by some 35 percent to a target price of 100 ECUs per ton, near world market levels. Farmers would then be compensated for their loss of income through a system of direct payments linked to the total acreage of each farm. Finally, compensation would be "modulated," so that small farmers would receive greater compensation than large farms, and in all cases compensation would be linked to a commitment to set aside acreage to avoid overproduction in the future. Although the Commission plan would not save money in the short term, and indeed might lead to a slight increase in agricultural spending to finance direct payments to farmers, in the long term the plan would reduce the CAP's incentive to overproduce, and hence the CAP's persistent pressures on the EC budget (Swinbank 1993). A final consideration, unspoken but implicit in the Commission's proposals, was that the proposed reforms would bring EC agricultural prices closer into line with world prices, and thereby reduce the trade-distorting effects of the CAP and the need for export subsidies which were the most sensitive issue in the GATT negotiations. In short, MacSharry's proposed reforms would increase the flexibility of the Commission's negotiating mandate, while at the same time drawing a clear and conspicuous bottom line beyond which the Community could refuse to go.

In Kingdon's (1984) terms, the stalled Uruguay Round negotiations and the budgetary pressures in early 1991 provided the Commission an important "window of opportunity" to press for a far-reaching reform of the CAP, which had been rejected or watered down by a coalition of farm lobbies and agriculture ministers in previous years. Nevertheless, MacSharry's proposals faced unanimous opposition among both the agriculture ministers and EC farm groups when he introduced them to Council in February 1991, and passage was by no means assured. Some member governments, such as Great Britain, Denmark, and the Netherlands, supported MacSharry's case for CAP reform, but opposed his plans for modulated payments, which they argued would benefit inefficient small farmers at the expense of the larger and more efficient British, Danish, and Dutch farmers. At the other extreme, France initially resisted the move from price support to direct payments, while Germany fought for price cuts considerably less draconian than the 35 percent cut in wheat prices sought by MacSharry. Community farm groups, finally, joined the agriculture ministers in their hostility to MacSharry's proposals, which they argued would decrease farm incomes and were being proposed only in response to bullying from the USA.

The twin pressures of the Uruguay Round and the budget, however, eventually led the member governments to support the broad lines of MacSharry's proposals, although several specific provisions of the plan were altered in Council bargaining during the first half of 1992. More specifically, in order to reach agreement, the Portuguese Presidency of the Council proposed a series of compromises in the Commission proposal, including the abandonment of the Commission's proposed modulation scheme to benefit small and medium-sized farmers, which MacSharry reluctantly accepted. More contentious, however, was the Presidency's proposed compromise on the cuts in the price of wheat, which were the linchpin of MacSharry's reform proposals. Whereas MacSharry had proposed a 35 percent cut in the price of wheat, the Portuguese proposed a compromise cut of 27 percent, largely to appeal to Germany, a high-cost producer. MacSharry, however, reportedly dug in his heels and refused to agree to such a cut, which would lead to continuing overproduction and sabotage the Commission's negotiating position within the GATT. Instead, he persuaded the Portuguese to propose a new price of 110 ecus, "a 29 percent cut close to the 30 percent the Commission had always set out to achieve, with a 1 percent psychological sweetener to enable Germany to feel it was in the 20s" (Gardner 1992a). The Germans accepted the proposal and the Council, after more than a year of bargaining, adopted the most radical reform of the CAP since the policy's inception in the 1960s. The Commission had compromised on modulation and on wheat prices, but the central, radical element of the Commission's reform—the shift from price support to direct payments—remained intact in the final Council bargain, leading one of the Commissioner's aides to label the reforms "son of MacSharry, definitely" (Gardner 1992b). Remarkably, the member governments had adopted in its essentials a reform plan which they, together with the EC's farmers, had been unanimous in rejecting only eighteen months earlier.

4.3. External bargaining: negotiating Blair House

Having secured the passage of CAP reform, MacSharry and the Commission returned to the agriculture negotiations with the USA, armed with the MacSharry reforms as the Community's new bottom-line negotiating position. The Uruguay Round negotiations were further complicated, however, by the emergence of a new agricultural dispute between the EC and the USA, involving EC subsidies to Community oilseeds producers. Under a 1962 GATT agreement, the EC had agreed to grant US oilseeds duty-free status, yet beginning in the 1970s the Community offered subsidies to European oilseeds-processing, contributing to a significant decline in the US share in the European oilseeds market. The US government accordingly took the oilseeds dispute to a GATT arbitration panel, which ruled in 1990 and again in 1992 that the EC subsidies were illegal, and in April 1992 the USA announced its intention to impose punitive tariffs on $1bn. worth of EC agricultural imports. Thus, while technically distinct from the Uruguay Round talks, the oilseeds dispute became linked for bargaining purposes with the outcome of the Uruguay Round, and led to hard bargaining between American and EC negotiators in October and November of 1992.

These negotiations led to conflict within the Commission when, on the eve of the US Presidential elections in early November, MacSharry and Trade Commissioner Frans Andriessen traveled to Chicago, along with British Agriculture Minister John Gummer as president-in-office of the Council, for last-minute talks with US Trade Representative Carla Hills and Agriculture Secretary Edward Madigan. In Chicago, MacSharry and Andriessen came close to reaching a global agreement with Hills and Madigan on the oilseeds dispute as well as the outstanding Uruguay Round issues of internal supports and export subsidies, when Commission President Jacques Delors again raised the issue of the Commission's negotiating mandate. As Ross tells the story,

Delors, with the French at his back . . . telephoned MacSharry to warn him that the proposed deal went beyond CAP reform and the Commission's negotiating mandate. Delors also announced that he would oppose the deal in the Commission and was confident of winning, and that were the deal to go forward, it would be vetoed by at least two member-states. MacSharry promptly resigned from his role as oilseeds negotiator and, with Andriessen, went back to Brussels to confront the Commission President, with whom neither was on cordial terms. . . . Delors was outvoted in the Commission on the issue of the negotiating mandate. (Ross 1995: 211–12)

On November 10th, five days after handing in his resignation, MacSharry therefore returned as the Commission's chief negotiator on agricultural issues, and resumed the agricultural negotiations with the lame-duck but activist team of Hills and Madigan.

Finally, on November 20th, the Commission and the Americans, meeting at Blair House in Washington, DC, signed the so-called Blair House "Pre-Agreement," resolving both the oilseeds dispute and the Uruguay Round agricultural issues. On oilseeds, the Community agreed to curtail domestic production by 10–15 percent in terms of acreage, responding to a key US demand. The Uruguay Round portion of the deal contained agreements on both internal supports and export subsidies, where the volume of exports receiving subsidies would be cut by 21 percent, rather than the 24 percent demanded by the Americans or the 18 percent offered by the EC. The Commission, finally, also obtained a so-called "peace clause," under which the USA agreed not to challenge EC agricultural subsidies for a period of six years (Preeg 1995: 144–7).

4.4. Reneging, renegotiating, and wrapping up: from Blair House to Marrakesh

At Blair House, the Commission had reached the long-sought-after agreement on agricultural issues with Washington, thereby clearing the way for the conclusion of the Uruguay Round, which would follow roughly a year later in December 1993. It had done so, however, by agreeing to a package which had not been explicitly approved by the member governments, raising the problem of ratification by the Council. In particular, the Blair House agreement came under persistent attack from France, where farmers burned US flags in the streets of Paris and Agriculture Minister Jean-Pierre Soisson argued that the Commission had exceeded its mandate, negotiating an agreement with the USA which went beyond the CAP reforms agreed to in May.

The British and Danish Presidencies avoided putting the Blair House agreement to an immediate vote in the Council, which in any case could be taken by qualified majority vote over French objections, but successive French governments carried on a year-long assault against the agreement even so, demanding a renegotiation of the Uruguay Round provisions of Blair House. Such a re-negotiation was resisted, however, by the new Trade Commissioner, Sir Leon Brittan, and by a majority of the member governments, which were concerned about reopening the difficult and delicate package agreed to at Blair House.

The French position, however, was strengthened by two factors. First, the member governments agreed in the autumn of 1993 to ratify the final Uruguay Round package by consensus, and not by qualified majority vote as specified in Art. 113, thus giving France a potential veto over the results of the Round. In fact, however, French Prime Minister Edouard Balladur preferred not to veto the overall results of the Round, from which France stood to benefit, and he still hoped to force a renegotiation of Blair House prior to the final vote on the Uruguay Round. Second, and more importantly, Balladur prevailed on German Chancellor Helmut Kohl at their August 28th summit meeting to support the French position in the interests of the wider Franco-German relationship. This German change of position was crucial, and in September the Council of Ministers instructed Brittan to ask for "amplifications or additions" to the Blair House agreement with Washington.

Against this European background, the Clinton administration, eager to reach agreement before the expiration of the US "fast-track" authority, agreed to a series of "clarifications" of the Blair House agreement at a meeting in Brussels on December 1–3, 1993, which went a considerable way toward responding to French demands (for details see Preeg 1995: 163–7). With the agricultural issue out of the way, the contracting parties of the GATT completed the final package of the Uruguay Round negotiations on December 15, 1993, and, in a complex intergovernmental bargain involving side-payments to France and Portugal, the Council of Ministers unanimously approved the outcome of the negotiations on the following day (Devuyst 1995). Formal signing of the Final Act took place on April 15, 1994, in Marrakesh.

In a postscript to the Round, however, a dispute arose regarding the respective competences of the Commission and the member-states in the ratification of the Final Act. The member governments had agreed to allow the Commission to act as the exclusive EC negotiator during the Round, but without prejudice to the final distribution of competence between the two levels. As ratification approached, the member governments insisted on the right to ratify individually the sections of the Round dealing with new trade issues such as services and intellectual property, while the Commission argued that the entire agreement should be ratified by the Community under Art. 113 of the Treaty. Concerned about the considerable difficulties that such individual ratifications might pose in future trade negotiations, the Commission appealed the question of competence to the European Court of Justice.

Rather surprisingly given our assumptions about the integrationist preferences of supranational organizations, the Court in November 1994 handed down a decision which largely supported the position of the member governments. While the Community did indeed possess exclusive competence to negotiate on trade in goods as well as on non-tariff barriers to such trade, the

Court held that in the areas of services and intellectual property rights, the Community and the member-states were jointly competent to negotiate agreements with third parties. The Court acknowledged in its ruling that such mixed competence would create problems in future trade negotiations, but held that the problem was to be resolved between the Commission and the Council. This adverse ruling has led Ludlow, among others, to conclude that the Court is now under pressure from the member-states "to act as a restraint on the central institutions as much as, if not more than, a catalyst of their advance" (quoted in Devuyst 1995: 462). Regardless of the Court's motives in this particular ruling, it is worth noting that the Santer Commission, in its opinion to the 1996 intergovernmental conference to revise the Maastricht Treaty, proposed modifying Art. 113 to give the Community exclusive competence to negotiate in the areas of services and intellectual property, but it was ultimately rebuffed by the member-states in the final text of the Treaty of Amsterdam.

Summing up this section, then, the case of the Uruguay Round agriculture negotiations presents yet another mixed picture of Commission influence. On the one hand, I have argued that the Commission was both purposeful and successful in harnessing external US pressures and internal budgetary pressures to produce and steer through the Council a reform of the CAP more rapid and more far-reaching than the Council would likely have adopted in the absence of Commission entrepreneurship. On the other hand, it must also be admitted that the Commission was less successful in securing member-state ratification of its GATT negotiations at Level 1, and in particular of the Blair House agreement, on which the Commission was forced into an embarrassing involuntary defection. In order to understand the Commission's lack of success in this area, consider the four factors mentioned in the introduction as the determinants of the Commission's autonomy and influence: preferences, decision rules, information, and transnational coalitions. In the case of the Uruguay Round agriculture negotiations, all four of these factors worked against the Commission's efforts to shape an agreement with the USA on agriculture: the preferences of the member-states, and in particular of France, were clear and intensely opposed to any major agricultural concessions; the decision rule for ratification of the final agreement, although legally QMV, was in practice unanimity, providing France with an effective veto over the Blair House agreement; with regard to information, the member-states monitored Commission behavior closely through the Art. 113 committee, providing the Commission with few informational advantages over recalcitrant member governments; and finally, the transnational coalition of agricultural interests was largely against any further concessions to the USA on agriculture, and opposed rather than supported the Commission vis-à-vis the member-states. In the absence of these four factors, the Commission's delegated powers as the Community's chief negotiator were insufficient to enable it to push through its preferences on agriculture in the GATT negotiations.

Finally, however, it should be pointed out that the agriculture case is not necessarily typical of Community trade policy as a whole. Because of the high political salience of agriculture within the member-states (including, but not only, France), member governments provided the Commission with a narrow and detailed negotiating mandate, monitored the Commission closely through the Art. 113 Committee, and were willing to risk a breakdown in the Round in order to respond to domestic pressures from politically powerful farmers. It seems likely that in other areas of less political salience, the Commission is granted greater discretion in defining the Community's negotiating position, and that ratification in the Council is less problematic than in the case of Blair House.

5. Conclusion

In this chapter, I have theorized the Commission's role in the European Union in terms of a principal–agent relationship between the Commission on the one hand, and the member governments on the other hand, and I have briefly examined the Commission's executive powers in the areas of structural policy, competition policy, and external trade policy in order to shed light upon the workings of this principal–agent interaction. The findings of these brief case studies are suggestive rather than definitive, but they do provide some preliminary support for the hypotheses presented above, and suggest further avenues for empirical research. For the sake of brevity, I focus here on four conclusions.

First, the three cases examined above suggest that the Commission does indeed have independent preferences, and is in fact a competence-maximizer along the lines suggested by Majone, Cram, and others. Across all of the areas surveyed, the Commission has attempted, in some cases successfully, to increase both EC and Commission competence in the planning and administration of the Structural Funds; in the establishment of Community-wide criteria for cartels, concentrations, state aids, and, especially, mergers; in the aggressive use of Art. 90 to liberalize telecommunications in the post-1992 internal market; and in the Commission's claim to exclusive Community competence to negotiate on the member-states' behalf in the new areas of services and intellectual property rights. Along the integrative dimension, therefore, the Commission's preferences have largely conformed to the predictions of neo-functionalist and institutionalist theorists.

Along other dimensions, on the other hand, and particularly along the Left–Right split mentioned earlier, the Commission has often been internally divided, and its preferences have been less predictable. In trade, for example, Commissioners were openly divided on agriculture, with MacSharry more willing than Delors to make concessions to the USA. Similarly, in the area of competition policy the Commission has been split between neoliberals such as Leon Brittan who advocate the strict competition criteria championed by DG IV, and other Commissioners like Delors who have been willing to weigh competition criteria against other, social and industrial policy criteria.

Second, all three cases suggest that the Commission enjoys considerable autonomy and influence in its implementation of Community policies. In structural policy, for example, the Commission successfully set the agenda for major 1988 reforms which increased its own powers, and it was subsequently able to build direct networks with subnational governments, and stand up to powerful member governments like the UK on the issue of additionality, at least in the short term. Similarly, in the area of competition policy, the Commission was able, with the support of the Court of Justice, to apply Art. 90 to the liberalization of the telecommunications sector, and to secure its long-sought goal of jurisdiction over European-level mergers and acquisitions. In the case of external trade policy, finally, Delors and MacSharry were able to exploit the external pressures from the USA and other EC trading partners to push through the Council a far-reaching reform of the Common Agricultural Policy, despite the initial resistance of all of the major EC farm groups and the Council of Agriculture Ministers.

Third, however, the cases examined above suggest that the Commission's ability to act on these preferences, and to press for "more Europe," should not be overstated, and varies widely across issue-areas and over time as a function of the preferences of the member governments, the rules governing the sanctioning or overruling of the Commission, the information available to both the Commission and the member governments, and the Commission's ability to strike up alliances with important transnational actors. In the case of the Structural Funds, for example, the Commission exploited member-government concerns about efficiency, and its asymmetrical access to information, to press for important new powers in the administration of the Funds—powers which it then used aggressively to pursue a Commission policy directly at odds with the concerns of the various member governments, including the UK. By 1993, however, the Commission's informational advantage had dissipated, and the decision rules favored those member governments seeking a revision of the Commission's powers. The resulting 1993 Fund Regulations did not remove all Commission discretion, but the ability of the Commission to move aggressively, and against the preferences of the member governments, had been substantially curtailed.

In the competition policy cases examined above, by contrast, the Commission's powers were laid down in Art. 90 of the Treaty and in the 1989 Merger Regulation, respectively. In both cases, therefore, the "default condition" for the Commission's delegated powers was the status quo, thus protecting the Commission from any member-government efforts to roll back its powers. Commission's powers were enshrined in the Treaties, making it more difficult for member governments to sanction Commission behavior of which they disapproved. Nevertheless, a lack of member-government and interest-group support has led the Commission to resist using Art. 90 to liberalize the energy sector, and the determined opposition of the UK and Germany has thus far prevented the Commission from mustering a qualified majority in the Council in order to lower the thresholds under the Merger Regulation.

Finally, in the area of trade, the Commission was generally unable to translate its role as chief negotiator into leverage vis-à-vis member governments such as France on the substance of the Uruguay Round agreement. Facing strong member-state preferences, a demanding de facto consensus rule for ratification, close monitoring from the Art. 113 committee, and intense opposition from agricultural lobbies, the Commission was forced to back down on the Blair House agreement in 1992–3. Once again, the agriculture negotiations of the GATT were an unusually controversial issue in EC trade policy, and are not necessarily representative of the Commission's influence in trade policy more generally. Nevertheless, these cases suggest that the Commission's formal Treaty powers are not sufficient to predict or explain actual Commission autonomy and influence, and that we need to look as well at preferences, decision rules, information, and the availability of transnational coalitions in any given case.

A fourth conclusion which emerges from the case studies is that the Commission's autonomy and influence also depends crucially on its rather complex relationship with the European Court of Justice. The Commission and the Court are, in Westlake's (1994) fortuitous phrase, both "partners and rivals" in the policy process. On the one hand, the Court shares with the Commission a broad or teleological reading of the Treaties, and a longstanding preference for deeper integration, which has led the Court to support the Commission's efforts to expand Community competence, as in the cases of merger control and telecommunications deregulation discussed above. On the other hand, however, the Court has also sought to defend the overall "institutional balance" among the various EC institutions, and to ensure that the Commission carries out its functions in a clear and transparent manner, and so the Court has often ruled against the Commission in the area of competition policy, and in the Commission's bid for greater negotiation powers in external trade policy. The Commission and the Court may, therefore, be the engines of integration, but as we have seen, the two engines do not always pull in the same direction.

9

Citizen Support for Policy Integration

RUSSELL J. DALTON AND RICHARD C. EICHENBERG

O NE of the most remarkable features of modern European politics has been the process of European integration. Beginning with the Coal and Steel Community, the nation-states of Europe have gradually and relatively steadily moved toward ever-closer union. Moreover, in the last decade the rate of progress has accelerated, as the European Union expanded its policy responsibilities and membership, and institutionalized its presence in European politics.

The initial process of European integration was dominated by the strategies and actions of political elites in line with the intergovernmental model described by Stone Sweet and Sandholtz (Chapter 1). Over time, however, this process has gradually moved toward a model of supranational governance that includes a range of other societal actors. Party leaders, parliamentary committees, transnational interest groups, and other political groups are now more involved in the process of building Europe.

Our research specifically focuses on the role of public opinion as a societal actor in the integration process. Only ten years ago, unification research often ignored public opinion for understandable reasons. The integration process began as intergovernmental bargaining, and factors such as international power, elite preferences, or the actions of organized interests dominated the frameworks of neofunctionalists and realists alike. When researchers did consider the role of public opinion, at most they concluded that the public offered a "permissive consensus" that provided political leaders with considerable latitude in carrying out the European project (Lindberg and Scheingold 1970). Others bluntly dismissed the significance of public opinion (Haas 1958: 17).

Several factors have contributed to an increased awareness of the significance of public opinion in the integration process. In retrospect, it appears that scholars underestimated the role of public opinion in defining the national preferences that guided elite bargaining during the early decades of the integration process. Adenauer's efforts to build a European identity among the Germans, the public debate that accompanied the failed attempt to develop a

We are grateful to Anthony Messina for a thorough reading of an earlier version of this chapter.

European defense force, or the popular endorsement of the Common Market concept were affected by public preferences, or at least elite perceptions of these preferences. Even under an intergovernmental model, public opinion is important in defining national preferences.[1]

In addition, as the integration process has evolved from intergovernmental bargaining toward "normal" politics, this expanded the role of public opinion in the process. EU policy is no longer a policy domain that is distant from the everyday life of Europeans. Just as in the formation and implementation of domestic policy, EU policy involves public debates about the political choices facing each member nation. For example, public opinion on integration policy contributed to Margaret Thatcher's political vulnerability toward the end of her administration. Similarly, public debates over currency union and public reactions to proposed cuts in government spending to meet EU targets are highly visible parts of French and German domestic politics. Public preferences inevitably condition the actions of interest groups, political parties, and elites toward EU policies. Furthermore, a changing framework for EU policymaking increases the potential ways in which public opinion can influence the integration process.[2] Today, public opinion (and the positions of other national and transnational actors) is politically relevant in determining the activities of the EU politics of the member-states to a degree that violates a simple intergovernmental model of the integration process.

Public opinion also plays a role in moving the integration process along the continuum from intergovernmentalism to supranationalism. The public's policy preferences can influence which areas are most susceptible to further integration efforts. When there is permissive consensus or positive support, national governments are more able to endorse European action. When the publics of the member-states disagree, this is likely to retard further integration. Moreover, discussion of the "democracy deficit" within the EU necessarily creates pressures to move away from intergovernmental modes of decision-making and toward institutional arrangements that increase the input from the public and other societal actors.

The recent history of the European Union illustrates that public opinion wields real influence. Public reactions to the reforms of the 1980s and 1990s—principally the Single European Act and the Maastricht accords—demonstrated that European citizens were neither "permissive" nor "consensual" in their appraisal of the dramatic relaunching of European integration. The Danish referendum of 1992 temporarily detracked the integration process, while the Irish, French, and Danish referendums of 1993 moved the process ahead. In

---

[1] Indeed, neofunctionalist writings in the second wave of integration research readily accepted the role of public opinion in the integration process (Haas 1971; Schmitter 1971). On the interrelationship of domestic preferences and intergovernmental bargaining see Moravcsik (1989).

[2] The introduction of a directly elected parliament gives the public a direct representation within the EU. In addition, the institutionalization of the integration process has increased the public's potential points of access into the process, such as contacting EU officials, to contacting national parliament officials, petitioning the ECJ, and other methods.

fact, one could argue that public opinion and the votes of citizens in the ratification of the SEA and Maastricht have been *a profound influence* on the recent
process of integration. In the wake of the Danish and French referendums on
Maastricht, sensitivity to public opinion became a hallmark of European integration.[3]

In summary, public opinion has grown from a relatively minor role in the
integration process to a principal focus of political and scholarly attention. We
acknowledge that public opinion has a broad and diffuse influence, and that
the policy positions of specific societal actors—such as political parties and
interest groups—may be more important in explaining the immediate course
of the integration process (see Chapter 3). But public opinion provides the
broad context for these policy debates, much as it does for the domestic politics
of the member-states. Public support for the European Union can facilitate the
process of further union, just as public skepticism toward the EU can slow the
integration process. As the Union moves toward further reform, it seems no
exaggeration to speak of a *Citizens' Europe*.

This research examines the patterns of citizen support for the process of
European integration. We focus our attention on support for policy integration
in specific issue areas. That is, to what extent do Europeans believe that policy
responsibility in specific areas such as health, environment, defense, and other
fields should be transferred from national governments to the European
Union. Like others in this research project, we are interested in explaining how
the integration process moves along the continuum from state-centered action
to supranational action—this time measured in public preferences (see Chapter
1). We believe that public opinion is one factor that can influence movement
along this continuum. In addition, the variations in public support for policy
integration provide a medium for testing theories of the integration process as
measured in public sentiments.

1. Public Opinion and Policy Integration

Even if European integration is described as a general political process, it involves separate decisions to take common action on discrete policies. Progress
comes not from a broad movement on all fronts, but by specific initiatives in
specific areas. Integration is a process by which the EU gradually accumulates
policy responsibilities.

However, most prior opinion research has focused on generalized public

---

[3] Further evidence of the relevance of public opinion comes from the European Union itself.
The European Commission has displayed its concern for public opinion by its efforts to monitor opinions in the member-states. In addition to the long series of biannual Eurobarometer
surveys of European public opinion, the Commission recently instituted a new series of
periodic "flash" surveys to gauge opinion in the wake of important EU reform initiatives and a
new monthly monitoring poll to keep the Commission abreast of public reactions.

support for the process of European integration (Eichenberg and Dalton 1993; Anderson and Kaltenthaler 1995; Gabel and Palmer 1995; Gabel 1998). Scholars have devoted less attention to the specific policy preferences of Europeans and their support for European action in specific policy domains.[4] Yet many theories of European integration stress the policy-specific nature of this process. The recent debates over the terms of the Single European Act or the Maastricht agreement reinforce the point that specific policy choices are being debated, and the relative speed of the integration process is a function of the specific policies being discussed.

Therefore, our analyses focus on public opinions toward specific policy domains. In what areas do Europeans feel that policymaking should be the responsibility of national governments, and in what areas should this be the responsibility of the European Union? More important, what factors determine these policy preferences? Although opinion research has not studied policy integration in detail, existing integration theory provides a fertile starting point for generating our hypotheses. The following sections review this literature.

1.1. Cross-policy variation

The question of how policy integration develops is directly linked to some of the central theoretical questions in integration research. The work of early functional theorists focused on the sequence of broadening policy responsibility for a supranational body that results from initial integration efforts (Haas 1958; Mitrany 1966). Partially because certain problems require it (Mitrany 1966), and partially because of the problem of overcoming national loyalties (Haas 1958), the neofunctionalist strategy begins integration in sectors of scientific, technical, or economic interdependence. Once in place, these initial steps lead to increased interdependence, which may create pressure for further integrative steps, a process labeled "ramification" by Mitrany and "spillover" by Haas.

Of course, there has been much debate about the theoretical and political merit of the functional strategy (e.g. Dougherty and Pfaltzgraff 1990: 433–42). What interests us here, however, are the theoretical implications for public support for policy integration in various domains. If public sentiments follow the neofunctionalist logic, then a direct implication of functionalism is that: *public acceptance of policy integration should be greater in narrow areas of scientific or technical integration.*[5]

For example, European publics may see mutual agreements on occupational safety standards as a technical matter and easily accept EU competency on

---

[4] Sinnott (1995) is one of the few exceptions; he presents European trends in support for policy integration.

[5] More precisely, we might expect that potential public resistance to integration will be lower in these areas, enabling elites to use them as an initial basis of integration. Then success in these areas will generate public awareness and support for the integration process.

this issue. However, issues that directly touch on employment practices or employment security may evoke different popular responses. In short, policy integration starts with "narrow" policy concerns and then broadens to more fundamental policy domains.

Functionalist theory generates additional hypotheses about the process of policy integration. The impact of *interdependence* is crucial for both Mitrany and Haas because it creates two types of effect.[6] First, it increases the mutual sensitivity of societies, and thus increases the need for policy coordination. Second, and perhaps more important, it increases the interest of the parties in a relationship of *mutual gain*. Haas's later work emphasized the successful provision of "welfare" as a factor contributing to integration (1984). This notion is nicely summarized by Nye: "Neofunctionalists prefer a strategy of increasing policy interactions and assume that identities and loyalties will gradually follow *interests* and expectations in clustering around (and supporting) institutions associated with policy integration" (1971: 44, emphasis ours). Interests, of course, must be seen as the successful provision of gains.

This version of neofunctionalist theory thus presumes that existing and potential international cooperation drive the integration process, a theme similar to Stone Sweet and Caporaso's research in this volume (Chapter 4). European action develops in areas where the potential benefits from international cooperation are greatest. If the public perceives Europe in these terms, then we might expect that: *public support for policy integration should be greater for those issues that are difficult to solve at the national level or which have clear potential benefits from international coordination.*

In contrast to the neofunctionalist approach, Stanley Hoffmann (1966; also see Moravcsik 1991) argued that the integration process is shaped by national interests. Integration proceeds most swiftly when it does not involve matters of essential national interests. In Hoffmann's terms, integration begins with "low-politics" issues such as the technical or scientific examples of neofunctionalist theory. In these cases, national elites (and the general public) are more willing to grant decision-making authority to a supranational body over which they will have less control. When significant accomplishments have been achieved in these areas, the integration process may move to other policy domains. Hoffmann argued that "high-politics" issues of national security or national identity would be the most resistant to policy integration. Thus, efforts to establish a customs union or a common foreign-aid program might gain broad support, but attempts to develop a single European Army would meet with popular (and elite) resistance. Hoffmann's definition of high and low politics issues was somewhat fuzzy; the former included such issues as national security,

---

[6] This approach is also compatible with Karl Deutsch's work on intersocietal transaction patterns and the development of "community" (Deutsch *et al.* 1957: 58). Deutsch saw public values and the integration process as interrelated: as societal transactions and interdependence increased, presumably values would change or perhaps converge. For Deutsch, then, the development of support for "community" was rooted in structural factors, especially the cross-border flow of goods and other international interactions.

control of the domestic economy, and general rights of national sovereignty. Low politics issues encompass such matters as welfare policies, tariff policies, and other lower priority policies. If we accept this broad distinction, then: *public support for policy integration should be greater for "low-politics" issues than for "high-politics" issues.*

An even more utilitarian argument assumes that the integration process is based on national calculations of specific policy gains from unification. The expansion of the EU's policy authority results from relationships of interdependence and calculations of gain derived from the integration process. Elites may start the ball rolling, but eventually they have to deliver the goods. Prior research generally supports this utilitarian assumption of public opinion. Richard Eichenberg and Russell Dalton (1993) show that Europeans evaluate the policy performance of the EU in two senses. First, gains from intra-European trade are strongly related to overall public support for the European Community. Second, there is now ample evidence that Europeans evaluate the EU on the basis of economic performance, that is, based on such factors as unemployment, economic growth, and inflation (Eichenberg and Dalton 1993; Gabel 1995; Gabel and Palmer 1995). Further, Matthew Gabel's recent work (1998) demonstrates that Europeans are quite sophisticated in their evaluation of the costs and benefits of integration. Drawing skillfully on the theory of gains from trade in the customs union context, Gabel shows that Europeans seem well aware of the implications of trade liberalization given their particular combination of education and compensation, that is to say, their skills and (relative) wages. Although Europe as a whole has experienced huge gains in prosperity from trade, Gabel shows that individual Europeans are aware that there will be winners and losers in the process, and they adjust their support for integration accordingly. This leads to another prediction about public opinion: *public support for policy integration will reflect a utilitarian calculation of the costs and benefits of European action.*

1.2. Cross-national patterns

The preceding discussion has focused on possible differences in policy integration across specific policy domains; but, of course, another source of variation involves differences across nations. The debates on the Single European Act clearly demonstrated that nations varied in the priority they attached to various policy domains and their willingness to support European action in specific domains. For instance, Southern Europeans advocated a social charter and greater EU efforts on social policy, while the Danes and the Dutch wanted the EU to assume greater responsibility for environmental policy. Even the specifics of trade and economic policy varied across nations; while some nations strongly endorse monetary union, others are openly skeptical about the idea.

In addition to indicating the general evaluation of a policy area, utilitarian theories may explain why nations differ in their support for policy integration. For instance, Matt Gabel's research on the class bases of support for the EU suggests that utility calculations may vary across nations (Gabel 1997). However, it is not entirely clear how to translate the general utilitarian logic into hypotheses linking costs and benefits in specific policy areas. We will develop the utilitarian hypotheses in more detail below when we examine the levels of policy integration in specific domains, but the general logic is clear: *national differences in support for policy integration may be a function of specific national costs and benefits*.

Rather than a narrow utilitarian logic, cross-national comparisons of attitudes toward European integration may emphasize the importance of national traditions, culture, and values as an explanation. An early work in this genre was Karl Deutsch's *Political Community and the North Atlantic Area* (1957). Although Deutsch placed heavy emphasis on the impact of intersocietal communication theory, he also emphasized the "mutual compatibility of major values" as a variable crucial to the integration process. The strength of national identity, or nationalistic sentiments, has been a major factor in explaining national support for European Union (Shepard 1975; Inglehart 1977). Even if phrased in more modest terms, national traditions and experiences with the European Union can create a national response to European integration that is apparent across specific policy domains. For example, Gabel and Palmer (1995) show that World War II experiences still condition overall levels of national support for the EU; Eichenberg and Dalton (1993) find that "national traditions" exert a significant impact on support for the EU even when a multitude of other factors are included in a multivariate model.

Still, it is unclear whether such broad national characteristics hold promise for explaining national levels of policy integration across domains. While this literature suggests which factors should be associated with the decline of national identity and support for the general process of European integration, support for integration of specific policy areas actually varies greatly across societies (as we will see below), highlighting the question of what factors differentiate policy areas from one another. Nonetheless, this research does provide a possible cross-national hypothesis: *public support for policy integration should be greater among those societies with the highest level of support for the general project of European integration*.

By examining the levels of public support for policy integration in several policy domains and across the member-states of the EU, we can both assess the prospects for further expansion of the EU's policy authority, and use this evidence to test prior theorizing about the nature of the integration process.

2. Patterns of Support for Policy Integration

We are primarily interested in explaining public support for policy integration in areas that were involved in the SEA/Maastricht agreements or that may represent the next steps of the integration process. On the one hand, public acceptance of EU action in specific policy domains marks areas that are most susceptible to further integration, or at least domains where the "permissive consensus" is most developed. On the other hand, by understanding what influences the public to shift their preferences along the national–supranational dimension, we can better understand the theoretical basis for policy integration.

Our empirical base is the rich series of Eurobarometer surveys that the Commission of the European Community has conducted (Reif and Inglehart 1991). Since the 1970s the EU has asked Europeans about their willingness to see various policy areas handled at the national level or at the European level (Dalton 1978). Then, beginning in the mid-1980s the EU began a new series using a different survey question:

Some people believe that certain areas of policy should be decided by the (National) government, while other areas of policy should be decided jointly within the European Community. Which of the following areas of policy do you think should be decided by the (National) government, and which should be decided jointly within the European Community?

Our analyses focus on the percentage of the public who respond that particular policy areas should be "decided jointly" within the EU.

2.1. Variation across policy issues

Table 9.1 shows the percentage support for policy integration for the fullest set of items over the 1989–97 period. We present the overall responses for the Europe of the twelve (EU12), that is, for those twelve states who were members of the Community during the full period of these surveys.[7] (Statistics for 1985–9 are shown in italics because question wording diverged from subsequent surveys and thus are not fully comparable.)

Focusing first on the overall *level* of support for policy integration, the Community finds itself in a "half empty/ half full" situation. Across all policy areas, support for policy integration is about 50 percent. In more recent surveys, which include additional policy areas, support has occasionally dropped to below that level, standing at 49 percent in 1993 and 1994. However, these data also show that support varies widely across issue areas. Taking the extremes, only 35 percent of Europeans favored integrating "personal data" policy (in 1993), but almost 80 percent have at times favored integration in "cooperation with developing countries."

Fig. 9.1 ranks policy domains according to the overall level of support for EU decision-making. An "above average group" contains six policy areas: developing countries, scientific research, foreign policy, environmental protection,

---

[7] Percentages are based on the Community-wide sample, weighted to reflect national populations 15 years of age and over.

Table 9.1. Percentage of respondents favoring policy integration at the EU level

	1985	1987	1988	1989	1990	1991	1992	1993	1994	1995	1996	1997
Cooperation with developing countries	77	42	51	76	74	79	79	74	76	78	74	70
Scientific and technological research	70	60	63	77	75	76	76	70	72	74	72	68
Foreign policy toward non-EC countries		44	50	66	64	70	71	68	69	71	68	64
Protection of the environment	69	61	68	67	66	70	71	67	63	69	63	61
Security and defense	58	60	57	48	47	50	55	48	49	56	49	50
Currency		43	48	57	51	57	55	51	51	61	56	53
Rates of value added tax				51	48	51	53	48	48	52	48	47
Basic rules for broadcasting (radio/tv)				47	45	46	45	38	41	43	41	41
Codetermination/worker participation				36	37	39	38	32	33	42	42	41
Health and social security				38	39	39	39	34	31	40	35	33
Education				34	38	38	39	33	30	35	35	34
Average of above 11 issues				54	53	56	56	51	51	56	53	51
Political asylum regulations							58	54	55	58	53	53
Immigration policy							59	54	54	59	54	54
Industrial policy							57	48	48	56		
Fight unemployment	59						51	46	50	60	51	51
Worker health and safety							48	40	40	48		
Cultural policy							47	38	36	39	34	34
Protection of personal data				39	39	39	41	35				
Average of full response set							55	49	49	55	53	51

Note: Some Eurobarometers contain additional (policy) responses not shown here; when two surveys are available in one year, the mean of the two is displayed.

Sources: Eurobarometer number: (1985) 24; (1987) 28; (1988) 29; (1989) 32; (1990) 33; (1991) 35/36; (1992) 37/38; (1993) 39/40; (1994) 41/42; (1995) 43/44; (1996) 46; (1997) 47.1.

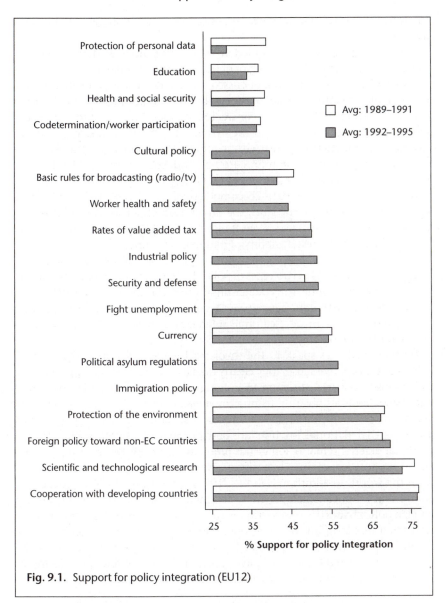

Fig. 9.1. Support for policy integration (EU12)

asylum regulations, and immigration policy. Where comparisons to earlier periods are possible (Dalton 1978), there was broad support for European action on foreign policy and environmental policy long before the initiatives of the SEA and Maastricht. This is a fairly diverse set of policy areas, but they are characterized by at least one of the following traits: they deal with the external environment (foreign policy, developing countries, immigration issues); with classic interdependence issues (environment, immigration); and they do not have substantial *immediate* implications for individual standards of living.[8]

The "average" group basically contains two sorts of policies: defense and economic management. The ranking of defense is understandable in terms of the "high–low" politics distinction discussed earlier—defense is, after all, the basic function of protecting *national* territory—but it is significant that this aspect of external relations is apparently considered separate from the broader task of foreign policy, which is listed in the first group. The remaining items in this "average" group essentially deal with economic management and market management: support for a common currency, industrial policy, VAT rates, and unemployment policy.[9] Similarly, Dalton (1978) found that in the 1970s there was broad public acceptance of EU competence on economic issues of fighting employment and inflation. Thus, the broad economic role of the EU is generally accepted by its citizens, even if monetary and employment policies still primarily remain the responsibility of national governments.

Finally, the public appears least willing to grant the European Union policy-making responsibility on two types of policy issues: individual rights and standards of living (worker health; codetermination; social security; education), and policies dealing with national culture—what we earlier referred to as "identity issues" (education, privacy, cultural policy). Similar patterns have been observed for the 1970s (Dalton 1978).

Do these statistics speak to the theoretical issues raised above? In both a positive and negative sense, they clearly do. First, there does not appear to be a "high–low" politics distinction in judging policy integration. To the extent that "high" politics meant pursuing the *national interest* in relation to the external environment, these surveys suggest that Europeans have long adopted the view that national interests are best pursued in the European context. National defense remains somewhat problematic in this regard,[10] but there is broad support for a joint EU position on issues of Europe's foreign relations with the world. In addition, Dalton's (1978) early study of policy integration found that Europeans had generally accepted EU competence on a variety of foreign policy issues (relations with the superpowers, control of multinationals, and defense). European elites may once have emphasized the difficulties of co-ordinating foreign and defense policies among the European states (Rabier and Inglehart 1981), but these views have apparently changed (European Commission 1996). European publics see this as a natural area of joint action.

---

[8] Immigration perhaps deserves further discussion. We treat it as an interdependence issue, because the experience of the 1990s suggested to Europeans that it was to some extent a collective problem that no state could solve alone. Of course, immigration may have budgetary and welfare (employment) implications, although its ranking here suggests that Europeans see it as a problem concerning the external environment.

[9] VAT taxation might be considered an exception, but in the EU context it has long been discussed as an aspect of market liberalization rather than fiscal policy.

[10] e.g. *Eurobarometer* 44 (spring 1996) found that 44% of the citizens in the twelve favored national action on defense issues, and 52% favored EU action; thus a majority do support a European alternative. Furthermore, a 1996 survey of European elites found very high levels of support for European action on defense and foreign policy in general (CEC 1996).

"High-politics" issues no longer retain a special status among Europeans, if they ever did. In the early stages of the Community, overcoming traditional national sovereignty was clearly near the top of the psychological and political agenda for elites. As time has passed, however, it became clear that separate national positions on many international issues were less likely to succeed than a joint position. Beginning in the mid-1970s, moreover, a number of issues convinced European leaders—and apparently their constituents—that European interests were being neglected (principally by the senior alliance partner). Serious European efforts to construct joint positions began. Beginning most earnestly with the "Nixon shocks" of 1971, there ensued disharmony on the Middle East, energy policy, defense spending, nuclear weapons in Europe, the Soviets in Afghanistan, and the Iranian hostage crisis. Throughout this period, Europe attempted to increase its room for maneuver by laying the groundwork for a common foreign policy (Ginsberg 1989). Interestingly, when the Community first began surveying citizens on policy integration, it phrased the "foreign policy" item in the following terms: "make [our] presence felt in discussions with the superpowers." In short, as early as the 1970s, for Europeans, "high politics" meant aggregating their influence to balance the superpowers, and that could only be done on an EU level (Eichenberg 1997).

If the "high–low" politics distinction seems to have outworn whatever usefulness it once had, other aspects of integration theory find more support in these data. Clearly, there is something to the neofunctionalist logic and strategy. Problems of interdependence and technical complexity attract high support, either because the logic of interdependence seems to demand it (environment, immigration) or because the issue is distant from the citizen's concerns (scientific research). Similarly, past research has shown that market liberalization conditioned overall support for the Community, presumably because of the prosperity to be gained from trade. We see moderately high support for the management of that market (currency regulations, VAT).[11]

Finally, support for policy integration decreases when the issue turns from the management of the market to two sets of issues: the *definition of the national culture* (education, cultural policy, privacy) and the *distribution of national welfare*, including questions of income distribution (social security) and workplace rights (codetermination, health and safety). Education spans both categories; and European elites also see education as primarily a national policy domain (CEC 1996). These latter patterns confirm the enduring utility of the early emphasis on national values, culture, and identity, as well as Dalton's (1978) emphasis on the personal salience of public policy as a factor conditioning support for policy integration.

In summary, public support for policy integration suggests that the EU faces three distinct sets of political problems as it moves beyond the market emphasis of the SEA to the policy emphases of Maastricht. There is a broad basis of

---

[11] In 1996 European elites rated currency as the top policy domain for European action (CEC 1996). This is an apparent change from earlier elite opinions (Rabier and Inglehart 1981).

support for European action on issues of interdependence and relations with the outside world. There is moderate support, although not overwhelming, for the policy mechanisms that "regulate" the internal market. However, there is little support—indeed there is outright resistance—to any interference in the national state's traditional role as the final arbiter on questions of *the national culture* and *the distribution of national welfare.*

2.2. Variations across nations

Citizen support for policy integration varies among the EU member-states as well as across policy domains. For example, generalized sentiments toward European integration may extend across policies; nations that favor policy integration in one sector may also favor integration in others. Conversely, there are strong reasons to expect substantial national differences in the patterns of policy integration. Some nations may see benefits from integration in some areas, but neutral or negative consequences from integration in other sectors. Indeed, the process of integration has often involved balancing these contrasting national priorities to strike a European-wide bargain.

Table 9.2 presents the national patterns in the percentage preferring Community action in each of the eleven core policy areas (also see Dalton and Eichenberg 1993). Comparing across nations, the greatest net support for European-level action is found among the six founding nations, with most policy areas showing a plurality of support for EU action. It is noteworthy that the Germans fall noticeably below the other founding states. Germans are less enthusiastic than their neighbors about the seemingly consensual issues for European action—science and technology, foreign aid, and environmental protection—and are hesitant to yield national autonomy on matters such as currency reform and VAT rates. While Germans and their government voice strong support for the European ideal, they are now more cautious in actually transferring authority to Brussels.

A hesitancy toward policy integration is displayed among all six "new" states. The Danes and British express less support than average for policy integration in nineteen of the twenty-two areas presented in the table. Support for European action is equally restrained in Greece, Spain, and Portugal.

Taken in aggregate, support for policy integration across a range of policy areas appears to be an extension of overall support for the European project. Indeed, it would be surprising if this did not occur, since those publics which endorse the EU overall should generally endorse greater policy responsibility for the Union. However, these aggregate patterns often coexist with substantial and different patterns at the national level. Such variations may be a function of national values or utilitarian calculations.

Table 9.2. Support for Community decision-making by nation across eleven policy areas

	France	Belgium	Holland	Germany	Italy	Luxem.	Denmark	UK	Ireland	Greece	Spain	Port.	EU avg.
Cooperation with developing countries	83	75	81	77	83	78	67	65	77	63	73	66	77
Scientific and technological research	84	76	79	65	76	81	73	66	75	62	70	66	72
Foreign policy toward countries outside the EC	74	75	75	72	78	74	61	62	68	51	62	59	70
Protection of the environment	67	61	83	67	60	62	52	59	46	45	59	51	59
Security and defense	53	61	70	58	57	69	34	41	27	22	42	41	51
Currency	61	60	58	47	67	60	48	29	58	40	48	39	50
Rates of VAT	65	63	71	48	47	44	40	33	47	27	39	32	47
Basic rules for broadcasting and the press	47	41	45	48	46	55	24	30	39	28	36	31	41
Codetermination	34	32	33	39	32	43	12	33	39	27	23	31	33
Health and social welfare	21	27	39	33	35	37	10	31	26	35	26	37	30
Education	26	22	33	32	41	45	21	21	22	27	27	26	29
Country Average	55	54	61	53	57	59	40	42	48	39	46	44	51

Note: Table entries are the percentage replying that each policy area should be decided jointly within the Community *minus* those who believe the area should be decided by the respective national governments.

Sources: Eurobarometer 42 (Fall 1994).

3. Case Studies of Policy Integration

In our understanding the construction of the European project comes from developing public support where it is lacking, and building compromises between the differing policy priorities of societal actors and their national governments. In some areas the public may accept European action, facilitating policy integration in these areas. For instance, the public in the six EC founder states lean toward EC decision-making on foreign policy and security issues, and this support has increased in the post-Cold War period. The publics in the remaining nations prefer national policymaking on security and defense issues.[12] In other areas, the opinions of the public lag behind policymakers; in several member-states a plurality of the public still favors national action on monetary and currency union.

This section explores support for policy integration in three specific sectors: environmental policy, security and defense policy, and monetary union. These focused analyses will enable us to examine how national preferences differ and how these differences vary across time. Our goal is to determine how domestic policy preferences are formed and how they interact with policy change at the EU level.

3.1. Environmental policy

Our first case study deals with public support for EU or national decision-making on environmental policy. We selected this area for several reasons. Environmental policy is one of the most visible new issues of European politics, and thus enables us to examine the formation of preferences in a new area that has not previously been integrated into the policymaking process of either the EU or national governments. Environmental policy also represents an area where the international dimension of the problem is obvious, but where industry and consumers may bear real economic costs through stricter environmental policy. Thus it is an area that contains a diverse mix of factors that might encourage or discourage a shift toward supranational policymaking. We also know that environmental policy is an area where EU responsibility has changed as a result of the SEA and Maastricht accords—thus we can track the interaction of public opinion and policy change.

Environmental policy has a long, albeit sometimes surreptitious, policy history within the European Union (Sbragia 1993a; Vogel 1993). The European Community formed before environmental protection was a salient political issue. Thus, the Treaty of Rome makes no mention of environmental policy,

---

[12] However, when given the choice between NATO or the EU as a forum for international security, the public in Mediterranean Europe favors the EU.

and the early Community possessed no formal authority on environmental matters. Environmental issues began to gain the attention of policymakers in the early 1970s, as public pressure and international meetings brought this issue onto the political agenda. At the 1972 Paris Summit the heads of government called for the EC to develop an environmental program. The first EC environmental action plan followed in 1973; it assessed the state of the European environment and suggested a series of potential policy reforms. A second action plan was published in 1977 and a third in 1983. In 1981 the Community formed DG XI, which was responsible for environmental issues. During this period the issue received some attention from the EC institutions. However, economic recessions in the 1970s and 1980s focused EC attention on economic issues. In addition, the EC lacked formal legal authority to act on environmental matters, except through consensual regulations and directives. The Community issued a number of directives on environmental issues over this time, but these were fairly modest proposals because of the unanimity requirement. As late as the 1980s, therefore, environmental policy remained primarily a policy domain of national governments.

Although the environment remained off the EU's formal list of responsibilities, there was mounting public and interest group pressure during the 1980s for the EU to become more active on environmental matters. European-wide environmental problems, such as acid rain or periodic environmental crises, reminded Europeans that environmental problems spread across national borders. This was also a period of heightened public interest and activism on environmental issues (Dalton 1994). The public and environmental groups pressed Brussels to become involved in environmental policymaking, a role that was encouraged by DG XI.

The Single European Act transformed the EU's role on environmental issues. A revision of Art. 100 gave the Commission the legal right to set environmental policy. Additional changes to Art. 130 set the standards for environmental protection and mandated that environmental protection requirements be considered in other Community policy areas. Beyond the legal standing the EU gained by these provisions, these reforms also changed how environmental policy would be decided in the future. Instead of unanimous consent, as was the rule prior to 1987, Community action could be taken by a qualified majority when market-related issues were involved. The Maastricht Accords then extended the EU's environmental areas subject to a qualified majority and increased the European Parliament's role on environmental matters. Thus a single polluter nation no longer can block environmental protection policies at the EU level. A series of decisions by the European Court of Justice also expanded the EU's ability to promote strict environmental regulations (Vogel 1993).

By the 1990s, the EU had become a significant arena for the making of environmental policy in Europe. Much if not most of the policy responsibility still lies with the national governments. However, the EU is increasingly involved in setting environmental standards, arbitrating between conflicts involving economic interests and environmental protection, and establishing European-wide environmental policies.

This is an area where there has been a considerable shift from intergovernmental decision-making in the 1970s to supranational decision-making in the 1990s. Thus, it is interesting to examine the relationship between public preferences and the activities of the Community. Did the public follow elite cues, as the intergovernmentalists would suggest, or is there evidence that public opinion existed separately from the EU's own actions?

Because the Eurobarometers have changed their question wordings over time, we cannot exactly track the trends in public opinion over the past three decades. Yet the evidence from different questions presents a single picture. When questions on environmental policy were first asked in the 1970s, there was already surprisingly high public interest in these issues. In the 1973 European Community Survey, a large majority in each member-state (except Ireland) already felt that environmental protection was an important or very important issue. Subsequent surveys showed that public interest in environmental matters remained widespread over the next decade, despite the economic recessions Europe experienced at the same time (Dalton 1994: ch. 3). In the late 1980s and early 1990s, public interest increased even further.

The first EU public opinion surveys on this issue also found that a clear majority of Europeans favored EU action on environmental issues in the early 1970s. As early as 1974 and 1975, two-thirds of the European public favored Community-level decision-making on policies to fight pollution and protect the environment. Even after the economic recessions of the next several years, surveys in 1983 and 1984 found even higher levels of support for European action.[13]

Table 9.3 summarizes public support for EU decision-making on environmental matters over the last decade. Two findings are apparent from these data and earlier research. First, public support for European action *preceded* EU responsibility for this policy area. Since the early 1970s Europeans have generally favored EU policymaking, recognizing the international dimension of this issue and the need for common action on setting environmental standards. The European public created a "permissive consensus" for action on this issue —a consensus that took the EU more than a decade to translate into formal authority. Furthermore, the development of formal EU authority on this issue has apparently little impact on public sentiments.

Second, national differences in support for European action are fairly consistent and fairly stable over time. Southern Europeans, such as the Greeks, Spaniards, and Portuguese, are least supportive of EU action on environmental

---

[13] Sinnott (1995) notes that the wording changes in Eurobarometer 6 and 10 appeared to lessen support for European action on all issues, and attributes this to a methodological artifact of the question wording. For this reason we will not discuss these two surveys.

Table 9.3. Percentage of respondents favoring integration of environmental policy

	1985	1987 (Fall)	1989 (Fall)	1990 (Spring)	1991	1992	1993	1994	1995	1996	1997
Netherlands	81	79	82	81	83	83	84	82	84	86	75
Germany	79	82	77	68	73	73	75	69	72	72	69
France	81	49	73	62	69	70	65	68	69	67	70
Italy	84	56	64	68	71	74	62	61	68	67	65
Greece	48	58	50	55	61	60	57	52	67	60	57
Luxembourg	83	78	63	63	63	65	67	59	65		63
UK	70	62	63	71	70	70	65	60	65	57	48
Spain	69	57	63	64	73	69	62	59	63	64	66
Belgium	72	53	69	66	69	67	66	62	63	69	64
Denmark	60	85	44	55	57	61	60	49	60	48	55
Portugal	59	51	42	43	61	67	58	52	59	49	45
Ireland	50	47	44	51	55	56	49	48	57	55	48
EU12	69	61	67	66	70	71	67	63	69	65	62
Eurobarometer	24	28	32	33	35/36	37/38	39/40	41/42	43/44	46	47.1

Note: Where two Eurobarometers are displayed, the mean for the two biannual surveys is shown.

matters. The Irish also display significant reservations. In contrast, support is greatest in the Netherlands, which has a very active environmental movement and some of the strongest national environmental regulations in Europe.

This cross-national pattern tends to undercut a narrow self-interest explanation of national opinions. If we assume that EU standards would reflect an "average" of present national environmental policies, then EU policymaking would raise environmental standards for most Southern European nations and might produce lower environmental standards in nations with strict legislation. However, support for EU action is greatest in nations with already strong environmental legislation, and weak in nations with less developed environmental protections (Spain, Greece, Portugal, and Ireland).

Rather than national self-interest, it appears that support for EU action on environmental matters mirrors general public support for action on this policy. Where publics favor strong environmental regulation, as in the Netherlands, the expansion of EU policy responsibilities can increase environmental standards across the continent. Where public support for environmental reform is weak, as in Southern Europe, then an expansion of government activism (even by a European government) is not supported. In other words, in this area policy integration at the EU level appears to be an extension of national policy activism by other means.

3.2. A common foreign and security policy

There is something of a paradox in the fact that Europe has found it most difficult to achieve progress on the integration of foreign and defense policy. To be sure, it is precisely in these areas that "high-politics" questions of national interest, national tradition, sovereignty, and territorial security are raised. Nonetheless, it is also the case that European unity and European institutions were conceived to serve the pursuit of a broad range of external political and security interests. Most obviously, since 1957 Europe has been a customs union, and the institutions of the Community have become thoroughly engaged in the diplomatic representation of foreign trade and other economic interests abroad. Second, the very creation of the European Community was strongly motivated by foreign and security policy considerations. With the failure of the European Defense Community in 1954, the creation of integrated European institutions offered the only option that would bridge the American-supported desire to rearm West Germany and the European (especially French) fears that this step understandably provoked. Like American participation in NATO, the new institutions of European unity served the dual purpose of deterring the Soviets through unity, while simultaneously integrating and containing the newly rehabilitated West Germany.

A united Europe was seen as a balance—or lever—in an external environment characterized by bipolar dominance. As DePorte has put it (1986: 222–3):

Finally, on the international level, [the Schuman plan] promised not only to strengthen Western Europe in face of the Russian threat but also—though this was less talked about—to strengthen it vis-à-vis its indispensable but overpowering American ally. These Frenchmen, like many West Europeans, did not doubt that they had to rely on American strength for their security. But they did not want to rely entirely on the Americans to manage relations with the East which involved no less than war and peace, that is, the lives of the European nations. At the least a more united Europe could better influence American decisions affecting its vital interests; at the best it could break through the rigidity and risks of bipolar Europe by becoming strong enough to cease to be a stake of the superpowers in cold or hot war.

However, this latter purpose of European foreign policy soon fell victim to the Cold War context of a Europe allied to the USA. Increasingly, foreign and security policy were defined as a stark choice between the Atlantic and European options, and the latter could not be pursued without risking the former. Although European integration was originally a child of the Cold War, in the ensuing years integration of foreign policy could not be seen as competing with the Atlantic connection. The very real threats and tensions of the Cold War (not to mention pressure from Americans) helps to explain why the choice was framed this way, but perhaps it also resulted from the fact that the most energetic proponent of a European voice was General de Gaulle, who complicated matters even further by making it clear that Europe should be led by France, and who in any case was a strong critic of supranational solutions (Grosser 1982; DePorte 1986).

Yet the French position always contained a contradiction. Given the Soviet Union's geographic advantage, its (perceived) conventional dominance, and its large nuclear arsenal, European security required a nuclear deterrent. However, the first and most emphatic principle of French security policy under DeGaulle was the insistence on independence, most particularly in the nuclear realm. In the absence of French willingness to share its deterrent, let alone integrate its defense forces, the remaining European states chose to privilege the Atlantic connection, a result that certainly slowed the evolution of common European positions in foreign and security policy.

There matters rested until the end of the 1960s, when the European challenge to US foreign policy began to grow. Beginning with the Vietnam War and the negative economic consequences for Europeans, there ensued a number of transatlantic quarrels, especially on policy in the Middle East, energy, nuclear weapons, and the coordination of economic policy. Not surprisingly, therefore, the "launching" of formal efforts to institutionalize European cooperation in the foreign policy field began in earnest in the early 1970s in the form of European Political Cooperation (EPC), a form of intergovernmental coordination of foreign policy that nonetheless produced some important European positions on foreign policy, most notably the 1980 Venice declaration on the rights of the Palestinians. Perhaps equally important, the institutionalization of EPC led to biannual meetings of Foreign Ministers to discuss foreign policy specifically, and it also created a dense web of administrative links among Foreign Ministries and between Brussels and the ministries (Ginsberg 1989; Wood and Yesilada 1996; Smith, Chapter 11).

Foreign policy received little attention in the Single European Act because it was largely a market reform; but the Maastricht Treaty made official what Europeans had long aspired to: that the European Union "shall define and implement a common foreign and security policy" (see Chapter 11). The provisions of the Treaty on Common Foreign and Security policy are quite complex, but substantively they include the aspiration to an integrated defense and security policy in addition to the actual adoption of a common foreign policy, as for example in Art. J.4: "the common foreign and security policy shall include all questions related to the security of the Union, including the eventual framing of a common defense policy, which might in time lead to a common defense." The Treaty also commits the member-states to close consultation, collaborative actions in international bodies and conferences, and it specifies the West European Union as the "defense arm" of the Union.

However, the most important aspect of the Treaty's foreign policy provisions is that intergovernmental rather than supranational decision-making is specified. In both areas, the Council must first decide by unanimous vote that "joint action" should be undertaken; subsequent decisions in the pursuit of these actions are to be taken by qualified majority vote. In summary, the language and indeed the symbolism of the Treaty pushes the Union quite a bit forward in the integration of foreign policy, but supranational integration of authority remains rather limited.

Does this situation reflect the views of European citizens? To the extent that the Treaty continues the European tradition of ambivalence in the integration of foreign policy, it closely parallels citizen views. In the 1970s and 1980s, for example, responses to Eurobarometer surveys as well as US government polls showed that Europeans supported common European foreign policies. For example, in 1974 and 1975, almost 70 percent agreed that the Community should decide jointly to "make [our] presence felt in discussions with the US and the USSR," and in 1976, 55 percent of Europeans agreed that the EC should decide jointly to "defend [our] interests against the superpowers" (Dalton 1978). In addition, there was an increase from the 1970s to the 1980s in the percentage of Europeans who wanted Europe to conduct security policy "together" rather than "separately" (Eichenberg 1989: 14). However, throughout this same period, a substantial plurality of Europeans continued to believe that European security was best pursued within the NATO Alliance when survey questions provided that alternative (Eichenberg 1989: 118–58). Thus, although Europeans responded favorably to the idea of a common foreign or security policy, when phrased as an alternative to NATO, they turned distinctly less favorable.

The same is true of more recent polls. Table 9.4 summarizes the Eurobarometer policy integration questions on foreign and defense policy. It includes three separate questions on EU-level decision-making: cooperation with developing countries; foreign policy toward non-EC countries; and security and

Table 9.4. Percentage of respondents favoring integration of foreign and defense policy

Cooperation with developing countries

	1985	1987	1989	1990	1991	1992	1993	1994	1995	1996	1997
Italy	88	34	83	82	84	84	79	83	83	84	85
Netherlands	75	48	75	73	76	77	80	80	82	86	84
France	84	37	81	74	79	82	77	83	82	80	77
Spain	80	52	70	77	80	75	71	72	78	74	78
UK	79	50	76	80	81	80	72	73	76	67	66
Belgium	79	40	76	73	77	74	73	72	75	73	65
Ireland	83	43	73	72	73	77	72	75	75	75	74
Germany	79	51	77	68	76	78	76	76	75	72	76
Luxembourg	85	45	72	78	79	79	75	77	75		75
Denmark	57	48	64	63	68	70	69	68	74	64	68
Greece	72	37	56	58	64	64	58	61	71	64	57
Portugal	62	39	54	55	70	74	61	65	70	67	59

Foreign policy toward non-EC countries

	1985	1987	1989	1990	1991	1992	1993	1994	1995	1996	1997
Netherlands		48	68	66	79	74	78	76	79	82	82
Italy		37	78	74	75	80	75	78	79	79	83
France		42	73	63	72	73	70	74	76	74	72
Belgium		49	78	70	76	73	72	74	74	69	66
Germany		58	67	60	68	72	70	70	73	73	71
Luxembourg		51	63	65	65	72	72	71	73		76
Spain		39	58	69	71	65	64	61	70	70	69
Ireland		36	64	62	60	67	64	66	66	68	70

Table 9.4. (cont.)

Foreign policy toward non-EC countries

	1985	1987	1989	1990	1991	1992	1993	1994	1995	1996	1997
Portugal		24	41	47	59	67	55	60	63	58	56
UK		53	61	64	68	65	61	61	62	56	55
Denmark		50	47	47	56	57	58	60	62	57	58
Greece		33	36	42	54	55	50	49	61	59	53

Security and defense

	1985	1987	1989	1990	1991	1992	1993	1994	1995	1996	1997
Netherlands	64	54	63	67	66	70	75	71	77	76	75
Luxembourg	74	60	63	68	57	63	64	63	69		66
Belgium	64	60	58	53	63	57	57	56	65	61	54
Italy	71	53	56	60	59	69	54	60	64	60	64
Germany	61	57	58	50	53	57	58	59	60	61	62
France	61	72	51	42	46	53	42	51	56	52	54
Spain	60	58	37	40	48	48	43	41	52	50	54
Portugal	46	40	24	26	41	52	41	38	52	36	33
UK	51	64	39	42	42	41	39	39	42	37	35
Denmark	55	69	33	42	41	45	35	37	40	33	36
Greece	51	49	23	31	38	43	33	25	34	33	33
Ireland	53	50	25	24	29	29	23	26	30	26	28
Eurobarometer	24	28	32	33	35/36	37/38	39/40	41/42	43/44	46	47.1

Note: Where two Eurobarometers are displayed, the mean for the two biannual surveys is shown.

defense. There are several notable features in Table 9.4. First, comparing the levels of support across the three questions, there is much stronger support for the notion of integrating foreign policy generally than for integrating defense and security specifically. Why might this be the case?

First, as noted above, the Union already has a long tradition of coordinating its relations with the external environment. The most obvious example, of course, is the Union's role representing Europe on trade matters, but there is also the long experience of EPC as well as the Union's active program of trade and development assistance with the poorer nations (Lomé conventions). Second, the questions on foreign policy integration speak to general issues, while the integration of defense and security policies has quite specific operational (and perhaps budgetary) implications. Especially in the context of Cold War Europe, or even in specific situations with obvious implications for the Union, such as the conflict in Yugoslavia, the potentially unpleasant implications of defense policies surely affect the responses.

The cross-national differences in responses to these items also merit discussion. Unlike the responses to many of the policy integration items, the first two foreign policy items in Table 9.4 reveal substantial cross-national consensus; in no country is there consistently less than 60 percent support for integration of foreign policy and relations with the Third World, and the gap between the states showing the strongest and weakest support is much less than was the case in responses to the item on environmental policy integration. In summary, as concerns the general integration of foreign policy, there is both national and cross-national consensus.

The same is not true of defense and security policy, where there is substantial polarization between the oldest members of the Union and the newer members. In addition, the United Kingdom, now the inheritor of the Gaullist mantle in Europe, is substantially more negative than its continental partners. Most important, the three most important players on the issue of security policy integration—France, Germany, and the UK—are clearly divided in their level of support.

Finally, it is worth noting that the EU remains bedeviled by the debate concerning the compatibility of an EU defense policy and a defense based on NATO. Whether the debate is necessary is a subject beyond the terms of this chapter, but it is worth noting that, when faced with the choice in recent US government surveys, European support for the NATO Alliance remains surprisingly strong, given the decline in the Soviet/Russian threat, but it is also the case that, on a number of questions concerning an integrated European defense, citizens remain strongly supportive. Indeed, there is evidence that support for NATO and support for an integrated approach to European security are not perceived by citizens to be incompatible (USIA 1995). It therefore comes as little surprise that NATO and the EU in 1996 institutionalized a situation of "dual competence" for security policy in which NATO endorsed the concept of a specific "European Defense Identity" within NATO but also reaffirmed the primacy of the NATO Alliance (Art. 1996; NATO 1996; Eichenberg 1997).

3.3. **Economic and monetary union and the politics of convergence**

The final policy area we examine is citizen support for EU sovereignty on economic and monetary issues—one of the main issues of contention in current EU politics (see Chapter 7). The politics of European monetary cooperation can be usefully divided into three historical periods. A first phase might be called the *fixed exchange-rate phase*, encompassing the series of attempts beginning in the early 1970s to coordinate monetary policy by binding members to a more or less narrow band of exchange-rate fluctuations vis-à-vis other member currencies. Several characteristics of this phase (the European Monetary System and its variants) are noteworthy. First, in its inspiration and justification, the EMS was fairly narrow, technical, and indirect in its implications for fiscal and macroeconomic policy. It was essentially designed to manage and protect European markets from the uncertainties of exchange-rate fluctuations. By reducing uncertainty and exchange-rate cost of transactions, the system aimed to promote investment, trade, and growth. Equally important, the EMS had a *direct* impact only on the monetary instrument of government economic policy. Although it had indirect implications for fiscal and macroeconomic policy, these were not explicitly covered by the system. Thus, the politics of taxing, spending, and employment were left outside the direct purview of EU policy harmonization. Second, a substantial motivation for the system was the combination of annoyance and uncertainty that resulted from the perceived inconsistency and unpredictability of American monetary and fiscal policy after the breakdown of the Bretton Woods system. In summary, although the system was certainly embodied with some of the symbolism of European unity, one could argue that, in its public presentation and justification, it was designed largely as a management tool to facilitate the operation of the common market.

The EMS was not without its difficulties, of course, but a second phase began with the signature of the Maastricht Treaty and the commitment of the Union to economic and monetary union (EMU). From this point forward, the Union was committed to something far beyond the coordination of monetary policy through exchange-rate management, for Maastricht requires EU members to merge their sovereignty in monetary affairs by creating a single European currency, a single set of (politically independent) institutions for managing and regulating that currency, and perhaps most important, a single set of fiscal and economic policy objectives (termed convergence criteria) that are deemed necessary for a single currency to function effectively.

The immediate post-Maastricht phase certainly contained some continuity with the past. Especially when viewed in the context of the single-market program, the need to remove the uncertainties and costs associated with fluctuating exchange rates continued to hold a prominent place in the official rationale for the policy. What is more, European annoyance and concern for the vicissitudes of American economic policy continued to inform the policy dialogue that animated both the SEA in the 1980s and the monetary provisions of the Maastricht Treaty.

However, with Maastricht two new elements entered—and came to dominate—the public discussion. The most prominent was the central innovation of EMU itself: the establishment of a supranational authority and institutions to supplant national sovereign authority over monetary policy. Equally important, the politics of national symbols came to dominate the political reaction to EMU, as the theme of debate focused on the issues of national pride and identity that were combined in the visible symbols of history and culture that are imprinted on each nation's currency. Whereas monetary debates once turned on the width of the band in the "snake," after Maastricht the question was whether the loss of the nation's currency did not also mean the loss of its history and identity.

Not surprisingly, the politics of national identity proved troublesome enough as the Union and member-states worked through the ratification of the Treaty, but no sooner had they surpassed the ratification hurdle than members found themselves embroiled in a third, continuing phase of the public debate. This is the phase of the *convergence criteria*, and it has become increasingly clear that the potential negative impact of the criteria concerning interest rates, inflation, and budget deficits have been brought home to the European public by recent debate and experience. Unlike the relatively narrow and technical features of the former exchange-rate regime, which at least in public perceptions probably concerned exchange-rate coordination and little else, the convergence requirements of EMU now require coordination of budgetary and macroeconomic policy, and perhaps a significant dose of austerity. In short, the prior system had concerned exchange rates only, but after Maastricht the core of national governments' functions are at issue; political leaders must struggle to square domestic priorities on taxes, spending, growth, and employment with the politics of convergence. These developments come as an additional blow to domestic audiences already troubled by slow growth, stubbornly high unemployment, and pressure on public spending programs that arise from demographic developments and international competition. Finally, divergent economic and budgetary policies among the member-states further complicate a political problem that is already delicate. In summary, as the Union moves toward final implementation of EMU, the constraints and choices required by convergence exacerbate a consensus problem within and among EU members that was already complicated by the symbolic politics of identity and nationalism that initially greeted the Treaty.

However, whether these political complications will prove fatal to successful transition to EMU remains as yet an open question. In the first place, as Cameron describes so clearly in Chapter 7, the Union has moved decisively to remove doubts that it was committed to a clear timetable for implementation of EMU. In the initial post-Maastricht phase, there remained a hypothetical quality to the commitment to full EMU. However, with the declarations of the Turin and Dublin summits and the subsequent deliberations of Finance Ministers, the Union is now squarely on record as committed to implementation. Second, the key players in EMU, especially France and Germany, have reaffirmed their commitment to implementation and have worked closely to surmount both public doubts and squabbles among member governments. Finally, even absent these developments, it is not at all clear that public opinion totally rejects either the general aspirations or the technical details of EMU. As we have noted elsewhere (Eichenberg and Dalton 1993), European public opinion is sensitive to inflation and seems to ascribe some responsibility to Brussels for its successful management. To the extent that EMU is sold as a policy tool to bring non-inflationary growth, there is therefore some basis for believing that the public would greet it positively. Similarly, as described in an earlier section of this chapter, there is ample evidence that European public opinion supports "market-management" mechanisms at the EU level, precisely because they perceive an important goal of the EU to be the promotion of prosperity through intra-European trade. Thus, to the extent that EMU can be sold as a mechanism for reducing the cost and uncertainties of the market, it appeals to a basis of support that already exists in public opinion. Finally, the role of EMU and the Euro as "buffers" against American economic policies remains explicit, and thus has an appeal on economic grounds as well as appealing to a sense that the Union and its policies are designed to promote European influence more generally.

Whether the final "convergence" phase of transition to full EMU will founder on public rejection remains an open question. Table 9.5 displays national patterns of public support for joint EU decision-making in three policy areas that are relevant to EMU: "currency," "fighting unemployment," and "health and social security." Although these survey questions do not inquire in detail what the EU's precise responsibility in these three areas would be, clearly the first of the three items does sensitize respondents to the central issue of a common currency. In addition, the "unemployment" and "social security" questions highlight the new salience of the "post convergence" Union in areas such as economic growth and unemployment. These policies are also related to the budgetary convergence criteria; health and social policy represent the largest categories of public spending in Western Europe.

Table 9.5 reveals that support for policy integration in these areas has followed a generally similar cross-national pattern over time: there was a period of declining support in the initial post-Maastricht period (perhaps affected by a deteriorating economy as well), followed by a period of recovery in support that continued into 1995. Of the three policy areas, support for integration of currency policy is the highest in all countries but two (the UK and Portugal). By 1995, support for joint decision-making on currency matters enjoyed majority support in ten of the twelve member-states shown here, and in many members the support is quite strong. In fact, in every member-state but the UK and Germany, the negotiation, debate, and ratification of the Maastricht Treaty *increased* support for currency integration from its level prior to the signing of the Treaty.

Similarly, joint EU efforts to fight unemployment enjoy majority support in most member-states, a pattern that has been in evidence since the 1970s (Dalton 1978: 20). Moreover, this support also grew in the aftermath of the

Table 9.5. Percentage of respondents favoring integration of currency and related policy issues

Currency

	1987	1988	1989	1990	1991	1992	1993	1994	1995	1996	1997
Netherlands	40		53	50	58	58	57	57	77	70	58
Italy	32		68	66	71	77	69	67	75	74	76
France	60		72	63	69	65	58	64	70	64	60
Luxembourg	59		56	54	57	63	61	58	70		64
Belgium	46		67	62	65	66	62	57	62	62	57
Spain	35		46	41	57	54	53	50	62	59	56
Ireland	41		57	56	55	57	52	56	66	61	56
Greece	52		44	47	53	59	51	44	57	51	52
Germany	51		59	44	53	46	46	45	55	50	44
Portugal	27		28	33	47	57	44	39	52	51	41
Denmark	49		54	50	52	53	46	49	51	35	41
UK	32		42	42	36	32	27	30	43	29	25

"Fight unemployment"

	1987	1988	1989	1990	1991	1992	1993	1994	1995	1996	1997
Greece						57	53	51	67		55
Italy						70	57	56	69		67
Ireland						57	47	53	65		54
Portugal						61	52	53	61		47
France						58	50	60	61		57
Netherlands						49	48	48	61		53
Belgium						50	47	56	61		58

Table 9.5. (cont.)

"Fight unemployment"

	1987	1988	1989	1990	1991	1992	1993	1994	1995	1996	1997
Spain						44	37	37	56		51
Germany						46	46	50	59		52
UK						36	32	40	53		28
Luxembourg						42	43	51	56		54
Denmark						26	43	35	49		36

Health and social security policy

	1987	1988	1989	1990	1991	1992	1993	1994	1995	1996	1997
Greece			45	52	54	53	44	41	52	45	41
Portugal			36	39	45	55	42	34	51	37	31
Italy			48	56	54	52	39	38	48	46	48
Spain			40	40	47	42	33	27	41	34	36
Netherlands			41	44	39	38	45	38	45	44	39
Germany			37	35	37	40	41	33	42	34	34
Belgium			35	39	32	33	29	28	37	36	36
Ireland			35	31	29	37	28	29	39	32	29
UK			35	36	33	31	30	31	38	30	25
France			34	30	28	30	23	23	31	29	28
Luxembourg			31	40	34	33	33	36	40		37
Denmark			11	15	14	15	14	10	17	12	15
Eurobarometer	28	29	32	33	35/36	37/38	38/39	41/42	43/44	46	47.1

Treaty, in some countries by substantial margins. To be sure, this question on "fighting unemployment" might be seen as rather anodyne, since it is hard to imagine respondents rejecting *any* measure that might relieve Europe's most significant economic and social problem, and the increase in support on this question came over a period of economic difficulty. Nonetheless, it is worth recalling (from Table 9.1), that there *are* issues concerning the integration of social and employment policy about which respondents are far more negative (worker codetermination and health and safety regulations, for example). Thus, it seems at least plausible that respondents view the currency question and the unemployment question as issues of *market management*, a function that has long formed part of the EU's rhetoric and responsibilities (in the customs union, SEA, and EMS), and a function for which citizens seem to hold the EU responsible. In summary, the responses to these questions suggest that citizens are receptive—and certainly not resistant—to the EU's argument that the functioning of the single market requires economic mechanisms that reduce the uncertainties and costs of doing business in that market.

The same is not true of support for joint decision-making in the area of "health and social security." As we discussed earlier, rejection of EU action in this policy domain does not require the EMU to explain: the fact that the welfare state represents the unique combination of *national* values and compromises that form the basis of the postwar reconciliation of class and partisan interests in Europe. Perhaps it is not surprising that Europeans would be wary of introducing a supranational policy mechanism to supplant national *welfare traditions* and policies that represent such a historic and potentially fragile set of national compromises. In fact, the opposition to involving the EU in policies dealing with "income inequality" is actually longstanding (Dalton 1978: 20).

Equally important, the welfare state programs represent the largest categories of public spending, and to that extent they are obvious targets of budget austerity as the EMU convergence criteria force governments to reduce deficits. Interestingly, whereas the citizens of the more wealthy, older members of the EU had supported the market-management policies described earlier, here several of them fall at or below the average level of support for integration (France, Luxembourg, and Belgium are prominent examples). Since the modern welfare state is both older and larger in these states, there is some suggestion that citizens are reacting to the potential retrenchment that EMU might bring to social policy. These suspicions are reinforced by the fact that support for integration in this area *has actually declined* since 1989 in the older, wealthier member-states.

Other comparisons across the member-states are also noteworthy. There is a fairly clear pattern of strong support for currency policy among the group of wealthy, founding members who conduct a substantial amount of trade within the EU (that is, those for whom the market-management argument holds strongest sway). The exception, of course, is Germany, where support has stagnated over the period of the Maastricht debate and where questions about the costs of reunification and the fate of the deutschemark (and the economic policies that support it) are reflected in the ambivalence of the German public. Secondly, Greece, Spain, and Portugal were initially skeptical, but support for joint currency decision-making has grown substantially in these countries, leaving only Denmark and the UK in the familiar roles of rejectionists. Perhaps most interesting, on the health and social security question, the now-familiar pattern of strongest support among the older, founding members of the community is reversed: on this issue, only the newer members—especially Greece, Portugal, and Spain—show near-majority support for integration, a result of the fact that support has actually grown in these countries since the late 1980s.

Two perspectives compete to explain this pattern. First, to the extent that the measure taps vulnerability to EMU-caused budgetary austerity, the newer, less wealthy EU members may simply have less to lose than the older members with larger, well-established health and pensions systems (to name just two). Second, to the extent that the measure taps aspirations to social *policy harmonization*— perhaps on market-management and convergence grounds—the cross-national patterns suggest that the newer, poorer societies see some self-interest in harmonization (presumably because it would raise welfare standards), while the older members do not (presumably because it would mean a lowering of their own standards).

In any case, the combination of these patterns suggests clear lessons and perhaps predictions concerning the politics of EMU. First, there is moderate support within and among member-states for the harmonization of currency policy. This support has actually edged upward after the initial negative reaction to Maastricht. This support may depend on the logic of *market management*, a logic that Europeans are sensitive to because of its importance to the functioning of the single market and its prior history in the EMS. To be sure, the problems of German ambivalence and Danish and British recalcitrance are evident here as well, but this is hardly new, and in any case it occurs in the context of a generally warming public reception to monetary coordination.

However, as suggested earlier, the Achilles' heel of EMU may turn out to be the low levels of support that most citizens feel toward harmonizing health and social security. This is already evident in the domestic debates of France and Germany, both of which have made difficult budgetary cuts and reforms in their efforts to meet the convergence criteria.

4. Policy Integration and the Implications for the European Union

As the European Union moves beyond the market liberalization provisions of the Treaty of Rome and the Single European Act, our results can make a significant contribution to our understanding of how the integration process moves from state-centered action to collaborative policymaking within the European

Union. At a theoretical level, we would argue that our findings have much to say about the nature of the integration process. The first lesson is the importance of disaggregating the integration process. Although European integration may be a general process, it is comprised of specific steps on specific policy matters. Thus, it is more realistic to speak of a process of *policy integration* in which EU responsibility can be judged for specific policy areas. The building of a European Union progresses by the cumulation of policy integration, and the factors affecting policy integration may vary from issue domain to issue domain.

Generalizing patterns across multiple policy areas, it appears that some theoretical perspectives seem outworn, such as the "high–low" politics distinction that framed discussions of European integration in the 1960s and 1970s. While it is true that support for a truly unified European defense policy is moderate at best, one might argue that even this moderate support is higher than the "high-politics" framework would have predicted. Moreover, support for a joint European approach to the broader array of international relations is high and it is arguably more resistant than other policy areas to short-term perturbations. As we have argued, the staleness of the "high–low" distinction probably occurs because the analysts of earlier periods failed to notice that the Community's hesitant ventures into foreign policy collaboration masked a fundamental transformation in East–West relations (as well as Atlantic economic relations) that was propelling Europe into a posture of increased independence. With the end of the Cold War and the gradual reduction of the US presence in Europe, that trend is likely to continue.

Other theoretical perspectives are more useful in predicting where there is public support for policy integration. Clearly, theories that stressed the importance of values, culture, and identity are helpful in understanding public opinion toward specific policy domains. Perhaps this is not surprising; Karl Deutsch, for example, was an astute student of state- and nation-building. Our results show that scholars lost sight of the fact that Europe represents an experiment in the fundamental transformation of an international system. To the extent that this experiment impinges on the substratum of cultural and national identification built over hundreds of years, it is likely to meet resistance. If our results suggest anything, it is that support for policy integration is lowest in areas that touch on issues of national identity and culture.

Ironically, however, the *neofunctionalist strategy*—so much criticized for its imprecision and indeterminacy—stands up well in our analysis. First, as Mitrany suggested so long ago, citizens seem capable of identifying issue-areas characterized by interdependence, that is, those that are difficult to address on a national basis alone. Opinion series show, for example, that Europeans favored international action on environmental policy before national elites were willing to grant the EU policy responsibility. Second, the interdependence aspect of neofunctionalist theory is confirmed by the general public support for the liberalization of the market and for the instruments for managing that market. Perhaps the history of the community does not provide evidence of a mechanical process of integration–spillover–integration, but it is not entirely clear that neofunctionalist theory would have predicted such a simple process in the first place.[14]

Of course, the most interesting test of the neofunctionalist argument is yet to come, and this in two senses. First, the maturation of the internal market should yield a substantially different pattern of economic and political cleavages, based on the new division of labor of a fully functioning customs union. In this respect the work of Gabel (1998) is crucial; he demonstrates that support for integration varies along the lines suggested by a model of trade integration.[15] Thus, the predictions of the neofunctionalists might finally come to pass in the form of shifting patterns of interest aggregation to the European level.

This is a crucial subject for further research that would include the study of public opinion as well as analyses into the actual patterns of politics and policy-making. The best example is the so-called Social Charter of the Maastricht Treaty. As might be predicted from the data in this chapter, the Social Charter provoked some of the stormiest conflict in the final phase of negotiation (and ratification, as Danish voters showed). The provisions of the Social Charter are actually quite modest, confined to issues of workers' rights and working conditions. The core of the welfare state—the income transfers that constitute the largest share of public budgets—remain untouched (Lange 1992).

Nonetheless, once in place, the Social Charter might create pressure for further policy integration—spillover—for it is difficult to conceive of a truly liberalized labor market that has large discrepancies in compensation levels. Comparative advantage, after all, encompasses not just wages, but also the overall compensation package.[16] How this political process will play out is, of course, an open question, but it does suggest that there was more to the neofunctionalist logic than critics have given due.

---

[14] Actually, it is also not entirely clear that such spillover did not take place, but this is not the place to debate the issue.

[15] It is also apparent in work that goes beyond public opinion. Jeff Frieden, for example, has shown that trade has shifted coalitions on EU issues in ways that might promote further integration. See Frieden (1994).

[16] If our analysis is correct, two divergent results are likely to occur. First, an "opportunistic" approach may very well be taken by workers in societies with relatively limited social benefits—essentially the poorer members, but perhaps others whose relative social compensation is low (UK). Second, this approach is likely to be resisted by workers (and perhaps their elected representatives) in societies seeking to preserve relatively more generous social benefits—essentially the central and northern Europeans.

10

Institution-Building
from below and above:
The European Community in Global
Environmental Politics

ALBERTA M. SBRAGIA

T HE European Community was created in a postwar world of proliferating regional and global institutions. Its unique characteristics did not
insulate it from the international environment. How the Community
was to relate to that environment was contested both within the Community
and within its counterpart international institutions. What role should the
Community play on the international stage?

The member-states which formed the Community retained their sovereign
right to negotiate unilaterally in the myriad international organizations created
after World War II. Their participation in the Community did not automatically preempt their right to negotiate and represent themselves at international
bargaining tables. The one exception was clearly the GATT as the Treaty of
Rome gave the Community exclusive competence for commercial policy (although the Community itself did not become a signatory to the GATT). (See for
example Woolcock and Hodges 1996.) Given the retention of national sovereign rights in the international field outside of the GATT, the Community's
role in external relations was problematic. Many of the member-states assumed
that the international powers of the Community would be "enumerated"
powers and that they, the member-states, would control that process of institutionalization.

In 1997, as we examine the international role of the Community, we find it
playing a major role in many international fora concerned with "civilian"
issues. While its negotiating cohesiveness is not as stellar as the proponents of
a federal Europe would wish, its international presence is far more significant
than the Treaty of Rome would predict. This is particularly true in the global
environmental arena. How did the Community gain the power to be represented when the Treaty of Rome did not even mention the notion of

environmental protection? How did this international presence emerge? What were the dynamics? For its part, how did the global system react to the Community's representation once it was legitimated within the Community itself?

The emergence of the European Community as a player on the stage of global environmental politics raises two questions: (i) how did the Community qua Community gain the powers to act and (ii) how did the international system respond to the Community's demands for participation? The first question leads us to consider the process of institutionalization at the Community level while the second leads us to the process of institutionalization at the global level.

1. The European Union and External Relations

The power to negotiate and make treaties quickly emerged as one which the Commission wanted to institutionalize as a competence of the Community rather than resting primarily with the member-states. In the words of Eric Stein:

[I]n its earliest years the Community was understandably absorbed in the demanding internal task of building the common market; but because it was born into an interdependent world economy it was from the outset compelled to deal with third countries and the proliferating international organizations. By the nature of things, the treaty power was the principal instrument for the Community to replace bilateral relationships between its members and third countries and to create new relationships (Stein 1991: 141).

The Treaty of Rome specifically granted the Community the power to conduct external relations in the area of foreign commercial policy. The external role of the EEC in the trade arena was exercised without contestation. The EEC was not a signatory to the GATT, but given that it was the sole negotiator for the Community, its status was not challenged by the USA (see, for example, Meunier 1996). The EC did however become a member of the World Trade Organization in its own right. (The EU's member-states also became contracting parties.) In fact, the EC's newly found status in the international trade arena "gives formal international recognition to the role of the EC as laid down in the Treaty of Rome" (Scheuermans and Dodd 1995: 35).

More recently, the European Court of Justice has given the member-states a much greater role in negotiations having to do with trade in services than they were given in trade in manufactured goods. Nonetheless, the capacity of the Community and the Commission in trade can be viewed as the most "federal" of all external relations. The Community, represented by the Commission, is generally able to act as a unitary actor in trade negotiations.[1] It is important to

---

[1] Woolcock and Hodges (1996: 323), for example, conclude that in the Uruguay Round, "in fourteen of the fifteen negotiating groups, the EC performed on a par with, for example, the USA, if not better, in terms of presenting coherent consistent positions."

note here that the European Parliament plays a minor role in the formulation of external trade policy. That is not surprising. National governments, when operating in the international arena, are executive-driven: foreign affairs are relatively insulated from legislative control in all democratic systems. The process of democratization (as well as judicial review) was held at bay when it came to foreign affairs.

In contrast to the Community's role in trade relations, its position in other global arenas has been viewed as weak. The external (as well as EU) dimension of internal security policy (pillar 3) is widely viewed as ineffective, and studies of common foreign and security policy (CFSP) often argue that it is embryonic. The Community's international environmental relations, however, have received very little scholarly attention in spite of the explosion of activity in that area and the high level of scholarly interest in global environmental politics generally.

The Community's international environmental relations are at first glance interesting because they reside in pillar 1 (typically viewed as the most effective pillar) but their subject matter is not economic in the strict sense of the word. The legal status of environmental policy as a Community policy was unusual until the Single European Act, in that the Community approved environmental directives and entered multilateral environmental agreements without having the environment mentioned in the Treaty of Rome. It is a policy area in which the Community and the member-states share competencies, rather than being in the same category as trade, agriculture, or fisheries. In environmental policy, the Community's powers are of a "concurrent nature" and are characterized by "the (only) partial delegation of power" (Hession and Macrory 1994: 157). Therefore, international environmental agreements are known as "mixed agreements" (O'Keeffe and Schermers 1983; Groux and Manin 1985: 61–9; Lang 1986).

Looking at the question from the perspective of the Community's internal arrangements, how did the Community organize itself to deal at the international level? How were the relative competencies of the Commission and member-states sorted out? How did the balance between the Commission and the member-states manifest itself in this area of external relations?

Finally, the global (and often regional) dimension of environmental policy is addressed within the UN framework. The United Nations and its specialized agencies are perhaps the most prototypical of international organizations. The Community is merely an observer rather than a member.

The politics of global environmental politics highlight the barriers the international system qua system poses for the EU as an external actor outside the trade arena. Institution-building at the EU level does not merely involve sorting out the various competencies of the Commission, the member-states acting within the Community context, and the member-states acting unilaterally. It also involves the circumvention by the member-states of the structural barriers within the system to the EU's emergence as an international "actor." It is important to note here that the system is not only hostile to the juridical representation of an organization such as the Community but that it is not set up to even acknowledge the institutionalized "pooling of sovereignty" at the global level. Thus, how did the Community come to have international status as a party to some treaties? Given that it is not a sovereign state, and that contracting parties to treaties are in fact typically sovereign states, how has the Community acquired that status?

2. The EU and the International Arena

The role of the EU in the international arena, the environmental arena included, has been nurtured by the implications of creating a common market on the one hand and by the European Court of Justice on the other. The institutionalization of the Community's international role occurred gradually, driven by the substantive aims of the Community, the ambitions of the Commission, and the decisions of the ECJ.

2.1. The common market

The attempt to create a common market led the Commission in 1968 to propose a program to harmonize national regulations which threatened to create non-tariff barriers and distort competition. The national regulations which concerned the Commission included those in the field of environmental protection. The first environmental directives therefore were based on Art. 100 of the EEC Treaty, for they involved ensuring the free movement of goods. In general, the Commission used the objective of ensuring free movement to enhance its own reach; environmental protection was one avenue to such enhancement (Dietrich 1996; Pollack 1996).

Although the Commission became more concerned with environmental protection as such, the implications of environmental regulations for the functioning of the common market were always a major concern. As Frank Boons has pointed out, "environmental programmes that are adopted in one country can have substantial consequences for economic actors in other countries" (Boons 1992: 85). Furthermore, environmental regulations often raise questions of economic competitiveness (Golub, forthcoming). The economic implications of environmental protection led the Community to focus on international environmental agreements.

As the member-states became active in negotiating and signing multilateral environmental agreements, the Commission began to fear that "differences in national implementation measures would lead to disparities which, in turn, would hamper the proper functioning of the Common Market." The Commission therefore included "cooperation" with third parties as a component of the very first environment action program (Leenen 1984: 94). It subsequently became a party to a large number of multilateral conventions.

At a substantive level, therefore, the concern with the construction of the common market focused attention on international environmental agreements as these began to proliferate. National governments, acting unilaterally in negotiation and implementation, could well create non-tariff barriers under the rubric of environmental protection, barriers detrimental to the functioning of the market. Furthermore, the Commission saw environmental protection as giving it a policy reach which had not been included in the Treaty.

But while the substantive reasons might well have been compelling, the ability to be represented at the international level in the arena of environmental protection was not in the Treaty. In fact, environmental protection itself was not mentioned in the Treaty. The member-states had certainly not expected the Community to be represented in international environmental fora. How did the Community manage to become represented? Why was the international dimension able to be included in the very first action program on the environment? Here we turn to a key Community institution—the European Court of Justice.

The ERTA decision by the Court coupled with the decision by the heads of government to include the environment in the Community's policy competence gave the Community the opening to participate in international environmental politics. The SEA and Maastricht reinforced the ability to participate. The Court, through its case law, institutionalized the power of the Community to exercise external powers once the member-states decided that environmental protection was an arena in which EC legislation could be adopted.

2.2. The European Court of Justice

The fact that the EU has emerged as an identifiable international actor in the field of environmental protection is rooted in the actions of the European Court of Justice. In Nollkaemper's words:

[T]he field of the external relations of the Community is, together with the problems of the direct application and priority of Community law, the field in which the Court of Justice has played its most innovative part. The extent to which the Community has become able to claim a place on the international plane over the years is mainly a consequence of the substantial body of case-law developed by the Court (Nollkaemper 1987: 61).

The ERTA (1971) case served as the keystone to the Community's emergence as an international actor because it created the "link . . . between internal and external powers." The Court ruled that if the Community had been given the power to legislate internally to the Community, it implicitly had been given powers to act externally as well. In its judgment it ruled that

[E]ach time the Community, with a view to implementing a common policy envisaged by the Treaty, lays down common rules, whatever form these may take, the member States no longer have the right, acting individually or even collectively, to contract obligations towards non-member States affecting these rule. (Mastellone 1981: 104)

The ERTA case has emerged as the most significant benchmark for delineating the Community's role in international environmental politics. Typically, the Community first legislates and then exercises external jurisdiction. The Court's case law did not, however, clarify whether the Commission or the Council Presidency would represent the Community in international fora. There is no automatic assumption that in external relations the Commission is the Community; the Council Presidency can fulfill that role. Furthermore, the Court's decision did not change the international status of the Community's member-states. In Eric Stein's words:

[R]egardless of the scope of the horizontal and vertical transfer that distinguishes the Community from any other international organization, the Member States remain undisputed subjects of international law and retain their international personality. We thus have no less than thirteen international persons, that is twelve sovereign states with a partially circumscribed sovereignty, as well as a new international person . . . endowed with a substantial international capacity and external relations powers (Stein 1991: 129).

2.3. Community and member-states entangled

International treaties highlight the entangled situation described by Stein. They cover areas not covered by the Community's directives—areas which therefore remain in the competence of the member-states. Because the implementation of international environmental treaties will involve the competencies of both the Community and the member-states, such agreements are signed by both the Community and the member-states. They are known as "mixed agreements" and reflect the "mixed competence" intrinsic to environmental policy.[2] Mixed agreements are legally very complex,[3] but for our purposes, it is enough to say that they involve ratification by both the Community and the individual member-states. They symbolize the complex intertwining of member-state governments and supranationality which characterizes the Community.

The importance of the link drawn between internal and external powers lies in the fact that

the EC's external powers expand without the express approval of the Member States

---

[2] Pillar 1 includes areas of exclusive competence—trade in manufactured goods—and areas of so-called "mixed competence." The latter is seen by many Commission officials as far from ideal. In the words of one, "pillar one is being polluted by 'mixicity'—the notion of mixed competencies."

[3] John Temple Lang defines a mixed agreement in the following fashion: "International agreements are described as 'mixed' when both the European Community and some or all of its Member States become, or are intended to become, parties. In practice this is usually where the Community has exclusive competence over part of the subject matter of the agreement and non-exclusive or concurrent competence over the rest of the subject matter. However, the phrase 'mixed agreements' is also used to describe the much rarer situations in which either part of the subject matter of the agreement is outside the competence, even the concurrent competence, of the Community, or the Community becomes a party even though it has no exclusive competence over any part of the subject matter" (Lang 1986: 157–8).

simply in the course of developing the EC's internal policies. An extra constraint has therefore been added to EC internal policymaking, since the Member States should now always consider whether the adoption of some desirable item of EC legislation might not result in the undesirable (to them) loss of external competence. (Haigh 1992: 239)

For example, member-states refused to approve a directive on the dumping of wastes at sea which the Commission "had put forward at least partly to be able to accede to international dumping conventions (the Oslo and London Conventions)" (Haigh 1992: 240).

The member-states have never recognized international environmental relations as belonging to the exclusive competence of the Community and have gone to some length to ensure that their role is safeguarded. In the case of the Basel Convention on the transport of hazardous waste, for example, the member-states used "two marginal provisions . . . on technical assistance and research to argue that the convention did not come into the sphere of exclusive competence of the Community, but that it was a mixed agreement, i.e. that it contained provisions for which the Community was responsible and others which were of the competence of Member States" (Kramer 1995: 85–6).

While the member-states have worked to ensure that they will not be excluded from the international arena, they have also ensured that the Community would be a presence in that same arena. The SEA and subsequently the Maastricht Treaty gave "express competence to the Community to conclude international environmental agreements, which then are binding on the institutions of the Community and on the Member States" (Kramer 1995: 84). Before the coming into force of the SEA, however, the Community became a party to a number of important conventions. In Ziegler's words, the Community's "own competence to do so and the autonomous possibilities for its member-states were clarified only later by the jurisprudence of the Court of Justice" (Ziegler, n.d.: 2). For example, in 1975 it became a party to the Paris Convention of June 4, 1974 for the prevention of marine pollution from land-based sources, in 1977 to the Barcelona Convention of February 16, 1976 for the protection of the Mediterranean Sea against pollution, and to the Bonn Convention of December 3, 1976 for the protection of the Rhine against chemical pollution, in 1981 to the Bonn Convention of June 23, 1979 on the conservation of migratory species of wild animals, in 1982 to the Bern Convention of September 19, 1979 on the conservation of European wild life and natural habitats, and in 1981 to the Geneva Convention of November 13, 1979 on long-range transboundary air pollution (ibid. 2–3).

The link between the Community and other international bodies was explicitly recognized by the European Council held in Stuttgart in June 1983. The Council stated it saw "the necessity to take coordinated and effective initiatives both within the Community and internationally, particularly within the ECE" in combating pollution (Johnson and Corcelle 1995: 22). The Single European Act, for its part, in Art. 130r (5) stated that "within their respective spheres of competence, the Community and the Member States shall cooperate with third countries and with the relevant international organizations." It gave the

Community a legal basis for the negotiation of international environmental accords. In 1987, the heads of state and government at the Dublin Summit decided that the Community should play a key role in the area of international environmental activity.

The Maastricht Treaty reflected that commitment. Art. 130r included a new objective for Community action: Community policy on the environment should contribute to "promoting measures at international level to deal with regional or worldwide environmental problems."[4] That new provision indicated how far-reaching the internationalization of environmental problems had become. It also strengthened the Community's prerogative in the international field. In Hession's and Macrory's words, the new language in the Treaty

confirms the independent nature of the Community's external power. This latter point is important as the Community previously had to rely on the existence of internal measures to justify external competence in application of the ERTA principle. [It] strengthens the argument that the Community's interest is general and is unrelated to any functional relationship with internal problems or measures (Hession and Macrory 1994: 158).

3. The Commission and International Organizations

The framers of the Treaty of Rome were well aware of the international organizations whose universe they were joining. The role of the EEC multilateral fora was explicitly dealt with in the Treaty of Rome. The Treaty in fact gave short shrift to external relations (other than foreign commercial policy) except in regard to international organizations. In particular, the UN, GATT, OEEC (later OECD), and the Council of Europe were given special mention. Art. 229, for instance, specifically empowered the Commission to handle relations with international organizations, with specific reference to the UN, its specialized agencies, and GATT. In 1971, the EEC was only just about to upgrade the head of its Washington office to Director-General and yet it maintained "permanent liaison, falling only just short of diplomatic missions with GATT in Geneva and OECD in Paris. When OEEC become OECD a special protocol gave to the EEC Commission the task and right to be involved in its work" (Henig 1971: 10).[5]

Although the Community was only given observer status in those organizations, it is important that the Commission was explicitly given the role of representing the Community with regards to the international organizations

---

[4] The other three objectives are preserving, protecting, and improving the quality of the environment, protecting human health, and the prudent and rational utilization of natural resources.

[5] With regards to the OECD, the Commission points out that "although the Community is not a member of that Organization, its status there is higher than that of an observer. Supplementary Protocol No. 1 to the Convention on the OECD stipulates that the Commission shall take part as of right in the work of the Organization and that representation of the Communities shall be determined with the institutional provisions of the Treaties" (CEC 1989: 19).

mentioned. In what is known as pillar 1 in the post-Maastricht era, therefore, the Commission was given an international role although it was constrained by the very important fact that the Community was not a member of the organizations named. Furthermore, Art. 229 does not authorize the Commission to engage in binding commitments (Macrory and Hession 1996: 135). As the Community de facto became more important in the international arena and its competencies expanded, its official role within the international arena became more complicated.

In a report examining the relationships between the Community and global and regional intergovernmental organizations, the Commission wrote:

Not only does the Community have wide ranging relations with these intergovernmental organizations, but these have also undergone a certain evolution. New policies such as that relating to the environment, have involved it in new fields. Similarly, a larger place has increasingly been made for the Community by the international organizations such as the UN system, since in the exercise of its competence it has come to play a larger role (CEC 1989: 21).

The Community's participation in intergovernmental organizations, however, is often problematic. Given that the Community is now far more than an international organization but is not a state and that its unique structure is not recognized in international law, its role in international organizations is an awkward one. In the Commission's words:

The Community often shares observer status with intergovernmental organizations of the traditional type and is therefore in practice placed on the same footing as those organizations, at least for the present. The Community should be given a status higher than that of observer when the international organization in question is discussing matters falling within the jurisdiction of the Community, but in practice an approach along those lines often runs into difficulties. The basic problem is that traditional international law can accommodate only nation states, or groupings of nation states. Therefore, there has been some resistance to the implied change which is necessary in order for the traditional doctrine to accommodate the new legal entity constituted by the Community (CEC 1989: 19).

The key issue for the Commission has been to gain for the Community a separate "right of access to, and participation in, the work of the deliberative organs of international organizations and conferences." It was not sufficient for the member-states to agree to a common position among themselves and then have one of them state it within an international organization. The Community wanted to be recognized as a distinct entity with an international personality, and the acquisition of a separate status within international organizations symbolized that recognition. The recognition of such status was of "great importance" (Groux and Manin 1985: 43).

In fact, the right of the Community to "have a seat" in the sense of taking part in meetings (but still officially as an observer and therefore without a vote) at international conferences or within international organizations did not come easily. In the case of the UN General Assembly, the Community did not receive the right to participate until 1974.[6] (While the Commission can speak at meetings of commissions of the UN General Assembly, it is not allowed to address the Plenary Assembly.) By the mid-1980s, "this battle [could be] considered as almost over since the great majority of permanent international organizations have officially allowed . . . the EEC to take part in their proceedings" (Groux and Manin 1985: 43, 49). Nonetheless, the Community has no status with the Security Council, the Trusteeship Council, and the International Court of Justice (Brinkhorst 1994: 610).

In the case of UN international conferences for specific negotiations, the Community must receive the right to participate in each case. The Community is represented at the UN by the Head of the Delegation of the Commission who, however, does not hold ambassadorial status and by the Permanent Representative of the country holding the Presidency of the Council (Brinkhorst 1994: 610). Brinkhorst, the former Director-General of DGXI, the DG responsible for international environmental negotiations, argues that "there is a growing disparity between this patchy legal situation of the Community and its political projection at the United Nations" (ibid. 611). The Community as such has less legal standing than its political profile would suggest.

In the case of the environment, the Commission has had contacts with UNEP since the latter was founded in December 1972. The relationship was formalized in an exchange of letters between Dr. Mostafa K. Tolba, Executive Director of UNEP, and Gaston E. Thorn, President of the Commission in June 1983. Those letters call for regular contacts between the two institutions, exchange of documentation, participation of the Community in UNEP meetings, and consultations on the Regional Seas program, activities pertaining to the assessment of the environment, and environment and development (CEC 1989: 85–6).

Up until the mid-1980s, however, the Community generally did not try to be recognized as an official member of an international conference organized under the auspices of the United Nations. The refusal of the Soviet Union and the East European countries to recognize the Community in any fashion was thought to bode ill for any such initiative (Groux and Manin 1985: 45–6). As we shall see, the Commission did make a strenuous effort at the negotiations leading to the Vienna Convention to become a contracting party to that Convention—that effort as well as its eventual success signaled a new era for the Community in the international arena.

In many cases, the Commission is a non-voting participant but the member-states are members of the international organization and field national delegations. Furthermore, the organization often deals with matters which fall under

---

[6] Much to its dismay, however, the Community has the same formal status vis-à-vis the UN General Assembly as the Commonwealth Secretariat, the International Committee of the Red Cross, the League of African Unity, and the Organization of the Islamic Conference. It is certainly true that such organizations have little similarity with the Community, representing "both in law and in their factual position a totally different political reality" (Brinkhorst 1994: 610).

both member-state and Community jurisdiction. Those areas are known under the rubric of "mixed competence." Thus, Community representation is often that of "dual representation." In such cases, the Community is represented by both the Commission and the member-state holding the Presidency of the Council. The Commission typically speaks on those issues which fall under the Community's exclusive competence although it may also be asked to speak in areas of mixed competence. Such "dual representation," for example, is in place at the UN General Assembly, the Economic and Social Council, and UNCTAD (CEC 1989: 21).

It is important to note that "dual representation"—which includes the Commission and the Presidency as representatives of the Community—incorporates both the "supranational" and the "intergovernmental" in the Community's external face. That type of representation in bodies such as the United Nations does not date from the going into force of the Maastricht Treaty with its provisions for CFSP. Rather, it has its institutional roots in the original mandate in the Treaty of Rome which gave the Commission the right to be involved with the United Nations and the ECJ's ERTA decision which coupled internal and external powers.[7] Institutionalization has been influenced by a wide variety of factors—not the least of which has been the new prominence of environmental regulations as challenges to cross-border trade—but clearly the Court has played a pivotal role in setting out the essential framework within which the Community's external representation would evolve. Over time, the Community has become a unitary actor more frequently, has worked out a working relationship between the Commission and the Council Presidency, and has secured international recognition. Each step in this process was hard-fought, but the Community is clearly more unitary, more "balanced," and more recognized than it was in 1973 when environmental policy was added to its competencies.

4. Global Environmental Politics

The dynamics found in the field of global environmental politics reflect the tensions found in the international arena more generally. Although environmental protection is a relatively new field within global politics, the Community did not find it easy to be accepted by the global system. Although unique, the Community was not a state, and the system (the USA in particular) had difficulty in accepting it as a negotiating counterpart. The legal complexities of

---

[7] The trade arena stands as a contrast. In the case of the Uruguay Round, member-states did not field national delegations. The Commission was the sole representative and the Presidency was not a partner nor was it included in the negotiating team. The member-states gave the Commission the right to negotiate for the Community even in those areas (such as services and intellectual property rights) characterized by "mixed competence" (Woolcock and Hodges 1996: 302).

"mixed agreements," the shifting patterns of competencies over time, the evolution of power from the member-states acting unilaterally to their collective
action on the international stage in partnership with the Commission, the
general lack of precedents and benchmarks in understanding the Community's international role, and the problems for monitoring compliance of these
ambiguities were instrumental in making it difficult for the diplomats to accept
negotiating with the Community. From the point of view of third parties, it
was difficult to know which authority—Brussels or the national governments—
would be responsible for implementation and enforcement. That ambiguity
made acceptance of the Community particularly problematic.

4.1. Internationalization of environmental issues

The Community has had to face the question of its international standing in
the field of environmental protection because of the explosion of multilateral
activities in this area. In Edith Brown Weiss's words

In 1972 international environmental law was a fledgling field with less than three dozen
multilateral agreements. Today international environmental law is arguably setting the
pace for cooperation in the international community in the development of international law. There are nearly nine hundred international legal instruments that are
either primarily directed to international environmental issues or contain important
provisions on them. This proliferation of legal instruments is likely to continue (Weiss
1994: 30).

The density of environmental negotiations at the international level is
striking. According to Weiss, "between 1990 and 1992, there have been about a
dozen highly important multilateral negotiations occurring more or less in
parallel" (Weiss 1994: 30). Not surprisingly, the implications of this much
activity for traditional notions of sovereignty have not gone unnoticed.[8]
   Scholars have increasingly paid attention to the creation of global institutions (regimes) in the environmental arena (Young 1989, 1991, 1993; Hurrell
and Kingsbury 1992; Alker and Haas 1993; Haas et al. 1993). The United Nations play an important role in such an effort. In particular, the establishment
of the UN Environment Program (UNEP) at the 1972 UN Conference on the
Human Environment in Stockholm "was probably the most important institutional consequence of increased concern with global environmental change
in the Cold War era" (Alker and Haas 1993: 15). UNEP's impact has been felt at
the regional as well as at the global level. The Mediterranean Action Plan was an
offshoot of UNEP, for example (Haas 1990).
   The most recent example of such global institution-building is the Framework
Convention on Climate Change, signed at the UN Conference on Environment
and Development (UNCED) in Rio de Janeiro in June 1992, the Conference on
Environment and Development with its resulting Rio Declaration, Agenda 21,

---

[8] See e.g. Hurrell and Kingsbury (1992); Conca (1994); Litfin (1995).

and Commission on Sustainable Development, and the Convention on Bio-diversity also signed at Rio.

4.2. International negotiation

EU participation in international negotiations is complex. Its participation in binding commitments is rooted in Art. 220. Typically, in areas characterized by mixed competence, the Commission will be the negotiator acting under a mandate unanimously agreed to by the Council. The Commission, while it is negotiating, "continuously consults with a special committee composed of member-states' representatives. In practice, member-states also participate in the negotiation of the environmental agreements" (Kramer 1995: 84). In areas where the member-states retain jurisdiction, they will negotiate on their own. Given the institutional evolution of the Community, each treaty negotiation has had a different dynamic. The actual representation of the Community is more flexible than the legal scholars might predict. At times the Commission may be asked by the Council to speak for the Community in areas which do not fall within the exclusive competence of the Community while at other times the Presidency may speak even in such areas. When the Presidency speaks for the Community, it will do so using the formula "on behalf of the Community and its member states" (Macrory and Hession 1996: 136).

The following cases give a brief sketch of the key elements of the institution-building process—and its interaction with what can be seen as "the" key third party, the USA—which has characterized the Community's involvement in international environmental negotiations.

4.3. Global treaties and institution-building

4.3.1. CITES

In the case of the 1973 Convention on International Trade in Endangered Species, the major global treaty on nature protection, the Community was not a signatory but did enact a regulation implementing the Treaty (EEC/3626/82) which protected more than 250 species of fauna and flora more stringently than did the CITES Convention itself (Johnson and Corcelle 1995: 306). The fact that the Community was not a signatory was at least partly a question of timing—it did not have competence for environmental protection at the time the Treaty was negotiated. The member-states in 1977 agreed that it should become a signatory, but the Treaty did not allow for the accession of regional economic integration organizations (Johnson and Corcelle 1995: 417; Weiss 1996). In 1983, an amendment to the Treaty (the so-called Gaborone Amend-ment) was negotiated with the USA acting as the principal negotiator. The Gaborone Amendment would have allowed the Community to accede to the Treaty, but the USA, concerned that the institutional structure of the EC would not be able to effectively implement CITES restrictions, decided not to follow through and accept the amendment. The Community is therefore not yet a signatory, primarily because of American opposition.

The knotty question of whether the EC can actually ensure compliance with global treaties as effectively as can national governments operating at the national level has remained largely unresolved from the American point of view. It is the concern with whether the EC can comply on the ground that has undergirded a sustained American skepticism or opposition to the EC's being recognized as an actor in international environmental negotiations.

Although the Community was not a signatory, the member-states' participation in the Conference of the Parties held in 1985 in Buenos Aires was co-ordinated on a daily basis by the Italian Presidency. It must be remembered that in 1985 no treaty basis for environmental protection existed and the Community had not been allowed to sign—yet a regulation implementing CITES had been approved at the Community level and the member-states were acting in the EC framework because of that regulation. In those areas where a common position had been formulated, those positions "were presented to the Conference on behalf of the Community by the presidency, the Commission, or by the delegation of the member states having a special interest or specific knowledge on the matter" (CEC 1985a: 729, final, 2).

Nonetheless, in the Commission's words, "the Conference witnessed a number of Community incidents" (CEC 1985a: 729, final, 2). The member-states disagreed with the Commission on a variety of issues as well as disagreed with each other. In some contentious areas, no common position was arrived at.

Thus, both the Commission and the Presidency played an important role in the negotiations. While the Community did act in a unitary fashion on some issues, disagreements in both discussions and voting indicated that it was not yet ready to act in a unitary fashion. Clearly, the Community would have been more influential if it had been able to act more cohesively. Yet it is un-precedented for a non-signatory to have the kind of influence which it did have on some issues.[9]

4.3.2. Ozone

American (as well as Soviet) opposition to the Community's emergence as a signatory to global treaties persisted throughout the 1980s. The USA originally opposed the EC signing both the Vienna Convention on the ozone layer and the Montreal Protocol, at least partially because treating the Community as one political unit had implications for how individual member-states might or might not comply with the treaty (Haigh 1992: 242; Hampson with Hart 1995: 265). In those treaties, however, the member-states backed the Commission's insistence on the Community becoming a contracting party.

The politics of ozone, however, have one clear feature. The Commission's "insistence on special statutory treatment" became a key negotiating point,

---

[9] For a more in-depth discussion of the EU's role in CITES, see Sbragia with Hildebrand (1998).

one which, from the point of third parties, was typically shrouded in confusion over what the power of the Community in the area actually was. The question of whether and when the Community exercised exclusive competence was particularly difficult to answer from a legal standpoint. The political ramifications of an answer to that question were often too problematic. As the Community's legal adviser John Temple Lange put it, "precisely because the limits of exclusive competence are politically important, they are particularly difficult and controversial to define" (cited in Benedick 1991: 95). The confusion over the entanglement between Community and member-states fuels concern over compliance. Who is responsible for ensuring compliance with the final treaty —Brussels or national capitals? Given the importance for economic actors of the Montreal Protocol, it was particularly important for many countries, the USA included, that the accountability for compliance be relatively straightforward.[10]

In spite of the irritations caused to third parties (and at times to the member-states themselves) by the Commission's relentless pursuit of ensuring its international status, the Community was so important it could not be ignored or dismissed. The cohesion of the Community in the area of ozone generally has been such that it has emerged as a key actor (Szell 1993: 36; Litfin 1995). During the Vienna Convention negotiations, the European position was so cohesive in its opposition to binding commitments that a framework convention laying out general principles only was seen as the only feasible option. The Community was in fact a unitary actor, with the member-states and the Commission acting in unison (Jachtenfuchs 1990: 264).

Leaving aside the content of the environmental restrictions adopted, the Commission strenuously negotiated to be allowed to become a contracting party without restrictions (Benedick 1991: 95). Given the lack of explicit competence for environmental protection before the adoption of the SEA, the Commission viewed the negotiations as a way to "obtain greater competence in environmental affairs within the Community. Had it succeeded, it could claim the right to propose Community legislation to implement the ozone convention and future protocols" (Jachtenfuchs 1990: 263). The Council had agreed in January 1982 that the Community should become a contracting party, and in October 1984 had agreed that the Community should be allowed to become a contracting party without any conditions being attached. However, both the USA and the USSR had proposed restrictions. The USA wanted "a prior participation by one member-state" and the USSR wanted prior participation by a majority of the member-states (CEC 1985b: 8, explanatory memorandum). A compromise was finally reached which was acceptable to the Commission.

Negotiations over the Montreal Protocol to the Vienna Convention had

---

[10] The politics of ozone depletion have been very much concerned with economics. As Jeffrey Berejikian argues, "the central concern of the EC was the economic impact of ozone layer protection" (Berejikian 1997: 790).

some of the same features. The status of the Community—which had both symbolic and substantive implications—was the subject of heated debate and only a last-minute compromise put forth by New Zealand's Environment Minister allowed the negotiations to conclude (Hampson with Hart 1995: 265). Richard Benedick, the American negotiator, gives a sense of how important the dispute became:

After a nerve-racking midnight standoff over this issue, during which the fate of the protocol hung in the balance, a compromise was reached at the last possible moment. . . . this concession would obtain only if all member countries plus the EC Commission became parties to the protocol and formally notified the secretariat of their manner of implementation (Benedick 1991: 96–7).

However, the issue of competence was highlighted when the issue under discussion was a fund to help developing countries obtain advanced technology. The Community could not be involved, and "on this point the member-states acted on their own" (Haigh 1992: 241).

During the Protocol negotiations, the Community again kept the agreement from being as stringent as the USA and the Scandinavians wanted. After a political change at the Community level which transformed the politics of ozone, the Community emerged as a policy leader during the negotiations for the London and Copenhagen amendments. Regardless of whether the Community was a "leader" or a "laggard," however, the Community was cohesive enough to emerge as a key negotiating partner.

4.3.3. Climate change
By the time the climate change negotiations began officially in February 1991, the EC had become a recognized power in the area of international environmental politics. The UN General Assembly had created the Intergovernmental Negotiating Committee (INC) for a Framework Climate Convention under whose auspices the negotiations were conducted. Within that framework, "the EC assumed a lead role in the negotiations by virtue of its commitment to returning its joint carbon dioxide emissions to 1990 levels by the year 2000" (Porter and Brown 1996: 95).

While the Community's commitment did indeed provide a benchmark, the Commission's role in the actual negotiation of the Framework Convention was rather limited. The member-states, however, were involved.

Given the role of the USA in international politics, environmental politics especially, it was essential for the success of the Rio Conference (at which the UN Framework Convention on Climate Change was to be signed) that President Bush personally attend. The American position, however, was opposed to binding commitments to reduce carbon dioxide emissions to a specific level by a specific date. The European Community was viewed by the USA as a key adversary, and President Bush demanded the Europeans change their position. Bush "personally called German Prime Minister Helmut Kohl to ask him to drop his government's demands for the stabilization commitment in return for

Bush's participation in the Earth Summit (Porter and Brown 1996: 96). Whether that call was to Kohl as a German or whether it was to Kohl as a key player in the EC's politics of climate change is impossible to say, but it may be irrelevant. By that point, the European Community and its member-states were so entangled in a way which does not easily fit the legal language of "competencies."

Member-states used their bilateral contacts with Washington to lobby the Bush administration to support the EU's position (unsuccessfully of course). The member-states and the Community were intertwined in such a way that the EC could be seen as a unitary actor using multilateral diplomatic channels to convince the USA to change its position (Porter and Brown 1996: 95). In the context of transatlantic negotiations, the member-states have been in a much stronger position than has the Commission (a situation which began to change under the Clinton administration).[11] The member-states clearly dominated that exchange—but acted in a unitary fashion. From the American point of view, it was the EC/Germans/Dutch/British who were lobbying rather than the member-states acting unilaterally.[12]

The entanglement of the Community and the member-states when dealing in transatlantic negotiations is evident in the negotiation of Art. 4 (2) of the Convention. In Nigel Haigh's words,

[T]he UK Secretary of State for the Environment, Michael Howard, allegedly with the encouragement of some other Environment Ministers from EC member-states, traveled to the United States and agreed a form of words with US officials which forms the basis of Article 4(2) of the Convention. Whether this can be regarded as an EC contribution to the framing of the Convention is a matter of opinion. Formally it was not since no formal Council decisions were taken on the subject, but without the machinery provided by the EC for discussion between ministers it may not have happened (Haigh 1996: 181–2).

The USA is such an important actor that it is difficult to analyze the EU's role without taking into account the impact of American policy. Given that climate change policy is essentially an issue of international political economy because of the wide-ranging impacts on industrial activity and structure of carbon dioxide emission reductions,[13] the economic interdependence within the industrialized world cannot be ignored by the EU. It is for that reason that in 1992 EU Finance Ministers insisted that any EU carbon tax be implemented only on condition that the USA and Japan acted in kind. Japan agreed on condition that the USA enact some kind of carbon tax. The Clinton administration refused. Although there are significant member-state differences on the carbon tax issue (the UK opposes it in principle), there is no doubt that a change in the

---

[11] For a discussion of how the Clinton administration began to view the Community as a more important transatlantic partner, see Gardner, A. (1997); Sbragia (1996).

[12] The member-states, however, maintained control of the negotiations over the Global Environmental Facility. The Community is not a member of the GEF but is trying to become one. At least some of the member-states, however, are opposed to the Community's membership.

[13] Michael Grubb has argued that the impact of reducing greenhouse gases will be significant. In his words "No previous environmental problem has been at once so closely related to major sectors of economic activity." Cited in Sell (1996: 106–7).

American position would transform the politics of the carbon tax debate within the EU as well as the international politics of climate change (Zito 1995; Porter and Brown 1996: 149).

The climate change negotiations once again highlighted the concern of third parties that implementation be transparent. Art. 22 (2) specifies that regional economic integration organizations which accede to the Convention (i.e. the Community) must "declare the extent of their competence with respect to matters governed by the Convention" (Macrory and Hession 1996: 114). The entangled legal situation in areas of "mixed competence" and "mixed agreements", however, makes this difficult. Thus far the Community's statement is lacking specifics. That perhaps is not surprising, especially given the lack of specifics in the Framework Convention on Climate Change itself. As Macrory and Hession point out, "[i]n the absence of a clearly defined area of exclusive Community competence for climate change and in the absence of a clear obligation detailing specific action it is extremely difficult to isolate Community and member-state obligations" (ibid. 1996: 114).

4.3.4. UNCED

Once the General Assembly in December 1989 decided to convene a UN Conference on Environment and Development in 1992, the question of the European Community's participation arose. In March 1992, the Council of Ministers approved the full participation of the Community in the UNCED—"on equal terms with the member-states" (Jupille and Caporaso 1996: 20). However, as Jupille and Caporaso point out, when Portugal, in the exercise of the Community Presidency, asked during the New York PrepCom (IV) meeting that Commission President Delors be treated during the concluding ceremonies at Rio as if he were a head of state, a fierce dispute erupted with the USA and the member-states themselves were unwilling to go that far (ibid. 1996: 21).[14]

A compromise position was put together which acknowledged the special position of the Community in the world of international affairs. The compromise allowed the Community to participate fully in the UNCED deliberations—the only international organization to be given that privilege. This privileged position was however not to be viewed as a precedent, and the Com-

---

[14] I have drawn heavily from Jupille and Caporaso's excellent paper. Preparatory committees were very important in the UNCED process. In Stanley Johnson's words, "Few international conferences can have been so thoroughly prepared as the UN Conference on Environment and Development. UNCED's Preparatory Committee (which became known as PrepCom) held four meetings, each of them four or five weeks in length, which were attended by most of the member-states of the United Nations, by the intergovernmental bodies both inside and outside the UN system, by a host of non-governmental organizations including the business, scientific, and academic communities, as well as the representatives of 'green' groups and charitable and other bodies interested in the environment and development. The task of these successive meetings of UNCED's PrepCom was to define the issues, to help shape the programs and other proposals, to assess financial implications where this was possible and, finally to narrow down the areas of disagreement so that the Rio Conference might ultimately be confronted with a manageable agenda" (Johnson 1993: 19).

munity would still not be allowed to vote. The following excerpt summarizing the compromise gives a sense of how the Community's actual participation was to take place:

The EEC will represent exclusively the Community's position to the Conference on issues falling within the EEC's exclusive competence. In cases of mixed competence, the EEC and its member-states will determine which, as between them will represent the positions of the Community and its member-states. The EEC shall inform the UNCED secretariat prior to consideration of an agenda item by the Conference if the EEC will be representing a position of the Community and its member-states with respect to specific matters within the scope of that agenda item. (Jupille and Caporaso 1996: 21)

On April 13, 1992, the General Assembly approved a special decision to grant the Community's request to be granted "full participant status." Brinkhorst, then the Director-General of DGXI, describes the content and significance of that decision in the following terms:

This status conferred on the EEC rights enjoyed by participating states, including representation in committees and working groups of the conference, the right to speak and to reply, and to submit proposals and substantive amendments. On two counts the position would be different from that of member-states: the EEC would not have the right to vote (including the right to block a consensus) nor to submit procedural motions. Although EC representatives made it clear from the beginning that the EC would not request a 13th vote, no new ground could be broken on this point n view of the clear language to the contrary of the UN Charter . . . the decision was considered as an important breakthrough of the general procedural rules prevailing at meetings of UN conferences (Brinkhorst 1994: 612).

The Community had played what Brinkhorst characterizes as a "certain mediating role" between developing countries on the one hand and the USA and Japan on the other. The G-77 therefore actively supported the granting of "full participant status" to the Community (Brinkhorst 1994: 613).

The Council Presidency played an active role during the negotiations. According to one negotiator from a non-member-state, at certain points the Presidency on behalf of the Community was negotiating with the G-77 with the USA and Russia sitting on the sidelines. In his words, "the Community was a powerhouse." Although the Commission's presence was weakened by the refusal of the Commissioner for the Environment to attend, the Community played an important role. The Commission's civil servants were involved and the Council Presidency was very visible. Third parties certainly interpreted the Presidency's actions as those of the Community. Given the codes of international negotiations, the fact that Ken Collins, the Chair of the important parliamentary committee on the environment, did not attend mattered much less than did the fact that the Council Presidency was active.

The relationship between the Commission and the Presidency seems to have been relatively smooth. The Council of Ministers had decided in March 1992 that the Presidency would typically represent and negotiate for the Community in areas of mixed competence but that the Commission could act in the same fashion if it were so agreed. In areas where important EC directives had been approved—toxic chemicals, waste, and fisheries—"the Commission represent-atives spoke exclusively on behalf of the Community" (Brinkhorst 1994: 613).

The Community in fact was able to act in a unitary fashion more easily on environmental issues than on those dealing with development aid policy. No common EC position had been developed, and the Community in that area was unable to exert the kind of influence it did in the environmental arena (Brinkhorst 1994: 614).

The Community did sign Agenda 21 even though it is not a legally binding document. From a legal perspective, such a signature was unusual. Martin Hession argues that "the general powers of the Commission to maintain all ap-propriate relations with organs of the United Nations (Art. 229) cannot be con-sidered sufficient for such general political declarations" (Hession 1995: 156).

In fact, the Community has been active in its relations with the Committee for Sustainable Development (CSD) which was established by Chapter 38 of Agenda 21 as a Commission of the UN's Economic and Social Council. The General Assembly, in establishing the CSD in January 1993, explicitly called for the full participation of the Community. The Council of Ministers had on November 23, 1992 accepted a Commission recommendation that the Com-munity should participate fully in CSD activities. The member-states which were elected to membership on the Commission (the Community itself would not seek election) would, on issues within the Community's exclusive compet-ence," exercise their votes on the basis of a Community position decided on in Community coordination. On issues of mixed competence, coordination would take place with a view to securing a common position of the basis of which the Community members of the CSD should vote" (Brinkhorst 1994: 615).

The Council of Ministers in its meeting of March 4, 1996 laid out the guide-lines to be used by the Union during the 4th Session of the Commission which met in New York from April 18 to May 3, 1996. These guidelines were also to be used in the preparation for the European Union's participation in the 1997 spe-cial session of the UN General Assembly which is to review the progress made in the implementation of the commitments made at Rio (Council of Ministers 1996: 5309/Presse 45: 5–7).

5. Conclusion

The European Community has over time developed the international standing and the capacity to become an important international actor in the area of international environmental relations. Third parties as well as the UN system have gradually acknowledged the Community's unique status vis-à-vis its member-states and are in the process of adapting international institutions to accommodate its unusual demands.

What is striking about the Community's role is that an institutionalized balance between the Commission and the member-states acting collectively within the framework of the Union is being constructed at the same time that the Community is emerging as an important actor in the global environmental context. The Presidency is a key Community institution in the foreign environmental affairs of the Community. The Commission, for its part, is playing a role much more important than might have been expected given the importance of states in the international system. The member-states, although in constant conflict with the Commission over the internal allocation of responsibilities, are nonetheless consistently agreeing to have the Community play an important international role in the environmental arena.

The institutionalization of "dual representation" represents an innovative way for the Community to be represented while maintaining a central role for the member-states. The Community has found a way to incorporate both intergovernmentalism (in the form of the Council Presidency) and the "federal" (in the form of the Commission) in its external personality.

Significantly, the external role of the Commission was legitimized by the European Court of Justice. The Court, as it has so often, gave a powerful "federal" impetus to the Community by recognizing the external dimension of what we now know as pillar 1. It, however, did not exclude the member-states. The entanglement between the Community and the member-states is packaged under the rubric of "mixed competence" and "mixed agreements." The arcane and convoluted legal spiderwebs which make up the area of "mixed competence" and "concurrent powers" are in fact the foundation stones for the balance between Brussels and national capitals which makes the Community both so complex and so successful as an instrument of integration.

The environmental arena has proven to be a fruitful arena for institution-building. The Community has been able to increase its stature, its international reach, and its effectiveness within international organizations. Each global treaty has proven to be a step in a process of institution-building which is still ongoing. Its future role in the Commission for Sustainable Development and General Assembly activities in the post-Rio period is likely to continue on a similar trajectory—incremental steps which increase its status as well as its access to the decision-making centers within international fora (such as informal meetings), and therefore the likelihood that it will be able to act in a unitary fashion.

The Council Presidency, flanked by the Commission, and the Commission, flanked by the Council Presidency, are likely to force the international system to acknowledge an entity which does not require the constituent units to subordinate themselves to a "federal" government or to a "center" as conventionally understood. The ever-more institutionalized coupling of the "supranational" and the "intergovernmental" in the conduct of international environmental politics represents a case of institution-building at both the Community—and the global—level.

11

Rules, Transgovernmentalism, and the Expansion of European Political Cooperation

MICHAEL E. SMITH

THE European Community (EC)[1] reached a milestone in 1991–2 with the Maastricht Treaty on European Union, which featured foreign and security cooperation as pillar 2 of its three-part institutional structure. Yet the Common Foreign and Security Policy (CFSP) was not pulled out of thin air at Maastricht; it relied on more than two decades of quiet, patient teamwork under a informal mechanism, "European Political Cooperation" (EPC). Indeed, despite the failures of the European Defense Community and the European Political Community in the 1950s, and of the Fouchet plans for closer political integration in the 1960s, the EC has persistently attempted to intensify foreign policy cooperation among its member-states to increase its influence in world politics. In the hope of becoming "a cohesive force in international relations," and encouraging "political union" (Art. 30.2[d], Single European Act), EC governments gradually developed EPC to help reinforce European economic integration.

While EC foreign policy cooperation—in the form of EPC or the CFSP—is underdeveloped compared to its other policy domains, it is still an impressive achievement. Why does this enterprise deserve our attention? That states as interdependent as those of the EC should cooperate in foreign policy is not

I gratefully acknowledge the financial support of the Council European Studies and the 1995–6 US Fulbright European Union program. For advice and assistance I would also like to thank Viscount Etienne Davignon, Roy Ginsberg, Patrick Morgan, Simon Nuttall, John Peterson, Philippe de Schoutheete, Penny Turnbull, the EC and EPC officials who agreed to be interviewed for this research, and the other contributors to this volume.

[1] To avoid confusion, this chapter stresses a distinction between the terms "European Community" (EC) and "European Union" (EU) since EPC structures were separate from those of the EC for many years. I use "EU" to refer only to the three-pillar structure created by the Treaty on European Union (Maastricht Treaty), featuring the EC, the CFSP, and the third pillar, Justice and Home Affairs cooperation.

noteworthy by itself; many internal and external forces might have encouraged EC states to coordinate their foreign policies over the past several decades (Ginsberg 1989). Equally, that such states—already embedded as they were in the economic integration project—should establish modest institutional support for such cooperation is not very puzzling. In this sense the initial *creation* of EPC could be viewed in part as a product of functional or sectoral "spillover"; it was intended to augment the expanding economic policies of the EC in the face of its first enlargement.

What *is* remarkable about EPC is the extent to which its member governments felt increasingly obligated to forge and adhere to common policies, and the extent to which the EPC system became inseparably entangled with EC procedures. More surprisingly, this happened with a very weak—indeed, nonexistent at first—organizational structure and with severely limited involvement (compared to other EC policy domains) by supranational Community actors. Hence it is difficult to claim that the institutionalization of EPC was primarily a product of political spillover, whereby powerful EC actors, chiefly the Commission and European Court of Justice (ECJ), expand their authority over a policy domain.[2]

In other words, there are two questions to be explored here. First, how could a supposedly feeble agreement—and one external to EC actors and procedures —have such pervasive effects on its member governments, even in a "difficult" issue-area such as foreign policy cooperation? Second, how could this happen with little or no involvement by EC actors? For unlike many EC socioeconomic policy domains, EPC did not have a well-defined bureaucracy or constituent. European interest groups did not pay much attention to political cooperation, and domestic politics in the form of public opinion, lobbying, or electoral competition rarely intruded on EPC. Moreover, since previous attempts to "Communitarize" defense cooperation had failed so spectacularly, EC member-states took special care to keep EPC from being "contaminated" by existing supranational procedures in the EC. As a result, governments easily dominated EPC at first; EC-level actors such as the Commission and the European Parliament were marginally involved; the ECJ was specifically excluded; and EPC decision-making rules—unlike those eventually used to establish the single market— relied on the consensus principle. Hence a formidable barrier was deliberately erected between EC foreign economic policymaking and EPC; there seemed to be little opportunity for any dynamic interaction between interest groups, businesses, a European-level technocracy, or other EC actors to make EPC less intergovernmental and more like the supranational European Community.

---

[2] For more extensive discussions on the application of functional spillover arguments to EPC, see Ifestos (1987), and Ginsberg (1989). On the general distinction between types of spillover, see Caporaso and Keeler (1995). It should also be noted that one of the founding fathers of neofunctionalism, Ernst Haas, explicitly excluded security and defense from his expansive logic of sectoral integration, which emphasized socioeconomic issues. See Haas (1972).

However, the story does not end there. Instead, EPC developed as a peculiar European institution among national diplomats by reinforcing informal rules of behavior established through trial and error, and to a much lesser extent, by permitting and legitimating the involvement of EC actors and procedures. Informal EPC rules and formal EC-level rules changed EPC from a forum for sharing information among governments (as it was designed) to a more institutionalized, collective, binding, and "Community-sensitive" system despite the efforts of some governments to resist this process. As EPC habits and procedures were institutionalized into a coherent body of European values and rules, they even caused member-states—large and small—to change their attitudes and preferences in certain situations, despite the absence of any real compliance or enforcement mechanisms besides peer pressure.[3] To explain why EPC and its successor, the CFSP, often appear to be "less than supranational but more than intergovernmental," this chapter analyzes the mechanisms by which EPC conditioned member-states to behave in three ways: first, to respond automatically and collectively to changing currents in world politics; second, to preserve these responses as a body of policies and procedures; and third, to increasingly frame these responses in terms of EC policies and rules.

The argument is presented in five stages. First, I outline a theoretical argument challenging the view that governments dominate the EPC/CFSP decision-making process, although EPC originated as an informal intergovernmental arrangement. Second, I show how EPC began to change (against the wishes of some governments) from an intergovernmental system due to the development of an innovative transgovernmental network, which linked and harmonized foreign policymaking in EPC member-states. Third, I explain how this network led to the establishment of EPC rules, and how these became associated with EC rules and procedures. Fourth, I show the extent to which the EPC mechanism encouraged the involvement of EC actors to preserve the rules previously established in the transgovernmental network.[4] Fifth, I continue this argument by briefly examining the replacement of EPC with the more formal and Community-bound CFSP under the Treaty on European Union. As the CFSP's rules are still somewhat distinct from supranational EC procedures, such cooperation is being challenged by the EU's hopes to expand its instruments into the military sphere, and more importantly, by its hopes to absorb a dozen or more new member-states in the near future. Accordingly, in 1996 the EU began yet another intense debate about changing the institutional foundations of political cooperation among its member-states.

---

[3] This chapter relies in part on interviews and informal conversations, conducted during 1995–6, with more than sixty officials involved in EPC/CFSP between 1970 and 1996. These include officials from Foreign Ministries, the Commission, the Council Secretariat-General, the Committee of Permanent Representatives, EC legal services, and the European Parliament.

[4] Since EPC ceased to exist with the creation of the CFSP, I write of it in the past tense although most of its procedures live on in the new mechanism.

1. Intergovernmentalism, Institutions, and the Origins of EPC

It is not necessary to recount here the tortured history of European foreign and security policy cooperation before 1970. It should only be recalled that the 1957 Treaty of Rome (EEC Treaty) does not mandate such cooperation; hence, one cannot look to it for much guidance about the development of this policy domain (Lak 1992). Indeed, one might even expect that such cooperation would not develop at all, given the way these treaties condition other EC policy domains.[5] In view of the origins, formal organizational structure, and goals of EPC, it is probably an exaggeration to consider it as an institution or even as a specific EC policy domain. EPC was established by the 1970 Luxembourg Report as a compromise between supranational and intergovernmental structures. Given the economic difficulties of the times, concerns about the impact of the first enlargement on the EC's political cohesion, and perceptions of American inattentiveness (if not hostility) to European problems, all EC member-state governments recognized that radically different national foreign policy positions could harm the EC, its policies, and relations between its members and between it and the outside world (Nuttall 1992; Allen and Wallace 1982; Wallace and Allen 1977).

Since they agreed only on the need for some measure of foreign policy consultation, the Luxembourg Report specified that governments would dominate and define any such coordination, and that it would be separate from EC policies and procedures. For the EC's external economic affairs (such as trade policy), the "EC method" was used to produce legally binding negotiating positions; the "EPC method" simply established a context in which consultation and coordination (and possibly joint action) in foreign and security policy could occur (Ginsberg 1989). In EPC, then, all states were equal, with no system of voting or weighted votes as in the EC Council of Ministers. Governments took turns leading the system; the one holding the six-month rotating EC Presidency also set the agenda for EPC discussions, represented EPC abroad, served as the meeting place for such discussions, and provided temporary staff support as needed. In terms of formal rules, EPC was not linked to the EC, not supported by a permanent organization or bureaucracy, and not even negotiated as a treaty. It had no permanent budget or staff for many years, no resources of its own, no meeting place, no secretariat-general or chief official, and no specific areas of competence. It had no compliance standards, legal obligations, or enforcement mechanisms to speak of, and it formally required little more than a commitment (not an obligation) among member-states to consult with each other and to coordinate their foreign policies if possible. In sum, at first it was little more than an exclusive "gentlemen's club," run by diplomats

---

[5] For a comparison, see Ch. 3.

for diplomats, subject to the goodwill of its members and closed to outside scrutiny. EPC simply was what its member governments said it was.[6]

Superficially, then, the EC compartmentalized its external economic and political relations. EPC had different ground rules, working methods, policy issues, legal foundations, instruments for action, timetables, venues for meetings, working languages (English and French only below ministerial level), and its own political culture. Its administrative infrastructure was centered in the Foreign Ministries of its member-states, and did not include other Ministries involved in EC affairs (Agriculture, Finance, and so on). Additionally, the "low politics" of EC affairs were handled by the economics or EC section in most Foreign Ministries; EPC was "high politics" handled by the political section. Finally, EPC's most important founding documents between 1970 and 1981 (the Luxembourg, Copenhagen, and London Reports) did not have treaty status, nor were they submitted to national parliaments for approval. In short, for states who wished to cooperate informally, EPC exhibited all the requisite characteristics: states avoided explicit, formal, visible pledges; agreements were not ratified; states could quickly change or renegotiate their commitments according to circumstances, and they could use and develop (or abolish) the system at will (Lipson 1991).

In theoretical terms, these characteristics have led some analysts to apply general models of intergovernmentalism (Bodenheimer 1967; Pijpers 1991; Taylor 1982; Wallace 1983) or more sophisticated "two-level games" theories (Bulmer 1991) to European foreign policy cooperation. These approaches focus on the role of governments, usually emphasize bargaining, and pay minimal attention to both institutional structures and historical context. I argue, however, that narrow intergovernmental or multilevel games approaches do not capture key elements of the EPC policy process. The cumulative impact of EPC deliberations created a far more institutionalized (i.e. rule-based) and binding system than that desired or expected by member-states. In addition, state preferences were often formed endogenously, within the EPC system. This argument challenges the view that political cooperation was a multilevel bargaining game by emphasizing the institutional development of EPC in terms of four factors.

First, governments did not monopolize the EPC system to the extent assumed by intergovernmental approaches. To be sure, domestic actors rarely had an opportunity or even a desire to ratify EPC agreements. Agreements were rarely open to public scrutiny or approval, public opinion was unaware of or uninterested in EPC, and there were few access points to relevant policymakers.[7]

---

[6] This description is broadly based on Wallace and Allen (1977); Wessels (1982); Wallace (1983); Ginsberg (1989); Nuttall (1992); and interviews with former EPC officials, Brussels, 1995–6.

[7] As Hill (1983) notes, even after ten years of EPC, "public opinion within the member-states [was] sadly ill-informed about and remote from EPC. . . . In none of the member-states [was] there evidence to suggest that awareness of what EPC entails has percolated very far even into the circles of educated opinion."

However, EPC's administrative infrastructure—based on a highly complex network of transgovernmental communications—developed in such a way that it limited the ability of senior-level government officials to dominate the entire policy process. To an extent surprising even to those who designed it, EPC outcomes became far less based on ad hoc political discussions than on the socialization of lower-level officials in national capitals and, later, the involvement of EC actors in Brussels. Shared ideas and understandings were pursued in this network, and this sensitivity to European issues among lower-level policymakers filtered up to governments in terms of the issues and options that were considered. With EPC's low-key network of transgovernmental consultation, state preferences were changed in some cases and practically created out of thin air in others.[8]

Second, EPC was novel in the extent to which its customs developed into rules, often to the irritation of member governments. Produced and stabilized within the transgovernmental network, EPC rules did not emphasize bargaining, as intergovernmental approaches often assume. The system was not used as a forum for making side-payments, threatening sanctions against each other, or linking issues into broad package deals (deals which regularly occur in other EC policy sectors or during Intergovernmental Conferences) to solve incomplete contracting problems. Member-states were not that ambitious at first; hence, it was inappropriate to use overt bargaining tactics to make policy in EPC. Officials honestly attempted to avoid power politics and confrontation during their discussions. It was intended to be a system for an exchange of views; if states discovered a common interest during discussions they could act in common, but there was neither an obligation to do so, nor provisions for trading favors to forge a common action. In general, EPC discussions reflected a "problem-solving," not bargaining, style of decision-making thanks to the reserve of trust built up in the transgovernmental network. Indeed, insiders often stress EPC's social dimensions, and the importance of persuasion; even during difficult discussions over the imposition of sanctions for political ends, officials usually avoided hard bargaining.[9] Once these informal rules proved their usefulness, they were preserved in a coherent body of policies and procedures, occasionally linked to EC procedures, and they conditioned later EPC outcomes.

Third, the relationship between EC actors and EPC, although strictly controlled by member governments, expanded somewhat beyond what was expected in the beginning of the system. The European Court did not become a

[8] Interviews, Brussels, 1995–6. Also see Hill (1983, 1996); Serre (1988); Smith (1998*b*); and EPC case studies on Central America (Smith 1995); South Africa (Holland 1987, 1995); the Middle East (Ifestos 1987); and the CSCE (Groll 1982).

[9] Interviews, Brussels, 1995–6. Conversely, Martin (1992) has argued that EC states did bargain during the Falklands Islands crisis, a major event in EPC's history. Nuttall (1992) rejects this interpretation: "It is going too far to suggest that a link between the price decisions (on EC agricultural prices) and the Falklands sanctions was ever established, but it is certainly the case that the climate of sympathy which had been created for the United Kingdom which had been created by the Argentinian invasion was in the process of being dissipated by the feeling that in the eyes of Whitehall Community solidarity was a one-way street."

major player in the codification of EPC rules, nor was the Commission the driving force behind the development of the EPC transgovernmental network. Instead, the system relied on domestic actors in its member-states to establish and reinforce its rules. But the Commission and the EPC secretariat did provide some administrative guidance, informal policy input, and institutional memory, helping to link EPC with the existing Community policy domains. This happened for a number of reasons which will be discussed in detail below.

The fourth element in this analysis is time, in two senses. First is the long-term historical development of EPC, in particular its "path-dependent" effects, or the way individual policy decisions coalesced and stabilized so that they conditioned future choices.[10] As these decisions were often the product of behind-the-scenes procedural debates among diplomats, in this story there are few dramatic leaps forward, signal events or cases, or decisive breaks with the past. A "historical institutionalist"[11] perspective alerts us to the incremental effects of informal rules and procedures on social behavior. Indeed, since EC foreign policy cooperation was driven by a tension between two competing rule systems—the informal one of EPC and the EC's own treaty-based legal system—and was always subordinate to the wishes of governments, EPC innocently and slowly encouraged government subordination to more formal and binding EC rules. Second, I note that the short-term EPC policy process always exhibited elements of both intergovernmentalism and supranationalism: the broad EPC agenda often was (and still is) set by EC heads of state/government acting in the European Council. During later phases of the process (policy choice, implementation, funding, etc.), other actors, rules, and EC procedures can exert their effects, but only within the context set by officials at the highest level. This fact, the exclusion of the ECJ, and the limited use of majority voting procedures in foreign policy cooperation, have kept this domain from ever becoming truly supranational.

In general, then, a more sophisticated view of policymaking than intergovernmentalism suggests that the system demonstrated a paradox of institutional strength: although EPC was an informal, decentralized, non-coercive institution, and did not enjoy strong public support or interest, and was conceived as a system external to the EC, it resulted in an expansion of foreign policy cooperation and changed state interests and preferences. EPC expanded in ways unanticipated or opposed by many member-states, and authority in this area was increasingly influenced by EC procedures. In practice, then, EC foreign policy cooperation was simultaneously institutionalized and became less intergovernmental: EPC rules and policies became more coherent and stable while the system itself became linked to the Community. The next three sections of this chapter examine the mechanisms by which this change occurred.

---

[10] On path-dependency, see Krasner (1984) and Ch. 2.

[11] Historical institutionalism is most often associated with studies of comparative political economy, but its insights can be effectively applied to the EC as well. For an overview, see Steinmo *et al.* (1992).

2. The Institutionalization of EPC: Transgovernmental Relations

In spite of its modest origins and fragile structure, EPC resulted in decisive changes in the way the EC conducted its external political relations. Its first direct tools were merely declarations, démarches, and collective approaches to international organizations and conferences. For example, after years of uni-lateral action in the UN General Assembly, voting among EC states increased from 30–40 percent unanimity in the 1970s up to 80 percent at some points in the 1980s. Performance in the CSCE was even better.[12] From this timid start, EPC tools expanded to include codes of conduct, written conventions, economic aid and sanctions, peace and democratization plans, fact-finding missions, and other measures. In terms of tasks, EPC became useful during crisis situations, in drawn-out negotiations to resolve conflicts or foster development, and in the increasing tendency of the EC to bunch external negotiations into "package deals" which included a political dialogue. EPC also expanded the EC's political relations geographically. And as Ginsberg (1989) has observed, after EPC was created the EC also began to take what he calls "self-styled" foreign policy actions, which reflected:

[T]he EC's own internal deliberations, both within the EC bodies themselves and be-tween the member-states and EC bodies. Self-styled actions reflect the EC's own sense of mission and interest in the world. They are not solely dependent on the need to respond to external stimuli but instead are products of (A) habits of working together; (B) EC and member-state initiatives; and (C) a sense of what Europeans want in foreign policy questions.

Equally importantly, EPC changed the ways its members determined and pursued their interests. Governments which previously had no interest in cer-tain problems took on EPC positions or even helped bring them about simply due to their participation in the mechanism.[13] Foreign policies became more transparent and somewhat more predictable, while compliance with positions became more common despite the absence of sanctioning mechanisms. For example, the Euro-Arab dialogue, one of the longest-running EPC initiatives, helped the positions of pro-Arab France and pro-Israel Germany and the Netherlands converge (Allen 1982; Ifestos 1987). Even strong states succumbed to EPC actions they opposed (such as Britain and Germany on sanctions against

[12] Cooperation at the UN was probably even stronger than statistics suggested. Resolutions adopted by consensus were usually not included in the data, and some have argued that dif-ferences in voting more often than not reflected tactical differences rather than fundamental variations on policy. See the discussions in Hurwitz (1976); Lindemann (1976, 1982); Foot (1979); Groll (1982); and Nuttall (1992).

[13] Witness Ireland's surprising (and effective) activism during the 1975 Portuguese crisis and the first difficult years of the Euro-Arab dialogue, or the way Greece's extreme foreign policy positions were moderated within EPC.

South Africa), and states opposed to certain aspects of EPC for other reasons (Denmark because of potential ratification problems and its sensitivity to NATO; Greece because of Turkey; Ireland because of neutrality, etc.) permitted more discussion of security affairs in EPC. One major case study, Europe and Central America, suggests that not only did EPC help its member governments focus their efforts into a coherent policy, but European policy in the end was more effective than that of the USA (Smith 1995). Finally, EPC did not always produce lowest-common-denominator positions either; instead, they often converged around a dominant or "median" point of view once taken up in the system (Nuttall 1992). Thus, very soon after the creation of EPC, Henri Simonet, acting President of the Council, could state before the European Parliament that "The practice of political cooperation has become more enduring and more scrupulous than the actual texts intend" (*Proceedings of the European Community*, Appendix 223, 15 November 1977). As a German participant, Otto von der Gablentz (1979) similarly observed, EPC acted "as a delicate system of incentives and sanctions imposing a European discipline on its member-states."

This section and the two that follow show the extent to which the influence of EPC can be understood as the cumulative product of a dynamic and multifaceted process of institutionalization, as EPC became less intergovernmental (like NATO) and more supranational (like the EC). Toward this end I explore three intervening processes—a middle-range theoretical framework—that evolved between the policies of individual national governments and the risks and opportunities provided by the international system to account for the way informal EPC foreign policy coordination resulted in an enduring, rule-based, EC-sensitive body of behavior and policies. In addition to the influence of time, the institutionalization of EPC can be broken down into three linked elements, in order of decreasing importance: transgovernmental relations, the development and codification of EPC rules, and the involvement of EC actors.

In this section I consider *transgovernmental relations*. Analysts of EC policy-making (and of international cooperation in general) have argued that transnational links between interest groups, businesses, or other actors can play an important role in determining cooperative outcomes. These links are likely to emerge in dense, complex issue-areas, especially those which involve international institutions (Keohane and Nye 1972, 1974; Sandholtz and Zysman 1989; Risse-Kappen 1995). Transnational groups can mobilize in support of, or opposition to, an agreement between states (or its implementation), which affects the final product. In EPC, links between *governments and diplomats* were far more important and strongly developed than those between non-state actors such as interest groups. Also, these links did not "emerge," nor did the Commission encourage them; they were *deliberately created* by states (though on the basis of a non-treaty instrument) as an alternative to EC control, but quickly expanded beyond the original plan. Finally, these links were originally forged to serve *no specific purposes or policy ends*. EPC basically created a novel communication system between officials without a very clear goal to be served by that system. Officials were first directed to share information as they saw fit; policy outcomes were a peripheral consideration.

Indeed, transgovernmentalism was *the* key feature of EPC from the beginning. European Council summits of heads of state and government were supposed to dominate the EPC process and provide the main link between the EC and EPC. Among other functions, the summits were supposed to set EPC guidelines, coordinate EC/EPC policies and solve disputes when they clashed, and make declarations on European foreign policy issues (Bulmer 1985; Bulmer and Wessels 1987). The Council Presidency became an important part of EPC in this regard (Schoutheete de Tervarent 1988; Wallace and Edwards 1976). Yet on a practical, day-to-day basis, governments could not ignore the fact that delegation and communication below the European Council/Presidency level were required, especially in the absence of an EPC bureaucracy. In most cases the European Council was not even involved in policy details; it was more often preoccupied with EC, not EPC, affairs. In fact, Foreign Ministers dominated EPC discussions, meeting at least four times a year at first. EPC thus began to involve Foreign Ministries more, to their delight, and it "brought them back" to EC affairs at a level equal to other domestic ministries (agriculture, finance, etc.) who often acted as "foreign" ministries in EC discussions. Smaller states in particular saw a revolution—terms of reorganization and expansion—in their Foreign Ministries to cope with the EPC workload. With their limited representation outside the EC, they especially benefited from information shared by larger states.[14]

With EPC, officials enjoyed somewhat more freedom of movement since rules and sanctions were not yet as well developed as in the EC. Progress was encouraged by the fact that governments permitted coordination below the highest levels to harmonize their views in the hopes of producing common positions. Without a permanent staff to manage EPC and keep it separate from the EC, the creation of a transgovernmental infrastructure was an acceptable, low-cost alternative, but this was the first step toward institutionalizing foreign policy cooperation. While the rules of EPC eventually emerged through a sometimes painful process of trial and error, few states could object to seemingly innocuous lower-level links between professional bureaucrats and diplomats. Several characteristics of the system became especially important in the day-to-day workings of EPC.

For example, below the level of Foreign Ministers, coordination was achieved through regular contacts between Foreign Ministries, primarily through the designation of a *Political Committee* (PoCo) composed of Political Directors (senior officials from each Foreign Ministry). PoCo began to meet at least four times a year (it eventually met once a month or more) and agreements reached in its unusually casual group atmosphere could then be defended to individual

---

[14] EPC's role in enhancing the stature of Foreign Ministries in the EC is described in many of the contributions to Hill (1983). Also see Hill and Wallace (1979); Wallace (1982); Hill (1996); and Smith (1998).

national governments. The PoCo was also permitted to set up *working groups* composed of experts from foreign or other appropriate ministries (and eventually also from the Commission). These were organized along both functional (UN, CSCE, non-proliferation) and geographical (Asia, Middle East, Eastern Europe) lines according to the needs of EPC; hundreds of meetings of such groups took place each year. Below the PoCo, a system of European Correspondents was set up to manage EPC on a daily basis in the absence of a secretariat. Liaison between EC capitals was the primary task of this group. Cohesion within this group became especially close over the years, and it fostered many personal friendships. With their common bureaucratic roles, esprit de corps, and devotion to a new policy system that privileged their input, European Correspondents and EPC working groups made common analyses of problems rather than bargained on behalf of their governments.[15]

To further help with information-sharing in EPC, the highly innovative and effective *correspondance Europeène* (or COREU) telex network was established in 1973. The number of COREUs exchanged quickly mushroomed to hundreds per week, and the system enabled points of view to be shared between all member-states (and eventually the Commission) within a matter of hours. In addition to this quantitative change, officials familiar with the system also acknowledge a *qualitative* change in the subject matter of COREUs over the years, with more security and military matters being discussed via telex (such as arms-control issues) than in the beginning. Political cooperation (like EC membership in general) also encouraged states to reduce their own internal conflicts before considering common European options. States cannot pursue an unlimited agenda at the EC level; priorities must be set at home and with partners to make the most of their influence in Brussels. Especially in small states, EPC fostered a convergence of many foreign policy positions among officials and political parties.[16]

This formal system encouraged other informal transgovernmental relationships in the EPC system, helping to break down the desired distinction between EPC and EC affairs. Missions of EC member-states to third countries expanded considerably during the first decade of EPC. Diplomats in these missions (and their local interlocutors) rarely if ever observed the formal distinction between EPC and the EC, and they could hardly be made to do so by their foreign ministries. EC officials thus informally coordinated their EC/EPC efforts in third countries, and they were eventually directed to do so by the London Report and the Single European Act (SEA). EC ambassadors prepared joint reports (which was not expressly called for or even desired by EC states), shared information, and made policy recommendations to higher officials at home. They also conducted common démarches in third countries (most often on human rights issues), held common debates with high representatives of third

---

[15] Interviews, Brussels, 1995–6. The transgovernmental component of EPC is also described in Wallace (1982); and Nuttall (1992: 14–25).

[16] Interviews, Brussels, 1995–6. Also see Hill (1983) and Nuttall (1992).

countries, and cooperated during crisis situations without much guidance from EC capitals. Frequently missions of large EC states acted on behalf of small EC members who had limited representation in the developing world. Especially when small or remote states were the object of action, links between missions became a vital "back-door channel" to achieving political cooperation. This was occasionally resented by Foreign Ministers and by the PoCo; the French even attempted to put a halt to such activity during the 1980s.[17]

In sum, these day-to-day transgovernmental contacts helped reduce COGs' monopoly of the EPC process. They acted in much the same way as transnational links between interest groups and EC actors do in other EC policy domains. Direct communication between governments was institutionalized at all levels, even in departments and embassies, while the EPC working groups especially played a greater role than originally anticipated. They often suggested collectively derived options to higher officials. A distinct "mobilization effect" or "coordination reflex" could be observed in Foreign Ministries and missions: when a problem came up, officials *automatically* activated the COREU network to exchange opinions, consider options, and build consensus *before* individual national positions were established.[18] Government actors at all levels both gradually adapted to each other and oriented themselves toward "Europe" when considering problems. By directly involving and empowering domestic bureaucrats in the process, EPC created some sense of European loyalty among foreign policymakers in its member-states (Wessels 1982). As one participant put it, a "European dimension" was built into a process which previously had been exclusively based on national considerations (Schoutheete de Tervarent 1980).

Thus, EPC encouraged joint gains and common perceptions: a distinct *communauté de vue*. In other words, transgovernmental relations were structured to produce a European consensus, not for the confrontational purpose of exploiting divisions in each other's domestic politics, as one analyst of two-level games has suggested (Knopf 1993). Personalities mattered of course, but thanks to the tendency toward information-sharing and consultation, most officials felt committed to the EPC *communauté de vue* since they had been closely involved in its articulation. As I discuss below, the set of common viewpoints which expanded through transgovernmental discussions became more explicitly codified, and were loyally defended, as substantive EPC rules, while the involvement of EC actors was gradually permitted (if not encouraged) to protect those rules.

[17] Also, in at least one case (South Africa) the EC ambassadors to that country were invited back to Brussels as a group to help EPC form a response to anti-apartheid sentiment. Interviews, Brussels, 1995–6.

[18] The "reflex of coordination" was first described in the 1973 Copenhagen Report; it is also stressed in all of the most well-known personal accounts of EPC (see Schoutheete de Tervarent (1980); Fonseca-Wollheim (1981); Hurd (1981); and Nuttall (1992)), and in interviews, Brussels, 1995–6.

3. The Codification Process: EPC and EC Rules

The transgovernmental network was a major step in EPC, but this communication had more far-reaching effects than trust, common views, and friendship. Continuous interaction and information-sharing encouraged the preservation of effective working procedures and policies as EPC rules. However, as noted, a distinctive feature of EPC was that it operated for years outside any legal or treaty arrangements. Due to the sensitivity of the issue-area and EPC's informal nature, rules and substantive policies took time to develop and arduous debates took place whenever any actor attempted to formalize them. Indeed, the system would not have been created at all if states had attempted to impose legal rules on themselves. As Simon Nuttall, a former EPC participant, once observed (1992), "The first decade and a half of Political Cooperation [was] marked by extreme conservatism in the drafting of theoretical papers and bold innovation on the ground." Additionally, for some states (such as Denmark and Ireland) debates over procedure were far more difficult than those over substance because of the thorny domestic constitutional issues they raised; thus they were avoided as much as possible. According to another observer, "Pragmatism is one of the main features governing political cooperation. The fixing of rules and procedures in official texts before they have proven their usefulness is alien to EPC procedure" (Regelsberger 1991).

However, it is equally true and important that EPC procedures, once established, were respected as much or even more than the actual substance of policy. States generally supported the "correct" use of informal procedures on good faith, even if they did not agree with specific policies. Thus coalitions within EPC continually changed within the context of its procedures according to the problem at hand, and cut across issues or regions, rather than hardening into blocs of states with dominant shared interests or forming permanent cleavages. As Hill (1983) once observed, alignments in EPC were usually issue-centered, informal, and shifting. Although EPC rules were not formally codified for many years, and they were usually "enforced" through intra-group politics of reputation and persuasion rather than by reference to legal obligations or sanctions, nonetheless a peculiar set of unwritten laws emerged during EPC discussions according to those familiar with the system. These influenced state behavior in profound ways and found increasing legitimacy as rules, the violation of which brought down heavy condemnation from other EC members, while defecting states felt increasingly obliged to defend themselves to their EPC partners.

This section focuses on the most important and explicit EPC rules, both procedural (those concerning the way policy is made) and substantive (those outlining specific EPC policies or actions), which showed increasing and enduring EC-wide legitimacy.[19] Since there is not the space here to engage in an

---

[19] This is not a firm distinction, of course; e.g. cooperation within the UN could be viewed as

extended discussion of the differences between principles, unwritten laws, norms, rules, conventions, decrees, and the like, I rely on a fairly simple distinction between informal and formal rules and follow Friedrich Kratochwil's (1989) treatment of rules as problem-solving or choice-simplification mechanisms. Informal rules are defined here as explicit, shared standards for behavior; formal rules are behavioral standards expressed in terms of rights and obligations; these are codified in written form (though not necessarily in a treaty).

3.1. Procedural rules

EPC did not even exist at first according to international law, but officials conducted their relations in EPC—which itself was established as an explicit "gentlemen's agreement"—according to improvised habits which became an increasingly binding set of rules. Governments generally recognized the power of precedent in EPC, even if actors such as the ECJ were excluded from the process. EPC rules were informal and vague at first; they acted as de facto "opt-out clauses" since interpretations over their application could vary. As Holland (1987) put it, EPC provided the best of both worlds: "collective foreign policy harmony together with virtual domestic autonomy."

However, states became less inclined to opt-out as rules were codified. Most important at first were the general rules of *confidentiality*, *consensus*, and *consultation*, which encouraged problem-solving instead of bargaining. Thus, EPC discussions were private; states could not use information shared during them to embarrass or blame other states. The engineering of trust was a foundation of the system; secrecy encouraged confidence among states since they typically did not have to fear public politicization of issues brought up for discussion, embarrassment at failure, or that information shared would be used against them. EPC discussions were also conducted with unanimity; any state could block discussion of a sensitive matter without justification. This rule became increasingly challenged over the years with enlargement and the growing number of difficult issues on the EPC agenda, but in the early years it made discussions less threatening since states felt they could terminate them at will. Finally, states adopted a general rule to consult with each other before adopting final positions of their own so that policies of their partners would not catch them by surprise. These three basic rules, practiced and reinforced in the EPC transgovernmental network, fostered a nascent *communauté de vue* on what constituted "European interests."[20]

In terms of explicit working procedures, governments discovered that consistency of the EPC process would be difficult in a system with no central

a policy end by itself (a substantive rule) or a procedure to advance particular goals of the EC. However, as the discussion will show this distinction between procedure and substance has been made by EPC officials and texts; hence I rely on it as well.

[20] Interviews, Brussels, 1995–6. Also see Schoutheete de Tervarent (1980); Fonseca-Wollheim (1981); and Wessels (1982).

bureaucracy and with rotating directors (the Presidencies) every six months. In 1976 Denmark suggested the idea of the *coutumier* ("custom"), a compilation of all formal and informal working procedures which became the "bible of EPC" for European Correspondents in foreign ministries. This was done primarily to smooth transitions between Presidencies in the absence of a permanent secretariat (Haagerup and Thune 1983). A number of procedures found their way into the *coutumier*, which became a kind of "EPC common law." Coordination of positions became a rule in organizations and conferences, the most visible expression of EPC at first. Additionally, EC states who were members of the UN Security Council (Britain and France) were required to take account of EPC positions in that forum and inform their EC partners about its deliberations. EPC was intended to produce medium- and long-term positions, but after Afghanistan and Iran crisis procedures (*consultations d'urgence*) were reinforced; these were first successfully invoked during the 1982 Israeli invasion of Lebanon. Finally, the role of the Presidency became more central as EPC's main contact with outsiders, which reduced the importance of bilateral "special relationships" in some cases (Wallace and Edwards 1976). Such changes also made it necessary to clarify the role of EC actors in EPC, as I discuss below.

The expansion of the *coutumier* over the years, and the eventual expression of many of its procedures in treaty form, showed how rules could develop in a legitimate and authoritative manner merely through routine interactions and self-policing, even without the involvement of a bureaucracy or court. Although, as Wessels (1982) observed, "Legalistic discussions which aim[ed] to avoid or produce precedents rarely occur[red] in EPC," EPC participants increasingly acted as if its rules were binding. Besides improving the working relationships among foreign policy officials, such rules also helped placate the small states in particular, who were always sensitive to the idea of an intergovernmental EPC being run by a *directoire* of large states. Instead of "balancing" against the large states, small states (with the notable exception of Denmark) tried to turn EPC into the more rule-based regime it became (they also pushed for more involvement by the Commission for the same reason; see below). As in the EC, small states in EPC attempted to overcome their dependency by constructing a system based on law, not power. A more stable partnership between large and small states was forged in EPC by the principle of equality under the law.

Thanks to the *coutumier* procedures, long before the SEA many began to suggest that the informal, extra-legal arrangements worked out between governments in EPC were sufficiently constraining to be considered *legally* binding. As Belgian Foreign Minister Henri Simonet told the EP in 1977, in EPC "a kind of law of custom has emerged . . . which naturally does not envisage any sanctions but which has nevertheless taken on the character of a recognized rule which can be occasionally broken but whose existence one still recognizes" (*Proceedings of the European Community*, 15 November 1977). Maarten Lak (1989) argues that even without formal codification, the reports and practices of EPC "could well have come to form a beginning of customary European law as far as applied in practice, as implementation pursued consistently would have provided validity by precedent."

However, as Dehousse and Weiler (1991) once observed, while international commitments such as EPC can arise without a formal treaty, their binding quality always rests on the consent of member-states. Similarly, the "guidelines" of the European Council on EC/EPC were also of dubious legality, since it too was not an EC body. Instead, these arrangements seemed to be a part of what international law scholars began to call "soft law," or the body of international conventions, codes of conduct, and declaratory texts which aim at changing state behavior but which do not necessarily establish legal rights and obligations. Dehousse and Weiler argue that a "sociological" view of such soft laws makes them legal, and interviews with EPC participants typically confirm this view. Also, the fact that sovereignty in EPC was pooled or ceded to a center created the impression that it had legal personality, although EPC was of course
• not an international organization (Lodge 1989).

Given the persistence of these problems of interpretation, it was not until 1987 that Title III of the SEA "legalized" EC foreign policy cooperation as a treaty for the first time, but the debate over the extent to which the SEA set down legal obligations was never clearly resolved. Thus EPC was not formally "Communitarized" with the SEA, and like the Treaty on European Union (see below), it merely codified existing practices in an attempt to clarify and preserve what had been achieved.[21] But it did create stronger legal obligations than had ever existed under EPC. According to Dehousse and Weiler, the SEA provision (Art. 30) that parties shall "endeavour" to formulate a European foreign policy created an obligation to act in good faith, a recognized concept in international law. The real problem was the lack of effective adjudication or enforcement mechanisms in EPC, not the lack of specific legal obligations (problems which exist in many other international agreements).[22] Those who did not support an act could, out of respect for the majority, decide not to oppose them, already a standard EPC practice. This enabled states to avoid the terribly difficult issue of majority voting in EPC, and since the Luxembourg compromise has effectively disappeared, this seemed to put EPC and the EC on nearly the same footing where voting and consensus were concerned.

In addition to this general elevation of EPC to a legal status closer to that of the EC, an equally vital procedural link between the two rule systems developed when EC governments wished to use EC instruments for EPC ends. Such decisions usually provoked heated procedural disagreements; gradually,

---

[21] According to Title I of the SEA, the EC was still based on the EC Treaties; EPC was still based on its various reports and the "practices gradually established among the member-states" (the *coutumier*). Also, the reference to EPC in the SEA was to "cooperation in the sphere of foreign policy" in the hopes of forming "a European foreign policy" rather than to a *common* foreign policy. Finally, there was also no stated *obligation* to achieve common positions.

[22] Also note that the Irish Supreme Court felt the EPC provisions in the SEA were legally binding, which required a constitutional amendment to change Irish neutrality, and the Danes had similar difficulties with the SEA (and later with the Treaty on European Union).

however, they led to a greater recognition of both the legitimacy and efficiency of EC competencies. At first EPC sanctions were imposed on a national basis with only a symbolic invocation of EC procedures. However, the rigid distinction between the European Council/EPC and the Council of Ministers/EC began to disappear as Foreign Ministers considered how EC resources or procedures could give more weight to EPC actions (Holland 1991). More specifically, when EPC decisions affected an EC competency (such as the use of sanctions) invoking certain articles of the EC Treaties automatically made EPC a more rule-based and Community-sensitive regime than usual practice warranted. As Maarten Lak (1989) observed, the interaction rules of the SEA constituted the most "legal" of its EPC provisions given the language used, in part because these rules made Commission involvement in EPC mandatory.

Several articles of the Rome (EEC) Treaty have been invoked (more than one article in some cases)[23] in the context of EPC discussions to enable the mechanism to legally mobilize EC resources or actions for political ends; portions of Arts. 113, 223, 224, 228, 229, and 238 in particular:

Article 113   Empowers the Commission to recommend to Council when accords with third states are needed. Council directs the Commission to open and conduct negotiations (typically for economic policies).

Article 223   Protects EC members from the disclosure of information which may damage their security. It effectively permits the protection of domestic arms industries and policies from the requirements of the common market, and provides for the creation of a list of products which are to be excluded from the common market project.

Article 224   Calls for member-states to consult to prevent the functioning of the common market from being disrupted from serious internal or international disturbances, such as war.

Article 228   Empowers the Commission to negotiate accords with third states and international bodies.

Article 229   Empowers the Commission to ensure the maintenance of relations with international bodies (such as the UN and GATT) and their specialized organs.

Article 238   Permits the EC to conclude accords with a third state, a union of states, or an international organization. Such accords may involve reciprocal rights and obligations, common action, and special procedures.

Arts. 113 and 228 were often cited when EC and EPC actions were taken parallel to each other and decided with their separate procedures. Art. 113 (the common commercial policy) was later invoked to provide a makeshift legal basis for an EPC decision to use EC tools, although there were doubts as to whether Art. 113 could be legally used for political ends. After many intense

[23] e.g. EPC–EC actions against apartheid in South Africa involved years of procedural debates and the application of nearly all EPC/EC foreign policy tools: démarches, statements, codes of conduct, economic sanctions and assistance, a European Coal and Steel Community embargo, and other measures. See Holland (1995).

debates over procedure in the 1980s (provoked by the Iran and Afghanistan crises), Art. 113 EC legislation which referred to "discussions in the context of EPC" became standard practice for sanctions; this opened the door to other "interactive" EC/EPC external political actions and the production of "dualist" EC/EPC case law. This was done as much for efficiency's sake as it was to respect EC competencies, as states realized it was difficult to ensure compliance with EPC economic measures without EC regulations and the monitoring of member-state behavior by the Commission. After years of dual agreements, a 1989 EC regulation on controlling weapons-grade chemicals finally provided an acceptable legal formula for EC/EPC procedures to be combined in a single text.[24]

In sum, states gradually found ways to bridge the "legal gap" between the EC and EPC, another procedural rule which developed from pragmatic habits or customs shared by officials who were responsible for the EPC system. Many of these rules were developed after crises: EPC procedures changed notably after states were caught off-guard by international problems in the late 1970s and late 1980s. Once customs and draft texts proved their usefulness, they were more likely to be codified in the *coutumier* at first and in the SEA later. These procedures also brought EPC closer to the EC in two ways: they reflected a growing sensitivity to the greater legitimacy and efficacy of treaty-bound EC rules, and they justified more involvement of EC actors to protect both EC and EPC rules and to encourage compliance. This is even more extraordinary when one considers that, as Weiler (1985) noted, all instruments of national policy (including sanctions) could have been used in EPC given enough political will. Instead, states increasingly chose to respect and utilize EC rules, resources, and actors when acting in EPC to make the system more efficient and forceful, and the two systems became more closely linked than in the beginning.

3.2. Substantive rules

This section focuses on EPC policies or actions designed to serve certain collective goals or interests of EPC/EC member-states. Since there was no formally institutionalized representation of European political interests, it may be tempting to consider EPC's substantive policies or rules as the sum of its member-governments' interests. Any EPC policy would reflect a lowest-common-denominator consensual position, possibly forged by the state holding the EC Presidency. This was not always the case. First, EPC was embedded in the same broader normative structure which gave birth to the EC itself and which influenced liberal democratic states in and out of the EC. This structure generally emphasized free and open government, respect for the rule of law, protection of human rights, economic liberalism, the indivisibility of security in Western Europe, multilateral cooperation in the UN and CSCE, the peaceful resolution of disputes, and so on. The EC has occasionally attempted a

---

[24] Council Regulation (EEC) 428/89 of 20 Feb. 1989, OJ L 50/1/1989. Also see Nuttall (1992).

formal definition of "European interests,"[25] but such efforts often were premature, vague, and difficult to conclude when divorced from positions already forged within EPC.

Second, instead of being established in treaty form, or being produced in an ad hoc way depending on the leadership of individual Presidencies, most substantive EPC rules were codified as customs, which later influenced member-state positions. To be sure, respect for EPC procedures was greater than that for substantive EPC policies, but in neither case could the rules associated with these processes be understood as lowest-common-denominator outcomes. According to many participants, "medianism" prevailed: the extreme positions of governments changed to reflect the most common position, not the one minimally acceptable to all states. In the case of substantive EPC rules, these were usually described as a component of "political union," a vague notion; in practical terms, discussions in the framework of EPC enabled states to bridge many previously divisive cleavages over a number of issues. These include the East–West and North–South conflicts, the question of ending colonialism, the debate between justice and human rights versus economics and strategy, differences between nuclear and non-nuclear states, the interests of large versus small states, neutral states versus alliance members, the Arab–Israeli conflict, and many specific cleavages over tactics.[26] The collective positions that emerged from these debates were increasingly codified in EPC reports and treaties as substantive rules. Thus, EPC polices persisted beyond each Presidency.

Specifically, substantive EPC rules were still generally based on the informal *communauté de vue* or *acquis politique* produced during discussions on major foreign policy questions in the EPC network. These comprised a package of "unified basic foreign policy standpoints." At the initiative of the British Presidency in 1977, officials decided to compile the substantive EPC texts of each Presidency into the *recueil* ("collection"). Although the *recueil* expanded in unforeseen ways over the years, EPC was first and foremost a defensive measure to protect the EC. As such, it could be considered a "regime of common aversion;"[27] member-states generally agreed on the need to shield the still-evolving EC from unilateral foreign policy actions of its own members. This "damage-limitation" function has been emphasized since the Luxembourg Report; it also justified the role of the Commission to give its views on how EPC might affect the EC. The importance of this rule was quickly revealed in practice during the chaotic response of the EC to the first oil shocks in the 1970s. The lack of cooperation here directly led to one of the longest-running EPC initiatives: the Euro-Arab dialogue. By the time of the SEA, this damage-limitation rule had expanded into a rule that the twin pillars of the EC and EPC must also

[25] e.g. see the "Document on the European Identity published by the Nine Foreign Ministers" (Copenhagen, 14 Dec. 1973); the "Solemn Declaration on European Union," (Stuttgart Declaration, 19 June 1983); and the "Declaration of Principles of Human Rights," *European Documentation Bulletin 1986*.

[26] For a review, see Fonseca-Wollheim (1981) and the Federal Republic of Germany (1988).

[27] On regimes of common aversion, see Stein (1983). The use of EPC as a means to protect the EC is described in detail in Bonvicini (1982).

be *consistent*: action in one domain had to support action in the other. The Presidency and the Commission were directed to make sure EC/EPC consistency was sought and maintained (Arts. 30.3–30.5, SEA).

Beyond protecting the EC from reckless independent foreign policies, a number of other rules emerged from EPC deliberations. The expansion and codification of substantive rules was difficult, but it occurred. It is impossible to cite all of them here; instead they might be classified as sets of policy orientations surrounding a geographic and/or functional domain. Based on the most ambitious and highest-profile EPC initiatives of its early years, it is clear that issues were chosen based on their proximity and importance to the EC, not on their chances for resolution. At first, the emphasis was typically on long-term goals with third countries or regions closest to the EC (hence the CSCE, the Euro-Arab dialogue, a working group on Mediterranean issues). These plans generally emphasized progressive conflict-resolution as opposed to crisis management. In part to distinguish itself from the USA, EPC declarations on these issues showed what behavior or principles would result in a favorable response from the EC.

Despite achievements in these broad areas, EPC was initially confounded by the specific *domaines réservés* of its members. At first, an unwritten rule made taboo the consideration of issues which were known to be sensitive to certain member-states (former colonies; Greece and Turkey; Britain and Ireland; East and West Germany; etc.). Thanks to this understanding, substantive rules in EPC were more easily defined in terms of what subjects were off limits rather than what issues could be discussed. The most important functional expansion of EPC involved the inclusion of security affairs on its agenda. Although Art. 224 of the Rome Treaty obliged member-states to consult each other when considering unilateral action on security issues which may impact the functioning of the EC, at first security or defense matters were rarely the object of serious discussion in EPC. Defense in particular was usually left to NATO, but EPC enabled its members to carve their own role in such matters while recognizing their status as junior partners of NATO, even in the face of domestic difficulties over this role for EPC. After these positive developments, and after the Iranian and Afghanistan crises, the 1981 London Report finally recognized the necessity of discussing in EPC "foreign policy questions bearing on the political aspects of security."[28]

Later, when the EC's tools of economic sanctions began to be used in EPC, substantive rules were formalized and used as precedents for later acts. After more heated debate against the backdrop of renewed USA–USSR tension during the early 1980s, the SEA finally included a reference to cooperation on the "political and economic aspects of security" within the framework of EPC (Art. 30.6), a major advancement of the agenda. This opened the door to more consideration of security-related questions, non-proliferation measures, and arms-control issues in EPC, despite their controversy for some member-states (Ireland in particular), since economics were not emphasized in NATO and

---

[28] "Report on European Political Cooperation issues by the Foreign Ministers of the Ten on 13 October 1981" (London Report), Part I.

security concerns were not emphasized in the EC. But military crises were still hard to handle in EPC as member-states diverged over the means and ends of defense policy (and defense ministers of course were not permitted to meet in Council or EPC). This disagreement directly led to the "reactivation" of the Western European Union (of which Denmark, Ireland, and Greece were not members) in 1984 as a quasi-defense arm of the EC, and it increasingly challenged the ability of EPC to handle the rapid changes in the USSR in the late 1980s. Except perhaps for military instruments, then, EPC thus quietly and persistently led to a major expansion of the EC's foreign affairs agenda, in both geographic and functional terms, and a simultaneous contraction of the *domaines réservés*, often to the irritation of member-states. The veto was used less frequently; even when it was attempted, the system rarely "gave up" on important matters. Officials at all levels simply wore each other down with arguments until previously taboo subjects were considered in EPC.

To summarize, codification of rules (procedural and substantive) in the SEA essentially meant putting soft law into hard law, making fragmented practices a coherent whole and elevating them to real legal status. Governments were supposed to take obligations more seriously; violations had higher costs (if only reputational at first); aggrieved parties had legitimate avenues for redress (but in international courts, nor the ECJ; see below); and the treaty was ratified by, and had the formal support of, national parliaments and/or citizens. The legality of the SEA was also important for its impact on the socialization process, consolidating the *acquis politique* previously created through trial and error. The *acquis politique* was not as clearly articulated or as binding as the *acquis communautaire*, of course, but it was important nonetheless. Later, the SEA enhanced the stability and acceptability of the EPC process by combining the institutional instruments of both EPC and EC. As Dehousse and Weiler observed (1991), the total separation of the two (legal) systems (of EPC and the EC) had become untenable; because of the progress they achieved in the European Community, member-states effectively abdicated part of their autonomy as EPC partners.

Equally importantly, the SEA officially excluded any differentiated participation in EC/EPC, which would have an effect on future enlargements. New members had to accept the *acquis politique* to join the EC, a condition first imposed during Greece's accession to the EC (and later made part of the SEA). Documents on EPC procedures and the "European identity" were given to Greece, and they were asked to take part in EPC with all its associated rights and obligations. But a notable difference was made: acceptance of EPC procedural texts (the *coutumier*) was required, but not of the substantive ones (the *recueil*) (Nuttall 1992). This reflected the difference between procedure and substance, and between the EPC *acquis* and the EC *acquis* discussed above. But EPC deliberations and the power of precedent continually raised the status quo of procedures and policies so that states felt the costs of exit or defection were often higher than the costs of compliance, even if there were no specific sanctions involved in the cost-benefit calculation.

4. EPC Actors: The Commission and Secretariat

To this point in the analysis I have stressed the importance of transgovernmental relations and the development of EPC rules. This is not to say that EC actors have had no influence on EPC's institutionalization, only that they mattered far less than in other EC policy domains.[29] From the very beginning of EPC, member governments took great care to emphasize the distinction between EPC and Community affairs to prevent the "contamination" of one by the other. They also resisted the establishment of any permanent bureaucracy for EPC. Yet governments began to realize that EPC would become more consistent, if not efficient, if they could draw upon the resources of the EC. The two most important developments in this area were the increasing involvement of the Commission, and to a lesser extent, the creation of a permanent EPC secretariat.[30] Again, it should be emphasized that, for most of its history, the involvement of EC actors and the secretariat was far less important than the mechanisms of transgovernmentalism and rule codification. But the limited involvement described in this section set the stage for more far-reaching institutional changes at Maastricht.

4.1. The European Commission

Between the Luxembourg Compromise and the creation of EPC and the European Council, the Commission was in the midst of losing authority vis-à-vis EC member-states. Likewise, the Commission was highly suspicious of the way both EPC and the European Council could reduce its own authority in EC affairs and contaminate the EC with intergovernmentalism. In general, the Commission was more often concerned with expanding (or at least preserving) its given authority in other EC policy domains than with extending its participation in political cooperation. Thus, the Commission played a fairly limited role in EPC. The privileged role of Foreign Ministries in EPC tended to strengthen them against the Commission in this domain. As an issue-area, EPC also was not very conducive to the kind of power the Commission has been especially adept at mobilizing: generating support for European policies among businesses and other interest groups.

[29] For comparison, see Chs. 5 and 8.

[30] The EP and ECJ played very limited roles in the institutionalization of EPC, although the EP has been a vocal advocate of making political cooperation a more supranational process (such as the "Report on European Political Cooperation and the Role of the European Parliament" (Elles Report), *EP Working Document*, 1981: 1–335/81; and the "Draft Treaty on European Union" (1984), prepared by the EP. For details on the EP, see Corbett (1989) and Elles (1990). ECJ rulings established a non-restrictive view of sanctions under Art. 113, which enabled them to be used with EPC (the first of the so-called EC–EPC "parallel powers"). Other ECJ cases expanded the EC's right to be a member of certain international organizations, its treaty-making powers, and the use of export controls for political ends (Pescatore 1979; Govaere and Eeckhout 1992; Cheyne 1994; Sack 1995). These are the primary ECJ decisions that indirectly affected the EPC policy process.

Yet Commission involvement in the early years of EPC was vital at least for one reason: making sure EPC decisions did not adversely affect the Community. Again, most small states appreciated the Commission's role as an independent functional link between EPC and the EC. At first it could be invited to EPC discussions as an observer or source of expertise on the EC, but nothing more. It performed such a role during the first EPC initiatives: advising CSCE and Euro-Arab dialogue working groups on economic cooperation (against the wishes of France). Also, the fact that trade policy for Eastern Europe had been taken over by the EC at the beginning of 1973 provided the Commission with a convenient procedural excuse to be consulted on CSCE issues, and it attempted to make the most of this opening. But Commission officials were admitted to EPC meetings only when specific points relevant to the EC were on the table, then they were often quickly ushered out. Also, the Commission was not even linked to the COREU network until 1981, although it was occasionally supplied with COREUs by "EC-friendly" diplomats.[31]

From the Commission's highly circumscribed role in EPC at first, it became more valued and involved in the policy process. Its status changed from that of an invited guest to that of an active participant, not least because of its neutral position toward EPC members. Involvement here took several forms. First, the Commission was especially useful as a source of information and expertise, especially when states were considering the use of EC tools for EPC purposes. It became an alternative resource when departments in Foreign Ministries neglected to share information with each other, or when Foreign Ministries did not share information with other ministries involved in EC affairs (due, for example, to bureaucratic rivalries or time constraints).[32] It was especially helpful in filling the information gap between states' Foreign Ministries and their economics ministries, and the information gap in Brussels between the Committee of Permanent Representatives and EPC officials when EC tools were being considered since the Commission's representative was usually the only person to participate in both fora. In addition to ensuring "consistency" of EPC and EC external policies (Art. 30.3, SEA), the Commission was charged with monitoring state behavior when EC/EPC mixed agreements (such as the control of dual-use goods for political ends) were established.

Second, the Commission became an informal policy entrepreneur (albeit a subtle one), as it did not enjoy the same exclusive "right of initiative" it held in the EC and could not launch EPC actions on its own. It granted emergency economic aid in part for political reasons (Cyprus and Portugal were notable early efforts) and suspended economic negotiations on others (Spain). It also con-

[31] The Benelux states were especially generous in providing the Commission with EPC information that other states had wanted to keep from it. Interviews, Brussels, 1995–6.

[32] In most EC states EPC was (and the CFSP still is) handled by the political section of the Foreign Ministry and EC affairs were handled by the economics section. Only Britain and Belgium included European Correspondents in the economics or EC departments. In anticipation of the Treaty on European Union, Denmark combined parts of its economics and political departments into a unit for Northern hemisphere/EU affairs in 1991. Sweden also merged its departments in spring 1996 after joining the EU.

trolled the disbursement of development aid thanks to the Lomé Convention and other agreements, and occasionally made such aid subject to political criteria on an ad hoc basis. These efforts were not always controlled or even approved within the EPC framework, and some (such as the Ortoli declaration on Spain) were more the result of individual Commissioner action than that of the body as a whole. In part to prevent it from becoming a "loose cannon" in EC foreign policy,[33] the London Report finally called for Commission involvement in all EPC working groups (which had been taking place already to some extent). The SEA slightly expanded this by permitting a formal association with the Commission in all EPC discussions (Art. 30.3).

Third, the Commission began to represent the EC abroad on EPC matters. Unanimity was usually necessary for the Presidency to contact a third country; this could be difficult to achieve. A compromise in 1983 first allowed the Commission to accompany the Presidency in contacts with third countries at the ministerial and directorial levels, and to be involved in all regional groupings (Regelsberger 1991). The Commission now has well over 100 diplomatic missions and is continually opening new ones; its foreign network is more extensive than that of many member-states. The Commission was increasingly lobbied by outside actors to undertake EPC initiatives, and it received diplomats and other leaders from non-EC states. It became an especially important actor when member-states chose to delegate to it external responsibilities which inevitably allowed it to use both economic and political criteria to make its decisions. This occurred during the development of the Mediterranean policy noted above, and later with the Commission's control of the huge PHARE and TACIS programs used to disburse billions of European Currency Units (ECUs) to Eastern Europe and the former Soviet Union after 1989.

Finally, EPC affected the Commission as well. It was increasingly expected to take into consideration a more comprehensive approach to problems of democracy, stability, and development rather than view only the economic dimensions of issues facing the EC. Its position between the EC and EPC had a general stabilizing effect on the EC's external relations, which compensated for the lack of continuous attention by the European Council. It recognized the potential for mutual gains when the EC and EPC acted in unison. Although its position markedly improved in EPC, the Commission never had any real autonomy in this domain; its power here always rested on the evolving attitudes and goodwill of member-states. The holder of the Presidency in particular largely controlled how much influence the Commission had in EPC (Nuttall 1988, 1996; Cameron 1997). Thus it would be an exaggeration to say that the Commission was an instrumental actor in the institutional development of EPC, although its position has improved since the late 1980s and the Treaty on European Union.

---

[33] French Foreign Minister Claude Cheysson, a former Commissioner, is believed to have played a major role in permitting such involvement of the Commission in EPC. Interviews, Brussels, 1996.

4.2. EPC secretariat

As noted, EPC lacked its own bureaucracy for many years; governments intended it to be self-administering. Although a secretariat was discussed when EPC was founded, enough states opposed this to prevent the creation of any permanent staff. However, the expansion of the EPC agenda, the increased burden placed on the Presidency by such an agenda, and the limitation felt by small states when they held the Presidency resulted in some important informal changes which led to a permanent secretariat for EPC. Although it was not an EC institution at first and it played a limited role, in recent years this body has become part of the EC's institutional structure.

The secretariat had its roots in the informal "troika" practice of sharing some of the burden of the Presidency among the previous, current, and following holders of the office. This developed in the 1970s in part to support the Euro-Arab dialogue. In 1977 EC states quietly adopted the practice of seconding a few of their junior officials to the next Presidency state as a support team to assist with the transition. This practice of lending diplomats was formalized in the London Report (section 10) and it became especially useful to help maintain EC/EPC contacts with Turkey after the accession of Greece to the EC. It also helped educate officials about the national foreign ministries of their EPC partners (Nuttall 1992). Over the next several years an intense debate raged over whether to create a permanent secretariat to do preparatory work for EPC and to reduce the load on the Presidency country. The creation of an EPC working group of policy planners under the German Presidency in 1983 helped, but the question of a secretariat was not resolved until the SEA in 1986 when France finally accepted that the secretariat would serve EPC, not the European Council, and it gave up its long-held insistence that any EPC secretariat must be based in Paris.

Indeed, the secretariat was the SEA's most important and controversial organizational change, one which took years of intense debate. The idea posed an especially difficult problem for small states: they often needed help during their Presidencies, but were still wary of any permanent EPC institution. Hence, its tasks at first were administrative and organizational, it was based in Brussels, and it was supposed to serve the Presidency (or the Political Committee). It consisted of only five diplomatic officials plus a head, supported by a small administrative staff; all were seconded from national foreign ministries. It was not nearly as strong as Franco-German proposals had suggested, with no budget or authority of its own. Nor was it involved in political dialogues or actions.[34] The head of the secretariat did not emerge as an influential neutral policy-broker; he had limited personal autonomy which always depended on the Presidency state.

---

[34] The EPC Secretariat is described in the "Decision of 28 February 1986 by EC foreign ministers meeting in the framework of European Political Cooperation on the occasion of the signing of the Single European Act," *EPC Bulletin*, 1986, Doc 86/090.

But the secretariat did engage in some limited conceptual work, such as drafting texts and preparing speeches for the Presidency. It also drafted responses to the growing number of questions asked by the European Parliament (EP) about EPC, an important example of how actions of one EC actor helped justify the creation of another institution to ensure the consistency of replies to the questions. The head of the secretariat also regularly appeared before the EP's relevant committees to discuss EPC issues. The secretariat competed to some extent with the European Correspondents in national capitals, although a beneficial working relationship eventually developed between them, and it became important as an institutional memory for EPC beyond the *coutumier* and *recueil* collections. As Regelsberger (1993; also see Da Costa Pereira 1988) has noted, after the SEA a gradual integration of the secretariat's personnel with the external activities of the Presidency could be observed, and there was concern that secretariat decisions may have unexpected external repercussions.

In sum, I have shown how the institutionalization of EPC proceeded along three dimensions: the development of a decentralized but complex and resilient transgovernmental network; the codification of EPC habits as rules; and the involvement in EPC of entrenched EC actors such as the Commission. Trust, habits, and interests emerged mainly through a distinctive set of diplomatic ties at all levels of government. Communication and the lending of officials to each other provided an environment conducive to the establishment of rules. After habits proved their practical usefulness to the officials involved in the system, governments were more likely to treat such customs as binding rules and to accept that they be codified as legal rules. These rules in turn increasingly involved the EC itself and EPC became a valuable component of European integration. However, in recent years the gains achieved in EPC have been threatened by internal and external pressures as its members attempted to formally institutionalize this pragmatic, informal system into a Common Foreign and Security Policy (CFSP). How innovative and successful has the transition from EPC to the CFSP been? It is to this final question that I now turn.

5. Toward Supranationalization?
The CFSP from Maastricht to the IGC

The Treaty on European Union (TEU, or Maastricht Treaty) brought foreign policy cooperation closer to the European Community than ever before. Although the CFSP is much less ambitious than many of the convenors of the Intergovernmental Conference on Political Union had hoped (Baun 1995–6; Corbett 1992; Laursen and Vanhoonacker 1992), it does include several important, though incremental, changes to foreign policy cooperation in Europe. These should not be interpreted, however, as major moves toward supranationalization. Like the SEA before it, the TEU's provisions on the CFSP (Title V) are generally based on a set of existing practices established by informal custom. Its decision-making rules still deliberately set it apart from those of the EC, and the most significant changes are still vague enough to cause confusion and debate among officials when CFSP actions are taken (Nuttall 1993; Eaton 1994; Edwards and Nuttall 1994).

In general, the TEU reflects some degree of progression along the three dimensions of institutionalization mentioned above. The transgovernmental network was enhanced by centralizing the links between governments in Brussels: the Committee of Permanent Representatives (COREPER) now prepares all Council meetings, and it has the last word to ensure consistency between its preparation of EC matters and the PoCo's preparation of CFSP matters. To aid COREPER in this task, "CFSP counsellors" were established by each member government and relevant EC and EPC working groups were merged. Procedural changes in voting and budgeting were instituted, and rules on security and consistency were enshrined in the TEU. The Commission reorganized and expanded its external relations directorate (creating DG-IA) to accommodate the CFSP.[35] Additionally, in a decision taken immediately after Maastricht, the Lisbon European Council (June 26–7, 1992) defined a number of specific geographical and functional areas open to joint action in the CFSP. When the CFSP entered into effect in November 1993, these areas had been made the subject of the first CFSP joint actions. Finally, the old EPC secretariat was formally attached to the Council of Ministers and directed to serve it, not to the Presidency alone.

However, the CFSP clearly did not meet the expectations of officials, observers, or citizens—all of whom now find the CFSP policy process confusing and inefficient. Many critics have also pointed to a number of problems inherent in the institutional design of the CFSP.[36] In general, the TEU's dual structure for external relations (the EC and the CFSP) opened up a new battle between intergovernmental and supranational visions of political cooperation. Since the wording of Maastricht was unclear on a number of issues (like EPC before it), states fear that any new decisions will set precedents for the CFSP which may bind them later, or will involve the Commission or EP to a greater degree than they would like. The fact that the Commission and Council legal services are deliberately attempting to legalize far more vigorously than under EPC/CFSP decisions and set precedents exacerbates this fear. Difficult yet valuable experiments in creating "model common positions" and EC and CFSP "mixed agreements" have been attempted to avoid tedious, time-consuming debates over the wording of texts and the choice of voting procedures.[37]

[35] "*Creation du groupe de conseillers PESC,*" internal COREPER document, 26 July 1994. This change was based on a decision of the Political Directors on 1/2 July 1994, "Recommendations of the Political Committee to the General Affairs Council," internal Council document, 18 July 1994. Interviews, Brussels, 1995–6. Also see Nuttall (1995).

[36] For a more detailed analysis of CFSP performance, problems, and prospects, see Holland (1997); Regelsberger *et al.* (1997); Smith (1998*a*, 1998*b*).

[37] See the "*Mode d'emploi concernant les positions communes sur la base de l'Article J.2 du Traite sur l'Union Europeenne,*" internal Council document 5194/95 of 6 Mar. 1995. Interviews, Brussels, 1995–6.

Unsurprisingly, qualified majority voting for the CFSP has not been successfully attempted, although this is one of the TEU's most important CFSP provisions (Art. J.3). Even in seemingly uncontroversial areas (such as disbursing
previously set-aside CFSP funds for Mostar), decision-making and funding
problems have resulted in money being taken "illegally" from existing EC
budgets on an ad hoc basis to avoid having to create a permanent CFSP line in
the budget which the EP can control. While the CFSP line is now part of the
Commission's budget, CFSP disbursements still have to be approved by the EP
(Monar 1997). The system has also seen Council jealously over Commission involvement in security-related areas, which has limited the number of security-
related CFSP actions. Finally, officials complain that the informal, club-like
atmosphere of EPC has been damaged by the legalization and bureaucratiza-
tion of foreign policy cooperation. This change of policymaking style and the
sensitivity of states to legal precedents makes CFSP decision-making a far more
demanding and contentious process than that of EPC.

Maastricht, then, left much to be desired among those who are anxious for a
more forceful EU political presence. The present system for foreign policy cooperation is still one designed for a dozen members at most. The CFSP does not
enable the EU to focus its formidable economic resources quickly, consistently,
and effectively to meet external challenges. Homogeneity, flexibility, and in-
formality were hallmarks of EPC, but these characteristics are being threatened
in the new EU. The TEU also demonstrates the extent to which Commission
involvement in a European policy area is necessary to make the process more
efficient if not supranational. Commission influence in turn depends on its
ability to mobilize support among domestic actors, who are usually more concerned with socioeconomic problems than with foreign policy.[38] The Commission's role vis-à-vis the East in development and enlargement policy, might
enhance its influence—though indirectly and in the long run—over the CFSP,
but a few member-states are still on the defensive.

Finally, the TEU shows how institutional changes can backfire, as they
disrupted the fairly harmonious EPC with ideological disputes about CFSP
procedures and the new division of labor. The dual structures of the CFSP and
the EC now conflict, with the PoCo and COREPER unsure of their specific roles
and often unable to resolve differences of opinion. Some states are still determined to avoid serious institutional changes (such as majority voting, involvement of the ECJ, or effective compliance mechanisms) to meet these concerns.
It is still questionable whether the CFSP will lead to a full-scale common European external policy or merely improve the coordination of national foreign
policies started under EPC. Thus, during the 1996–7 IGC, governments looked
to (among other ideas) changes in CFSP decision-making rules, a permanent

---

[38] The Commission has, however, turned its attention to defense equipment cooperation,
where it may be able to influence support for a European-wide security and defense policy
through the "backdoors" of industrial policy and the single market. See the *Commission Communication on the Challenges Facing the European Defence Industry*, released by the Commission's
Spokesman's Service, Brussels, 25 Jan. 1996.

CFSP policy-planning and analysis unit, regularly using EC funds for the CFSP, and gradually merging the EU and WEU to enhance the CFSP and prepare the EU for the next enlargement. Yet the fact that the ECJ is still excluded from the CFSP lends credence to the view that states truly fear the unpredictable power of the ECJ to advance integration (by "judicializing" diplomatic processes) further than governments would like.

6. Conclusion

The case of EPC reveals two fascinating tendencies. It shows that, if governments are insulated, and domestic interest or pressure is absent in a policy area, EC actors are indeed less able and willing to expand their authority (or they expand it very slowly). EPC also shows, however, that intergovernmental systems can still be altered with rules that are more powerful than analysts appreciate, and that neither the ECJ nor the Commission are necessarily needed to develop and reinforce them. In EPC, institutionalized transgovernmental relations helped produce these rules, not revolutionary EC legal doctrines or Commission activism. Of course, a number of internal and external factors stimulated the EC to act, resulting in policy change. These include: enlargements of the EC, changes in US–Soviet relations; crises; interdependence; the ability of large states to lead the system; the persistence of small states' arguments to legalize EPC; the willingness of "EC-friendly" member-states to include the Commission in EPC; and the efficiency and entrepreneurship of the Commission when it was involved. But without the transgovernmental network, *coutumier* procedures, *recueil* policies, and the establishment of an EPC secretariat to preserve these elements, they stood little chance of lasting longer than each six-month EC Presidency.

Now that defense is included in the CFSP, and the CFSP itself is closer to the EC than ever before, supranationalization of this domain is no longer an impossible goal. It is clear that although the CFSP (like EPC) is understood to be a major component of political union, as a policy process it can not be treated in terms of supranational institutionalism or federalism. Member governments still exert most influence in the CFSP, the CFSP executive (in the form of the Presidency or the Commission) is very weak, and there is little consistency in terms of budgetary resources or ECJ involvement. And domestic politics in the form of public opinion or party influence are unlikely to exert significant pressures for the supranationalization of the CFSP. However, although states still have ultimate authority here, only a small minority of member-states is holding up the transfer of more foreign policy power to EC institutions; even these states recognize the system is necessary but unworkable (or will be, after the next enlargement) if they demand consensus at every stage of the policy process. The EU is a unique, vibrant arena where the demands of interdependence and the limits of institutional engineering continually engage each other. Conventional notions of territoriality, authority, and sovereignty are sadly outmoded in many regions of the world—especially in Western Europe—and the technology of international cooperation, not to mention the analytical tools of international relations, has not caught up with many changes (Ruggie 1993).

In short, sovereignty over foreign policy need not be directly confronted (as it has been in other EC policy areas) with majority voting, regulations, directives, ECJ rulings, or in the glare of public IGC bargains. It can be subverted in some cases, through back channels and at lower levels of administration, so that states find themselves producing common positions and conducting joint operations even while they loudly proclaim their sovereign rights to refrain from doing so. Even if member-states support the improved efficiency brought about by an institutional change, they are often hesitant to commit themselves to such an institution (as during an IGC) for fear of being forced into behavior that was not anticipated when the institution was created, or for fear that the public will think they gave up too much sovereignty to the EC. This is especially true of political cooperation, where it is difficult to measure the costs and benefits of common action and concerns about national sovereignty are intense.

However, when a cooperative system such as the CFSP moves from codifying institutional changes to normal policymaking, the transgovernmental network will resume its operations to effect changes in state behavior and promote cooperation from the "bottom up" in ways I have outlined in this chapter. Thus, the battle over institutional control of political cooperation is not yet over. In fact, now that the Commission, COREPER, and the Parliament have legitimate roles to play (even if they are often prevented from fully playing these roles), the decisive battle between supranational and intergovernmental visions of European political integration may be just beginning.

12

Regional Integration Theory: Understanding Our Past and Anticipating Our Future

JAMES A. CAPORASO

A S regional integration studies enter the fifth decade, they continue to attract the interest and attention of many scholars in international relations and comparative politics. Such interest is testimony to the fact that the bold and somewhat risky experiments of the 1950s have succeeded in surpassing their original objectives of establishing a security community, free-trade area, and common market. Indeed, the very fact that virtually no attention is paid to devise ways to prevent the outbreak of hostilities among countries of Western Europe indicates that the member-states have transcended their original objectives. While integration is a process and not an "end-state," many aspects of that process have been consolidated in structures, rules, and practices that are enduring. There is a European Community (EC) architecture and a EC *acquis* (the accumulated laws and institutions) which, while changeable in principle, present themselves as ongoing structures.

By focusing on the institutional accomplishments of the EC, this book mirrors the vitality of European integration at the same time that it tries to identify and trace its essential movements. Taken collectively, the authors of the chapters, in varying degrees, argue that the EC has experienced broad institutionalization, moving into areas not originally part of the Rome Treaty mandate (environment, consumer affairs) and deep institutionalization (qualified majority voting, judicial interpretations of Art. 119 on "equal pay for equal work," the cooperation and co-decision procedures). The result of these developments is a parametric change in the structure of the EC and its mode of governance which goes far beyond simple quantitative change in particular variables. Deep and broad institutionalization increases the importance of rules (by definition), modifies and constrains power-based bargaining, and shapes the interests and presumptions of states, e.g. the presumption concerning which arena should be used for problem-solving. Power politics is far from gone, but the resources of states—their capabilities, whether political, military, or economic—must increasingly be channeled through European institutions.

Viewed against the impressive achievements of the past, the contributions of this book are less typological, less marked by thick description of particular policy domains, and more motivated by explanatory theory of a distinctive cast. The chapters are less concerned with "What the EC is" (a federation? a regime? a multilevel polity?) than with proposing explanations for why we find variation across important policy areas, across time, and across different institutional settings. The central conceptual device is not the isolated ideal type but rather a continuum running from pure intergovernmental politics (a classic balance of power system) to a supranational polity in which EC institutions possess jurisdiction and authority over the individual member-states in specified policy areas. The form of the supranational polity is an open question. It could be organized along federal lines as explored by Sbragia (1992); it could take the form of islands of regulatory authority corresponding to discrete tasks (Majone 1993, 1994); or it could take the form of a strongly member-state-driven process where delegated authority is carefully circumscribed, monitored, and controlled (Moravcsik 1993). But on balance, the authors spend little time asking whether the EC resembles a state system, a domestic polity, a multilevel polity, or some other idealized mode of governance. Instead, we have tried to move the discussion in the direction of positive theory.

The effort to write explanatory theory, and the commitment to evaluate theoretical claims empirically, implies a dual modesty. Theories cannot be overly abstract, too sweeping in their claims, and cannot ride roughshod over differences in contexts, national situations, policy areas, or historical epochs. A crucial requirement of testable theory is that it generate "middle-level" propositions, specific enough to suggest operational indicators, yet general enough for the empirical results to reassemble at a higher (i.e. more abstract) level,[1] so as not to be isolated from one another. While it may be apparent, it bears emphasizing that all the authors have done original research, thus not relying on yet another opportunistic recycling of data presented by someone else.

In the remainder of this concluding chapter, I focus on three themes inspired by this book. While the individual contributions are obviously important, I do not simply rediscuss them here. The chapters speak for themselves and the editors have done an admirable job of introducing them and tying them together. The three themes are as follows: (i) the growing institutionalization of the EC; (ii) the changing relevance of different theories over time; and (iii) the present state of the theoretical debate.

---

[1] Middle-level theory does not imply the abandonment of either general theory or empirical analysis. Such theories simply attempt to provide an intermediate language to connect the concrete and the general.

1. Growing Importance of Institutions in the EC over Time

An interesting thought experiment is animated by the following question: why is it that the research program of Ernst B. Haas and not that of Karl W. Deutsch came to dominate the field of integration studies? Both men have distinguished scholarly records, are richly steeped in history, and have produced powerful arguments and evidence regarding the processes of national and international integration. The answer to the question of which approach would predominate would not have been so obvious in 1960. Deutsch and his collaborators published *Political Community and the North Atlantic Area* in 1957, a book which advanced powerful insights about integration, insights based on very detailed historical evidence. Deutsch's analysis of the Hanseatic League, the union between Norway and Sweden, relations among cities and regions in Germany and Italy, the formation of modern Switzerland out of smaller and quite autonomous cantons, as well as the emerging prenational capabilities of the American colonies (and later states), all served to place his communication theories on a firmer footing. These historical findings were far from recondite and fragmentary. Quite the opposite. In separate contributions, and not simply as a tautological restatement of the historical data, Deutsch advanced a powerful cybernetic theory of human interaction. It simultaneously placed the individual narratives of state-formation on a firm material basis (economic exchange, migrations, wars, the mobilization and transfer of resources) and symbolic basis (ideas, shared values, the development of a "we-feeling"). Quite contrary to Charles Tilly, Deutsch did not find that "war makes the state, the state makes war" (Tilly 1975). While Haas strongly diminished the importance of ideology, dismissing "Europeanism" as "merely a mood, an ambiance that remains compatible with the attenuated national consciousness" (Haas 1968: p. xxix), Deutsch makes the symbolic content of transactions central.

In addition, the continuing influence of Haas's work cannot be attributed to sociological factors or to subsequent intellectual currents not dictated by his own work. Deutsch as well as Haas had a host of excellent graduate students intent on spreading the word. One has only to mention Hayward Alker, Bruce Russett, William Foltz, Donald Puchala, and Richard Merritt, all of whom followed in the Deutschian tradition and made important contributions of their own.[2] Regarding the subsequent intellectual currents mentioned above, the two primary developments since the main contributions of these two authors are rational choice theory and political economy. The first is orthogonal to the work of Haas and Deutsch. Neither one chose to express himself in this idiom though of course neither rejected the view of individuals as thinly rational. The second development (political economy) is also ambiguous in terms of how it has shaped our subsequent views of these two scholars. If anything, macro-

---

[2] Haas's students include Philippe C. Schmitter and Leon N. Lindberg among others.

political economy (rather than rational-choice political economy) arguably advantaged a more favorable later reading of Deutsch (the focus on exchange, flows of goods and productive factors, his view of the economy as an inter-related system). Finally, Deutsch's central preoccupation with communication, language, and meaning (how people interpret events) situated him nicely to reap the benefits of the linguistic and symbolic "turns" in the social sciences. To put it bluntly, cybernetics and constructivism have natural elective affinities.

The compelling reason is neither sociological nor does it have to do with subsequent intellectual paradigms. The Haasian approach is durable for very good intellectual reasons of its own. It provides a theory of institutions, or at least insists on their importance, to go along with the emphasis on socioeconomic interests as agents of change. Perceptively, Haas himself noted the difference between his approach and that of Deutsch and his collaborators.

This picture of political community differs in some essential respects from the kindred concept of "security community" proposed by some contemporary students of nationalism and community formation. In both formulations, the absence of violence as a means of political action among the participant groups is given a central place. Deutsch's concept, however, does not insist on the presence of a specified institutional structure, contenting itself with the consecration of non-violent means of achieving social change as the major criteria differentiating "community" from ordinary international relations. The scheme used here, by contrast, makes the existence of political institutions capable of translating ideologies into law the cornerstone of the definition (Haas 1958: 4).

Both neoclassical economists and neorealist theory typically carry out their analyses as if institutions did not matter. For the economist the basic model is driven by the interaction of relative scarcities (generating supply conditions) and relative preferences (generating demand conditions) under specified technological constraints. Individuals strive to maximize but they do so within an environment where supply and demand conditions are decided exogenously. Agents inside markets use productive assets (including money) to influence outcomes. Agents inside the interstate system use power. Given the fewness of states, and the concentration of power, strategic interaction is possible, a condition open to economic agents only when the market is distorted (e.g. oligopoly). In both models, rules do not influence outcomes.

When rules are introduced, it becomes clear that actors will behave differently. Some rules are prohibitions (don't sell votes or child labor; don't use chemical weapons); others change relative costs (e.g. rules that require pollution cleanup); and still others make possible exchanges that would not otherwise occur (e.g. rules that specify international property rights more firmly, assuring better enforcement of contracts).

The formation of the European Economic Community (EEC) brought into being a complex institutional architecture, even more so than the formal organizational chart suggests.[3] It fostered an environment among states that

---

[3] For an excellent account of the functioning of the Community Institutions see Noel (1973).

gradually became saturated with rules. The Council of Ministers is a legislative body which adopts or denies regulations and directives in a variety of areas. It is composed of the relevant ministers of each member-state. As such it represents the territorial interests of the states. The state-centric institution is somewhat offset by the Commission, which drafts legislation, helps to establish the agenda, and mediates bargains among the member-states. The European Court of Justice is also a more supranational institution, though the full powers of the Court were certainly not recognized in 1958. Finally, the Rome Treaty provided for a European Parliament, a deliberative body whose representatives were not at the time directly elected.

Along with the Committee of Permanent Representatives and the Economic and Social Committee, the above institutions provided the basic architecture of the EC. However, this architecture was just a shell, a broad framework within which the relations among institutions would play themselves out. Relations between the Council of Ministers and Commission, at once synergistic and competitive, are important in our understanding of the Common Agricultural Policy (CAP) as well as current struggles over the limits of the Commission's power. In addition, the limited role of the ECJ in the early period, before direct effect and superiority of Community law had taken place, and before the full implications of the Art. 177 procedure had been realized, has now given way to a conception of an activist court with power of judicial review, a power which many of the member-state judiciaries do not themselves possess. Indeed, the signal importance of the law, as developed through the ECJ's jurisprudence in conjunction with national courts, was nearly completely missed by political scientists.[4]

Does the growing institutional strength of the EC imply a strong state, i.e. a strong European state? Majone (1997) is correct when he answers this questions in the negative. As Majone points out, the framers of the Rome Treaty were dirigistes. They came from countries where public ownership, government intervention in the economy, and large-scale income redistribution were done as a matter of course (1997: 4). Yet the economic constitution of the EC is progressively liberal. Thus the institutional framework surrounding the European market is regulatory rather than one that advances redistribution, public ownership, and sectoral intervention.

The move to the single European market provides a fascinating story in the history of political economy. The "depolitization of the Common Market" (Majone 1997: 4) opened up a large space for economic exchange beyond the direct reach of state control. Regulation by experts and regulatory commissions replaced public ownership in many cases. As the EC developed, the stress on planning and direct intervention gave way to a more arm's-length emphasis on creating the "right" economic climate (inflation, money supply, stable currency) as well as regulating the economy in such a way as to assure social goals

---

[4] There were numerous lawyers and legal scholars who called our attention to the influence of European law. See Stein (1981) and Weiler (1981, 1991).

other than efficiency. Far from implying the absence of politics or a lessened role for institutions, the expansion of the market in the mid-1980s took advantage of the bargaining power of capital (its mobility and hence increased exit opportunities) to weaken the control of labor over the national market. This point is so basic yet it is often lost in the discussions of the awesome technical efficiency of the single market and the role of the Commission in bringing it about.[5]

The editors of this volume attach importance to the political and institutional dimensions of integration. Integration is not defined as an end state, nor as the construction of a European identity or super-state. The focus instead is on supranational governance, defined as "the competence of the EC to make binding rules in any given political sector." (Stone Sweet and Sandholtz, Chapter 1). Such an approach is cognizant of institutional variation across sectors while at the same time it is open to macro-conceptions of governance that transcend specific issue-areas.

The individual chapters play out this general theme, giving life to the continuum stretching from intergovernmental relations to supranational governance. In Chapter 3, Fligstein and McNichol concern themselves with the institutional architecture of the EU. They take a constitutive approach, focusing on the ways in which policy fields come into being, organizational resources are mobilized, and actors are empowered. Michael Smith (Chapter 11) starts with a hard case in two interrelated senses: first, cooperation in the security field presents the actors with the least harmonious configuration of interests, hence the smallest collective gains to reap (indeed, absolute loss is possible through cooperation); second, the security arena is attached to a very decentralized, if issue-specific, international system where states are most jealous of their sovereignty, where a formal organization does not exist,[6] where no treaty basis has been laid before 1991, and where practically no well-organized societal interests are present to push the process. Even in an institutionally hostile environment, as predicted by both functionalism and Olsonian interest group theory, institutionalization has occurred—often glacially and informally but it has occurred.

In Chapter 8, Mark Pollack examines the contingent autonomy and influence of supranational institutions. He does not argue in favor of or against either but instead attempts to specify the conditions under which autonomy and influence are enhanced and diminished. Institutional agents (of the Commission) may have great discretion, may enjoy asymmetries regarding information of local contexts, and may simply be too costly to monitor. On the other hand, the Council of Ministers or European Council may "rein in" the

---

[5] For a view of the single market which contradicts the view expressed here, see Fligstein (1996).

[6] The North Atlantic Treaty Organization concerns the entire Atlantic world. Its concerns only partially overlap with the countries of the EU. The Organization for Security and Cooperation in Europe (OSCE) is composed of fifty-two countries, many of them outside the Europe identified by the EC, and some not in Europe at all.

Commission or, by rewriting the Treaty, they may more precisely specify the jurisdiction of the ECJ. The point is not to settle the issue once and for all but simply to remind ourselves than any analysis of the EU is by necessity an analysis within a dense institutional context.

2. The Changing Relevance of Different Theories

Theories may be wrong, irrelevant, and/or inadequate. It is important to distinguish among all three. A theory is wrong (unconfirmed, falsified) if its basic explanatory structure does not account for the evidence, holding constant all extraneous factors that might affect the outcome. I do not underestimate the difficulty of knowing when a theory is incorrect, though the conditions are much laxer than those required for confirmation. A theory is irrelevant when applied to an observational domain (i.e. to certain facts) for which it makes no predications. It is of course a metatheoretical mistake to do so but this does not prevent the mistake from being made. Applying dependencia theory to voting compliance in the United Nations as a result of trade reliance is an egregious example of inappropriate application of a theory. Using theories of market competition in oligopolistic settings would yield incorrect predictions not because the theory is wrong but because it is the wrong theory. Thirdly, theories can simply be inadequate (underspecified) in the sense that, taken by themselves, they do not contain enough information to make accurate predictions, even through they may isolate the most important causal factors at work.[7] Nearly all theories are underspecified in the sense that countless factors outside the basic model may affect outcomes.

When Haas wrote *The Obsolescence of Regional Integration Theory* (1975) I believe he had the irrelevance of neofunctionalist theory in mind. Neofunctionalist theory was not so much wrong as simply inapplicable to the circumstances of complex interdependence among advanced capitalist countries. The EC had ceased to be a system in the throes of deep transformation and resembled more a collection of countries pursuing separate goals within a turbulent and interdependent setting. To some, Haas's article signaled the death of integration theory (and integration) but this would be the correct inference only if the events of the 1970s predicted the decline of integration.[8] This is controversial at the very least.

I am not sure if Haas was right. Scholars (Haas included) did not adequately distinguish between the magnitude of values of the explanatory factors in the theory on the one hand (the independent variables) and the validity of the

---

[7] What this implies is that there are other factors lying outside the theory and that these other factors do not function as random disturbance terms. This means that the theory, even if perfectly valid, may yield incorrect predictions, indeed they may even be incorrect on average.

[8] All of this assumes that integration did in fact slow down during the 1970s. On this point see Weiler (1981) and Caporaso and Keeler (1995).

theory on the other. As the values of the explanatory variables become weak, we do not reject the theory; instead we should simply draw out the implications for variation in the phenomena to be explained—generally the smaller the values, the less the impact. Even vanishingly small scores on the independent variables do not present a problem, either theoretically or methodologically. Instead of looking at integration as a set of conditional relationships, scholars in the 1960s and 1970s expected integration to always move forward, and did not specify the conditions under which this would occur and not occur. There was a sense, completely unsubstantiated either theoretically or empirically, that the European Community was a perpetual motion machine, "doomed to succeed" even in the face of statist holding actions such as the "Empty Chair" crisis precipitated by de Gaulle, a *federateur malgré lui*. Thus, when integration slowed down, in the eyes of the theorists, integration theory was thought to be disconfirmed. But rather than being wrong, it was simply less relevant.

As we argue in favor or against particular theories, it rarely occurs to us that our changing subject matter might require more than patchwork repair and refinements at the margins. The EC has changed in important ways. It has gone far beyond its original goals of establishing a free-trade area, customs union, and common agricultural policy. It has added new policy sectors, as Pollack demonstrated so nicely in "Creeping Competences" (1994), has altered inter-institutional relations among the Council of Ministers, Commission, Parliament, and ECJ—not always in a more supranational direction! And it has deepened and elaborated a legal framework that has gone far beyond what most experts (even legal experts) forecast.

Understandably perhaps, a newer generation of scholars, uninspired by debates between intergovernmentalism and neofunctionalism, and bemused by all the fuss over abstract terms such as spillover, sovereignty, autonomy, and a non-territorial approach to problem-solving, struck out on their own. Some of them tried the route of policy analysis (Hix 1994; Heritier 1996). Having grown up with the EC as a fact of life (rather than a novel experiment in international organization), young scholars accept it as a partial polity, within which policymaking can be carried out as if the setting were national. Thus, banking, competition, pharmaceuticals, environment, commercial policy, and social policy can be examined with the standard tools of agenda-setting, coalitions, policymaking, and implementation.

While there is much value in these studies, we should note that for better or worse, many of them have given up the integration project (not a sin of course, and not necessarily even bad for intellectual progress). Some problems are best dealt with by abandoning them. Perhaps the message of the new policy analysts is that "the EC has arrived" and that, therefore, questions of systems-transformation have been supplanted by questions related to the governance of Europe in multiple policy sectors, taking the basic institutional structure of the EC as given. This is certainly a legitimate strategy. To say anything at all, we must take numerous other things as given, and there should be no special pleading about omitting the EC's institutional structure or level of integration.

The policy analysis and sectoral approach will inspire its own critics, some of whom will evaluate policy studies on their own terms, others who will be troubled at what has been left out. On this latter point, both intergovernmentalism and neofunctionalism are in partial agreement, even if the process behind this agreement is unsurprisingly different. Moravcsik, the most vigorous spokesperson of the intergovernmentalist position, would disagree with the assumption that the EC is an institutionalized polity and argue instead that "the EC can be analyzed as a successful intergovernmental regime designed to manage economic interdependence through negotiated policy coordination" (1993: 474). Neofunctionalists, institutionally minded analysts, and those who see the EC from the standpoint of the development of state structures, however different from the Westphalian model, are also likely to be troubled, and for obvious reasons. The EC has made important progress but viewed within the long-term historical framework required for analysis of state-building, such progress is only a beginning. Few would deny the continuing importance of nation-states, whether in the hard-wiring of the EC (the Council of Ministers, the European Council, the numerous oversight committees) or in the grand bargains that provide the Community's foundation (Moravcsik 1993). And for scholars who are interested in Europe's social-democratic character, the unfinished business is indeed enormous (see Streeck and Schmitter 1991; Streeck 1994, 1995b; Rhodes 1995).

In addition to policy analyses and the enhanced role of comparative politics in EC research, a number of other perspectives have been advanced. I can only mention them and not do them justice in this chapter. Gary Marks has proposed a model of multilevel governance (1993) to capture the multiple levels of activity in the Community, the splitting and sometimes sharing of competence, and the importance of interrelationships among levels (see also Marks *et al.* 1996). Along similar lines, Leibfried and Pierson (1995) conceptualize European social policy as taking place within a multitiered polity, which resembles *grosso modo*, the essential institutional features of a federal system. Fritz Scharpf (1988, 1994) has also conceptualized the EC as at least a two-level system and has drawn out some of the prominent decision-making features of such systems. Finally, Alberta Sbragia (1992) has elaborated and applied to Europe the "federal idea," as opposed to distinct federal systems. This maneuver has allowed her to move beyond typological work ("the EC is more like Germany than like the United States") to theoretical and empirical questions of great interest.

In sum, as the EC has developed, the relevance of comparative politics has increased, along with its offshoots in policy analysis, interest groups analysis, and liberal theories of preference formation. Even realism, once a favored theory for why the EEC came into existence in the first place—the Cold War, bipolarity, the US foreign policy goal of a politically secure, wealthy, non-warring Western Europe—has fallen into disuse, not so much wrong as simply irrelevant to most of today's problems in Europe. So the newer approaches have enriched our understanding of the Community's achievements. They have done this in part by reminding us that, while the EC has a long way to go, nevertheless much has been achieved. While these achievements may fall short of political or scholarly goals, for analytical purposes there is enough in place to make analysis of policy and politics among territorially differentiated units worthwhile.

3. The State of the Theoretical Debate

The subject matter of European integration is inherently dynamic. It involves changes over time in the structure of supranational governance, the scope and depth of political institutions, the emergence of regional authority structures, the formation of a European public space, and the relocation of political functions (e.g. interest articulation, interest aggregation at the European level). To develop coherent explanations of constantly moving phenomena presents a daunting challenge.

No one denies that explaining the transformation of a system is more difficult than explaining behavioral outcomes within a fixed structure. Yet, or perhaps precisely because of this, we have innumerable theories of regional integration. Indeed, regional integration studies could uncharitably be criticized for providing a refuge for homeless ideas. And the comparativists lament, "so many variables, so few cases," applies in the extreme here, since there is only one case but numerous proposed explanatory factors. Of course, the EC can be broken down into constituent parts such as policy sectors or issue-arenas and it can be analyzed in terms of how it changes over time. There are various ways to decompose the macrosystem in order to extract variance. However, to the extent that the EC has one overall constitutional structure, or any other macrocharacteristic that is invariant over time and applies to all sectors, the single-case issue is a problem.

It is important to remind ourselves that early scholarship in regional integration was genuinely comparative. Karl Deutsch and his collaborators, in *Political Community and the North Atlantic Arena* (1957), undertook a study of huge historical and comparative dimensions, encompassing the Austro-Hungarian Empire, the nation- and state-building experiences of numerous countries (the UK, the USA, Italy, Switzerland, and Germany among others). Similarly, Ernst Haas, remembered mostly for *The Uniting of Europe*, also wrote about the Nordic Council, the Council of Europe, the North Atlantic Treaty Organization, the Western European Union, and the European Free Trade Association (1966). In addition, along with Philippe Schmitter, Haas explored the dynamics of integration in Latin America (1966). Joseph Nye wrote about African economic integration (1966). Other scholars studied the Caribbean, Central America, and South America.

The increasing interest in EC studies went hand in hand with the exclusion of other cases. As the EC grew more complex, developed its own corpus of policies and laws, and elaborated its own nuanced history, the demands on scholarship also increased. Knowledge of language, history, and institutions now seemed necessary. The same pressures for mastery that characterize area studies bore down on students of European integration. As the sunk costs and asset-specific knowledge of European integration increased, the desire to "leave," even for the purpose of drawing comparisons, decreased.

There are two (non-exclusive) ways to counter these narrowing pressures, one empirical and the other theoretical. Comparativists such as Robert Bates and David Laitin argue that comparative scholarship should be problem-driven. Interest in a problem should direct us to the appropriate "field" setting. This implies that our research include other cases than simply the EC. The second route is theoretical. The distinctive mix of properties that makes for the EC need not prevent us from conceptualizing it in more abstract terms. A first step in the direction of better understanding where the EC "fits" or "what the EC is an instance of" is to reconnect EC studies with theories of comparative politics and international relations (Moravcsik 1993: 473–4).

The two baseline theories on which I comment here are neofunctionalism and liberal intergovernmentalism. Other perspectives, such as policy analysis, do not qualify as full theories of the integration process in the same way. Policy analysis is analysis of public policy within an integrated framework rather than a theory of how integration takes place. Regulation theory, an impressive achievement associated with the names of Majone (1993, 1994, 1997) and Egan (1995), accurately portrays and explains part of the emerging transnational political structure of the EC, i.e. those matters that are capable of being governed through European-wide regulatory structures. What this theory does it does well. But it is far from comprehensive.

Functionalism's primary focus is on the relationship between concrete tasks and practical problem-solving on the one hand, and the territorial organization of political authority on the other. For Mitrany, the territorial structure of the nation-state system was badly adapted to meeting the challenges of the modern world, which often crossed national frontiers in complex ways. For this same reason, Mitrany was against regional union; to him regionalism was simply "territory writ large", a point he made in his polemic against Briand's and Coudenhove-Kalergi's schemes for European union (1930: 457).

The general outlines of neofunctionalism are well known (Haas 1958, 1968; Caporaso and Keeler 1995). Neofunctionalism identifies two important components of the integration process. The first is societal and the second has to do with the importance of international experts and supranational organizations. Functionalists such as Haas and Monnet both felt that the primary stuff of politics was in society. The raw material of political life started with family, factory, school, professional organizations, unions, corporations, and so on. Haas examined the fabric of social life in great detail in *The Uniting of Europe*. Monnet insisted on *unité des faits* (a broad consensus of the societal level) as a precondition of political cooperation.

Societal actors created the demand, the raw material of politics, but demand by itself is not enough. Societal wants do not automatically translate into outcomes or policies, cooperative or otherwise, without an explicit political process. Scholars such as Haas, Schmitter, and Lindberg specified the theoretical no-man's-land between Mitrany's social groups and political integration. They placed great emphasis on rules, institutions, and political organization.

The second component, supranational organizations, is a continuation of the same story. Neofunctionalism joined society's demands to the capacity of supranational organization. This aspect of the theory emphasized the power of the expert, the ability of supranational technocrats to structure the agenda, and the variable ability of the Commission to broker deals. It is important to note that these two theoretical components work together. Without transnational society, there is nothing to fuel the integrating process. As with pluralism, the stuff of politics is ultimately rooted in society. But transnational society, whether organized or not, would be inert and ineffective without some form of leadership, some arena within which politics could give shape to the mass of inchoate demands. This leadership was to be provided by the institutions of the EC, in particular by the Commission.

The appeal of functionalism and neofunctionalism was enormous. It provided a theory of advanced capitalist society which glossed over the conflict between labor and capital in favor of technical areas where problem-solving and cooperation pointed to positive gains. It made a threefold distinction between background conditions, conditions at the time of union, and process conditions, thus anticipating my earlier point about the changing importance of different variables at different points during the integration process. The background conditions suggested where integration was most likely to occur while the process conditions addressed the secondary dynamics, including spillover.

While neofunctionalism held sway during the early period of integration, it soon became apparent that its predictions were insufficient to explain the ups, downs, and plateaus of the integration process. Neofunctionalism seemed to rely on a naive faith that societal demands for cooperation were without limit. This is not necessarily true even with increasing interdependence (powerful groups may be hurt by interdependence) and there is no economic reason (let alone political reason) that interdependence should increase forever. Neofunctionalists badly needed a hypothesis about the secular trend of trade, capital movements, and economic interdependence in general.

Part of the reason that neofunctionalism "failed to generate an enduring research programme" (Moravcsik 1993: 476) is that it did not adequately theorize societal interests; in particular, it did not provide a theoretically productive way of organizing societal interests. Instead, it thought of societal groups as functionally specific or diffuse, controversial or non-controversial, populated by experts or generalists and so on. These early efforts at creating a typology did not work so well, in large part because the criteria used blended together phenomena that were quite different in terms of theoretical implications. By comparison, today we have several schemes for ordering societal interests that seem superior (Lowi's typology of distributive, redistributive, regulatory, and constitutive (Lowi 1964)); and a large number of interest configurations drawn from microeconomics (e.g. coordination, prisoners' dilemma, chicken, assurance games, and so on). These typologies result in more homogeneous groupings and also provide a clearer picture of the incentives facing individuals making decisions.

The second major theory is liberal intergovernmentalism. In a 1993 article, "Preferences and Power in the European Community: A Liberal Intergovernmental Approach," Andrew Moravcsik proposed a two-stage theory of preference formation and intergovernmental bargaining. It has since come to be thought of as a new synthesis in many quarters, bringing together a liberal theory of preference-formation with an intergovernmental focus on hard power-bargaining among states. A core assumption is that states are rational self-interested actors, that they "read" the demands of society (through lobbying), that these demands are somehow aggregated into a preference function for chiefs of government (COGs), and that COGs negotiate over differences in international fora. This approach attempts to capture the best of both worlds: the interests of domestic and transnational society are captured in preferences while governments pursue these preferences in international bargaining. There is no need to choose between state and society. They simply have different roles.

Comparing the societal dimension of liberal intergovernmentalism and neofunctionalism, I would argue that Moravcsik's formulation is superior. Neofunctionalism did look at societal activities, groups, transnational contacts, and even the prospective gains from international cooperation. But neofunctionalism had no explanation for which groups should succeed, form coalitions, mobilize interests, have access to policymakers, and affect policy. The conception of international problem-solving was technocratic and somewhat naive. If there was a problem cutting across frontiers, if there was a felt need, and groups of people aware of their common condition, then tasks would be identified, resources mobilized, and problems solved.

But needs are not always satisfied, even given adequate resources and technology. This may be because the agents who would benefit are not those who decide, or in the case of collective-action problems, failure may be linked to problems of organizing, to opportunism, and to difficulties related to the monitoring and enforcement of agreements. Even when collective, net gains can be reaped, agreement may not be forthcoming.

Moravcsik draws on Olsonian interest-group theory which tells us that the interest-group system is biased against large, diffuse interests, that producers are more likely to be favored than consumers, and that successful collective action is more likely in settings where small groups will be strongly motivated to act since they fully internalize the benefits. This partly ratifies what Schattschneider (1960) already knew, that "in the pluralist heaven the celestial chorus sings with a strong upper class accent." However, Olson's analysis goes beyond the rich–poor divide or the predictions of resource-based theories of power.

The second component of liberal intergovernmentalism relates to negotiations. Liberal theories are useful in understanding how states form their goals but are of little help advancing the story from here. The interplay of interest-group pressures gives way to a second set of dynamics, negotiations—qualitatively distinct from the first. Few would deny the continuing power of states and the hard bargaining among them, even in arenas characterized by high levels of interdependence and institutionalization. States are always calculating opportunities and constraints, even while they are not formally negotiating.

The emphasis on negotiations, and inevitably power, should be welcome to students of integration. Power has been strangely downplayed in the EC. I can see two reasons for backgrounding power. The first reason is that integration studies, as a field, has a "technicist" orientation in a certain sense. The central problem, approached from a self-interested perspective, is how states can coordinate their actions in such a way as to further their joint goals. The task of the analyst is to find solutions which benefit everyone, and to downplay problems which require winners and losers except as second-order phenomena. Regime theory, for example, focuses overwhelmingly on strategies which move the Pareto frontier outward in a northeast direction.

In the final analysis, I would not argue that power is excluded by analyses which focus on mutual gains. Asymmetries in benefits may exist (powerful states may assure it), some states may have the power to shape agendas, to force some things into the decisional arena and keep other things out. These examples may not imply the power of negative sanctions but they do represent power at another level.

A second, but very much related, reason for downplaying power has to do with the nature of the EC itself. As a political system, the EC has avoided highly conflicted areas where redistribution and symbolic clashes reside. The EC is a consensus-seeking system based on rational deliberation, appeals to evidence, and suasion strategies. These strategies are even hardwired into formal voting rules, especially in areas where unanimity is required. Unanimity voting provides the procedural guarantee of the Pareto principle, assuring that no change takes place if even one actor opposes new legislation. This is a "first-cut" principle to be sure, since resistant actors can be bribed to go along by compensating them out of the gains of others. Nevertheless, the veto provides a strong mechanism against new legislation, unless there is very broad, even total agreement.

Thus, to the extent that unanimous agreement is called for, behavioral power (the power to make others comply) will be diminished since any potential loser can prevent action. As we move from unanimity to qualified majority voting (QMV), the power to compel increases, though exactly how is a function of voting weight, linkages to other areas, and coalition partners.

To repeat my main point, regardless of how we conceptualize power, power resources, voting power, go-it-alone power (Gruber 1996)—we are better off with power "in" rather than power "out".

The liberal intergovernmental framework has made contributions regarding preferences and bargaining. Yet it is vulnerable on some grounds and deserves to be interrogated on others. The focus on "major decisions" (Moravcsik 1993: 517) and "celebrated intergovernmental bargains" (1993: 473) should be questioned. Why are major decisions appropriate cases even if the prediction is that this is where hard bargaining is to be found? Good case selection implies that we look where we don't expect the outcome also. Otherwise we run a stronger risk of falsely "proving" our theory. Surely "major decisions" is not a viable, self-contained category, qualitatively set off from other variables. Most sensibly, it would seem to occupy a region on a continuum running from "minor to major" decisions, "consolidating to agenda-setting" decisions or some equivalent. We need to know two things: what is the full continuum on which "major decisions" presumably occupies a special location, and what are some representative cases of major decisions and hopefully minor and intermediate decisions?

A second point is neither criticism nor agreement per se. It involves the interpretation of liberal intergovernmentalism in light of other theories of integration. Liberal intergovernmentalism muddies the waters in terms of a straight-up, comparative evaluation of neofunctionalism and itself. This is due to the way Moravcsik incorporates societal influence (domestic and transnational) into domestic preferences. These preferences draw on the same influences as neofunctionalism. In addition, to a certain extent, liberal intergovernmentalism plays down the societal component of neofunctionalism in favor of the supranational organizational component. By so doing, LIG severs neofunctionalism's organic tie between societal pressures and interests on the one hand, and supranational institutions and leadership on the other. It thus simultaneously deprives neofunctionalism of some of its societal force propelling transnational collaboration, frees itself from systemic realism[9] while still holding on to states as central and sovereign actors, and reattaches society to government bargaining through a stepwise linkage between liberal preference formation and government negotiations. Much that is functionalist terrain is absorbed into LIG and some that is realist is dropped from the intergovernmental model. No one can criticize Moravcsik for pruning and sifting, for getting rid of the weak branches and holding on to the strong. But the lines between classical realism and neofunctionalism have been blurred. Realism can now embrace economic goals, can reject the hierarchy between security and economic issues, and can thoroughly disassociate itself from the systemic determination of preferences.

Finally, I disagree with LIG's assessment that international institutions are relatively unimportant and function mostly as passive devices to reduce the transaction costs and enhance the efficiency of international negotiations and

---

[9] By "systemic realism" I refer to the realism of Waltz, Mearsheimer, and many other classical realists who theorize national preferences as due to the location of states in the international system, particularly the international distribution of power. Moravcsik's version of realism relies upon states, sovereignty, and power bargaining but state leaders are open to a wide variety of motivations, and are likely to be affected by domestic and transnational economic factors more than overall security calculations.

agreements. In part, this is an empirical question to be resolved through research. Moravcsik's theory hasn't ruled this out a priori but it does make predictions that international organizations embody the delegated authority of the member-states, and that these states can instruct, police, monitor, and rein in supranational actors at any time. This point of view is not supported by almost all of the research in this volume. I will not belabor the point here, but will return to it shortly.

Let me now turn to the approach outlined in the volume and try to make three points. The first concerns microfoundations, the second relates to the re-thinking of the relationship between transnational society and supranational institutions, and the third is a commentary on path-dependence.

The editors of this volume, as well as the contributors, secure their analyses on solid microfoundations. Individuals are first situated within their material and symbolic environments and these incentives, motivations, and beliefs are taken as important. Thus, macrobehavior—whether aggregate transactions, political institutionalization, or decision-making—is rooted in the world of individuals.[10] These individuals pursue goals in an environment of inter-dependence which provides opportunities as well as interference. But a central claim, a "first-cut" hypothesis, is that as transnational activity goes up, pres-sures on governments to adjust their policies go up too. Governments can of course resist, pull back from these transactions, try to rewrite the rules govern-ing these transactions, and so on. But they are likely to do so only by bearing increasing costs and this is likely to be intolerable electorally.

The general approach is open to numerous ways of conceptualizing issues, policies, decisions, institutional arenas, and so on. The editors of this volume, as well as many contributors, including myself, are dissatisfied with the typo-logies and categories of both neofunctionalism and liberal intergovernmental-ism. Indeed, perhaps the single biggest misdirection of neofunctionalism was that it prompted us to organize our subject matter on the basis of a number of dichotomies: technical–nontechnical areas, functionally specific–diffuse con-cerns, controversial and noncontroversial issues, etc. Agriculture, security, social policy, and competition are all highly technical but agriculture and security are certainly not non-controversial and do not easily present the pros-pect for collective gains, except at the expense of outsiders. This book has made a break with prior issue typologies and has explored the possibilities of alternat-ive ways of conceptualizing societal interests, some of them based on micro-economic schemes of interest configurations (as in Chapter 4), others that are motivated by sociological conceptions of organizational fields (Chapter 3), and still others who take on issue-areas previously thought to be resistant to cooperation (Chapter 2, social policy; Chapter 11, security) and scrutinize the logic of cooperation in these "hard cases."

The second contribution of this book is that it charts and exploits a different

---

[10] This is an ontological, not a causal proposition. It says nothing regarding whether the source of explanations is individual or social.

link between transnational society and supranational institutions. Contrary to some accounts, liberal intergovernmentalism does take transnational society into account but it funnels the demands through the domestic political processes of the member-states. If transnational factors "count," it is because member-states represent these factors in international negotiations. While not denying the importance of this sequence of factors, this book emphasizes another route. Agents in transnational society, in their attempts to solve problems, may go directly to supranational institutions. This is true to some extent of the direct lobbying activities of interest groups on the Commission. It is also true with regard to the way individuals and groups take their grievances directly to the ECJ. Regarding the transnational relations literature, the crucial point about the ECJ's doctrine of direct effect is that it opens a space for transnational actors at the level of supranational institutions.

The third point concerns path-dependence. A proper understanding of the EC today, as opposed to the EEC in its early years, implies an answer to the following question: what accounts for the direction of the EC's development? The EC has grown in membership, in the scope of its policy competences, and the breadth and depth of its institutions. Analysis of the Community at any point in time, or even comparative statics, is likely to miss much of what the EC is about (a point forcefully made in Chapter 2).

Simplifying greatly, there are two approaches for understanding the temporal path of the EC. The first approach sees the Community's upward movement resulting from a series of exogenous shocks: the political demands of agriculture during the 1950s and 1960s, the global competition with the USA and Japan during the 1970s and 1980s, resulting in the single-market initiatives, and so on. Each time the EC faces a challenge it responds through institutional restructuring and policy changes. These changes, then represent adaptations to shifting pressures from outside and inside. They do not reflect an indigenous internal dynamic and they can be reversed with no greater effort than that required for the initial changes.

The second approach rests on a path-dependence logic (see David 1985; Arthur 1989, 1994; and Chapter 2). Its theory of change is completely different from the one presented above. If a process is path-dependent, its present behavior is heavily constrained by the past. Path-dependent processes are strongly biased in one direction. Reverse movement is possible but there are forces working against it. In physics and chemistry, once certain processes have unfolded (especially if molecular change is involved), going back is nearly impossible. Try, for example, to unmake a stew, starting from finished product and ending with the original ingredients. One mechanism underlying path-dependent processes is increasing returns, the opposite of what one expects in classical and neoclassical economic models. Increasing returns may lie at the bottom of the knowledge invested in the Community's institutions and decision-making procedures, network externalities may exist, and there may be political economies of scale derived from bringing together many issues and processing them within a common framework.

A second mechanism is lock-in. Community policies are often difficult to pass but, once passed, they are difficult to revert to the former status quo. This is simply because the rules operate in such a way as to inhibit change. Strictly speaking, there is no asymmetry here. All that we have said is that "it is difficult to do and difficult to undo." But suppose there is a political process embedded in the EC which brings about change by interpretation of the rules, including the Treaty and secondary legislation. If the ECJ decides that "equal pay for equal work" implies that vacation time, company cars, and pensions must be distributed equally between men and women, then such an interpretation can only be reversed by unanimity of heads of state acting as a constituent assembly.

Rules that make it hard to undo policies, taken along with an activist court, provide a long-term bias in favor of the Community's institutional development. Indeed, the Commission can be reined in and the Council may clip the Court's wings. Yet who can doubt that the Community has grown and Europe continues to be transformed?

BIBLIOGRAPHY

European Community Legislation

Commission Directive 88/301/EEC, *of 16 May 1988, on competition in the markets in tele-communications terminal equipment.*

Commission Directive 90/388/EEC, *of 28 June 1990, on competition in the markets for telecommunications services.*

Commission Directive 94/46/EEC *amending* Directive 88/301/EEC *and* Directive 90/388/EEC *in particular with regard to satellite communications.*

Council Directive 71/305/EEC, *Concerning the Coordination of Procedures for the Award of Public Works Contracts.*

Council Directive 77/62/EEC, *Coordinating Procedures for the Award of Public Supply Contracts.*

Council Directive 86/361/EEC *on the initial stage of the mutual recognition of type approval for telecommunications terminal equipment.*

Council Directive 91/263/EEC *on the approximation of laws of the Member States concerning telecommunications terminal equipment, including the mutual recognition of their conformity.*

Council Regulation 428/89/EEC of 20 February 1989, OJL 50/1/89.

Council Resolution 92/C8/01 *of December 1991 on the development of the common market for satellite communications services and equipment.*

Council Resolution 93/C213/EEC *on the review of the situation in the telecommunications sector.*

European Court of Justice Decisions

ECJ (1963). Van Gend en Loos, Case 26/62, *ECR* 1963: 1.

——(1964). Costa, Case 6/64, *ECR* 1964: 585.

——(1974a). Van Duyn, Case 41/74, *ECR* 1974: 1337.

——(1974b). Dassonville, Case 8/74, *ECR* 1974: 837.

——(1974c). French Merchant Seamen, Case 167/73, *ECR* 1974: 359.

——(1976). Defrenne II, Case 43/75, *ECR* 1976: 455.

——(1978). Simmenthal, Case 106/77, *ECR* 1978: 629.

——(1979). Cassis de Dijon, Case 120/78, *ECR* 1979: 649.

——(1981). Jenkins, Case 96/80, *ECR* 1981: 911.

——(1982). Commission *v.* UK, Case 61/81, *ECR* 1982: 2601.

——(1984). Von Colson, Case 14/83, *ECR* 1984: 1891.

——(1985a). Italy *v.* Commission, Case 41/83, *ECR* 1985: 873.

——(1985b). CBEM, Case 311/84, *ECR* 1985: 3261.

——(1985c). European Parliament *v.* Council of Ministers, Case 13/83, *ECR* 1985: 1513.

——(1986a). Marshall (I), Case 152/84, *ECR* 1986: 723.

——(1986b). Nouvelles Frontières, Joined Cases 209–213/84, *ECR* 1986: 1425.

——(1990a). Barber, Case 262/88, *ECR* 1990: 1889.

——(1990b). Marleasing, Case C-106/89, *ECR* 1990: I-4135.

——(1990c). Hertz, Case, 179/88, *ECR* 1990: 3979.

ECJ (1991*a*). Francovich, Case C-6 & 9/90, *ECR* 1991: I-5357.

——(1991*b*). Dekker, Case 177/88, *ECR* 1990: 3941.

——(1991*c*). Höfner, Case 41/90, *ECR* 1991: I-1979.

——(1991*d*). ERT, Case 260/89, *ECR* 1991: I-2925.

——(1991*e*). France *v.* Commission, Case 202/88, *ECR* 1991: I-1223.

——(1992). Spain, Belgium and Italy *v.* Commission, Joined Cases C-271/90, C-281/90 and C-289/90, *ECR* 1992: I-5833.

——(1993*a*). Marshall II, Case 271/91, *ECR* 1993: 4367.

——(1993*b*). Lagauche, Joined Cases C-46/91 and C-93/91, *ECR* 1993: I-5267.

——(1993*c*). Ministére Public Decoster, Case 69/91, *ECR* 1993: I-5335.

——(1993*d*). Ministére Public *v.* Taillandier, Case 92/91, *ECR* 1993: I-5383.

——(1994). Webb, Case 32/93, *ECR* 1994: 3567.

Other Documents

Commission of the European Communities (CEC) (Serial). *Directory of the Commission of the European Community*. Luxembourg: Office for Official Publications of the European Communities.

——(1969). *Memorandum of the Commission to the Council on the Coordination of Economic Policies and Monetary Cooperation within the Community, 15 February 1969*. Luxembourg: Office for Official Publications of the European Communities.

——(1979). Commission of the European Communities: *Air Transport: A Community Approach*. Bulletin of the European Communities, Supplement 5/79. Luxembourg: Office for Official Publications of the European Communities.

——(1983). *Communication from the Commission to the Council on Telecommunications: Lines of Action*. COM (83) 573.

——(1984*a*). *Civil Aviation Memorandum No. 2, Progress towards the Development of a Community Air Transport Policy*. COM (84) 72.

——(1984*b*). *Communication from the Commission to the Council on Telecommunications: Lines of Action*. COM (84) 277.

——(1985*a*). *On the Main Results of the Fifth Meeting of the Conference on the Parties to the Convention on International Trade in Endangered Species of Wild Fauna and Flora*. COM (85) 729.

——(1985*b*). *Concerning the Negotiation for a Global Framework Convention on the Protection of the Ozone Layer*. COM (85) 8.

——(1987*a*). *Treaties Establishing the European Communities*. Luxembourg: Office for Official Publications of the European Communities.

——(1987*b*). *Towards a Dynamic European Economy: Green Paper on the Development of the Common Market for Telecommunications Services and Equipment*. COM (87) 290.

——(1988). *The Community Budget: The Facts in Figures*. Luxembourg: Office for Official Publications of the European Communities.

——(1989). *Relations between the European Community and International Organizations*. Luxembourg: Office for Official Publications of the European Communities.

——(1990). *Green Paper on a Common Approach in the Field of Satellite Communications in the European Community*. COM (90) 490.

——(1992). *Treaty on European Union*. Luxembourg: Office for Official Publications of the European Communities.

——(1993*a*). *The Community Budget: The Facts in Figures*. Luxembourg: Office for Official Publications of the European Communities.

——(1993b). *Community Initiatives*. Luxembourg: Office for Official Publications of the European Communities.

——(1993c). *Communication on the Consultation on the Review of the situation in the telecommunications services sector*. COM (93) 159.

——(1993d). *RACE 1993*. Brussels.

——(1994a). *The Future of Community Initiatives under the Structural Funds*. COM (94) 46.

——(1994b) *Guide to the Community Initiatives*, 1st edn. Luxembourg: Office for Official Publications of the European Communities.

——(1994c). *Green Paper on the Liberalization of Telecommunications Infrastructure and Cable Television Networks. Part One: Principles and Timetable*. COM (94) 440.

——(1994d). *Towards the Personal Communications Environment: Green Paper on a Common Approach in the Field of Mobile and Personal Communications in the European Union*. COM (94) 145.

——(1994e). *Green Paper on the Liberalization of Telecommunications Infrastructure and Cable Television Networks. Part Two: A Common Approach to the Provision of Infrastructure for Telecommunications in the European Union*. COM (94) 682.

——(1995a). *Directory of Community Legislation in Force*. Luxembourg: Office for Official Publications of the European Communities.

——(1995b). *RACE 1995*. Brussels.

——(1995c). *Conclusions of the Presidency, Cannes, 26–27 June 1995. Bulletin of the European Union no. 6*. Luxembourg: Office for Official Publications of the European Communities.

——(1995d). *Conclusions of the Presidency, Madrid, 15–16 December 1995. Bulletin of the European Union no. 12*. Luxembourg: Office for Official Publications of the European Communities.

——(1996a). *Top Decision Makers' Survey: Summary Report*. Luxembourg: Office for Official Publications of the European Communities.

——(1996b). *Commission Communication on the Challenges facing the European Defence Industry*. Brussels: Commission's Spokesman's Service.

——(1997a). *Eurobarometer 46: Autumn 1996*. Luxembourg: Office for Official Publications of the European Communities.

——(1997b). *European Economy, 1997. Broad Economic Policy Guidelines, 64/1997*. Luxembourg: Office for Official Publications of the European Communities.

Committee for the Study of Economic and Monetary Union (1989). *Report on Economic and Monetary Union in the European Community (with Collection of Papers)*. Luxembourg: Office for Official Publications of the European Communities.

Committee of Governors of the Central Banks of the Member States of the European Economic Community (1987). *Report on the Strengthening of the EMS: Memorandum to Council of Economics and Finance Ministers*. Basle: Bank for International Settlements.

——(1990). *Draft Statute of the European System of Central Banks and of the European Central Bank*. Basle: Bank for International Settlements.

Council of Ministers of the European Communities (Serial). *Report on the Activities of the European Council of Ministers*. Luxembourg: Office for Official Publications of the European Communities.

——(Serial). *Guide to the Council of Ministers*. Luxembourg: Office for Official Publications of the European Communities.

——(1996). *105th Council Meeting, Environment* (4 March 1996), 5309/96 (Presse 45). Brussels.

European Communities (1970). *Report to the Council and the Commission on the Realisation by Stages of Economic and Monetary Union in the Community. Supplement to Bulletin II–1970 of the European Communities.* Luxembourg: Office for Official Publications of the European Communities.

European Council (1986). *Presidency Conclusions.* European Council 34th Meeting (internal EC documentation).

European Monetary Institute (1994). *Annual Report 1994.* Frankfurt am Main: EMI.

——(1995*a*). *Annual Report 1995.* Frankfurt am Main: EMI.

——(1995*b*). *The Changeover to the Single Currency.* Frankfurt am Main: EMI.

——(1996). *Progress towards Convergence 1996.* Frankfurt am Main: EMI.

House of Lords (1980). *Select Committee Report on the European Communities. European Air Fares.* London: HMSO.

——(1985). *Select Committee Report on the European Communities. European Air Transport Policy: Report of the Select Committee on the European Communities.* London: HMSO.

NATO (1996). *Final Communiqué, Ministerial Meeting of the North Atlantic Council, Berlin.* Brussels: Press and Information Service.

General

Agence Europe (1993) 15 July.

Agra Europe (1991) 15 February.

Alker, H. R., and Haas, P. (1993). "The Rise of Global Ecopolitics," in N. Choucri (ed.), *Global Accord: Environmental Challenges and International Responses.* Cambridge, Mass.: MIT Press.

Allen, D. (1982). "European Political Cooperation and the Euro-Arab Dialogue," in D. Allen, R. Rummel, and W. Wessels (eds.), *European Political Cooperation: Toward a Foreign Policy for Western Europe.* London: Butterworths.

——(1983). "Managing the Common Market: The Community Competition Policy," in W. Wallace, H. Wallace, and C. Webb (eds.), *Policy-Making in the European Community.* London: John Wiley & Sons.

——(1996). "Competition Policy: Policing the Single Market," in H. Wallace and W. Wallace (eds.), *Policy-Making in the European Union.* Oxford: Oxford University Press.

——Rummel, R., and Wessels, W. (eds.). (1982). *European Political Cooperation: Toward a Foreign Policy for Western Europe.* London: Butterworths.

——and Smith, M. (1994). "External Policy Developments." *Journal of Common Market Studies,* 32: 67–86.

——and Wallace, W. (1982). "European Political Cooperation: The Historical and Contemporary Background," in D. Allen, R. Rummel, and W. Wessels (eds.), *European Political Cooperation: Toward a Foreign Policy for Western Europe.* London: Butterworths.

Alter, K. J. (1996). "The European Court's Political Power: The Emergence of an Authoritative International Court in the European Union." *West European Politics,* 19: 458–87.

——and Meunier-Aitsahalia, S. (1994). "Judicial Politics in the European Community: European Integration and the Pathbreaking Cassis de Dijon Decision." *Comparative Political Studies,* 26: 535–61.

Amato, G. (1988). *Un Motore per lo SME: Memorandum to the Council of Economic and Finance Ministers.* Rome: Ministry of Finance, 23 Feb. 1988.

Anderson, C., and Kaltenthaler, K. (1995). "The Dynamics of Public Opinion toward European Integration." *European Journal of International Relations,* 2: 175–99.

Anderson, J. J. (1995). "The State of the (European) Union: From the Single Market to Maastricht, from Singular Events to General Theories." *World Politics,* 47: 441–65.

Anderson, S., and Eliassen, K. (1991). "European Community Lobbying." *European Journal of Political Research*, 20: 173–87.

Art, R. (1996). "Why Western Europe Needs the United States and NATO." *Political Science Quarterly*, 111: 1–39.

Arthur, W. B. (1988). "Self-Reinforcing Mechanisms in Economics," in P. W. Anderson, K. J. Arrow, and D. Pines (eds.), *The Economy as an Evolving Complex System*. Reading: Addison-Wesley.

——(1989). "Competing Technologies, Increasing Returns, and Lock-In by Historical Events." *Economic Journal*, 99: 116–31.

——(1994). Increasing Returns and Path Dependence in the Economy. Ann Arbor: University of Michigan Press.

Bachrach, P., and Baratz, M. (1962). "Two Faces of Power." *American Political Science Review*, 56: 947–52.

Balladur, E. (1988). *The Monetary Construction of Europe: Memorandum from the Minister of Finance to the Council of Economic and Finance Ministers*. Paris: Ministry of Economics and Finance, 8 Jan. 1988.

Bar, F., and Borrus, M. (1987). "From Public Access to Private Connections: Network Policy and National Advantage." *Berkeley Roundtable on the International Economy Working Paper* 28. Berkeley.

Barber, L. (1996). "Brussels Seeks Control of Trade Deals." *Financial Times*, 5 Sept.

Bates, R. (1987). "Contra Contractarianism: Some Reflections on the New Institutionalism." *Politics and Society*, 16: 387–401.

Baun, M. J. (1995–6). "The Maastricht Treaty as High Politics: Germany, France, and European Integration." *Political Science Quarterly*, 110: 605–24.

Beck, N., and Katz, J. N. (1995). "What to Do (and Not to Do) with Time Series Cross-Section Data." *American Political Science Review*, 89: 634–47.

Beer, S. H. (1978). "The Modernization of American Federalism." *Publius*, 3: 53–95.

Benedick, R. E. (1991). *Ozone Diplomacy: New Directions in Safeguarding the Planet*. Cambridge, Mass.: Harvard University Press.

Berejikian, J. (1997). "The Gains Debate: Framing State Choice." *American Political Science Review*, 91: 789–806.

Berenz, C. (1994). "Hat die betriebliche Alterversorgung zukunftig noch eine Chance?" *Neue Zeitschrift fur Arbeitsrecht*, 11: 433–8.

Berlin, D. (1992). "Interactions between the Lawmaker and the Judiciary within the EC." *Legal Issues of European Integration*, 17: 17–48.

Bishop, M. (1993). *A Fairer Deal? Deregulation and Lower Air Fares—The Facts, A Report by British Midland*. Castle Donnington, UK: Public Affairs Department.

Bodenheimer, S. J. (1967). "The Political Union Debate in Europe: A Case Study in Intergovernmental Diplomacy." *International Organization*, 21: 24–54.

Bonvicini, G. (1982). "The Dual Stucture of EPC and Community Activities: Problems of Coordination," in D. Allen, R. Rummel, and W. Wessels (eds.), *European Political Cooperation: Toward a Foreign Policy for Western Europe*. London: Butterworths.

Boons, F. (1992). "Product-oriented Environmental Policy and Networks: Ecological Aspects of Economic Internationalization." *Environmental Politics*, 4: 84–105.

Brinkhorst, L. J. (1994). "The European Community at UNCED: Lessons to be Drawn for the Future," in D. Curtin and T. Heukels (eds.), *Institutional Dynamics of European Integration*. Dordrecht: Martinus Nijhoff.

Buckley, N. (1996). "Brussels Seeks More Power on Mergers." *Financial Times*, 10 July.

Bulmer, S. (1985). "The European Council's First Decade: Between Interdependence and Domestic Politics." *Journal of Common Market Studies*, 24: 89–104.

——(1991). "Analyzing EPC: The Case for Two-Tier Analysis," in M. Holland (ed.), *The Future of European Political Cooperation: Essays on Theory and Practice*. London: Macmillan.

——(1994a). "The Governance of the European Union: A New Institutionalist Approach." *Journal of Public Policy*, 13/4: 351–80.

——(1994b). "Institutions and Policy Change in the European Communities: The Case of Merger Control." *Public Administration*, 72: 423–44.

——and Wessels, W. (1987). *The European Council: Decision-making in European Politics*. London: Macmillan.

Burley, A.-M., and Mattli, W. (1993). "Europe before the Court: A Political Theory of Legal Integration." *International Organization*, 47: 41–76.

Caldeira, G. A., and Gibson, J. L. (1995). "The Legitimacy of the Court of Justice in the European Union: Models of Institutional Support." *American Political Science Review*, 89: 356–76.

Cameron, D. R. (1992). "The 1992 Initiative: Causes and Consequences," in A. M. Sbragia (ed.), *Euro-Politics: Institutions and Policymaking in the 'New' European Community*. Washington, DC: Brookings Institution.

——(1993). "British Exit, German Voice, French Loyalty: Defection, Domination, and Cooperation in the 1992–93 ERM Crisis." Paper presented at the Annual Meeting of the American Political Science Association, Washington, DC.

——(1995a). "From Barre to Balladur: Economic Policy in the Era of the EMS," in G. Flynn (ed.), *Remaking the Hexagon: The New France in the New Europe*. Boulder, Colo.: Westview.

——(1995b). "Transnational Relations and the Development of European Economic and Monetary Union," in T. Risse-Kappen (ed.), *Bringing Transnational Relations Back In: Non-State Actors, Domestic Structures and International Institutions*. Cambridge: Cambridge University Press.

——(1996a). "Exchange Rate Politics in France, 1981–1983: The Regime-Defining Choices of the Mitterrand Presidency," In Anthony Daley (ed.), *The Mitterrand Era: Policy Alternatives and Political Mobilization in France*. London and New York: Macmillan.

——(1996b). "National Interest, the Dilemmas of European Integration, and Malaise," in J. T. S. Keeler and M. A. Schain (eds.), *Chirac's Challenge: Liberalization, Europeanization, and Malaise in France*. New York: St. Martin's Press.

——(1997a). "Economic and Monetary Union: Two Transitional Issues." *Swiss Political Science Review*, 3: 121–7.

——(1997b). "Economic and Monetary Union: Underlying Imperatives, Transitional Issues, Third-Stage Dilemmas." *Journal of European Public Policy*, 4: 455–85.

——(1998). "EMU after 1999: The Implications and Dilemmas of the Third Stage." *Columbia Journal of European Law*, forthcoming.

Cameron, F. (1997). "Where the European Commission Comes," in E. Regelsberger, P. de Schoutheete de Tervarent, and W. Wessels (eds.), *Foreign Policy of the European Union: From EPC to CFSP and Beyond*. Boulder, Colo.: Lynne Rienner.

Caporaso, J. (1996). "The European Community and Forms of State: Westphalian, Regulatory, or Post-Modern?" *Journal of Common Market Studies*, 34: 29–52.

——and Keeler, J. T. S. (1993). "The European Community and Regional Integration Theory." Unpublished MS.

————(1995). "The European Union and Regional Integration Theory," in C. Rhodes and S. Mazey (eds.), *The State of the European Union: Building a European Polity?* Boulder, Colo.: Lynne Rienner.

Cheyne, I. (1994). "International Agreements and the European Community Legal System." *European Law Review*, 19: 581–98.

Colchester, N., and Buchan, D. (1990). *Europower: The Essential Guide to Europe's Economic Transformation in 1992*. New York: Random House.

Conca, K. (1994). "Rethinking the Ecology–Sovereignty Debate." *Millennium*, 23: 701–11.

Corbett, R. (1989). "Testing the New Procedures: The European Parliament's First Experience with its New 'Single Act' Powers." *Journal of Common Market Studies*, 27: 359–72.

————(1992). "The Intergovernmental Conference on Political Union." *Journal of Common Market Studies*, 30: 271–98.

Craig, P. P. (1991). "Sovereignty of the UK Parliament after Factortame." *Yearbook of European Law*, 1991: 221–56.

Cram, L. (1993). "Calling the Tune without Paying the Piper? Social Policy Regulation: The Role of the Commission in European Community Social Policy." *Policy and Politics*, 21: 135–46.

————(1994). "The European Commission as a Multi-organisation: Social Policy and IT Policy in the EU." *Journal of European Public Policy*, 1: 195–217.

Current Survey (1994). *European Law Review*, 19: 221.

Curtin, D. (1990). "The Province of Government: Delimiting the Direct Effect of Directives." *European Law Review*, 15: 195–223.

Da Costa Pereira, P. S. (1988). "The Use of a Secretaria," in A. Pijpers, E. Regelsberger, and W. Wessels (eds.), *European Political Cooperation in the 1980s: A Common Foreign Policy for Western Europe?* Dordrecht: Martinus Nijhoff.

Dalton, R. (1978). "The Uncertain Future of European Integration." Paper presented at the annual meetings of the American Political Science Association, New York.

————(1994). *The Green Rainbow: Environmental Interest Groups in Europe*. New Haven, Conn.: Yale University Press.

————and Eichenberg, R. (1993). "A People's Europe: Citizen Support for the 1992 Market and Beyond," in J. Ray and D. Smith (eds.), *The 1992 Project and the Future of Integration in Europe*. New York: M. E. Sharpe.

Dang-Nguyen, G. (1986). "Telecommunications: A Challenge to the Old Order," in M. Sharp (ed.), *Europe and the New Technologies*. Ithaca, NY: Cornell University Press.

Danielson, M. N. (1976). *The Politics of Exclusion*. New York: Columbia University Press.

David, P. (1985). "Clio and the Economics of QWERTY." *American Economic Review*, 75: 332–7.

De Grauwe, P. (1989). *International Money: Post-War Trends and Theories*. New York: Oxford University Press.

————(1994). *The Economics of Monetary Integration*, 2nd edn. New York: Oxford University Press.

————and Papademos, L. (eds.). (1990). *The European Monetary System in the 1990s*. London: Longman.

Dehousse, R. (1994a). "Comparing National and EC Law: The Problem of the Level of Analysis." *EUI Working Paper in Law 94/3*. San Domenico di Fiesole, Italy: European University Institute.

————(1994b). *La Cour de justice des Communautés européennes* (The European Court of Justice). Paris: Montchrestien.

Dehousse, R. (1994c). "Community Competences: Are there Limits to Growth?" in R. Dehousse (ed.), *Europe After Maastricht: An Ever Closer Union*. Munich: Beck.

——(n.d.). "Regulation by Networks in the EC: The Role of European Agencies." San Domenico di Fiesole, Italy: European University Institute.

——and Weiler, J. H. H. (1991). "EPC and the Single Act: From Soft Law to Hard Law?" in M. Holland (ed.), *The Future of European Political Cooperation: Essays on Theory and Practice*. London: Macmillan.

DePorte, A. (1986). *Europe Between the Superpowers*. New Haven, Conn.: Yale University Press.

Deutsch, K. (1953). *Nationalism and Social Communication: An Inquiry into the Foundations of Nationality*. Cambridge, Mass.: MIT Press.

——*et al.* (1957). *Political Community and the North Atlantic Area: International Organization in the Light of Historical Experience*. Princeton, NJ: Princeton University Press.

——(1967). *France, Germany and the Western Alliance*. New York: Scribner & Sons.

De Vries, M. G. (1976). *The International Monetary Fund 1960–71: The System under Stress*. Washington, DC: IMF.

Devuyst, Y. (1995). "The European Community and the Conclusion of the Uruguay Round," in C. Rhodes and S. Mazey (eds.), *The State of the European Union, III: Building a European Polity?* Boulder, Colo.: Lynne Rienner.

Dietrich, W. F. (1996). "Harmonization of Automobile Emission Standards under International Trade Agreements: Lessons from the European Union Applied to the WTO and the NAFTA." *William and Mary Environmental Law and Policy Review*, 20: 175–221.

Doganis, R. (1991). *Flying Off Course: The Economics of International Airlines*. London: HarperCollins Academic.

Dougherty, J., and Pfaltzgraff, R. (1990). *Contending Theories of International Relations*. New York: Harper & Row.

Dusek, D. (1995). "The Negotiation of the Czech-EC Association Agreement." Unpublished thesis. Cambridge, Mass.: Harvard University.

Dyson, K. (1994). *Elusive Union: The Process of Economic and Monetary Union in Europe*. London: Longman.

Eaton, M. R. (1994). "Common Foreign and Security Policy," in D. O'Keeffe and P. M. Twomey (eds.), *Legal Issues of the Maastricht Treaty*. London: Chancery Law Ltd.

Edwards, G., and Nuttall S. (1994). "Common Foreign and Security Policy," in A. Duff, J. Pinder, and R. Price (eds.), *Maastricht and Beyond: Building the European Union*. London: Routledge.

Egan, M. (1995). "Regulating European Markets: Mismatch, Reform, and Agency." Ph.D. thesis, Pittsburgh: University of Pittsburgh.

Eichenberg, R. (1989). *Public Opinion and National Security in Western Europe*. Ithaca, NY: Cornell University Press.

——(1997). "Do European Citizens Want a Common Security Policy (Any More than They ever Did?)." Paper presented to the Convention of the International Studies Association, Toronto.

——and Dalton, R. (1993). "Europeans and the European Community: The Dynamics of Public Support for European Integration." *International Organization*, 47: 507–34.

Eichener, V. (1993). "Social Dumping or Innovative Regulation? Processes and Outcomes of European Decision-Making in the Sector of Health and Safety at Work Harmonization." *EUI Working Paper 92/28*. San Domenico di Fiesole: European University Institute.

Eichengreen, B., and Frieden, J. (eds.). (1994). *The Political Economy of European Monetary Unification*. Boulder, Colo.: Westview.

Elles, J. (1990). "The Foreign Policy Role of the European Parliament." *Washington Quarterly*, 13: 69–78.

Ellis, E. (1991). *European Community Sex Equality Law*. Oxford: Oxford University Press.

Emerson, M., Gros, D., Pisani-Ferry, J., Italianer, A., and Reichenbach, H. (1992). *One Market, One Money: An Evaluation of the Potential Benefits and Costs of Forming an Economic and Monetary Union*. Oxford: Oxford University Press.

Eurecom (1993). May, vol. 5.

——(1995). November, vol. 7.

European Report (1990*a*). 3 February.

——(1990*b*). 9 June.

——(1990*c*). 24 October.

——(1990*d*). 10 November.

——(1993*a*). 13 March.

——(1993*b*). 29 September.

——(1993*c*). 17 July.

——(1994*a*). 1 October.

——(1994*b*). 15 October.

——(1994*c*). 29 October.

——(1994*d*). 19 November.

——(1994*e*). 24 December.

——(1995*a*). 15 March

——(1995*b*). 24 June.

——(1995*c*). 16 September.

——(1996). 1 March.

Evans, P., Jacobson, H., and Putnam, R. (eds.) (1993). *Double-Edged Diplomacy: International Bargaining and Domestic Politics*. Berkeley, Calif.: University of California Press.

Falkner, G. (1995). "The Maastricht Protocol on Social Policy: Theory and Practice." *Working Papers in Contemporary European Studies*. Sussex: Sussex European Institute.

Fernandez Esteban, M. L. (1994). "La Noción de Constitución Europea en la Jurisprudecia del Tribunal de Justicia de las Comunidas Europeas" (The Notion of a European Constitution in the Case Law of the European Court of Justice). *Revista Española de Derecho Constitucional*, 40: 241–89.

Financial Times (1987). 23 January.

——(1995). 10 November.

——(1996). 10 January.

——(1997*a*). 13 March.

——(1997*b*). 19 March.

Fligstein, N. (1996). "Markets as Politics: A Political Cultural Approach to Market Institutions." *American Sociological Review*, 61: 651–73.

——and Brantley, P. (1995). "The Single Market Program and the Interests of Business," in B. Eichengreen and J. Frieden (eds.), *Politics and Institutions in an Integrated Europe*. Berlin, FRG.: Springer-Verlag.

——and Mara-Drita, I. (1996). "How to Make a Market: Reflections on the European Union's Single Market Program." *American Journal of Sociology*, 102: 1–33.

Folkerts-Landau, D., and Mathieson, D. J. (1989). *The European Monetary System in the Context of the Integration of European Financial Markets*. IMF Occasional Paper 66. Washington, DC: IMF.

Fonseca-Wollheim, H. da (1981). *Ten Years of European Political Cooperation*. Brussels: Commission of the European Communities.

Foot, R. (1979). "The European Community's Voting Behavior at the United Nations' General Assembly." *Journal of Common Market Studies*, 17: 350–9.

Frattiani, M., and von Hagen, J. (1992). *The European Monetary System and European Monetary Union*. Boulder, Colo.: Westview.

Frieden, J. (1995). "European Monetary Union: A Political Economy Perspective," in B. Eichengreen, J. Frieden, and J. von Hagen (eds.), *Politics and Institutions in an Integrated Europe*. Berlin, FRG.: Springer-Verlag.

Fuchs, G. (1995). "The European Commission as a Corporate Actor? European Telecommunications Policy after Maastricht," in C. Rhodes and S. Mazey (eds.), *The State of the European Union, III: Building a European Polity?* Boulder, Colo.: Lynne Rienner.

Gabel, M. (1995). "Market Liberalization, Class Interests, and Public Support for European Integration." Unpublished MS, University of Kentucky.

——(1998). *Interests and Integration: Political Opinion and European Union*. Ann Arbor: University of Michigan Press.

——and Palmer, H. (1995). "Understanding Variation in Public Support for European Integration." *European Journal of Political Research*, 27: 3–19.

Gablentz, O. von der (1979). "Luxembourg Revisited, or the Importance of European Political Cooperation." *Common Market Law Review*, 16: 685–99.

Gaidar, Y., and Pöhl, K. O. (1995). *Russian Reform/International Money*. Cambridge, Mass.: MIT.

Gardner, A. L. (1997). *A New Era in US-EU Relations? The Clinton Administration and the New Transatlantic Agenda*. Brookfield, Vermont: Ashgate.

Gardner, D. (1992*a*). "Basis of a Deal on Radical CAP Reform in Sight." *Financial Times*, 21 May.

——(1992*b*). "Reforms with a Rain of Sense: The EC's Agricultural Package, Brokered by Ray MacSharry, Will Cut Output and Food Prices." *Financial Times*, 22 May.

Garrett, G. (1992). "International Cooperation and Institutional Choice: The European Community's Internal Market." *International Organization*, 46: 533–58.

——(1993). "The Politics of Maastricht." *Economics and Politics*, 5: 105–23.

——(1995). "The Politics of Legal Integration in the European Union." *International Organization*, 49: 171–81.

——(1996). "An Institutional Critique of Intergovernmentalism." *International Organization*, 50: 539–69.

——Kelman, R. D., and Schultz, H. (1996). "The European Court of Justice: Master or Servant? Legal Politics in the European Union." Unpublished MS.

——and Lange, P. (1994). "Internationalization, Institutions, and Political Change." Unpublished MS.

——and Tsebelis, G. (1995). "The Limitations of Intergovernmentalism: An Institutional Critique." Unpublished MS.

Geertz, C. (1980). *Local Knowledge*. Princeton, NJ: Princeton University Press.

Genscher, H. D. (1988). *A European Currency Area and a European Central Bank: Memorandum to the General Affairs Council*. Bonn: Ministry of Foreign Affairs, 26 Feb. 1988.

Gerus, V. (1991). "Comitology within the European Community's Policy-making Process: A Mechanism of Political Control in the Inter-institutional Relations of the Council of Ministers and the Commission." Unpublished MS.

Giavazzi, F., and Giovannini, A. (1989). *Limiting Exchange Rate Flexibility: The European Monetary System*. Cambridge, Mass.: MIT.

——Micossi, S., and Miller, M. (eds.). (1988). *The European Monetary System*. New York: Cambridge University Press.

Ginsberg, R. H. (1989). *Foreign Policy Actions of the European Community: The Politics of Scale*. Boulder, Colo.: Lynne Rienner.

Giscard d'Estaing, V. (1988). *Le Pouvoir et la Vie*. Paris: Compagnie 12.

Golub, J. (forthcoming). "Global Competition and EU Environmental Policy: Introduction and Overview," in J. Golub (ed.), *Global Competition and EU Environmental Policy*. London: Routledge.

Goodman, J. B. (1992). *Monetary Sovereignty: The Politics of Central Banking in Western Europe*. Ithaca, NY: Cornell University Press.

Gormley, L. (1985). *Prohibiting Restrictions on Trade within the EEC*. Amsterdam: Elsevier-TMC Asser Instituut.

Govaere, I., and Eeckhout, P. (1992). "On Dual Use Goods and Dualist Case Law: The *Aime Richardt* Judgment on Export Controls." *Common Market Law Review*, 29: 940–65.

Gowa, J. (1983). *Closing the Gold Window: Domestic Politics and the End of Bretton Woods*. Ithaca, NY: Cornell University Press.

Goyder, D. G. (1993). *EC Competition Law*. Oxford: Clarendon Press.

Green, D. P., and Shapiro, I. (1994). *Pathologies of Rational Choice: A Critique of Applications in Political Science*. New Haven, Conn.: Yale University Press.

Green-Cowles, M. (1993). "The Politics of Big Business in the Single Market Program." Paper presented at the Third Biennial Conference of the European Community Studies Association, Washington, DC.

Greider, W. (1982). *The Education of David Stockman and Other Americans*. New York: Dutton.

Groll, G. von (1982). "The Nine at the Conference on Security and Cooperation in Europe," in D. Allen, R. Rummel, and W. Wessels (eds.), *European Political Cooperation: Toward a Foreign Policy for Western Europe*. London: Butterworths.

Gros, D. (1996). *Towards Economic and Monetary Union: Problems and Prospects*. Brussels: Centre for European Policy Studies.

——and Thygesen, N. (1992). *European Monetary Integration*. New York: St. Martin's Press.

Grosser, A. (1982). *The Western Alliance*. New York: Vintage Books.

Groux, J., and Manin, P. (1985). *The European Communities in the International Order*. Luxembourg: Office for Official Publications of the European Communities.

Gruber, Lloyd G. (1996). "Ruling the World: Power Politics and the Rise of Supranational Institutions." Ph.D. dissertation, Stanford University.

Guitian, M., Russo, M., and Tullio, G. (1988). "Policy Coordination in the European Monetary System." *IMF Occasional Paper 61*. Washington, DC: IMF.

Haagerup, N., and Thune, C. (1983). "Denmark: The European Pragmatist," in C. Hill (ed.), *National Foreign Policies and European Political Cooperation*. London: Allen & Unwin.

Haas, E. B. (1958). *The Uniting of Europe: Political, Social and Economic Forces, 1950–1957*. Stanford, Calif.: Stanford University Press.

——(1961). "International Integration: The European and the Universal Process." *International Organization*, 15: 366–92.

——(1964). "Technology, Pluralism and the New Europe," in S. Graubard (ed.), *A New Europe?* Boston: Houghton Mifflin Co.

——(1966). "International Integration: The European and the Universal Process," in *International Political Communities: An Anthology*. New York: Doubleday.

Haas, E. B. (1967). "The Uniting of Europe and the Uniting of Latin America." *Journal of Common Market Studies*, 5: 315–43.

——(1968). *The Uniting of Europe*, 2nd edn. Stanford, Calif.: Stanford University Press.

——(1971). "The Study of Regional Integration," in L. Lindberg and S. Scheingold (eds.), *Regional Integration*. Cambridge, Mass.: Harvard University Press.

——(1972). "International Integration: The European and the Universal Process," in M. Hodges (ed.), *European Integration*. Harmondsworth: Penguin Books.

——(1975). "The Obsolescence of Regional Integration Theory." *Research Series No. 25*. Berkeley: Center for International Studies.

——and Schmitter, P. C. (1966; originally published 1964). "Economics and Differential Patterns of Integration: Projections About Unity in Latin America," in *International Political Communities: An Anthology*. New York: Doubleday.

Haas, P. M. (1990). *Saving the Mediterranean: The Politics of International Environmental Cooperation*. New York: Columbia University Press.

——Keohane, R. O., and Levy, M. A. (eds.). (1993). *Institutions for the Earth: Sources of Effective International Environmental Protection*. Cambridge, Mass.: MIT Press.

Haggard, S., and Simmons, B. A. (1987). "Theories of International Regimes." *International Organization*, 41: 491–517.

Haigh, N. (1992). "The European Community and International Environmental Policy," in A. Hurrell and B. Kingsbury (eds.), *The International Politics of the Environment: Actors, Interests, and Institutions*. Oxford: Clarendon Press.

——(1996). "Climate Change Policies and Politics in the European Community," in T. O'Riordan and J. Jager (eds.), *Politics of Climate Change: A European Perspective*. London: Routledge.

Hall, P. H. (1986). *Governing the Economy: The Politics of State Intervention in Britain and France*. Cambridge: Polity Press.

——and Taylor, R. C. R. (1994). "Political Science and the Three New Institutionalisms." *Political Studies*, 44: 936–57.

Hampson, F. O., with Hart, M. (1995). *Multilateral Negotiations: Lessons from Arms Control, Trade, and the Environment*. Baltimore: Johns Hopkins University Press.

Hay, R. (1989). "The European Commission and the Administration of the Community." *European Documentation*. Luxembourg: Office for Official Publications of the European Communities.

Henig, S. (1971). *External Relations of the European Community: Associations and Trade Agreements*. London: Chatham House.

Henning, C. Randall (1996). "Europe's Monetary Union and the United States." *Foreign Policy*, 102: 83–100.

Heritier, A. (1996). "Policy-Making by Subterfuge: Interest Accommodation, Innovation, and Substitute Democratic Legitimization in Europe." MS, San Domenico di Fiesole, Italy: European University Institute.

Hervey, T. K. (1994). "Legal Issues Concerning the Barber Protocol," in D. O'Keefe and P. M. Twomey (eds.), *Legal Issues of the Maastricht Treaty*. London: Chancery Law Ltd.

Hession, M. (1995). "External Competence and the European Community." *Global Environmental Change: Human and Policy Dimensions*, 5: 155–6.

——and Macrory, R. (1994). "Maastricht and the Environmental Policy of the Community: Legal Issues of a New Environment Policy," in D. O'Keeffe and P. M. Twomey (eds.), *Legal Issues of the Maastricht Treaty*. London: Chancery Law Ltd.

Hill, C. (1983). "National Interests—The Insuperable Obstacles?" in C. Hill (ed.), *National Foreign Policies and European Political Cooperation*. London: Allen & Unwin.

——(ed.). (1996). *The Actors in Europe's Foreign Policy*. London: Routledge.

——and Wallace, W. (1979). "Diplomatic Trends in the European Community." *International Affairs* 55: 47–66.

Hirsch, F. (1977). *The Social Limits to Growth*. Cambridge, Mass.: Harvard University Press.

Hix, S. (1994). "The Study of the European Community: The Challenge to Comparative Politics." *West European Politics*, 17: 1–30.

Hoffmann, S. (1966). "Obstinate or Obsolete: The Fate of the Nation-state and the Case of Western Europe." *Daedalus*, 95: 862–915.

——(1984). "Cries and Whimpers: Thoughts on West European Relations in the 1980s." *Daedalus*, 113: 221–52.

Holland, M. (1987). "Three Approaches for Understanding European Political Cooperation: A Case-Study of EC South African Policy." *Journal of Common Market Studies*, 25: 295–313.

——(1991). "Sanctions as an EPC Instrument," in M. Holland (ed.), *The Future of European Political Cooperation: Essays on Theory and Practice*. London: Macmillan.

——(1995). *European Union Common Foreign Policy: From EPC to CFSP Joint Action and South Africa*. New York: St. Martin's Press.

Hölzer, H. (1990). "Merger Control," in P. Montagnon (ed.), *European Competition Policy*. London: Royal Institute for International Affairs.

Hoskyns, C. (1986). "Women, European Law and Transnational Politics." *International Journal of the Sociology of Law*, 14: 299–315.

Hurd, D. (1981). "Political Cooperation." *International Affairs*, 57: 383–93.

Hurrell, A., and Kingsbury, B. (1992). "The International Politics of the Environment: An Introduction," in A. Hurrell and B. Kingsbury (eds.), *The International Politics of the Environment*. Oxford: Clarendon Press.

Hurwitz, L. (1976). "The EEC and Decolonization: The Voting Behavior of the Nine in the UN General Assembly." *Political Studies*, 24: 435–47.

Ifestos, P. (1987). *European Political Cooperation: Towards a Framework of Supranational Diplomacy?* Aldershot: Avebury.

Ikenberry, G. J. (1994). "History's Heavy Hand: Institutions and the Politics of the State." Unpublished MS.

Inglehart, R. (1971). "Public Opinion and Regional Integration," in L. Lindberg and S. Sheingold (eds.), *Regional Integration*. Cambridge, Mass.: Harvard University Press.

——(1977). *The Silent Revolution*. Princeton, NJ: Princeton University Press.

International Monetary Fund. (1996). *Direction of Trade Statistics Yearbook 1996*. Washington, DC: IMF.

Iverson, T. (1996). "Power, Flexibility, and the Breakdown of Centralized Wage Bargaining: Denmark and Sweden in Comparative Perspective." *Comparative Politics*, 28: 399–456.

Jachtenfuchs, M. (1990). "The European Community and the Protection of the Ozone Layer." *Journal of Common Market Studies*, 28: 261–77.

Jackson, K. T. (1985). *Crabgrass Frontier: The Suburbanization of the United States*. Oxford: Oxford University Press.

Jepperson, R. (1991). "Institutions, Institutional Effects, and Institutionalism," in P. DiMaggio and W. W. Powell (eds.), *The New Institutionalism in Organizational Analysis*. Chicago: University of Chicago Press.

Jervis, R. (1993). "Systems and Interaction Effects," in J. Snyder and R. Jervis (eds.), *Coping with Complexity in the International System*. Boulder, Colo.: Westview.

Johnson, S. P. (1993). *The Earth Summit: The United Nations Conference on Environment and Development (UNCED)*. London: Graham & Trotman/Martinus Nijhoff.

——and Corcelle, G. (1995). *The Environmental Policy of the European Communities*, 2nd edn. London: Kluwer Law International.

Jupille, J. H., and Caporaso, J. A. (1996). "The European Community in Global Environmental Politics." ECSA Workshop, The Role of the European Union in the World Community, Jackson Hole, Wyoming, 16–19 May.

Kassim, H. (1996). "Air Transport," in H. Kassim and A. Menon (eds.), *The European Union and National Industrial Policy*. London: Routledge.

Keeler, J. T. S. (1996). "Agricultural Power in the European Community: Explaining the Fate of CAP and GATT Negotiations." *Comparative Politics*, 28: 127–49.

Kenen, P. B. (1992). *EMU After Maastricht*. Washington, DC: Group of Thirty.

——(1995). *Economic and Monetary Union in Europe: Moving beyond Maastricht*. Cambridge: Cambridge University Press.

Kenney, S. J. (1992). *For Whose Protection? Reproductive Hazards and Exclusionary Policies in the United States and Britain*. Ann Arbor: University of Michigan Press.

——(1994). "Pregnancy and Disability: Comparing the United States and the European Community." *The Disability Law Reporter Service*, 3: 8–17.

——(1996). "Pregnancy Discrimination: Toward Substantive Equality." *Wisconsin Women's Law Journal*, 10: 351–402.

Keohane, R. (1974). "Transgovernmental Relations and International Organizations." *World Politics*, 27: 39–62.

——(1984). *After Hegemony: Cooperation and Discord in the World Political Economy*. Princeton, NJ: Princeton University Press.

——(1989). *International Institutions and State Power: Essays in International Relations Theory*. Boulder, Colo.: Westview.

——and Hoffmann, S. (1991). "Institutional Change in Europe in the 1980s," in R. Keohane and S. Hoffmann (eds.), *The New European Community*. Boulder, Colo.: Westview.

——and Nye, J. (eds.). (1972). *Transnational Relations and World Politics*. Cambridge, Mass.: Harvard University Press.

Kiewiet, R., and McCubbins, M. D. (1991). *The Logic of Delegation: Congressional Parties and the Appropriations Process*. Chicago: University of Chicago Press.

Kilroy, B. (1995). "Member State Control of Judicial Independence: The Integrative Role of the European Court of Justice, 1958–1994." Paper presented at the 1995 Annual Meeting of the American Political Science Association, Chicago, 31 August–3 September.

Kingdon, J. W. (1984). *Agendas, Alternatives, and Public Policies*. Boston: Little, Brown & Co.

Kirchner, E., and Schwaiger, K. (1981). *The Role of Interest Groups in the European Community*. Aldershot: Gower.

Knight, J. (1992). *Institutions and Social Conflict*. Cambridge: Cambridge University Press.

Knopf, J. W. (1993). "Beyond Two-Level Games: Domestic-International Interaction in the Intermediate Range Nuclear Forces Negotiations." *International Organization*, 47: 599–628.

Kramer, L. (1995). *E.C. Treaty and Environmental Law*, 2nd edn. London: Sweet & Maxwell.

Krasner, S. D. (1983). "Structural Causes and Regime Consequences: Regimes as Intervening Variables," in S. D. Krasner (ed.), *International Regimes*. Ithaca, NY: Cornell University Press.

——(1984). "Approaches to the State: Alternative Conceptions and Historical Dynamics." *Comparative Politics*, 16: 223–46.

——(1989). "Sovereignty: An Institutional Perspective," in J. A. Caporaso (ed.), *The Elusive State: International and Comparative Perspectives*. Newbury Park, Calif.: Sage Publications.

Kratochwil, F. V. (1989). *Rules, Norms, and Decisions: On the Conditions of Practical and Legal Reasoning in International Relations and Domestic Affairs*. Cambridge: Cambridge University Press.

Kruse, D. C. (1980). *Monetary Integration in Western Europe: EMU, EMS and Beyond*. London: Butterworths.

Lak, M. W. J. (1989). "Interaction Between European Political Cooperation and the European Community (External)—Existing Rules and Challenges." *Common Market Law Review*, 26: 281–99.

——(1992). "The Constitutional Foundation," in R. Rummel (ed.), *Toward Political Union: Planning a Common Foreign and Security Policy in the European Community*. Boulder, Colo.: Westview.

Landfried, C. (1984). *Bundesverfassungsgericht und Gesetzgeber* (The Federal Constitutional Court and Legislation). Baden-Baden: Nomos.

——(1992). "Judicial Policymaking in Germany: The Federal Constitutional Court." *West European Politics*, 15: 50–67.

Lang, J. T. (1986). "The Ozone Layer Convention: A New Solution to the Question of Community Participation in 'Mixed' International Agreements." *Common Market Law Review*, 23: 157–76.

Lange, P. (1992). "The Politics of the Social Dimension," in A. Sbragia (ed.), *Europolitics*. Washington, DC: Brookings Institution.

——(1993). "The Maastricht Social Protocol: Why Did They Do It?" *Politics and Society*, 21: 5–36.

La Tribune (1987). 24 January.

Laumann, E., and Knoke, D. (1989). *The Organizational State*. Chicago: University of Chicago Press.

Laursen, F., and Vanhoonacker, S. (eds.). (1992). *The Intergovernmental Conference on Political Union*. Maastricht: European Institute of Public Administration.

Leenen, A. T. S. (1984). "Participation of the EEC in International Environmental Agreements." *Legal Issues of European Integration*, 1984/1: 93–111.

Leibfried, S. (1992). "Towards a European Welfare State? On Integrating Poverty Regimes into the European Community," in Z. Ferge and J. E. Kolberg (eds.), *Social Policy in a Changing Europe*. Boulder, Colo.: Westview.

——and Pierson, P. (1995). "Semi-Sovereign Welfare States: Social Policy in a Multi-Tiered Europe," in S. Leibfried and P. Pierson (eds.) *European Social Policy*. Washington, DC: Brookings Institution.

Lenaerts, K. (1990). "Constitutionalism and the Many Faces of Federalism." *American Journal of Comparative Law*, 38: 205–64.

Levitsky, J. E. (1994). "The Europeanization of the British Style." *American Journal of Comparative Law*, 42: 347–80.

Lindemann, B. (1976). "Europe and the Third World: The Nine at the United Nations." *The World Today*, 32: 260–9.

——(1982). "European Political Cooperation at the UN: A Challenge for the Nine," in D. Allen, R. Rummel, and W. Wessels (eds.), *European Political Cooperation: Toward a Foreign Policy for Western Europe*. London: Butterworths.

Lindberg, L., and Scheingold, S. (1970). *Europe's Would-be Polity*. Englewood Cliffs, NJ: Prentice-Hall.

Lipson, C. (1991). "Why Are Some International Agreements Informal?" *International Organization*, 45: 495–538.

Lissitzyn, O. (1968). "Freedom of the Air: Scheduled and Unscheduled Services," in E. McWhinney and M. Bradley (eds.), *The Freedom of the Air*. New York: Oceana.

Litfin, K. T. (1995*a*). "Rethinking Sovereignty and Environment: Beyond Either/Or." Presented at SSRC Workshop, Rethinking Sovereignty and Environment, University of Washington, 13–15 Oct.

——(1995*b*). "Framing Science: Precautionary Discourse and the Ozone Treaties." *Millennium: Journal of International Studies*, 24: 251–77.

Lodge, J. (1989). "European Political Cooperation: Towards the 1990s," in J. Lodge (ed.), *The European Community and the Challenge of the Future*. New York: St. Martin's Press.

Lowi, T. (1964). "American Business, Public Policy Case Studies, and Political Theory." *World Politics*, 16: 667–715.

Ludlow, P. (1982). *The Making of the European Monetary System: A Case Study of the Politics of the European Community*. London: Butterworth Scientific.

——(1988). *Beyond Europe 1992: Europe and Its Western Partners*. Belgium: Center for European Policy Studies.

McAleavey, P. (1993). "The Politics of European Regional Development Policy: Additionality in the Scottish Coalfields." *Regional Politics and Policy*, 3: 88–107.

McCubbins, M. (1989). "Structure and Process, Policy and Politics: Administrative Arrangements and the Political Control of Agencies." *Virginia Law Review*, 75: 431–82.

——Noll, R., and Weingast, B. (1987). "Administrative Procedures as Instruments of Political Control." *Journal of Law, Economics, and Organization*, 3: 243–77.

——and Page, T. (1987). "A Theory of Congressional Delegation," in M. McCubbins and T. Sullivan (eds.), *Congress: Structure and Policy*. New York: Cambridge University Press.

——and Schwartz, T. (1984). "Congressional Oversight Overlooked: Police Patrols Versus Fire Alarms." *American Journal of Political Science*, 28: 165–79.

McGowan, L., and Wilks, S. (1995). "The First Supranational Policy in the European Union: Competition Policy." *European Journal of Political Research*, 28: 141–69.

McKendrick, G. G. (1987). "The INTUG View on the EEC Green Paper." *Telecommunications Policy*, 11: 325–9.

McNamara, K. R. (1993). "Common Markets, Uncommon Currencies: Systems Effects and the European Community," in J. Snyder and R. Jervis (eds.), *Coping with Complexity*. Boulder, Colo.: Westview.

Macrory, R., and Hession, M. (1996). "The European Community and Climate Change: The Role of Law and Legal Competence," in T. O'Riordan and J. Jager (eds.), *Politics of Climate Change: A European Perspective*. London: Routledge.

Magnifico, G. (1973). *European Monetary Unification*. New York: Wiley.

Majone, G. (1992). "Regulatory Federalism in the European Community." *Environment and Planning C: Government and Policy*, 10: 299–316.

——(1993). "The European Community between Social Policy and Social Regulation." *Journal of Common Market Studies*, 31: 153–70.

——(1994). "The European Community as a Regulatory State." Lectures given at the Academy of European Law, European University Institute, Florence.

——(1997). "State, Market, and Regulatory Competition in the European Union: Lessons for the Integrated World Economy." Unpublished MS.

Mancini, F. G. (1991). "The Making of a Constitution for Europe," in R. O. Keohane and S. Hoffmann (eds.), *The New European Community*. Boulder, Colo.: Westview.

Mangan, I. (1992). "The Influence of EC Membership on Irish Social Policy and Social Services," in S. O'Cinneide (ed.), *Social Europe: EC Social Policy and Ireland*. Dublin: Institute of European Affairs.

March, J., and Olson, J. (1989). *Rediscovering Institutions: The Organizational Basis of Politics*. New York: Free Press.

Marks, G. (1993). "Structural Policy and Multilevel Governance in the EC," in A. Cafruny and G. Rosenthal (eds.), *The State of the European Community 2: The Maastricht Debates and Beyond*. Boulder, Colo.: Lynne Rienner.

——(1996). "Decision-Making in Cohesion Policy: Charting and Explaining Variations," in L. Hooghe (ed.), *Cohesion Policy European Integration*. Oxford: Oxford University Press.

——Hooghe, L., and Blank, K. (1996). "European Integration and the State." *Journal of Common Market Studies*, 34: 341–78.

Marsh, David. (1992). *The Bundesbank: The Bank that Rules Europe*. London: Heinemann.

Marshall, T. H. (1975). *Social Policy*, 4th edn. London: Hutchinson.

Martin, A., and Ross, G. (1994). "Lessons from the Social Dimension of the European Union." Unpublished MS.

Martin, L. (1992). "Institutions and Cooperation: Sanctions During the Falklands Islands Conflict." *International Security*, 16: 143–78.

——(1993). "International and Domestic Institutions in the EMU Process." *Economics and Politics*, 5: 125–44.

Mastellone, C. (1981). "The External Relations of the E.E.C. in the Field of Environmental Protection." *International and Comparative Law Quarterly*, 30: 104–17.

Mattli, W. (1996). "Explaining Regional Integration." *Working Papers 96-4*. Irvine, Calif.: UC Global Peace and Conflict Studies Program.

——and Slaughter, A.-M. (1995). "Law and Politics in the European Union: A Reply to Garrett." *International Organization*, 49: 183–90.

Mazey, S., and Richardson, J. (1993). "Introduction: Transference of Powers, Decision Rules, and Rules of the Game," in S. Mazey and J. Richardson (eds.), *Lobbying in the European Community*. Oxford: Oxford University Press.

Meunier, S. (1996). "Divided but United: European Trade Policy Integration and EC-US Agricultural Negotiations in the Uruguay Round." Presented at the ECSA Workshop, The Role of the European Union in the World Community, Jackson Hole, Wyoming, 16–19 May.

Milward, A. S. (1992). *The European Rescue of the Nation-State*. Berkeley and Los Angeles: University of California Press.

Mitrany, D. (1930). "Pan-Europa—A Hope or a Danger?" *Political Quarterly*, 1: 457–78.

——(1947). "The International Consequences of National Planning." *Yale Review*, 37: 18–31.

——(1966). *A Working Peace System*. Chicago: Quadrangle Books.

——(1968). "The Prospect of Integration: Federal or Functional?" in J. S. Nye (ed.), *International Regionalism: Readings*. Boston: Little, Brown & Co.

Moe, T. (1984). "The New Economics of Organization." *American Journal of Political Science*, 28: 739–77.

——(1987). "An Assessment of the Positive Theory of Congressional Dominance." *Legislative Studies Quarterly*, 12: 475–520.

——(1990). "The Politics of Structural Choice: Toward a Theory of Public Bureaucracy," in O. E. Williamson (ed.), *Organization Theory: From Chester Barnard to the Present and Beyond*. Oxford: Oxford University Press.

Monar, J. (1997). "The Finances of the Union's Intergovernmental Pillars: Tortuous Experiments with the Community Budget." *Journal of Common Market Studies*, 35: 57–78.

Montagnon, P. (ed.). (1990). *European Competition Policy*. London: Royal Institute for International Affairs.

Moravcsik, A. (1991). "Negotiating the Single European Act: National Interests and Conventional Statecraft in the European Community." *International Organization*, 45: 19–56.

——(1993). "Preferences and Power in the European Community: A Liberal Intergovernmentalist Approach." *Journal of Common Market Studies*, 31: 473–524.

——(1994). "Why the European Community Strengthens the State." Unpublished MS.

——(1995). "Liberal Intergovernmentalism and Integration: A Rejoinder." *Journal of Common Market Studies*, 33: 611–28.

Mosley, H. G. (1990). "The Social Dimension of European Integration." *International Labour Review*, 129: 147–64.

Neuwahl, N. (1994). "Foreign and Security Policy and the Implementation of the Requirement for 'Consistency' Under the Treaty on European Union," in D. O'Keeffe and P. M. Twomey (eds.), *Legal Issues of the Maastricht Treaty*. London: Chancery Law Ltd.

Noam, E. (1992). *Telecommunications in Europe*. New York: Oxford University Press.

Noel, E. (1973). "How the European Community's Institutions Work." London: EC Information Office.

Nollkaemper, A. (1987). "The European Community and International Environmental Cooperation—Legal Aspects of External Community Powers." *Legal Issues of European Integration*, 1987/2: 55–91.

North, D. R. (1981). *Structure and Change in Economic History*. New York: Newton.

——(1990). *Institutions, Institutional Change and Economic Performance*. Cambridge: Cambridge University Press.

Nuttall, S. J. (1988). "Where the European Commission Comes In," in A. Pijpers, E. Regelsberger, and W. Wessels (eds.), *European Political Cooperation in the 1980s: A Common Foreign Policy for Western Europe?* Dordrecht: Martinus Nijhoff.

——(1992). *European Political Cooperation*. Oxford: Clarendon Press.

——(1993). "The Foreign and Security Policy Provisions of the Maastricht Treaty: Their Potential for the Future," in J. Monar, W. Ungerer, and W. Wessels (eds.), *The Maastricht Treaty on European Union*. Brussels: European Interuniversity Press.

——(1995). "The European Commission's Internal Arrangements for Foreign Affairs and External Relations." *CFSP Forum*, 2: 3–4.

——(1996). "The Commission: The Struggle for Legitimacy," in C. Hill (ed.), *The Actors in Europe's Foreign Policy*. London: Routledge.

Nye, J. (1966). "East African Economic Integration," in *International Political Communities: An Anthology*. New York: Doubleday & Co.

——(1971). *Peace in Parts*. Boston: Little, Brown & Co.

O'Keeffe, D., and Schermers, H. G. (eds.). (1983). *Mixed Agreements*. Boston: Kluwer Law and Taxation Publishers.

Oliver, P. (1988). *Free Movement of Goods in the EEC*. London: European Law Centre.

Olson, M. (1965). *The Logic of Collective Action: Public Goods and the Theory of Groups*. Cambridge, Mass.: Harvard University Press.

Organisation for Economic Co-Operation and Development (1996). *OECD Economic Outlook 60*. Paris: OECD.

——(1997). *OECD National Accounts, Main Aggregates, 1, 1960–1995*. Paris: OECD.

Ostner, I., and Lewis, J. (1995). "Gender and the Evolution of European Social Policies," in S. Leibfried and P. Pierson (eds.), *European Social Policy*. Washington, DC: Brookings Institution.

Padoa-Schioppa, T. (1994). *The Road to Monetary Union in Europe: The Emperor, the Kings, and the Genies*. Oxford: Clarendon.

——Emerson, M., King, M., and Mitteron, J. C. (1987). *Efficiency, Stability, and Equity: A Strategy for the Evolution of the Economic System of the European Community*. Oxford: Oxford University Press.

Pan, E. (1996). "Europe and the World: External Relations, Internal Dynamics." *Proceedings of the Thirteenth Annual Graduate Student Conference*. New York: Columbia University Institute on Western Europe.

Perrow, C. (1984). *Normal Accidents*. New York: Basic Books.

Pescatore, P. (1979). "External Relations in the Case-Law of the Court of Justice of the European Communities." *Common Market Law Review*, 16: 615–45.

Peters, B. G. (1992). "Bureaucratic Politics and the Institutions of the European Community," in A. Sbragia (ed.), *Europolitics: Institutions and Policymaking in the "New" European Community*. Washington, DC: Brookings Institution.

Philips, A. (1994). *Directory of Pressure Groups in the European Community*. Harlow: Longman.

Pierson, P. (1992). "'Policy Feedbacks' and Political Change: Contrasting Reagan and Thatcher's Pension-Reform Initiatives." *Studies in American Political Development*, 6: 361–92.

——(1993). "When Effect becomes Cause: Policy Feedback and Political Change." *World Politics*, 45: 595–628.

——(1994). *Dismantling the Welfare State? Reagan, Thatcher and the Politics of Entrenchment*. New York: Cambridge University Press.

——(1996). "The Path to European Integration: A Historical Institutionalist Analysis." *Comparative Political Studies*, 29: 123–63.

——and Leibfried, S. (1995). "Multi-tiered Institutions and the Making of Social Policy," in S. Leibfried and P. Pierson (eds.), *European Social Policy: Between Fragmentation and Integration*. Washington, DC: Brookings Institution.

Pijpers, A. E. (1991). "European Political Cooperation and the Realist Paradigm," in M. Holland (ed.), *The Future of European Political Cooperation: Essays on Theory and Practice*. London: Macmillan.

Pillinger, J. (1992). *Feminising the Market*. London: Macmillan.

Pinder, J. (1989). "The Single Market," in J. Lodge (ed.), *The European Community and the Challenge of the Future*. London: Pinter.

Pollack, M. A. (1994). "Creeping Competencies: The Expanding Agenda of the European Community." *Journal of Public Policy*, 14: 95–145.

——(1995a). "Obedient Servant or Runaway Eurocracy? Delegation, Agency and Agenda Setting in the European Community." Unpublished MS.

——(1995b). "The New Institutionalism and EC Governance: The Promise, and Limits, of Institutional Analysis." Unpublished MS.

——(1995c). "Regional Actors in an Intergovernmental Play: The Making and Implementation of EC Structural Policy," in C. Rhodes and S. Mazey (eds.), *The State of the European Union, III: Building a European Polity?* Boulder, Colo.: Lynne Rienner.

Pollack, M. A. (1996). "Ignoring the Commons: International Trade, the International Environment, and EC Environment Policy." Paper presented at the Council for European Studies Conference of Europeanists, Chicago, 14–16 Mar.

——(1997). "Delegation, Agency and Agenda Setting in the European Community." *International Organization*, 51: 99–134.

Porter, G., and Brown, J. W. (1996). *Global Environmental Politics*, 2nd edn. Boulder, Colo.: Westview.

Powell, W. W., and DiMaggio, P. (eds.). (1991). *The New Institutionalism in Organizational Analysis*. Chicago: University of Chicago Press.

Prechal, S., and Burrows, N. (1990). *Gender Discrimination Law of the European Community*. Aldershot: Gower-Dartmouth.

Preeg, E. H. (1995). *Traders in a Brave New World: The Uruguay Round and the Future of the International Trading System*. Chicago: University of Chicago Press.

Putnam, R. D. (1988). "Diplomacy and Domestic Politics: The Logic of Two-level Games." *International Organization*, 42: 427–60.

Rabier, J.-R., and Inglehart, R. (1981). "What Kind of Europe: Support for National Independence, Cooperation and Integration in the European Parliament." *Government and Opposition*, 16: 185–99.

Regelsberger, E. (1991). "The Twelve's Dialogue with Third Countries: Progress towards a Communaute d'Action?" in M. Holland (ed.), *The Future of European Political Co-operation: Essays on Theory and Practice*. London: Macmillan.

——(1993). "European Political Cooperation," in J. Story (ed.), *The New Europe: Politics, Government and Economy since 1945*. Oxford: Blackwell.

——Schoutheete de Tervarent, P. de, and Wessels, W. (eds.). (1997). *Foreign Policy of the European Union: From EPC to CFSP and Beyond*. Boulder, Colo.: Lynne Rienner.

Reif, K., and Inglehart, R. (eds.). (1991). *Eurobarometers*. London: Macmillan.

Rhodes, M. (1995). "A Regulatory Conundrum: Industrial Relations and the 'Social Dimension'," in S. Leibfried and P. Pierson, *European Social Policy*. Washington, DC: Brookings Institution.

Riker, W. (1955). "The Senate and American Federalism." *American Political Science Review*, 49: 452–69.

——(1986). *The Art of Political Manipulation*. New Haven: Yale University Press.

Risse-Kappen, T. (ed.). (1995). *Bringing Transnational Relations Back In: Non-state Actors, Domestic Structures, and International Institutions*. Cambridge: Cambridge University Press.

Ross, G. (1995). *Jacques Delors and European Integration*. Cambridge: Polity Press.

Roundtable of European Industrialists (1986). *Clearing the Lines: A User's View on Business Communications in Europe*. Paris and Brussels: European Roundtable Secretariat.

——(1989). *High Priority: Need for Renewing Transport Infrastructure in Europe*. Brussels: European Roundtable Secretariat.

Ruggie, J. G. (1993). "Territoriality and Beyond: Problematizing Modernity in International Relations." *International Organization*, 47: 139–74.

Sack, J. (1995). "The European Community's Membership of International Organizations." *Common Market Law Review*, 32: 1227–56.

Sandholtz, W. (1992*a*). "ESPRIT and the Politics of International Collective Action." *Journal of Common Market Studies*, 30: 1–22.

——(1992*b*). *High-Tech Europe: The Politics of International Cooperation*. Berkeley and Los Angeles: University of California Press.

——(1993*a*). "Choosing Union: Monetary Politics and Maastricht." *International Organization*, 47: 1–39.

——(1993*b*). "Monetary Bargains: The Treaty on EMU," in A. W. Cafruny and G. G. Rosenthal (eds.), *The State of the European Community*. Boulder, Colo.: Lynne Rienner.

——(1996). "Membership Matters: Limits of the Functional Approach to European Institutions," *Journal of Common Market Studies*, 34: 403–29.

——(1997). "Rules, Reasons, and International Institutions." Unpublished MS.

——and Zysman, J. (1989). "1992: Recasting the European Bargain." *World Politics*, 42: 95–128.

Sauter, W. (1995*a*). "The Relationship between Industrial and Competition Policy under the Economic Constitution of the European Union, with a Case Study of Telecommunications." Ph.D. thesis, Law Dept., European University Institute, San Domenico di Fiesole.

——(1995*b*). "The Telecommunications Law of the European Union." *European Law Journal*, 1: 101.

Sbragia, A. (1992). "Thinking about the European Future: The Uses of Comparison," in A. Sbragia (ed.), *Europolitics: Institutions and Policymaking in the "New" European Community*. Washington, DC: Brookings Institution.

——(1993*a*). "EC Environmental Policy: Atypical Ambitions and Typical Problems," in A. Cafruny and G. Rosenthal (eds.), *The State of the European Community*. Boulder, Colo.: Lynne Reinner.

——(1993*b*). "The European Community: A Balancing Act." *Publius*, 23: 23–38.

——(1996). "Transatlantic Relations: An Evolving Mosaic. International Conference, Policy-Making and Decision-Making in Transatlantic Relations," Universite Libre de Bruxelles, 3–4 May.

——with Hildebrand, P. (1998). "The European Union and Compliance: A Story in the Making," in E. B. Weiss and H. Jacobson (eds.), *Engaging Countries: Strengthening Compliance with International Environmental Accords*. Cambridge, Mass.: MIT.

Scharpf, F. W. (1988). "The Joint-Decision Trap: Lessons from German Federalism and European Integration." *Public Administration*, 61: 239–78.

——(1994). "Community and Autonomy: Multilevel Policymaking in the European Union." *Journal of European Public Policy*, 1: 219–42.

Schattschneider, E. E. (1960). *The Semi-Sovereign People: A Realist's View of Democracy in America*. New York: Holt, Rinehart, & Winston.

Schelling, T. (1978). *Micromotives and Macrobehavior*. New York: Norton.

Scheuermans, F., and Dodd, T. (1995). "The World Trade Organization and the European Community." *Working Paper, External Economic Relations Series, E-1*. Brussels: European Parliament, Directorate-General for Research, External Economic Relations Division.

Schmidt, H. (1990). *Die Deutschen und Ihre Nachbarn*. Bonn: Siedler.

Schmidt, S. K. (1996). "Sterile Debates and Dubious Generalizations: European Integration Theory Tested by Telecommunications and Electricity." *Journal of Public Policy*, 16: 233–71.

Schmitter, P. C. (1969). "Further Notes on Operationalizing Some Variables Related to Regional Integration." *International Organization*, 23: 327–36.

——(1970). "A Revised Theory of Regional Integration." *International Organization*, 24: 836–68.

——(1971). "A Revised Theory of Regional Integration," in L. Lindberg and S. Scheingold (eds.), *Regional Integration*. Cambridge, Mass.: Harvard University Press.

——(1992). "Interests, Powers, and Functions: Emergent Properties and Unintended Consequences in the European Polity." Unpublished MS.

Schneider, V., Dang-Nguyen, G., and Werle, R. (1994). "Corporate Actor Networks in

European Policy-Making: Harmonizing Telecommunications Policy." *Journal of Common Market Studies*, 32: 473–98.

Schneider, V., and Werle, R. (1990). "International Regime or Corporate Actor? The European Community in the Telecommunications Policy," in K. Dyson and P. Humphreys (eds.), *The Political Economy of Communications: International and European Dimensions*. London: Routledge.

Schoutheete de Tervarent, P. de (1980). *La Cooperation Politique Europeenne*. Brussels: Nathan Editions.

——(1988). "The Presidency and the Management of Political Cooperation," in A. Pijpers, E. Regelsberger, and W. Wessels (eds.), *European Political Cooperation in the 1980s: A Common Foreign Policy for Western Europe?* Dordrecht: Martinus Nijhoff.

Sell, S. (1996). "North-South Environmental Bargaining: Ozone, Climate Change, and Biodiversity." *Global Governance*, 2: 97–118.

Serre, F. de la (1988). "The Scope of National Adaptation to EPC," in A. Pijpers, E. Regelsberger, and W. Wessels (eds.), *European Political Cooperation in the 1980s: A Common Foreign Policy for Western Europe?* Dordrecht: Martinus Nijhoff.

Shackleton, M. (1993). "The Delors II Budget Package," in N. Nugent (ed.), *The European Community 1992: Annual Review of Activities*. Oxford: Blackwell.

Shapiro, M. J. (1980). *Courts: A Comparative and Political Analysis*. Chicago: University of Chicago Press.

——(1992). "The European Court of Justice," in A. M. Sbragia (ed.), *Euro-politics: Institutions and Policymaking in the New European Community*. Washington, DC: Brookings Institution.

——and Stone, A. (1994). "The New Constitutional Politics." *Comparative Political Studies*, 26: 397–420.

Shepsle, K. (1989). "Studying Institutions: Lessons from the Rational Choice Approach." *Journal of Theoretical Politics*, 1: 131–47.

Shepard, R. (1975). *Public Opinion and European Integration*. Lexington, Mass.: Lexington Books.

Sinnott, R. (1995). "Policy, Subsidiarity, and Legitimacy," in O. Niedermayer and R. Sinnott (eds.), *Public Opinion and International Governance*. Oxford: Oxford University Press.

Skocpol, T. (1992). *Protecting Soldiers and Mothers: The Political Origins of Social Policy in the United States*. Cambridge, Mass.: Belknap Press of Harvard.

Skowronek, S. (1982). *Building a New American State*. Cambridge: Cambridge University Press.

Slaughter, A.-M., Weiler, J., and Stone Sweet, A. (eds.) (1997). *The European Court and the National Courts: Legal Change in Its Social Context*. Oxford: Hart.

Smeets, H. D. (1990). "Does Germany Dominate the EMS?" *Journal of Common Market Studies*, 29: 37–52.

Smith, H. (1995). *European Foreign Policy and Central America*. New York: St. Martin's Press.

Smith, M. E. (1996). "Achieving the Common Foreign and Security Policy: Collusion and Confusion in EU Institutions." Paper presented at the 10th International Conference of Europeanists, Chicago, March 1996.

——(1998a). "What's Wrong with the CFSP? The Politics of Institutional Reform," in P. H. Laurent and M. Maresceau (eds.), *The State of the European Union, IV: Deepening and Widening*. Boulder, Colo.: Lynne Rienner.

——(1998b). "Beyond Bargaining: The Institutionalization of Foreign Policy Cooperation in the European Community, 1970–96." Ph.D. dissertation, Dept. of Politics and Society, University of California, Irvine.

Stein, E. (1981). "Lawyers, Judges, and the Making of a Transnational Constitution." *American Journal of International Law*, 75: 1–27.

——(1991). "External Relations of the European Community: Structure and Process." *Collected Courses of the Academy of European Law, 1, book 1*. Deventer: Kluwer Law International.

Steinmo, S., Thelen, K., and Longstreth, F. (eds.). (1992). *Structuring Politics: Historical Institutionalism in Comparative Analysis*. Cambridge: Cambridge University Press.

Stewart, T. (ed.). (1993). *The GATT Uruguay Round: A Negotiating History, 1: Commentary*. Deventer: Kluwer Law.

Stimson, J. (1985). "Regression across Time and Space." *American Journal of Political Science*, 29: 914–47.

Stoltenberg, G. (1988). *The Further Development of Monetary Cooperation in Europe: Memorandum to the Council of Economic and Finance Ministers*. Bonn: Ministry of Finance.

Stone, A. (1992). *The Birth of Judicial Politics in France*. New York: Oxford University Press.

——(1994a). "What is a Supranational Constitution: An Essay in International Relations Theory." *Review of Politics*, 56: 441–74.

——(1994b). "Judging Socialist Reform: The Politics of Coordinate Construction in France and Germany." *Comparative Political Studies*, 26: 443–69.

——(1995). "Constructing a Supranational Constitution: The Reception and Enforcement of European Community Law by National Courts." Proposal to the National Science Foundation, Global Perspectives on Socio-Legal Change Program.

Stone Sweet, A. (1998). "Constitutional Dialogues in the European Community," in A.-M. Slaughter, A. Stone Sweet, and J. H. H. Weiler (eds.), *The European Courts and National Courts: Doctrine and Jurisprudence*. Oxford: Hart Publishing.

——(forthcoming). "Judicialization and the Construction of Governance." *Comparative Political Studies*.

——and Brunell, T. (1998). "Constructing a Supranational Constitution: Dispute Resolution and Governance in the European Community." *American Political Science Review*, 92: 63–81.

Strange, S. (1976). *International Monetary Relations: International Economic Relations of the Western World, 1959–71*. Oxford: Oxford University Press.

Streeck, W. (1994). "European Social Policy after Maastricht: The 'Social Dialogue' and 'Subsidiarity.'" *Economic and Industrial Democracy*, 15: 151–77.

——(1995a). "From Market-making to State-building? Reflections on the Political Economy of European Social Policy," in S. Leibfried and P. Pierson (eds.), *European Social Policy: Between Fragmentation and Integration*. Washington, DC: Brookings Institution.

——(1995b). "Neo-Voluntarism: A New Europe Social Policy Regime?" *European Law Journal*, 1: 31–59.

——(1996). "The European Commission's Ability to Act under European Competition Law. The Example of Telecommunications and Electricity Policy." Paper presented at the German and American Young Scholars Institute on the Political Economy of European Integration at the University of Bremen, 4–16 Aug.

——and Schmitter, P. (1991). "From National Corporatism to Transnational Pluralism: Organized Interests in the Single European Market." *Politics and Society*, 19: 133–64.

Swinbank, A. (1993). "CAP Reform, 1992." *Journal of Common Market Studies*, 31: 359–72.

Szell, P. (1993). "Negotiations on the Ozone Layer," in G. Sjostedt (ed.), *International Environmental Negotiation*. Newbury Park, Calif.: Sage.

Taylor, P. (1982). "Intergovernmentalism in the European Communities in the 1970s: Patterns and Perspectives." *International Organization*, 36: 741–66.

——(1983). *The Limits of European Integration*. New York: Columbia University Press.

Thelen, K., and Steinmo, S. (1992). "Historical Institutionalism in Comparative Politics," in S. Steinmo, K. Thelen, and F. Longstreth (eds.), *Structuring Politics: Historical Institutionalism in Comparative Analysis*. New York: Cambridge University Press.

Tilly, C. (1975). "Reflections on the History of European State-Making," in C. Tilly (ed.), *The Formation of National States in Western Europe*. Princeton: Princeton University Press.

Triffin, R. (1961). *Gold and the Dollar Crisis*. New Haven: Yale University Press.

Tsebelis, G. (1994). "The Power of the European Parliament as a Conditional Agenda Setter." *American Political Science Review*, 88: 128–42.

——(1995). "Conditional Agenda Setting and Decision Making inside the European Parliament." *Journal of Legislative Studies*, 1: 65–93.

——and Kreppel, A. (1995). "The History of Conditional Agenda-setting in the European Union." Paper presented at the 91st Annual Meeting of the American Political Science Association, Chicago, 31 Aug.–3 Sept.

Tsoukalis, L. (1977). *The Politics and Economics of European Economic Integration*. London: Allen & Unwin.

——(1993). *The New European Economy: The Politics and Economics of Integration*. Oxford: Oxford University Press.

Ungerer, H., and Costello, N. (1988). *Telecommunications in Europe*. Brussels: Commission of the European Communities.

——Hauvonen, J. J., Lopez-Claros, A., and Mayer, T. (1990). "The European Monetary System: Developments and Perspectives." *IMF Occasional Paper 73*. Washington, DC: IMF.

USIA (1995). *The New European Security Architecture*. Washington, DC: United States Information Agency, Office of Research and Media Reaction.

Van Parijs, P. (1982). "Perverse Effects and Social Contradictions: Analytical Vindication or Dialectics?" *British Journal of Sociology*, 33: 589–603.

Van Tulder, R., and Junne, G. (1984). *European Multinationals in the Telecommunications Industry*. Amsterdam: Universiteit van Amsterdam.

Van Ypersele, J., and Koeune, J. C. (1985). *The European Monetary System: Origins, Operations and Outlook*. Luxembourg: Office for Official Publications of the European Communities.

Vogel, D. (1993). "Environmental Policy in the European Community," in S. Kamienecki (ed.), *Environmental Politics in the International Arena*. Albany, NY: SUNY Press.

Wallace, W. (1982). "National Inputs into European Political Cooperation," in D. Allen, R. Rummel, and W. Wessels (eds.), *European Political Cooperation: Toward a Foreign Policy for Western Europe*. London: Butterworths.

——(1983). "Political Cooperation: Integration through Intergovernmentalism," in W. Wallace, H. Wallace, and C. Webb (eds.), *Policy-making in the European Community*. Chichester: Wiley.

——and Allen, D. (1977). "Political Cooperation: Procedure as Substitute for Policy," in H. Wallace, W. Wallace, and C. Webb (eds.), *Policy-Making in the European Communities*. London: Wiley.

——and Edwards, G. (1976). "European Community: The Evolving Role of the Presidency of the Council." *International Affairs*, 53: 535–50.

Waltz, Kenneth N. (1979). *Theory of International Politics*. New York: McGraw-Hill.

Watts, R. L. (1987). "The American Constitution in Comparative Perspective: A Comparison of Federalism in the United States and Canada." *Journal of American History*, 71: 769–91.

Weaver, R. K., and Rockman, B. (1993). *Do Institutions Matter? Government Capabilities at Home and Abroad*. Washington, DC: Brookings Institution.

Weber, A. (1991). "Reputation and Credibility in the European Monetary System." *Economic Policy*, 12: 58–102.

Weiler, J. H. H. (1981). "The Community System: The Dual Character of Supranationalism." *Yearbook of European Law*, 1: 268–306.

——(1985). "The Evolution of the Mechanisms and Institutions for a European Foreign Policy." *EUI Working Paper 85/202*. San Domenico di Fiesole: European University Institute.

——(1987). "The European Court, National Courts, and References for Preliminary Rulings—the Paradox of Success: A Revisionist View of Article 177 EEC," in H. G. Schermers, C. W. A. Timmermans, A. E. Kellerman, and J. S. Watson (eds.), *Article 177 EEC: Experiences and Problems*. Amsterdam: TMC Asser Institute.

——(1991). "The Transformation of Europe." *Yale Law Journal*, 100: 2403–83.

——(1994). "A Quiet Revolution: The European Court and Its Interlocutors." *Comparative Political Studies*, 26: 510–34.

Weingast, B. R., and Moran, M. (1983). "Bureaucratic Discretion or Congressional Control? Regulatory Policy-making by the Federal Trade Commission." *Journal of Political Economy*, 91: 765–800.

Weiss, E. B. (1996). "The Natural Resource Agreements: The Living Histories." Unpublished MS.

——(1994). "International Environmental Law: Contemporary Issues and the Emergence of a New World Order." *Business and the Contemporary World*, 6: 30–44.

Wessels, W. (1982). "European Political Cooperation: A New Approach to Foreign Policy," in Allen *et al.* (1982).

Westlake, M. (1994). *A Modern Guide to the European Parliament*. London: Pinter.

Wheatcroft, S., and Lipman, G. (1986). *Air Transport in a Competitive European Market: Problems, Prospects and Strategies*. The Economist Intelligence Unit, Travel and Tourism Report No. 3. London: Economist Publications Ltd.

Whiteford, Elain A. (1996). "Occupational Pensions and European Law: Clarity at Last?" in Tamara K. Hervey and David O'Keefe (eds.), *Sex Equality Law in the European Union*. New York: Wiley.

Williamson, O. E. (1975). *Markets and Hierarchies: Analysis and Antitrust Implications*. Chicago: Free Press.

——(1993). "Transaction Cost Economics and Organization Theory." *Industrial and Corporate Change*, 2: 107–56.

Wilks, S., and McGowan, L. (1995). "Disarming the Commission: The Debate Over a European Cartel Office." *Journal of Common Market Studies*, 32: 259–73.

Wood, D., and Yesilada, B. (1996). *The Emerging European Union*. White Plains, NY: Longman.

Woolcock, S., and Hodges, M. (1996). "EU Policy and the Uruguay Round," in H. Wallace and W. Wallace (eds.), *Policy-Making in the European Union*. Oxford: Oxford University Press.

Young, O. R. (1989). *International Cooperation: Building Regimes for Natural Resources and the Environment*. Ithaca, NY: Cornell University Press.

——(1991). "Political Leadership and Regime Formation: On the Development of Institutions in International Society." *International Organization*, 45: 281–308.

Young, O. R. (1993). "Negotiating an International Climate Regime: The Institutional Bargaining for Environmental Governance," in N. Choucri (ed.), *Global Accord: Environmental Challenges and International Responses*. Cambridge, Mass.: MIT Press.`

Yuill, D., Allen, K., Bachtler, J., Clement, K., and Wishlade, F. (eds.). (1993). *European Regional Incentives, 1993–94*. London: Bowker-Saur.

Ziegler, A. R. (n.d.). "International Cooperation for the Protection of the Environment in the European Community: Shared Tasks and Responsibilities of the Community and the Member States." Unpublished MS.

Zito, A. (1995). "Integrating the Environment into the European Union: The History of the Controversial Carbon Tax," in C. Rhodes and S. Mazey (eds.), *The State of the European Community, III: Building a European Polity*. Boulder, Colo.: Lynne Rienner.

INDEX